CLINICAL DECISION MAKING IN BEHAVIOR THERAPY

A PROBLEM-SOLVING PERSPECTIVE

Edited by
Arthur M. Nezu
Christine M. Nezu

Research Press Company
2612 North Mattis Avenue
Champaign, Illinois 61821

Advisory Editor, Frederick H. Kanfer

For each other

In judgment be ye not too confident,
Even as a man who will appraise his corn
When standing in a field, ere it ripe.

Dante

He that judges without informing himself to the utmost
that he is capable, cannot acquit himself of judging amiss.

John Locke

Contents

Figures and Tables

Figures

Tables

Foreword

Programs for training problem-solving and decision-making skills have been widely used in treatment for clients having a range of different problems. Most of these programs are based on a five-stage model (D'Zurilla & Goldfried, 1971), whose origins have been traced to Dewey's five phases of reflective thinking. The therapeutic effectiveness of such programs has been documented by both research and clinical experience (D'Zurilla, 1986; Nezu, Nezu, & Perri, 1989). However, despite the proven value of the decision-making/problem-solving model with regard to clients, little formal attention has focused on its use to inform the clinical process. Traditionally, behavioral approaches have put a much heavier emphasis on treatment methods than they have on the structure of the therapeutic process.

In Part I of this book, Drs. Nezu and Nezu undertake the difficult task of describing how a decision-making model based on a problem-solving approach can be used as a framework to guide clinical thinking and action. One basic assumption of this proposed model is that clients' difficulties and dysfunctions are multiply determined. Consequently, depending on the idiosyncratic features of client characteristics and setting, different strategies may be appropriate even for similar complaints. The decision-making model offers a means for determining the best clinical approaches for particular clients and situations.

In their model, Drs. Nezu and Nezu describe the use of five problem-solving processes, guiding the reader through the judgments and decisions characteristic of the various stages of therapy (e.g., diagnosis and assessment, selection of specific treatment targets and methods, and evaluation of the effectiveness of treatment). Unlike most manuals on problem-solving and decision-making, which simply tell the clinician what to do, this book offers a rich conceptual background to justify each process and to explain its position in the clinical sequence.

Importantly, the editors draw not only on research from cognitive psychology and decision theory but also from literature dealing with the characteristic features of each stage of therapy. They also make the reader aware of the implications of each component of the problem-solving process for the further unfolding of treatment and point out the universal and personal biases that can, and frequently do, influence clinicians. Throughout, the editors blend clinical reality with the conceptual and technical analysis of the processes constituting the clinician's effective management of therapy. In this regard, the discussion represents a model of the effective combination of the craft of the scientist-practitioner.

In Part II, Drs. Nezu and Nezu bring together an impressive group of contributors to help illustrate how the decision-making model can be used in work with specific client populations. Writing from a cognitive-behavioral perspective, these authors apply the model to their particular areas of expertise, discussing the clinical issues that can be expected to arise in the therapeutic process. Not all types of behavior disorders are covered in Part II, but the variety offered will certainly allow the reader to generalize to those areas not specifically covered. In addition, these discussions are full of clinical wisdom, specific case examples, and excellent suggestions to help the clinician overcome problems in working with these populations. It is interesting to note in these chapters the similarities across different problem areas in what actually takes place in the interaction between therapists and clients. Indeed, these events commonly take place in most therapies, regardless of the theoretical school with which the therapist identifies.

Clinical Decision Making in Behavior Therapy provides the conceptual background and basic rules on how to proceed in therapy that, when supplemented with knowledge of specific treatment techniques, makes for the most effective interventions. The unusual combination of solid grounding in research and clear prescriptions for clinical implementation therefore cuts across different treatment paradigms, making the book appropriate for therapists from many different theoretical orientations working in many different areas. The strong blend of research and practice will also make the book an invaluable resource for persons in the early stages of training for psychotherapy.

FREDERICK H. KANFER
UNIVERSITY OF ILLINOIS AT URBANA-CHAMPAIGN

References

D'Zurilla, T. J. (1986). *Problem-solving therapy: A social competence approach to clinical intervention.* New York: Springer.

D'Zurilla, T. J., & Goldfried, M. R. (1971). Problem solving and behavior modification. *Journal of Abnormal Psychology, 78,* 107–126.

Nezu, A. M., Nezu, C. M., & Perri, M. G. (1989). *Problem-solving therapy for depression: Theory, research, and clinical guidelines.* New York: Wiley.

Preface

The impetus for this volume actually began over a decade ago, when we first attempted to answer the difficult questions our graduate students and interns posed concerning a variety of clinical decisions: "How do I go about selecting the correct target behavior for treatment?"; "Which behavioral approach should I use?"; "Do I teach assertiveness skills in a structured or informal manner?"; "The research article I read about the effectiveness of cognitive restructuring didn't include subjects like my patient. Should I use it anyway?"

Simultaneous with our struggle to provide useful answers to our students, we were also engaged in research attempting to assess the potential utility of social problem solving as an educational and therapeutic tool. Our continual efforts to teach our patients to become better problem solvers ultimately convinced us that a problem-solving model would be a useful metaphor for guiding the therapist's decision-making processes as well. With our colleague Mike Petronko, we first presented a model of clinical decision making for behavior therapy based on problem-solving principles at the annual convention of the Association for Advancement of Behavior Therapy in 1982. Since then, we have used this model as a guide for our own clinical practice and in our teaching and supervision of beginning behavior therapists.

As in all human endeavors, credit for the completion of this book cannot be solely ours. We would like to extend our appreciation to our coauthors and contributors, whose efforts truly make this book substantive. In particular, we would like to offer our thanks to our colleagues Mike Petronko, Mike Perri, and Tom D'Zurilla, who have collectively provided both creative inspiration and unconditional positive regard throughout the years. Further, it is important to acknowledge the significant influence of Fred Kanfer's scholarly work on our own writing and conceptualizations of the therapeutic process. Last, we would like to thank Ann Wendel and Karen Steiner at Research Press for the supportive manner in which they provided us with this opportunity to share our thinking about the complex process of clinical decision making and the way in which they facilitated its written articulation. Although these people certainly deserve credit, we alone accept responsibility for any "judgmental errors" we may have committed.

Introduction

Making decisions is always a difficult endeavor. This ubiquitous and constant human exercise permeates all aspects of our daily lives. Whether decisions involve getting married, buying a house, choosing a new car, obtaining a job, or naming a new baby, much of our existence is spent contemplating various options. When the choice involves only ourselves, the weight feels lighter than when it involves others. When as therapists we take on the responsibility for the psychological well-being of another human, our investment in making the right choice grows considerably. Moreover, the *process* of making accurate decisions becomes more complex. Therapists should not only understand their clients' problems in great detail, they should be thoroughly cognizant of the various treatments that are available.

This type of awareness is especially relevant for the field of behavior therapy. Because behavioral approaches are not meant to be applied regardless of the specific nature of patients' problems, effective decision making surrounding their application becomes crucial. Although a hallmark of behavior therapy is its insistence on a comprehensive assessment for the purposes of veridical treatment selection, to date only scant attention has been afforded to understanding how such clinical decisions are made. Moreover, few conceptual guidelines exist to aid practicing behavior therapists in choosing from among the vast array of potentially effective approaches.

The major purpose of this book is to provide such a conceptual model of prescriptive clinical decision making in the practice of behavior therapy. In the three chapters included in Part I, we describe conceptual issues associated with clinical decision making, behavior therapy, and problem solving. Specifically, chapter 1 describes a variety of judgmental errors and biases to which we are all prone and, as clinicians, wish to minimize. Chapter 2 proposes a problem-solving conceptualization of therapy and provides an overview of a prescriptive model of problem-solving training. Finally, chapter 3 describes in detail a model of clinical decision making based on a problem-solving formulation.

1

Optimal clinical decisions require not only avoidance of judgmental errors, but also expertise in the content area in which such decisions are made. The chapters included in Part II therefore illustrate the application of the clinical decision-making model to the treatment of a variety of common psychological disorders. The first of these applications, chapter 4, represents our own efforts in using the clinical decision-making model in treating clients with unipolar depression. Depression is often referred to as the "common cold" of psychological disorders. Perhaps because of its ubiquity, it has received a great deal of theoretical and research interest, much of it from those espousing a cognitive-behavioral perspective. Treatments based on this perspective have been found generally to be very effective. Even so, the temptation to use such approaches without considering individual differences should be scrupulously avoided. This chapter describes treatment issues in the area of depression in the effort to help decision makers overcome this type of judgmental error. In it, we also provide a step-by-step consideration of all five of the problem-solving processes involved in the decision-making model.

Chapter 5, written by Michael R. Petronko, discusses one of the more severe forms of anxiety disorder: agoraphobia. As the author points out, the agoraphobic patient presents the behavioral clinician with a host of decision-making dilemmas, not the least of which is, in the case of the homebound client, how and where to accomplish the first session. In using the framework of the clinical decision-making model, Petronko blends his clinical experience with the literature to capture the complexities involved in treating this kind of patient. Particularly noteworthy is the decision-making matrix he has developed to organize the many clinical strategies and tactics that may be used depending on the idiographic identification of target problems. Readers will also find his comments on pitfalls to avoid when using exposure procedures invaluable not only as concerns the treatment of agoraphobia but also with regard to anxiety disorders in general.

In chapter 6, one of the leading researchers in the field of obesity treatment provides a comprehensive and current picture of issues in this area. As Michael G. Perri points out, current models of obesity integrate biological, psychological, and social factors. As understanding of the causes and maintenance of this prevalent and severe health risk expands, so do the complexities involved in successful treatment. In the context of the clinical decision-making model, Perri addresses a variety of difficult treatment problems, including attrition, poor attendance, poor adherence, slow weight loss, binge eating, concomitant emotional difficulties, and relapse. In addition, he highlights a variety of patient-related factors important in deciding whether or not to provide treatment and, for the reader only rarely working in the area of obesity, provides a unique integration of structure and flexibility useful in approaching any type of clinical case.

Working with an individual patient provides ample clinical challenges; in our opinion, treating a couple for marital distress increases these complexities exponentially. In chapter 7, Mark A. Whisman and Neil S. Jacobson combine the most up-to-date research regarding marital therapy with an invaluable array of clinical recommendations. Drawing heavily on the empirical work of Jacobson and his colleagues, this chapter describes a flexible protocol that helps guide treatment planning with couples. The authors' approach, called *social-learning cognitive marital therapy*, reflects a focus on targeted problem areas beyond those usually identified in behavioral exchange programs. For example, recent research has documented the contribution to marital distress of cognitive factors such as unrealistic expectations or external attributions about the cause of one's marital difficulties. The authors not only underscore the importance of assessing the influence of such variables, they also provide helpful clinical suggestions to address them. In brief, we believe readers will find this chapter's "marriage" of empirical findings and clinical experience to be most useful.

Continuing the theme of couples therapy, Debra L. Kaplan and Adrian Sondheimer illustrate in chapter 8 the application of the decision-making model to the treatment of sexual dysfunction via a detailed case study. As they point out, behavior therapists have continued to develop and document highly efficacious procedures for a wide variety of sexual disorders. Nonetheless, treatment in this area continues to present clinicians with a multitude of complex decision-making issues. In their discussion, the authors correctly highlight the need to focus on parameters beyond the target problem of sexual dysfunction per se. Specifically, these include previous sexual relationships, developmental history, communication difficulties, and attitudes toward sex. Further, by noting a variety of biases therapists may have about human sexuality, Kaplan and Sondheimer clearly show how certain attitudes can influence the judgmental process.

As Neill S. Cohen and Christine M. Nezu point out in chapter 9, the concept of personality has not been a central focus within the behavioral framework. In fact, early behavior therapists argued vehemently against the cross-situational consistency of behavior, advocating instead the primacy of environmental influence. In view of the prevalence of the diagnosis of some forms of personality disorder, however, the need certainly exists to develop effective interventions in this area. In addition, these types of patients are often some of the most difficult to treat because, as the authors suggest, they rarely come to treatment complaining of personality difficulties but instead express various distress symptoms such as anxiety or depression. The challenges for clinicians early on thus revolve around accurate problem identification and formulation. Following the clinical decision-making model rather closely, Cohen and Nezu detail two different clinical cases, underscoring the importance of historic and developmental factors for treatment and pointing out the value of the patient-therapist relationship as a source of in vivo data about the patient's interpersonal style and as a treatment vehicle to engender more adaptive ways of relating to others. Readers will no doubt want to study this chapter carefully both because of the ubiquity of these types of problems and for the clinical gems contained in the case analyses.

The last decade has seen a dramatic increase in combat-related post-traumatic stress disorder (PTSD), especially in Vietnam veterans. In chapter 10, John A. Fairbank, a leading researcher in this area, applies the clinical decision-making model to provide a valuable assessment and treatment guide for this population. Although our understanding of this disorder is gradually increasing, treatment issues remain complicated. Clinicians who have worked with such patients can readily attest to the difficulties often encountered during treatment. As Fairbank points out, coexisting problems of alcohol or drug addiction can often confound both problem identification and treatment planning. Importantly, he also notes the impact that various notions about etiological factors have on the treatment process and emphasizes addressing variables related both to the traumatic event (i.e., severity of combat exposure) and to the individual (premilitary psychosocial adjustment). As a result of his current participation in a nationally based study of PTSD, Fairbank is able to provide the most recent information available on such factors. Although the focus of this chapter is on combat-related PTSD, the reader will find it applicable to patients who have experienced other types of traumatic stress, such as that resulting from crime or disaster.

In chapter 11, Philip C. Kendall and Lynne Siqueland highlight important issues in clinical decision making that cut across a variety of child and adolescent problems. They begin with a caveat reminding us to avoid the uniformity myth (i.e., that any one treatment approach will be effective for all cases), then use the basic tenets of the clinical decision-making model to outline a framework to help guide both assessment and treatment choices. Particularly noteworthy is their differentiation of childhood psychopathology based on behavioral (i.e., internalizing vs. externalizing) and cognitive (i.e., distortions vs. deficiencies) factors. Of even greater importance is their discussion of how the identification of such variables can lead to optimal treatment planning. In particular, they provide useful assessment and treatment recommendations for depressed and impulsive/aggressive children and adolescents. Although the main focus of this book is the application of problem-solving principles to the clinician's decision-making process, we are pleased to see that Kendall and Siqueland have pointed out the direct usefulness of problem-solving training for clients.

Focusing on a problem presenting perhaps the greatest challenge of all to the clinical decision maker, chapter 12 examines difficulties in managing chronic pain. Behavior therapists have contributed both useful assessment tools and effective treatment protocols to address this problem. As Arlinza E. Turner aptly points out, however, deeply in-grained biases in the clinician's problem orientation can seriously com-promise overall treatment planning. Health care programs, not traditionally based on a multidimensional approach, may not only provide inadequate care, they may even exacerbate an existing chronic pain problem. As a means of expanding our understanding of this area, Turner provides an overview of various theoretical views on concep-tualizing and treating pain, then goes on to illustrate the application of the decision-making model in three different clinical cases. The reader will find that this chapter contains helpful guidance in treating chronic pain patients, as well as in conceptualizing other medical problems often included under the general rubric of behavioral medicine.

Finally, in chapter 13, Thomas J. D'Zurilla and Arthur M. Nezu focus on the application of the decision-making model to the broadly conceived treatment strategy of stress management. Unlike the other contributions in Part II, this chapter thus does not center on a specific treatment area. However, an understanding of the decision-making model's relevance to this treatment strategy is important both because stress plays an etiological role in a wide variety of psychological and medical problems, and because stress management has become such a commonly employed behavioral intervention. As the authors point out, stress management has often become confused with anxiety manage-ment, in which the primary emphasis is on stress reduction. Adopting the more expansive viewpoint originally developed by Richard Lazarus, D'Zurilla and Nezu describe a transactional/problem-solving model that defines stress in terms of the interactive relation between the individual and the environment. They also draw parallels between the clinical decision-making model presented in Part I and the transaction-al/problem-solving model in order to illustrate various decision-making issues involved in the clinical practice of stress management. Readers familiar with the stress management literature will find that the chapter is replete with up-to-date information about social problem solving and its relation to psychopathology and that it also describes a novel approach to this area of clinical endeavor.

It is our concerted hope that this book can provide a conceptual model useful to other behavior therapists to aid in the difficult task of clinical decision making. At the very least, it is our wish to highlight the importance of this area to increase the empirical and theoretical attention we feel that it should be afforded.

Part I

Conceptual Issues

Arthur M. Nezu
Christine M. Nezu

Chapter 1

Clinical Prediction, Judgment, and Decision Making: An Overview

INTRODUCTION

With the idea that this book should be thought-provoking, we begin by asking the reader to solve a problem. Consider the following vignette describing the beginning and end of a common clinical situation. Upon reading this story, your task as the behavior therapist is to formulate a means-end analysis that provides for the middle portion, that is, the method by which to get from Point A (patient enters treatment) to Point B (successful termination).

> John Smith comes to your office to seek behavioral psycho-therapy. During the initial few sessions, he describes a series of complaints and symptoms that appear to have an impact on his general psychosocial functioning. In addition, John provides historical and demographic information pertaining to his previous and current life circumstances. Finally, he behaves in a manner indicative of a certain level of motivation to change. At the completion of treatment, a certain number of sessions (weeks or months) later, you and John agree that therapy has been successful and that he no longer requires any form of psychological intervention.

All of us would probably respond initially to the problem of what interventions to use with the statement "It depends!" It depends upon the specific nature of the symptoms and their course, John's unique developmental history, his current life circumstances, and so forth. In other words, we would want to ask several questions about John before attempting to provide a solution to the problem: What are the symptoms? How long were they present? When did he first begin to feel bad? Is he married? How old is he? Did he recently experience any traumatic events? We would all probably agree that these and a plethora of other inquiries would be necessary in order to help us formulate what we believed to be an effective treatment plan.

However, would we all ask the same kinds of questions? And, if so, assuming that we are all functioning as behavior therapists, would we use this information in a similar manner? In other words, would the *process* by which we utilize such information be reliable across therapists or over time by the same therapist? Our answers to these questions, based on the diverse literature, would be "Probably not." For example, Hay, Hay, Angle, and Nelson (1979) reported a study in which the reliability across a group of behavioral interviewers concerning the identification of specific problem areas was found to be low. Further, Wilson and Evans (1983) indicated that the reliability across 118 self-identified behavior therapists regarding target problem selection was modest at best. And Felton and Nelson (1984) concluded that inter-assessor agreement concerning hypothesized controlling variables and the formulation of treatment proposals was quite poor. As will be delineated later in this chapter, the cognitive processes of a therapist concerning issues of diagnosis, prediction, patient problem identification, treatment selection, and evaluation are not infallible.

These cognitive processes represent a complex series of clinical inferences, judgments, and decisions that a therapist constantly makes in attempting to travel successfully from the beginning to the end of therapy. Throughout the treatment process, the therapist is inundated with information that needs to be sorted, remembered, understood, and evaluated. Unlike mathematics and several of the physical sciences, psychotherapy, regardless of the underlying theoretical framework, is characterized by the lack of single, correct answers or solutions. The complex and multivariate nature of therapy tends to influence both the reliability and validity of the process of identifying effective treatment for a particular individual with a particular set of psychological symptoms.

For the moment, let us consider a second problem, this time of an arithmetic nature.

> Frank Brown, a 59-year-old farmer, has been a widower for the past decade. He currently lives alone on a farm that he in-herited as a young man. He often experiences periods of

despondency that he feels are due to loneliness. At his worst, he contemplates suicide by hanging. He defines his worst as those times when crop yields are poor and funds are insufficient to cover the monthly mortgage on the farm. However, he also remembers times as a child when he felt very sad even though the farm was thriving. One day, he goes to the local general store to buy some staples. After some time obsessing over his financial situation, he reluctantly decides upon the following purchases: three bags of potatoes at $2.99 per bag, one loaf of bread at $.89, seven cans of beans at $.49 a can, and two pints of whiskey at $3.99 per bottle. He slowly draws out a $20 bill from his pocket and hands it with trepidation to the store manager. Assuming that there is no state tax on food, how much more money does Mr. Brown need to cover his purchases?

Undoubtedly, your answer should be $1.27, regardless of the particular method you used to make the necessary calculations ("mental gymnastics," paper and pencil, hand calculator, or personal computer). You did not need to respond "It depends." There is no lack of information about Farmer Brown and his current life circumstances, history, and symptoms; however, in the present problem, these details are irrelevant. If these same details were used to describe John Smith in the first vignette, would they help us to better understand the context of the problem? On some level, of course they would. Yet it is still unlikely that all readers would provide the same (or even similar) means-end analyses. (Try this experiment on your colleagues.)

Why such divarications? The answer to this question can be found in the literature on clinical judgment, human inference, decision making, and information processing. These converging areas of research have consistently demonstrated that several ubiquitous impediments to accurate judgment negatively impinge upon the reliability and validity of people's decisions (Arkes, 1981; Kahneman & Tversky, 1973; Kleinmutz, 1984; Wiggins, 1981). Unfortunately, the clinical psychologist, psychiatrist, social worker, or counselor is not immune to such sources of error. In fact, due to the influence of overconfidence, trained clinicians might be even more susceptible to these problems (Arkes, 1981; Einhorn & Hogarth, 1978). One purpose of this book is to provide an overview of the sources of error or impediments that influence the reliability and validity of clinical decision making. Lest we leave the reader in despair (asking what good were all those years of clinical training), we quickly add that the remainder of this volume delineates a model of clinical decision making in the practice of be-havior therapy that attempts to overcome these sources of error. Before we describe the various types of errors in judgment to which we are all prone, we will provide a brief discussion of the general conceptual frameworks within which much of the research on these topics has been conducted.

MODELS OF REASONING AND INFERENCE

Perhaps the most well-known and controversial development in the history of the study of clinical judgment is Meehl's (1954) classic monograph on clinical versus statistical prediction. Based on a review of the pertinent experimental literature available at that time, Meehl concluded that intuitive or clinical predictions (i.e., the "art" of clinical psychology) were substantially less valid than those made through more formal actuarial or quantitative means (e.g., use of regression equa-tions). Interestingly, Meehl (1986) recently suggested that no more than 5 percent of what he wrote in 1954 can be retracted three decades later. In fact, he contends that what could be retracted would engender even more support for the actuarial approach to clinical prediction.

Meehl's (1954) original thesis spawned the development of one important area of research relevant to clinical decision making; simul-taneously, several additional subfields inside and outside of psychology explored similar topics. These include the fields of behavioral decision theory (Edwards, 1961; Einhorn & Hogarth, 1981), social judgment (Nisbett & Ross, 1980), information processing (Hunt & McLeod, 1979; Newell & Simon, 1972), and medical reasoning (Elstein & Bordage, 1979; Elstein, Schulman, & Spafka, 1978; Rachman, 1983).

Although these developments focus on different aspects of human inference and use different experimental paradigms, they provide substantial collective evidence that clinical judgment is often flawed. Further, many overlaps among these areas of research exist. One primary difference among them, however, involves the goals of inves-tigation. For example, studies within an information-processing perspective typically focus on *descriptive* approaches to clinical judg-ment, as compared to *prescriptive* or *normative* models. Descriptive models attempt to delineate the actual processes involved in making inferences without attempting to improve their validity. Behavioral decision theory, on the other hand, tends to be very prescriptive, with goals centering around ways of enhancing the accuracy of clinical predictions. Meehl's (1954) preference for actuarial approaches can be viewed as highly prescriptive in nature.

Clinical versus Statistical Prediction

As noted previously, Meehl's (1954) analysis of the existing literature led him to conclude that statistical approaches to clinical judgment were superior to those produced through more intuitive processes. Most of these investigations studied clinical, as compared to statistical, interpretations of psychological test data to predict, for example, college success, school drop-out rates, psychiatric diagnoses, and recidivism rates. Subsequent reviews and studies further confirmed Meehl's original thesis, particularly concerning the low performance rates of "experts." For example, Goldberg (1959) evaluated the efficacy with which different judges, using the Bender–Gestalt test, were able to distinguish between patients with and without organic brain damage. Results of this now-classic study indicated that judgmental accuracy was not significantly different among experienced psychologists, psychology trainees, and nonpsychologists (secretaries).

A similar study by Oskamp (1967) focused on the ability to make accurate classifications between patients hospitalized for medical versus psychiatric reasons using Minnesota Multiphasic Personality Inventory (MMPI) profiles. Among three groups of judges (MMPI experts, Veterans Administration psychological staff, and psychology trainees), no significant classification differences were found. More discouraging was the finding that overall performance levels barely exceeded chance.

One stream of research engendered by Meehl's (1954) pronouncement of the superiority of statistical versus clinical prediction involved the development of more sophisticated statistical regression models to enhance forecasting. Beyond a simple linear regression model, equations involving suppressor variables, moderator variables, and parabolic functions have been espoused (see Wiggins, 1981, for a more detailed explanation of these mathematical models).

In attempts to draw upon the strengths of clinical expertise and statistical approaches, other investigators sought to develop computer programs that provided formalized decision rules for making diagnostic judgments based on those of expert clinicians. For example, Kleinmutz (1967, 1975) developed a decision tree for MMPI interpretation that was based on decision rules articulated by experienced test interpreters. It was found that the computer program ultimately produced a higher "hit rate" (true positives) in various classification tasks than did the original diagnosticians. In general, such mathematical representations, or *models of man*, appear to be consistently more accurate in prediction tasks than are the individuals from whom they are originally derived (Goldberg, 1970).

Behavioral Decision Theory

A second approach to the study of clinical judgment emanates from investigations concerned with the decision-making process and choice behavior. Of the various research frameworks, decision theory tends to be the most prescriptive in nature. In it, investigators are concerned with developing models to improve rational choice, especially under conditions of uncertainty. Decision theory also involves understanding the process by which probability estimates are made and revised in light of new evidence.

Within this approach, decision making draws upon *utility theory* (Churchman, 1961; Edwards, Lindman, & Phillips, 1965), an extension of economic game theory and statistics. Such research has been concerned with the mathematical description of the processes involved in making choices and the assignment of values to these choices (Luce, 1959; von Neumann & Morgenstern, 1944). Utility theory itself involves a means-end conceptualization of decision theory whereby the expected utility of a given choice is a joint function of the consideration of both the value of the outcome of the choice and the probability of a given outcome of each alternative action. The value or desirability of each outcome should be distinguished and evaluated independently of the likelihood of its occurrence. Basically, a prescriptive decision-making model provides for a cost-benefit analysis concerning the consequences of a particular course of action (Payne, 1982).

When it comes to human decision making, this process is largely subjective because it is extremely difficult for individuals to predict with complete accuracy the consequences of certain actions. Edwards (1961) has described this process as the *subjective expected utility model* of human choice. In clinical decision making, this process becomes particularly complicated when data concerning a wide range of diagnostic, prognostic, and treatment information are absent. However, even when such data are available, the process of generating subjective probabilities is often fraught with error (Tversky & Kahneman, 1974). Consider the following example (adapted from Arkes, 1981) as an illustration of this strong potential for error.

> A new test to help diagnose depression in males has been developed. Preliminary investigations have shown that this test is 95 percent accurate (positive) for known depressed men and shows a positive finding 33 percent of the time among non-depressed men. In other words, a true positive hit rate is about three times the false positive rate. Assume that the general prevalence rate of clinical depression for males is about 5

percent. If this test is randomly given to a male, and the test is positive, what is the probability that he is actually depressed?

In giving this example to a wide range of students, colleagues, and workshop audiences, we have found that the majority of respondents provide answers that indicate a probability value of 65 percent or greater. The correct answer, in fact, is 13 percent. Admittedly, these data are based on uncontrolled research; however, they do illustrate the general tendency to estimate probability as a function of the high positive hit rate, without regard to the base rate probability value.

Demonstrating that the use of Bayes' Theorem to guide probability estimates decreases the likelihood of fallacious predictions is one outcome of decision theory research that has important implications for clinical situations (Arkes, 1981; Schwartz, Gorry, Kassirer, & Essig, 1973). This statistical approach helps determine the influence of new information with regard to testing hypotheses or making clinical judgments. In the preceding example, a Bayesian analysis would first define the problem in terms of *prior odds* and *posterior odds*. Calculating posterior odds helps to determine the correct probability value (i.e., the likelihood that a randomly selected male who tests positive is actually depressed). Prior odds are defined by *base rates* (i.e., those odds that a given male's depression can be discerned without the aid of any additional information, such as results from the newly developed test). Since the example indicates we should assume the prevalence (or base) rate for males to be 5 percent, prior odds would be 5/95 (i.e., 5 out of every 100 males are depressed). Using probability theory nomenclature, this could be expressed as

$$\text{prior odds} = \frac{p(D)}{p(\overline{D})} = \frac{5}{95},$$

where $p(\overline{D})$ represents the probability that a given male is depressed and $p(\overline{D})$ represents the probability that a given male is not depressed. In order to determine posterior odds, the prior odds are multiplied by the *likelihood ratio*, which is simply the probability of obtaining a certain result if the hypothesis is true (i.e., a positive test result for depressed males) divided by the probability of obtaining a certain result when the hypothesis is false (i.e., a positive test result for nondepressed males). This likelihood ratio, where T+ indicates a positive test result, is expressed as

$$\text{likelihood ratio} = \frac{p(D \mid T+)}{p(\overline{D} \mid T+)} = \frac{95}{33}$$

because a positive test result occurs 95 percent of the time when a male subject is depressed and 33 percent of the time when he is not depressed. Therefore, the posterior odds can be calculated as follows:

$$\frac{5}{95} \times \frac{95}{33} = \frac{475}{3,135} \ .$$

Because it is expressed as an odds function, this fraction should be read as "out of every 3,610 positive tests, 475 would be from a depressed patient and 3,135 would be from a nondepressed patient." Therefore, the probability that a positive test comes from a depressed person is

$$\frac{475}{475 + 3,135} = .13 \text{ or } 13 \text{ percent.}$$

Overestimations of this value reflect a general tendency to ignore base rates or prior odds. In the example, a 95 percent hit rate for depressed individuals appears rather high. Because substantial research has documented the extent to which this bias occurs (Tversky & Kahneman, 1974), many decision theorists have advocated the use of Bayesian analyses to improve clinical judgment and diagnostic decision making (Arkes, 1981; Lusted, 1968; Pauker, 1976).

Social Judgment

Social psychologists have long been interested in how people understand the meaning and causes of social events. This interest has engendered research in such areas as social judgment and social cognition. In a major review of this literature, Nisbett and Ross (1980) characterized as *intuitive scientists* those people who attempt to understand, predict, and control events in their social environments but who are influenced by a variety of inferential shortcomings. To some degree, these shortcomings represent people's failure to use in daily life judgments those normative principles and inferential aids that reflect formal scientific methodology.

One inferential flaw Nisbett and Ross described involves the use of a single, vivid case instead of summary statistics based on large samples. For example, a study by Borgida and Nisbett (1977) found that face-to-face interactions were more influential than summary statistics in influencing individuals' choices regarding upper level psychology courses. Specifically, introductory psychology students who indicated their intention to become psychology majors were randomly assigned to one of two conditions: (a) the face-to-face group, in which subjects listened to a panel of upper-level students provide evaluations about the courses, and (b) a statistical summary condition, in which subjects received written mean evaluation ratings concerning these same courses based on the responses of dozens of students. Subjects exposed to live reports indicated their intention to enroll in more of the highly evaluated courses and fewer of the poorly rated courses than did students receiving the summary statistics. Students in the former group also expressed greater certainty about their plans.

Another major area of interest to social psychologists, relevant for clinical settings, involves the construct of *causal attributions* (Jordan, Harvey, & Weary, 1988). In general, research has identified a robust actor-observer difference concerning attributions of behavior. Across a variety of settings, people, as actors, tend to attribute causality for their own behavior to external, situationally based variables, whereas observers of that same behavior tend to identify a variety of stable dispositions (i.e., "traits") of the actor as the relevant cause (Nisbett & Ross, 1980; Watson, 1982). Results of studies focusing on clinical judgment indicate that trained therapists may also be biased in the direction of attributing patients' behaviors to stable dispositions to the exclusion of situational factors (Batson, 1975; Harari & Hosey, 1981). This tendency is more pronounced among psychodynamic, as compared to behavioral, clinicians (Snyder, 1977). Likewise, cognitive-behavioral therapists (in whom the self-identified emphasis is on the cognitive side) may be more "trait-like" in their causal attributions concerning their patients' problems than may be warranted and may neglect important environmental factors. It would seem likely that, on the other hand, operantly oriented behavioral clinicians might seek for only causal information in the environment, tending either to minimize or exclude data about the person.

Information Processing

Another major influence on the investigation of clinical decision making involves information-processing models of cognitive operations. This body of research characterizes therapists as processors of information attempting to solve certain clinical problems. The mental activities of the clinician involve collecting, storing, retrieving, interpreting, and understanding bits of data regarding the clinical situation.

Within this paradigm, errors in clinical reasoning that can lead to ineffective problem resolution are hypothesized to be the result of the limited capabilities of humans to process large amounts of information at a given time. This concept has been referred to as *bounded rationality*

(Newell & Simon, 1972). More specifically, in order to cope efficiently with large amounts of information (as would be entailed in any clinical decision), humans resort to various strategies to help overcome their inherent limitations (e.g., limited short-term memory). Given these limitations, the clinician tends to focus only on what might be considered the more important pieces of information, to process such information in a serial (as compared to parallel) fashion, and to represent the clinical situation in very parsimonious terms. As should be pointed out very quickly, such strategies, or *heuristics,* are often necessary in order to solve any type of complex problem (Nisbett & Ross, 1980). However, these very strategies for coping more efficiently with complex problems can often lead to a variety of inferential errors, as will be described in greater detail in the next section.

One of the more prominent methodological procedures within the information-processing framework concerns the development of computer simulations patterned after the pioneering work on artificial intelligence by Newell and Simon (1972). In this approach, computer software programs are based on the problem-solving processes of experts. Similar to the work of Kleinmutz (1975), previously described, this procedure relies on direct observations of the behavior of experts, as well as on their thoughts, spoken aloud. Such an approach was used by Elstein et al. (1978) to study the reasoning of a group of experienced internists regarding a variety of medical and nonmedical problems. It should come as no surprise that findings were consistent with those from other research efforts. Specifically, inaccurate diagnoses were found to be related to problems in both data collection and interpretation (i.e., difficulties in manipulating large amounts of information). Further, when the physicians used data to help confirm or disconfirm hypotheses, they often overemphasized positive findings and discounted negative findings. Moreover, they often collected redundant data that bolstered their confidence in their diagnoses but added little new information. Based on such detailed analyses of internists' reasoning, researchers developed a set of computer programs that formalized the characteristic features of the diagnostic process (Elstein & Bordage, 1979). Such an approach can provide an excellent building block to facilitate theoretical development in the realm of clinical reasoning.

ERRORS IN CLINICAL DECISION MAKING

The investigations emanating from these various paradigms of clinical decision making have identified several specific errors in clinical reasoning and judgment. In one classic and influential paper, Tversky and Kahneman (1974) identified three heuristic principles commonly used to reduce complex tasks in assessing probabilities and predicting outcomes to simpler judgmental operations. These include *availability, representativeness,* and *anchoring heuristics.* All three of these "shortcut" cognitive processes have been shown to influence clinical decision making. Although these heuristics are necessary to process information in everyday living, as well as in clinical situations, they are often responsible for severe and systematic errors in judgment. Also responsible for judgmental errors are *biased search strategies, overconfidence,* and *hindsight bias.* After describing these various impediments to accurate clinical judgment (Arkes, 1981), or bad habits (Faust, 1986), we will discuss their implications for behavioral psychotherapy and assessment.

Availability Heuristic

People use the availability heuristic when they attempt to estimate the frequency of a class or probability of an event by the facility or ease with which examples or instances of that class or event can be recalled. In everyday life, an example might involve attempting to estimate the value of a new car based on the most recently viewed advertisements on television. Another example might be trying to predict the likelihood of winning a big lottery after reading in the newspaper about a person who won $1 million.

Because this heuristic principle is influenced by variables outside of veridical frequency and probability values, its use can lead to various biases and erroneous conclusions. If the size of a group is evaluated according to its availability, a group whose examples are more readily retrievable can appear to be more numerous than a class of equal or greater frequency whose examples are remembered less often. For example, a patient complaining of feelings of sadness would more likely be diagnosed as being depressed than as having a borderline personality disorder because the class of depression is more readily brought to mind. A patient in a state institution describing difficulties in relating to people might more likely be diagnosed as being paranoid schizophrenic than would the same individual in a Park Avenue private therapist's office, again because of the availability of the idea that schizophrenics are usually found in mental hospitals.

The salience or vividness and recency of an event can also affect availability estimates. Viewing a plane crash on the evening news would likely influence one's estimate of the frequency of such crashes in deciding how to travel on an upcoming vacation. Having recently interacted with a rude taxi driver in New York City might influence one to avoid this mode of transportation in the future because the availability principle would suggest a high prevalence of rudeness among all New York taxi drivers.

For the behavior therapist, a recent highly successful treatment of an individual with panic disorder using an exposure procedure may increase the probability that such a technique will be viewed as efficacious for the next patient who comes to therapy complaining of anxiety symptoms. With regard to assessment issues, the availability heuristic might affect one's prediction of a new patient's risk for suicide if a recent case involved a client who actually committed suicide when the initial risk was thought to be low.

Related to the availability heuristic is the influence of *preconceived notions* or *expectancies* (Arkes, 1981). This impediment to accurate clinical judgment involves using ideas about how things are "supposed to be," as compared to accurately perceiving how they really are. The classic clinical example involves the *illusory correlation*, first studied by Chapman and Chapman (1967). Essentially, these investigators were interested in how preconceived ideas can bias clinical judgments concerning the frequency with which two events co-occur. In their study, naive subjects were provided with the clinical diagnoses and Draw-A-Person (DAP) responses of certain hypothetical patients. The subjects were asked to judge the frequency with which certain features of the drawings (e.g., peculiar eyes) were associated with each diagnosis (e.g., paranoia or suspiciousness). Although the pairings were done randomly, judges in this study significantly overestimated the frequency of the covariation between "natural" associations such as large eyes and suspiciousness. The preconceived notion that large eyes are associated with the personality trait of suspiciousness persisted even when the veridical relation presented by the investigators was actually negative. A subsequent study using the Rorschach inkblot test confirmed the existence and robustness of the illusory correlation in a group of expert diagnosticians (Chapman & Chapman, 1969). Moreover, a more recent study by Kurtz and Garfield (1978) indicated that attempts to eliminate this bias by providing explicit training were not successful.

Representativeness Heuristic

To appreciate the ubiquity of the representativeness heuristic, consider the following scenario.

You are attending your 20th high school reunion and meet Steve, a classmate whom you have not seen since graduation.

You remember him as being somewhat shy and uninterested in sports, and as having a large comic book collection. You also recollect that he took no particular interest in school politics but always received above average grades. When you ask him about his current occupation, he says, "Take a guess! I'm either the assistant curator for the local art museum or a high school teacher." What would be your guess?

If you chose assistant art curator over high school teacher, you probably used the representativeness principle in making your decision. This heuristic is often invoked when people attempt to make predictions or decisions concerning the following types of questions: "What is the probability that X is associated with Y?" "What is the probability that A is a member of group B?" and "What is the probability that event A caused event B or that B caused A?"

When people attempt to assess such probabilities based on the degree to which A resembles B, then they are using the representativeness heuristic. For example, if A is thought to be highly representative of B, then the association between the two will also be evaluated as high, with the likely conclusion that A must be a class of B (or that A originates from B or causes B). Conversely, if A is not perceived as being similar to B, then the probability that A is an object of class B will be perceived as quite low.

Within the framework of cognitive psychology, characteristic A serves to access schema B, which in turn can access other characteristics. The representativeness heuristic, then, occurs when characteristic A accesses schema B due to perceived similarities between them. Schemata are cognitive structures that provide organized representations of various classes of information or rules. The schema of cat, for example, contains information regarding a wide variety of different types of cats (e.g., tabby, Siamese, Persian), various characteristics of cats across species (fur, whiskers, "meow" sounds), and idiosyncratic personalized information about cats ("I hate cats," "Cats are friendly animals," "Cats make wonderful pets"). Thus when the characteristics of friendly, furry, and whiskered are offered, the schema of cat tends to be automatically accessed.

As concerns Steve's profession, most people would tend to perceive the association between the characteristics of shyness, lack of interest in sports, and collectorship (even of comic books) and the schema of museum curator as high. In other words, these personality characteristics would tend to access a schema such as museum curator or librarian instead of other schemata. The resemblance between the characteristics of a high school teacher and Steve's earlier attributes is likely to be perceived as low. Thus, because the description of Steve does not bring the schema of high school teacher to mind, in this case similarity and probability tend to be evaluated in an equivalent manner.

Earlier in this chapter, we discussed the advantages of using Bayes' Theorem to increase the accuracy of one's predictions. The crucial point in that discussion involved paying particular attention to base rates. Using only base rates to help make the decision about Steve's current occupation (i.e., the number of art curators versus the number of high school teachers) would suggest that Steve is a high school teacher. Remember also that Steve's shyness and other "curator-like" qualities were observed two decades ago, further reducing the veracity of any strong association.

This insensitivity to base rates or prior probabilities is only one variable that affects representative thinking. Inattention to sample size can also influence the use of this heuristic (Dawes, 1986; Tversky & Kahneman, 1974). Sampling theory in inferential statistics suggests that, the larger the sample size from which a piece of data is generated, the more generalizable that information is to the entire relevant population. However, people generally tend to use the representativeness heuristic when evaluating the likelihood of obtaining a particular result in a sample obtained from a specified population. Scientists relying too heavily on results obtained from small samples also engage in the same judgmental error.

Misunderstanding the role of regression effects is another variable influencing the use of representative thinking. Basically, regression effects involve the natural phenomenon whereby extreme scores obtained on one occasion will tend to be either higher or lower on a subsequent occasion. For example, the student who receives the highest grade point average in college during her first year will likely be ranked lower at the end of the second year. Similarly, the student who obtains the lowest grade point average during the first year will likely be found to be somewhat higher in the ranks during the second year.

According to Tversky and Kahneman (1974), *regression to the mean* tends to be incompatible with the representativeness heuristic because this heuristic implies that a predicted outcome is maximally representative of the input. Thus the value of the outcome variable (i.e., highest test score at Time 2) can be expected to be just as extreme as the value of the input variable (i.e., highest test score at Time 1). These authors provide an example of this phenomenon that would appear to be particularly relevant for behavior therapy.

In a discussion of flight training, experienced instructors noted that praise for an exceptionally smooth landing is typically followed by a poorer landing on the next try. The instructors concluded that verbal rewards are detrimental to learning, while verbal punishments are beneficial. This conclusion is unwarranted because of the presence of regression toward the mean. As in other cases of repeated examination, an improvement will usually follow a poor performance and a deterioration will usually follow an outstanding performance, even if the instructor does not respond to the trainee's achievement on the first attempt. Because the instructors had praised their trainees after good landings and admonished them after poor ones, they reached the erroneous and potentially harmful conclusion that punishment is more effective than reward. (p. 1127)

The major problem caused by representative thinking occurs when a schema is accessed by a characteristic or event to the exclusion of other schemata. For example, during the assessment phase of treatment, if a particular schema (e.g., major depressive disorder) is accessed automatically, the probability of perceiving the patient's problems or diagnosis from the perspective of other schemata (e.g., medically related mood difficulties, personality disorders, anxiety-related problems) is greatly reduced. Further, representativeness errors are likely to occur if one's strategy for data collection and interpretation is based on such processes. In other words, when attempts are made to assess probabilities or make decisions based on searches specifically geared toward finding the schema that most resembles a characteristic, as compared to identifying a range of schemata that might provide possible alternatives, this bias becomes especially difficult to avoid. Thus errors in differential diagnosis, problem identification, target behavior selection, treatment planning, and evaluation can occur with high frequency when only a restricted range of ideas (i.e., schemata) are generated.

Anchoring Heuristic

The anchoring heuristic is a shortcut method of estimation or prediction involving situations in which final decisions are based more on initial impressions than on subsequent information. To make more accurate judgments, one should make adjustments in light of new or conflicting evidence. However, when insufficient adjusting occurs, the phenomenon of anchoring is responsible. In other words, different starting points can engender estimates that are biased toward the initial values.

An arithmetic example is provided by Tversky and Kahneman (1974) in a study in which two groups of subjects were asked to estimate the answers to the following numerical expressions within a 5-second time period.

$$8 \times 7 \times 6 \times 5 \times 4 \times 3 \times 2 \times 1,$$

as compared to

$$1 \times 2 \times 3 \times 4 \times 5 \times 6 \times 7 \times 8.$$

It was hypothesized that, due to the anchoring effect, insufficient adjustments based on initial rapid calculations would result in under-estimations for both groups. More important, however, it was hypothesized that subjects who received the descending sequence of numbers would judge the answer as being higher than would those who received the ascending order because the product of the first few steps of multiplication would be higher in the first expression. Results confirmed both predictions, in that the median estimate for the ascending sequence was 512, whereas the median estimate for the descending sequence was 2,250. (In fact, the correct answer to both is 40,320.)

More pertinent to the theme of this volume, several studies have documented the persistence of an anchoring effect in clinical situations. For example, Meehl (1960) noted that clinicians' identification of patients' personality traits stabilized between two and four sessions but differed insignificantly from identifications based on several months of therapy contacts. Bieri, Orcutt, and Leaman (1963) found the anchoring phenomenon to be present in a group of graduate social work students asked to estimate degrees of pathology in a series of clinical cases. Significant differences were found for identical cases as a function of the order of presentation. Friedlander and Stockman (1983) found a robust anchoring bias among a group of experienced clinicians (psychologists, psychiatrists, and clinical social workers) in their estimates of pathology and prognosis concerning a hypothetical patient. Behavior therapists are also susceptible to the anchoring effect, as shown by a survey conducted by Swan and MacDonald (1978) in which two-thirds of a sample of over 300 self-identified behavior therapists indicated that two or fewer sessions were required to conceptualize a client's problem. Delimiting such an important clinical task to so short a period of time would appear to facilitate the persistence of the anchoring phenomenon.

Biased Search Strategies

In situations that require gathering or searching for information to help make judgments, the strategy itself is often inadvertently responsible for producing erroneous conclusions. For example, selective attention to certain kinds of information can lead to biased estimates of covariation between two events. Consider the clinical situation in which a prediction about a person's potential for suicide is being assessed by the presence or absence of a particular diagnostic sign. Figure 1.1 represents the four different covariation possibilities between diagnostic sign and a person's risk for suicide. Research indicates that people generally focus mostly on Box 1 and, to a lesser degree, on Box 2 (Arkes, 1981), often ignoring Boxes 3 and 4. If one's search strategy is aimed at obtaining information contained only in Box 1, then a systematic bias in covariation can occur. Information contained in Box 3 is especially essential in predicting the veridical relationship between any two variables.

Figure 1.1 Four Possible Outcomes Concerning the Relationship between Two Variables

	Suicide potential High	Suicide potential Low
Diagnostic sign Present	1	2
Diagnostic sign Absent	3	4

Search strategies can also be biased if they tend to be confirmatory in nature. Such strategies involve searching for information or data that support one's original hypothesis rather than for facts that may help adjust one's initial impressions. Confirmatory search strategies have been documented as ubiquitous ways in which people attempt to verify inferences and make predictions (Wason, 1968, 1969). This bias was found even within a group of experienced statisticians, who should have been trained to seek for disconfirming evidence (Einhorn & Hogarth, 1978). Moreover, people tend to disregard evidence that actually contradicts their current judgment (Koriat, Lichtenstein, & Fischhoff, 1980).

Rigid adherence to one's theoretical orientation can influence a clinician to look only for data that are consistent with a certain conceptual viewpoint, rather than to conduct a broad-based assessment. For example, behavior therapists may tend to look only for environmental causal variables, whereas psychodynamic clinicians may seek only for intrapsychic pathogenic factors (Houts, 1984). In essence, "What we look for is what we get." The influence of theoretical persuasion can even occur among various schools within behavior therapy (e.g., cognitive versus operant; Swan & MacDonald, 1978). Confirmatory strategies can involve the type of questions we ask, attention to certain kinds of information to the exclusion of other types, and attempts to reproduce redundant information. With regard to this last area, research has indicated that increases in information serve to perpetuate biases, rather than reduce them (Lueger & Petzel, 1979), especially if this information provides nothing new (Elstein & Bordage, 1979).

It is also interesting to note that supposedly objective evaluations of the quality of scientific findings are also not immune to this type of judgmental error. In an attempt to understand better the nature of the peer review process involved in journal publications, Mahoney (1977) found a confirmatory bias among journal referees whereby articles consistent with reviewers' own theoretical orientations received good evaluations and those opposed received poor evaluations.

Overconfidence

Being overconfident in one's abilities can also serve as a source of systematic error in clinical reasoning (Arkes, 1981). Unfortunately, confidence has been found to be unrelated to clinical accuracy (Fischhoff, Slovic, & Lichtenstein, 1977). For example, Oskamp (1965) found that providing judges with more information served to increase their confidence in their decisions but did not necessarily increase the accuracy of these decisions. Even more damaging is the evidence indicating a significant negative relation between confidence and accuracy among a group of diagnosticians (Holsopple & Phelan, 1954). Einhorn and Hogarth (1978) suggested that overconfidence is related to difficulties in learning from experience in making judgments. For example, if clinicians tend to use confirmatory search strategies and neglect to pose disconfirming hypotheses, "Large amounts of positive feedback can lead to reinforcement of a nonvalid rule and hence to the illusion of validity" (p. 398).

Consider the situation in which a behavior therapist wishes to assess his effectiveness in treating a given psychological disorder according to a particular intervention. He may check the outcomes of a sample of patients treated during the past 2 years. If the proportion of good outcomes is high, the behavior therapist might infer that the judgmental procedure invoked in treatment planning was valid. However, in the absence of any systematic attempt to control for placebo or Hawthorne effects, a lack of disconfirmatory hypothesis testing can lead to erroneous conclusions. In essence, if a patient improves for any reason, the therapist providing behavioral treatment can attribute the improvement to the specific interventions that were implemented. Other treatment strategies that might be more efficacious, less costly, or require fewer therapy sessions might never be considered due to the therapist's confidence in his supposedly successful therapeutic planning.

Hindsight Bias

People engage in the hindsight bias when, knowing what a given outcome is, they claim they would have predicted it had they been asked to do so in advance of its actual occurrence. For example, in a study by Fischhoff (1975), several groups of subjects were presented with a variety of case histories and asked to judge the likelihood of four possible therapeutic outcomes. One hindsight group was told that, in fact, outcome A had occurred. These subjects were asked whether they would have been able to predict event A had they been asked to do so not knowing that it had occurred. A second hindsight condition involved telling subjects that event B was the true outcome. In comparison to the foresight group, both hindsight groups assigned substantially higher probabilities to those outcomes that they were told actually occurred. This finding suggests that either event A or event B was obvious only in hindsight. The hindsight bias also was evident among a group of 75 practicing physicians asked to assign probabilities to one of four possible diagnoses associated with an actual case (Arkes, Wortmann, Saville, & Harkness, 1981).

A relevant example comes from our own experience at a staff conference in presenting the case history of one of our clients. In describing this actual case, we purposely provided a large amount of assessment data across a wide range of problem areas. In addition to revealing a diagnosis of developmental disability, we told staff participants that this individual had been previously diagnosed as obsessive-compulsive. We then elicited feedback concerning various treatment issues and asked for confirmation of the dual diagnosis. Most of the staff agreed until we suggested that much of the clinical information implied that, rather than having an obsessive-compulsive disorder, our patient was actually borderline. Upon hearing this observation, the staff readily agreed and pointed to some of the clinical data we had presented as evidence in favor of this new diagnosis. When asked what the diagnosis should be, most staff indicated that it should of course be borderline, as if this would have been their choice all along.

IMPLICATIONS FOR BEHAVIOR THERAPY

The importance of identifying these judgmental errors for the field of behavior therapy is multiple. First, the evidence to support the ubiquity of these errors across judgmental tasks and settings is substantial. Second, these cognitive errors in decision making appear to occur in the general population; in addition, research has documented that experienced clinicians are not immune to these inferential problems. In fact, overconfidence in one's clinical acumen tends to decrease one's own awareness of the potential for making such errors (Arkes, 1981; Gauron & Dickinson, 1966). Third, there is no reason to believe that the specific training behavior therapists receive serves to prevent these inferential biases (Swan & MacDonald, 1978). Clearly, if the field of behavior therapy is to maintain its objectivity and empirical status, concerted efforts must be made to eliminate such judgmental biases.

The commitment to an empirical/scientific methodology is often cited as a major cornerstone of behavior therapy. In fact, this argument is often used to support behavior therapy's clinical superiority over such traditional approaches as, for example, psychoanalytically oriented psychotherapy. However, inattention to the area of clinical decision making might prove disastrous to the future of behavior therapy (Nezu, Petronko, & Nezu, 1982). Moreover, recent research has pointed to various discrepancies between behavior therapy as it is practiced and the empirical rigor with which its attempted validation is espoused in the literature. For example, Ford and Kendall (1979) reported that behavior therapists in professional practice do not generally operationalize their theoretical guidelines in clinical cases. As noted previously, Swan and MacDonald (1978) further suggested that factors such as school affiliations under the rubric of the behavioral approach (e.g., operant, cognitive, eclectic) can influence behavior therapists' perceptions of and clinical practice with patients. Barlow (1980) has previously warned behavior therapists of this gap: "I think if you examine the behavior of practicing clinicians, few, if any, of our clinical procedures are guided by the scientific training we received" (p. 323). Although some attention by behavior therapists has focused recently on issues regarding clinical judgment (Kanfer & Busemeyer, 1982; Turk &

Salovey, 1985), as Barrios and Hartmann (1986) note, "There appears to be a conspiracy of silence regarding the decision-making strategies used by behavioral clinicians" (p. 92).

One potential source of judgmental error specific to behavior therapy involves the relation between assessment and treatment. Unlike the omnibus treatment approach that other theoretical orientations might prescribe, behavior therapy endorses the concept that treatment be applied prescriptively, with concern being given to the nature of the disorder, prognosis, patient and therapist characteristics, and setting. In other words, behavioral treatment planning should focus on the unique characteristics, across a variety of patient and environmental variables, of a given individual. These individual differences among patients are not simply to be taken into consideration, but rather should serve as major determinants in our clinical decision-making efforts.

This idiographic application of behavioral techniques to a wide variety of psychological disorders presents a problem for the clinician beyond those posed by traditional clinical tasks (e.g., differential diagnosis or problem identification). The process of identifying the optimal intervention program for a given patient experiencing a particular dysfunction remains subject to error in cases where little consideration of the mechanisms guiding such choices is given. The continual escalation of interest in behavior therapy actually makes this concern even more salient. For example, in the recently published *Dictionary of Behavior Therapy Techniques* (Bellack & Hersen, 1985), no fewer than 158 entries are included as viable interventions within the behavioral armamentarium. The behavioral clinician is, then, faced with a very difficult practical problem—which approach or technique to use? If the answer to this question affords little credence to the potential negative impact of engaging in judgmental biases, the gap between scientific psychology and behavior therapy can widen even further. For example, Hersen (1981) expressed concern over the limited reading habits of behavior therapists and their unwillingness to take into consideration the different etiologic patterns of various disorders: "[Behavioral] therapies have been applied across the board consistent with the vested interests of their proponents" (p. 21).

If behavior therapy in practice is to enjoy a satisfactory marriage with science, this gap needs to close. Empirical findings need to be translated into clinical practice in nonresearch settings. However, the literature offers very little to facilitate this translation. For example, nearly two decades ago Kanfer and Phillips (1970) suggested that personal ingenuity and experience were the primary sources that behavior therapists have for selecting treatment approaches. Perhaps the heavy emphasis on technical expertise and implementation ignores the use of an overall conceptual framework to guide clinical judgment and decision making. Although others have provided various decision-making heuristics for behavioral clinicians (e.g., Goldfried & Davison, 1976) and despite calls for such approaches (e.g., Kanfer & Phillips, 1970), an overall model to guide clinical decision making for the practice of behavior therapy (Barrios & Hartmann, 1986; Nezu, Nezu, & Perri, 1988) is still lacking. The need for such a model becomes increasingly important as behavioral approaches become more accepted by mental health practitioners and more students are trained in this orientation.

In order to address this concern, the remaining two chapters in Part I will delineate a model of clinical decision making for the practice of behavior therapy based on a problem-solving framework (Nezu & D'Zurilla, in press; Nezu, Nezu, & Perri, 1989). Optimal clinical decisions require not only avoidance of such judgmental errors, but also expertise in the content area in which such decisions are made. Therefore, Part II will provide illustrations of the application of this model by experienced behavior therapists regarding a wide variety of common clinical problems. We hope that the model and clinical illustrations are helpful to practicing behavior therapists who paraphrase the question Paul (1969) asked over two decades ago as follows: "What behavioral procedures should I apply, with this specific patient, who has this particular disorder, and given these unique characteristics and circumstances?"

SUMMARY

The topic of clinical decision making and judgment has been the focus of several different research perspectives both inside and outside of psychology. These include the fields of clinical judgment, behavioral decision theory, social judgment and cognition, and information processing. As a result of substantial research efforts, several types of judgmental errors or biases have been identified. Such errors have been presented as characteristic of the ways that people generally process stimulus information in everyday living. Although these data-reducing strategies are necessary to cope with large amounts of information, they are also responsible for systematic judgmental errors. More important, research has demonstrated that expert clinicians are not immune to such biases. These judgmental problems include the availability, representativeness, and anchoring heuristics; biased search strategies; overconfidence; and hindsight bias.

We have underscored the importance of attending to this literature for behavior therapists, particularly in light of the espoused close association between assessment and treatment selection that a behavioral position advocates. A major purpose of assessment in behavior therapy is to help the clinician design an optimal treatment program for a given patient. Even individuals who may present similar symptom constellations should be treated differentially as a function of individual variations in a variety of patient and environmental characteristics (e.g., age, sex, severity of symptoms, life-style, race, etc.). Effective application of this idiographic perspective becomes increasingly more complex given increases in the array of treatment techniques available within the behavioral armamentarium. The need to understand and improve the means by which behavior therapists make such treatment choices is therefore crucial to the future of this theoretical orientation.

References

Arkes, H. R. (1981). Impediments to accurate clinical judgment and possible ways to minimize their impact. *Journal of Consulting and Clinical Psychology, 49,* 323–330.

Arkes, H. R., Wortmann, R. L., Saville, P. D., & Harkness, A. R. (1981). Hindsight bias among physicians weighing the likelihood of diagnoses. *Journal of Applied Psychology, 66,* 252–254.

Barlow, D. H. (1980). Behavior therapy: The next decade. *Behavior Therapy, 11,* 315–328.

Barrios, B. A., & Hartmann, D. P. (1986). The contribution of traditional assessment: Concepts, issues, and methodologies. In R. O. Nelson & S. C. Hayes (Eds.), *Conceptual foundations of behavioral assessment.* New York: Guilford.

Batson, C. D. (1975). Attribution as a mediator of bias in helping. *Journal of Personality and Social Psychology, 32,* 455–466.

Bellack, A. S., & Hersen, M. (1985). *Dictionary of behavior therapy techniques.* New York: Pergamon.

Bieri, J., Orcutt, B. A., & Leaman, R. (1963). Anchoring effects in sequential clinical judgments. *Journal of Abnormal and Social Psychology, 67,* 616–623.

Borgida, E., & Nisbett, R. E. (1977). The differential impact of abstract vs. concrete information on decisions. *Journal of Applied Social Psychology, 7,* 258–271.

Chapman, L. J., & Chapman, J. P. (1967). Genesis of popular but erroneous diagnostic observations. *Journal of Abnormal Psychology, 72,* 193–204.

Chapman, L. J., & Chapman, J. P. (1969). Illusory correlation as an obstacle to the use of valid psychodiagnostic signs. *Journal of Abnormal Psychology, 74,* 271–280.

Churchman, C. W. (1961). *Prediction and optimal decisions.* Englewood Cliffs, NJ: Prentice-Hall.

Dawes, R. M. (1986). Representative thinking in clinical judgment. *Clinical Psychology Review, 6,* 425–441.

Edwards, W. (1961). Behavioral decision theory. *Annual Review of Psychology, 12,* 473–498.

32   Chapter 1

Edwards, W., Lindman, H., & Phillips, L. D. (1965). Emerging technologies for making decisions. In T. M. Newcomb (Ed.), *New directions in psychology*. New York: Holt, Rinehart & Winston.

Einhorn, H. J., & Hogarth, R. M. (1978). Confidence in judgment: Persistence of the illusion of validity. *Psychological Review, 85,* 395–416.

Einhorn, H. J., & Hogarth, R. M. (1981). Behavioral decision theory: Processes of judgment and choice. *Annual Review of Psychology, 32,* 53–88.

Elstein, A. S., & Bordage, G. (1979). Psychology of clinical reasoning. In G. C. Stone, F. Cohen, & N. E. Adler (Eds.), *Health psychology*. San Francisco: Jossey-Bass.

Elstein, A. S., Shulman, L. S., & Spafka, S. A. (1978). *Medical problem solving: An analysis of clinical reasoning*. Cambridge: Harvard University Press.

Faust, D. (1986). Research on human judgment and its application to clinical practice. *Professional Psychology: Research and Practice, 17,* 420–430.

Felton, J. L., & Nelson, R. O. (1984). Inter-assessor agreement on hypothesized controlling variables and treatment proposals. *Behavioral Assessment, 6,* 199–208.

Fischhoff, B. (1975). Hindsight = foresight: The effect of outcome knowledge on judgment under uncertainty. *Journal of Experimental Psychology: Human Perception and Performance, 3,* 552–564.

Fischhoff, B., Slovic, P., & Lichtenstein, S. (1977). Knowing with certainty: The appropriateness of extreme confidence. *Journal of Experimental Psychology: Human Perception and Performance, 3,* 552–564.

Ford, J. D., & Kendall, P. C. (1979). Behavior therapists' professional behaviors: A survey study. *Professional Psychology, 10,* 772–773.

Friedlander, M. L., & Stockman, S. J. (1983). Anchoring and publicity effects in clinical judgment. *Journal of Clinical Psychology, 39,* 637–643.

Gauron, E. G., & Dickinson, J. K. (1966). Diagnostic decision making in psychiatry: I. Information usage. *Archives of General Psychiatry, 14,* 225–232.

Goldberg, L. R. (1959). The effectiveness of clinicians' judgments: The diagnosis of organic brain damage from the Bender–Gestalt Test. *Journal of Consulting Psychology, 23,* 25–33.

Goldberg, L. R. (1970). Man vs. model of man: Rationale, plus some evidence for a method of improving on clinical inference. *Psychological Bulletin, 73,* 422–432.

Goldfried, M. R., & Davison, G. C. (1976). *Clinical behavior therapy*. New York: Holt, Rinehart & Winston.

Harari, O., & Hosey, K. R. (1981). Attributional biases among clinicians and non-clinicians. *Journal of Clinical Psychology, 37,* 445–450.

Hay, W. M., Hay, L. R., Angle, H. V., & Nelson, R. O. (1979). The reliability of problem identification in the behavioral interview. *Behavioral Assessment, 1,* 107–118.

Hersen, M. (1981). Complex problems require complex solutions. *Behavior Therapy, 12,* 15–29.

Holsopple, J. G., & Phelan, J. G. (1954). The skills of clinicians in analysis of projective tests. *Journal of Clinical Psychology, 10,* 307–320.

Houts, A. C. (1984). Effects of clinician theoretical orientation and patient explanatory bias on initial clinical judgments. *Professional Psychology: Research and Practice, 15,* 284–293.

Hunt, E. B., & McLeod, C. M. (1979). Cognition and information processing in patient and physician. In G. C. Stone, F. Cohen, & N. E. Adler (Eds.), *Health psychology*. San Francisco: Jossey-Bass.

Jordan, J. S., Harvey, J. H., & Weary, G. (1988). Attributional biases in clinical decision making. In D. C. Turk & P. Salovey (Eds.), *Reasoning, inference, and judgment in clinical psychology*. New York: Free Press.

Kahneman, D., & Tversky, A. (1973). On the psychology of prediction. *Psychological Review, 80*, 237–251.

Kanfer, F. H., & Busemeyer, J. R. (1982). The use of problem solving and decision making in behavior therapy. *Clinical Psychology Review, 2*, 239–266.

Kanfer, F. H., & Phillips, J. S. (1970). *Learning foundations of behavior therapy*. New York: Wiley.

Kleinmutz, B. (1967). Sign and seer: Another example. *Journal of Abnormal Psychology, 72*, 163–165.

Kleinmutz, B. (1975). The computer as clinician. *American Psychologist, 30*, 379–387.

Kleinmutz, B. (1984). The scientific study of clinical judgment in psychology and medicine. *Clinical Psychology Review, 4*, 111–126.

Koriat, A., Lichtenstein, S., & Fischhoff, B. (1980). Reasons for confidence. *Journal of Experimental Psychology: Human Learning and Memory, 6*, 107–118.

Kurtz, R. M., & Garfield, S. L. (1978). Illusory correlation: A further exploration of Chapman's paradigm. *Journal of Consulting and Clinical Psychology, 46*, 1009–1015.

Luce, R. D. (1959). *Individual choice behavior*. New York: Wiley.

Lueger, R. J., & Petzel, T. P. (1979). Illusory correlation in clinical judgment: Effects of amount of information to be presented. *Journal of Consulting and Clinical Psychology, 47*, 1120–1121.

Lusted, L. B. (1968). *Introduction to medical decision making*. Springfield, IL: Charles C Thomas.

Mahoney, M. J. (1977). Publication prejudices: An experimental study of confirmatory bias in the peer review system. *Cognitive Therapy and Research, 1*, 161–175.

Meehl, P. E. (1954). *Clinical versus statistical prediction*. Minneapolis: University of Minnesota Press.

Meehl, P. E. (1960). The cognitive activity of the clinician. *American Psychologist, 15*, 19–27.

Meehl, P. E. (1986). Causes and effects of my disturbing little book. *Journal of Personality Assessment, 50*, 370–375.

Newell, A., & Simon, H. A. (1972). *Human problem solving*. Englewood Cliffs, NJ: Prentice-Hall.

Nezu, A. M., & D'Zurilla, T. J. (in press). Social problem solving and negative affective states. In P. C. Kendall & D. Watson (Eds.), *Anxiety and depression: Distinctive and overlapping features*. New York: Academic.

Nezu, A. M., Nezu, C. M., & Perri, M. G. (1988, September). *Clinical decision making in behavior therapy: A problem-solving perspective*. Workshop presented at the World Congress of Behaviour Therapy, Edinburgh, Scotland.

Nezu, A. M., Nezu, C. M., & Perri, M. G. (1989). *Problem-solving therapy for depression: Theory, research, and clinical guidelines*. New York: Wiley.

Nezu, A. M., Petronko, M. R., & Nezu, C. M. (1982, November). *Cognitive, behavioral, or cognitive-behavioral strategies? Using a problem-solving paradigm for clinical decision making in behavior therapy*. Paper presented at the annual convention of the Association for Advancement of Behavior Therapy, Los Angeles.

Nisbett, R., & Ross, L. (1980). *Human inference: Strategies and shortcomings of social judgment*. Englewood Cliffs, NJ: Prentice-Hall.

Oskamp, S. (1965). Overconfidence in case-study judgments. *Journal of Consulting Psychology, 29,* 261–265.

Oskamp, S. (1967). Clinical judgment from the MMPI: Simple or complex. *Journal of Clinical Psychology, 23,* 411–415.

Pauker, S. G. (1976). Coronary artery surgery: The use of decision analysis. *Annals of Internal Medicine, 82,* 8–18.

Paul, G. L. (1969). Behavior modification research: Design and tactics. In C. M. Franks (Ed.), *Behavior therapy: Appraisal and status.* New York: McGraw-Hill.

Payne, J. W. (1982). Contingent decision behavior. *Psychological Bulletin, 92,* 382–402.

Rachman, S. (1983). Behavioral medicine, clinical reasoning and technical advances. *Canadian Journal of Behavioral Science, 15,* 318–333.

Schwartz, W. B., Gorry, G. A., Kassirer, J. P., & Essig, A. (1973). Decision analysis and clinical judgment. *American Journal of Medicine, 55,* 459–472.

Snyder, C. R. (1977). "A patient by any other name" revisited: Maladjustment or attributional locus of problem? *Journal of Consulting and Clinical Psychology, 45,* 101–103.

Swan, G. E., & MacDonald, M. L. (1978). Behavior therapy in practice: A national survey of behavior therapists. *Behavior Therapy, 9,* 799–807.

Turk, D. C., & Salovey, P. (1985). Cognitive structures, cognitive processes, and cognitive-behavior modification: II. Judgments and inferences of the clinician. *Cognitive Therapy and Research, 9,* 19–33.

Tversky, A., & Kahneman, D. (1974). Judgment under uncertainty: Heuristics and biases. *Science, 185,* 1124–1131.

von Neumann, J., & Morgenstern, O. (1944). *Theory of games and economic behavior.* Princeton, NJ: Princeton University Press.

Wason, P. C. (1968). Reasoning about a rule. *Quarterly Journal of Experimental Psychology, 20,* 273–281.

Wason, P. C. (1969). Regression in reasoning? *British Journal of Psychology, 60,* 471–480.

Watson, D. (1982). The actor and the observer: How are their perceptions of causality different? *Psychological Bulletin, 92,* 682–700.

Wiggins, J. S. (1981). Clinical and statistical prediction: Where are we and where do we go from here? *Clinical Psychology Review, 1,* 3–18.

Wilson, F. E., & Evans, I. M. (1983). The reliability of target-behavior selection in behavioral assessment. *Behavioral Assessment, 5,* 15–32.

Chapter 2

Toward a Problem-solving Formulation of Psychotherapy and Clinical Decision Making

INTRODUCTION

In an attempt to provide a model of effective clinical decision making for behavior therapy, we adopt a problem-solving perspective. Although our approach is not the first to represent psychotherapy as a problem-solving process (cf. Haley, 1976; Kanfer & Busemeyer, 1982; Spivack, Platt, & Shure, 1976; Urban & Ford, 1971), we delineate a paradigm that focuses more explicitly on the judgmental processes of the behavioral clinician.

Our paradigm is based on the research and theory underlying *social problem-solving training*, as originally described by D'Zurilla and Goldfried (1971) and later revised by D'Zurilla and Nezu (1982). This particular prescriptive approach focuses on training clients to become better problem solvers as a means of dealing more effectively with stressful life circumstances (Nezu & D'Zurilla, in press; Nezu, Nezu, & Perri, 1989, in press), whereas the present model represents the clinician as a problem solver (Nezu, Nezu, & Perri, 1988; Nezu, Petronko, & Nezu, 1982).

Within this framework, each time a behavioral clinician makes an initial appointment with a prospective client, she is faced with a problem. This problem is providing an optimally effective treatment to a given individual, who is characterized by a unique constellation of complaints, symptoms, life circumstances, developmental history, and biological makeup. Solving this problem entails both identifying and implementing an intervention plan.

In this context, a problem can be defined as a clinical situation in which a therapist is presented with a set of complaints by an individual seeking help to reduce or minimize such complaints.[1] This situation is considered a problem because the client's current state (i.e., presence of complaints) represents a discrepancy from the individual's desired state (i.e., goals). A variety of impediments (i.e., obstacles or conflicts) prevent or make it difficult for the client to reach his goals without a therapist's aid. Such impediments may include variables relevant to the patient (e.g., behavioral, cognitive, and/or affective excesses or deficits) and/or the environment (e.g., lack of physical and/or social resources, presence of aversive stimuli). Behavioral treatment, then, represents the clinician's attempt to identify and implement a solution to this problem. An effective solution within this framework is characterized by treatment that reduces or minimizes the initial complaints by changing the nature of impediments and/or reducing the negative impact they exert on the patient. Depending upon the specific nature of the case, these goals can be accomplished in a variety of different ways.

Beyond this global representation of therapy as a problem-solving process, several major subproblems exist. These involve specific aspects of the therapeutic process, such as patient problem identification, target problem selection, treatment selection and design, treatment implementation, and treatment evaluation. Each of these components entails a variety of clinical decisions geared toward finding the best and most valid answers. How effectively each of these subproblems is resolved impinges greatly on the effective resolution of other therapeutic subproblems. For example, inaccurate problem identification would likely lead to poor treatment, however effective the decision-making process for selecting the treatment may have been. Thus successful

---

[1] Behavioral clinicians can be approached for help not only by individuals, but also by couples, families, groups, institutional or agency staff, and school systems. The term *client* or *patient* refers to any of these consumers of behavioral treatment.

treatment (i.e., actually achieving desired goals) requires that each of these subproblems be effectively solved. For each of these subproblems to be successfully solved, the therapist needs to avoid vigilantly the various reasoning biases delineated in chapter 1. Therefore, any model of clinical decision making should incorporate into its structure procedures geared toward minimizing such judgmental errors.

To illustrate this general formulation, consider Janice, a middle-aged woman who comes to treatment complaining of feelings of depression and anxiety and wanting to gain more control over her life. The general problem the therapist faces can be stated as "How can I help Janice feel less depressed and anxious and feel more in control?" Although this question is as yet ambiguous and ill-defined, it serves as a framework within which to begin the problem-solving process. Moreover, it reflects a close approximation of those goals initially articulated by the client herself, thus addressing issues of social validity (Kazdin, 1985).

Impediments that prevent or make it difficult for Janice to reach such goals on her own are potentially numerous: a difficult marriage, poor family relationships, cognitive distortions, heightened autonomic arousal potential, poor coping skills, dysfunctional attributional style, poor self-control skills, unassertiveness, maladaptive problem-solving skills, lack of financial resources, poor environmental support, medical difficulties, presence of severe stressors, recent traumatic events, poor social skills, and so on. One initial subproblem is, then, the accurate identification of those variables that serve as impediments (i.e., are causally and/or functionally related to the presenting complaints). A second subproblem relates to selecting target areas that appear to be the most relevant to goal achievement (i.e., successful resolution of the problem). Based on such identification, the therapist must develop an overall treatment program to address each of these target areas. Such a treatment plan may or may not incorporate several behavioral strategies for each of these target areas. For Janice, a treatment program may entail coping skills and relaxation training to help her deal with her heightened emotional response, parent training to address her family difficulties, and assertiveness training to increase her sense of mastery and control over her environment.

After developing such a plan, the therapist needs to implement and monitor it to determine whether it appears to be an effective solution. Continual scrutiny of Janice's progress is therefore necessary, including the constant eliciting of feedback from Janice herself. If progress is sufficient for goal attainment, then therapy can be terminated, and the therapist's problem is solved. Again, we are hypothesizing that the likelihood of successful termination is increased if the therapist avoids biased clinical judgments.

Although the case of Janice may appear to be rather straightforward, clinical reality dictates that the therapeutic process is rarely so uncomplicated. As Bellack and Hersen (1985) point out, "There are no simple cases" (p. 9). One complexity involves the situation in which the operational definition of the patient's goals alters as a function of changes (or lack thereof) made in therapy. For example, Janice may initially have thought that becoming happy involved a better marriage. Treatment might then incorporate some form of behavioral marital therapy. However, if attempts to enlist her husband's cooperation were unsuccessful, this particular strategy would appear impossible to implement. A change in her goals at that point might involve getting a divorce. In a different vein, Janice may have defined happiness as improved relationships with her children. Further discussion (or even attainment of this goal) might engender a reevaluation of her various roles and lead to her desire for a career outside the home in addition to being a mother and wife. Any model of clinical decision making, then, needs to take into account potential shifting or redefinition of goals throughout the therapeutic process (Kanfer, 1985; Kanfer & Busemeyer, 1982). This dynamic perspective is thus sensitive to the reciprocal impact among goals, treatment effects, treatment choices, and clinical decisions (Nezu et al., 1988).

Further, additional complexities can emerge when certain problems not identified early in the therapeutic process appear after initial treatment has begun. Consider an example provided by Bellack and Hersen (1985).

Even in the very few instances where a well-defined problem appears, exigencies in the patient's life experience undoubtedly will alter the therapist's game plan. Let us assume that we are treating a 26-year-old female phobic patient with standard systematic desensitization. Let us also assume that good progress has been attained after going up the hierarchy of items by the 9th treatment session. At the 10th session the patient appears for treatment one-half hour earlier than scheduled and visibly upset. She begins the session by recounting how she and her boyfriend just had a major quarrel over what she perceives to be his inattentiveness and neglect of her. During the course of the quarrel both partners have said things they now regret. Our patient, in particular, has alluded to the possibility of "breaking up." But, of course, this was said in the heat of the argument, and now she is fearful that he, too, feels rejected and that he may initiate separation in retaliation. (p. 9)

We agree with these authors that only the most insensitive or naive therapist would ignore this incident and proceed with the desensitization trials. As Bellack and Hersen (1985) imply, however, the interpersonal problem that this patient described may in fact be related to the phobia being treated by desensitization techniques. The emergence of this new problem may therefore entail reevaluation of the problem behaviors, goals, and treatment choices previously specified.

In summary, we have conceptualized psychotherapy within a problem-solving paradigm, wherein the discrepancy between the patient's initial state and his ultimate goal state is conceived as the problem the clinician must solve. Unique to a behavioral framework of intervention are several clinical subproblems. These include problem identification, target problem selection, treatment selection and design, treatment implementation, and treatment evaluation. In formulating any model to address the clinical decision-making process, we suggest that (a) the model incorporate within its structure means of minimizing various judgmental biases and (b) the model be dynamic in nature, taking into account the shifting nature of the therapeutic process, particularly changing goals. Before we describe such a model in chapter 3, we will present an overview of the various components of a general model of problem-solving training. These problem-solving processes represent the key principles of clinical decision making that should be applied across the various clinical subproblems.

THE PROBLEM-SOLVING PROCESSES

We conceive of the overall problem-solving process as a series of specific skills rather than as a single ability. These skills include five interacting component processes, each of which makes a distinct contribution toward effective problem resolution (Nezu & D'Zurilla, in press; Nezu et al., 1988). They include (a) problem orientation, (b) problem definition and formulation, (c) generation of alternatives, (d) decision making, and (e) solution implementation and verification. (See D'Zurilla & Nezu, 1982, and Nezu et al., 1989, for a more complete description of these problem-solving processes, as well as research supportive of their effectiveness in training programs.) Before we briefly describe each of these processes, it should be noted that this model is prescriptive in nature and does not represent how expert problem solvers or clinicians address problems in real life (see chapter 1). Nor does depiction of these five processes as stages imply that problem solving necessarily proceeds in an orderly, unidirectional fashion. Instead, effective problem solving is likely to be characterized by continual and reciprocal movement among the five processes (see Figure 2.1). In other words, the actual outcome of one stage can suggest changes in the outcomes of previous stages. For example, it is possible that the process of generating various treatment alternatives will lead the clinician and patient to reevaluate overall therapeutic goals. Despite

Figure 2.1 Interactive Relationships among the Five Problem-solving Processes

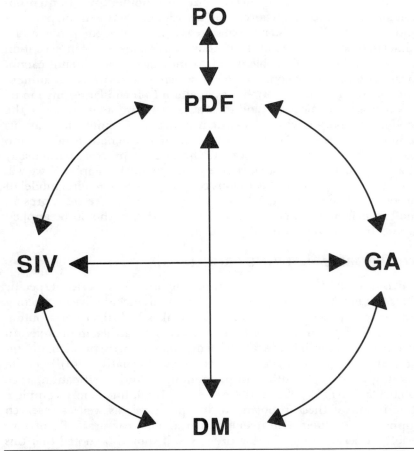

Note. PO = Problem Orientation; PDF = Problem Definition and Formulation; GA = Generation of Alternatives; DM = Decision Making; SIV = Solution Implementation and Verification.

their reciprocal nature, these processes are presented sequentially to reflect a logical and useful format to describe procedures.

Problem Orientation

This first problem-solving process reflects a general response set in understanding and reacting to problem situations. Orienting responses include an *attentional set* (i.e., sensitivity to problems) and a set of general and relatively stable beliefs, assumptions, appraisals, values, and expectations concerning life's problems and one's own general problem-solving ability. Depending upon the specific nature of these cognitive variables, a particular orientation may have either a facilitative or disruptive effect on later problem-solving activities. For example, if an individual believes that she has a major difficulty coping with problems, then it is likely that she would tend to avoid active attempts at problem resolution. Conversely, if a person appraises problem situations as challenges or opportunities for growth, then his attempts at solving problems would likely be effective.

Several orientation variables relevant to clinical situations cut across theoretical orientations; these mainly involve attitudes and values about mental health. For example, most clinicians, regardless of orientation, would view therapy as a viable and legitimate means for people to deal with their psychological difficulties. Willingness to adhere to legal and ethical standards concerning therapy (e.g., *Ethical Principles of Psychologists,* American Psychological Association, 1981) reflects another general set of values common to most clinicians. Although a thorough discussion of such beliefs is beyond the scope of this book, it is important to realize the influence they may have on clinical practice.

More relevant to the present discussion is the influence of one's *world view* on assessment and treatment planning. World views are cohesive philosophical frameworks within which people attempt to understand how the world works (Pepper, 1942). For mental health professionals, the major concern regarding a world view revolves around the way people function (i.e., having a perspective that helps one to understand, predict, and explain human behavior and psychopathology). World views incorporate, within a structured metaphor, several underlying assumptions concerning cause-effect statements pertaining to thoughts, emotions, behavior, the environment, and their interrelations.

Differential world views encompass different underlying assumptions. For example, a psychodynamic perspective could be classified, according to Pepper's (1942) schema, as an *organismic world view,* whereby one's behavior is explained according to the organic metaphor of stages of growth (i.e., psychosexual phases). Psychopathology, then, is viewed as being caused by immature or stunted growth in one of these stages. Social learning theory, on the other hand, can be classified as a *mechanistic world view* because it adopts the metaphor of a machine to explain behavior. Such perspectives identify the structures or aspects of the machine that produce or cause certain effects. Psychological distress, then, is viewed in terms of defective structures (e.g., poor self-efficacy).

Under the general rubric of the behavioral approach, antagonistic world views sometimes exist. For example, in contrast to the social learning model, a more radical behaviorist approach would be in keeping with a *contextualist world view* (Nelson & Hayes, 1986). This latter perspective focuses on the influence of the context in which events occur. Events are thought of as possessing properties only within a specific context, and, in a different context, would be characterized by a different set of properties. Within this framework, the structure of the machine is seen as superfluous because the effects of the machine can be understood only within a given context. Strict operant approaches within behavior therapy represent examples of the contextualist model.

By virtue of these different underlying world views or models of human behavior, fundamental differences emerge concerning content, focus, and methods of assessment and treatment planning. A functional analysis of overt behavior using behavioral observation procedures would be in keeping with a contextualist or operant model, whereas assessment of one's self-efficacy beliefs or assertiveness skills via self-report methods would reflect the mechanistic or cognitive-behavioral model. As Kazdin (1985) notes,

> The clinician's model of normal and deviant behavior and his or her therapeutic approach largely *dictate* [italics added] the type of behaviors (affect, cognitive, overt behavior) that will be assessed. Clinical work is not merely discerning the client's problem and then deciding on an assessment strategy. Rather, the clinical problem, as presented, is more likely to be reformulated and translated into assessment strategies to which the therapist may already be committed. (p. 34)

In light of the potential impact of such differences on the entire therapeutic process, we would go one step further and suggest that rigid adherence to any of these models by definition increases the likelihood that clinicians will engage in the various judgmental errors described in chapter 1. Precluding the plausibility of models other than the one embraced serves to facilitate the use of confirmatory search strategies, resulting in affirmations of only the model chosen. Maintaining that only certain schemata are proper for understanding behavior (e.g., "Behavior is always a function of the environment"; "Depression is always caused by cognitive distortions") would appear to engender the use of the availability, representativeness, and anchoring heuristics.

For the purpose of our clinical decision-making model, we advocate adoption of a *multiple causality perspective* within a biopsychosocial framework. This perspective implies that there are many paths by which a particular set of symptoms eventually become expressed and that a variety of biological (genetic, neurochemical, physical), psychological (affective, cognitive, overt behavioral), and social (social and physical environmental) variables may act or interact as causal factors.[2] Idiographic application of such nomothetic information is at the heart of this approach. Such a notion is consistent with a multiple response system approach to assessment (Evans, 1986), as well as with recent calls for multivariate analytic frameworks within which to understand psychopathology or deviant behavior (Craighead, 1980; Hersen, 1981; Nezu et al., 1988, 1989). It can be considered a synthesis of the mechanistic and contextualist world views.

This perspective also parallels a position advocating the use of *multiple operationalism* in the conduct of science. Such procedures include the multitrait/multimethod research design (Campbell & Fiske, 1959), multivariate (as opposed to univariate) causal modeling statistical procedures (Blalock, 1961), and meta-analysis, which uses multiple studies to test general theories (Glass, McGaw, & Smith, 1981). The perspective can further be viewed as an example of *planned critical multiplism* (Cook, 1985; Shadish, 1986), a methodological approach whereby attempts are made to minimize the biases inherent in any univariate search for knowledge. In this context, *multiple* can refer to both independent and dependent variables, methods to measure these

---

[2] *Cause* refers to the type of relationship that exists between two or more variables, where one variable reliably controls or influences certain aspects or parameters of the second variable. Such relationships might be either *distal* or *proximal*. A distal cause might be a genetic vulnerability to schizophrenia, whereas a proximal cause might involve increased negative life stress. Causes may also be *necessary, sufficient, interactive, contributory,* or a logical combination of these qualities. In other words, a causal relationship within our model does not necessarily imply a unidimensional (or unidirectional) pathway. Nor does it imply that such a relationship holds across all individuals experiencing similar presenting problems.

variables, and general constructs (e.g., multiple methods to assess a variable, multiple variables being assessed, multiple statistical procedures used to analyze data, and multiple hypotheses tested simultaneously).

Planned multiplism advocates heterogeneity, whereby the different options implemented have inherently competing biases. According to Shadish (1986), two key benefits can be derived from this perspective. First, multivariate approaches tend to provide for corroborative information of both a redundant and novel nature. Redundant information provides information about something that is already known; it offers no additional accounted-for variance. Novel information, being orthogonal to redundant information, adds new data, thus actually increasing the overall amount of variance accounted for. Second, using multiple options involves location of possible disconfirmations, inconsistencies, and biases. This method of searching for "truth" is a hallmark of the falsificationist school of philosophy of science, which contends that we learn as much or more about truth when we find out what is wrong with our theory as we can from novel corroborations (Popper, 1968). Both of these benefits can be accrued in clinical problem solving if a multiple causality perspective is adopted. Attention to the broad array of variables that may be causally related to the patient's presenting problems can serve to provide important new information and, when various disconfirmations occur, can highlight where certain biases might be operative.

Within our model of clinical judgment, these *focal problem areas*, embedded within the biopsychosocial conceptualization, are represented as impediments to achieving the clinician's goal of reducing or eliminating the client's presenting problems. Accurately identifying the relevant causal variables and the strategies that would be effective in changing them is the initial subproblem the clinician must solve. By conceptualizing patient complaints in this light, rather than by identifying and modifying unitary behavioral targets, we more closely approximate the difficulties inherent in clinical reality (Evans, 1985; Kazdin, 1985). This assertion is not to denigrate the vast contributions of the early behavioral assessment literature. However, within the behavioral literature, both single case and group comparison research studies have tended to address unitary target behaviors, neglecting the concept of *behavioral constellations* and *response covariations* (Kazdin, 1985; Voeltz & Evans, 1982) and the decision-making process by which such target responses are identified in the first place (Evans, 1985). This rather simplistic emphasis on the treatment of monosymptomatic patients is vulnerable to criticism from proponents of other theoretical orientations as well as from practicing, nonacademic behavioral clinicians. The latter might especially view this narrow focus as having little resemblance to clinical reality (Bellack & Hersen, 1985; Nezu et al., 1988).

In adopting the perspective of multiple causation, we do not advocate a haphazard, time-consuming search for all possible causal factors. Such an approach would represent the opposite extreme of a view restricted to unitary causation. Rather, *planned* multiplism is underscored. To identify variables potentially relevant to the individual patient and to delimit such a search, we suggest that a wide range of findings from the experimental literature be considered. This literature can also provide rich sources of competing hypotheses against which a preferred theory can be compared. As Shadish (1986) notes, "By planning multiple, heterogeneous options for any given intellectual task, rather than letting such options develop haphazardly or ignoring them altogether, investigators may more quickly find important biases in their knowledge claims" (p. 78).

To illustrate this approach clinically, consider the case of a depressed individual. Assume for the moment that the clinician's favorite causal model of depression leans heavily towards a cognitive formulation, of which there are several different types (see chapter 4 for a description of these approaches). Rigid adherence to such a model may influence the clinician to use biased and confirmatory search strategies in order to seek certain bits of information (e.g., presence of cognitive distortions, negative attributional style, poor self-control or regulatory skills). Doing so would entail the use of interview questions and self-report inventories geared to elicit clinical material relevant to only a cognitive model. Other information concerning the quality of the patient's marriage or social relationships might be relegated to a status of lesser importance, if acknowledged at all. In this case, the clinician should attend to studies highlighting the relevance of these social variables to the onset and maintenance of depression as a means of providing alternative hypotheses concerning the depression of this particular patient.

For some clients, the cognitive model may be more salient; for others, the social environment would be the more appropriate focal problem area. For still others, both problem areas might be causally operative. Because little evidence has been forthcoming to support a hypothesis of depression involving anger turned inward by a harsh superego, the behavioral clinician would not likely include this as one of several working hypotheses. However, all hypotheses would serve to suggest possible areas of assessment. As a broad-based assessment is conducted, incoming data of both a confirmatory and disconfirmatory nature can be used to evaluate each of these competing tentative hypotheses in a more empirical fashion. Moreover, anchoring errors can be avoided.

Related to this perspective of multiple causality is the characterization of behavioral intervention as a *strategic*, as compared to a *tactical*, approach to therapy. We define a strategy as a general approach that incorporates statements about subgoals and/or focal problem areas. Examples would include anxiety reduction, coping skills training, stress management, and relationship enhancement. Tactics are specific means by which such strategies are implemented (i.e., by which subgoals are achieved). With regard to an anxiety reduction strategy, for example, tactics might include relaxation training, biofeedback, flooding, exposure, cognitive restructuring, and diaphragmatic breathing.

By conceptualizing behavior therapy in this light, one tends to avoid making availability and representativeness errors in deciding which interventions to apply with a given patient. If various strategies are initially considered, a wide range of tactics can then be identified. However, if behavioral treatment is viewed as only a set of techniques, misapplication of treatment procedures is likely to occur. Biased judgments can engender use of the tactics without regard for idiographic differences. Automatically teaching a patient relaxation techniques solely as a function of patient statements concerning the presence of anxiety symptoms (or on the basis of elevated self-report anxiety scores) can potentially lead to ineffective treatment. Beyond a technique's potential efficacy for anxiety reduction per se, several additional factors may greatly affect successful implementation. These factors include the therapist's experience and competence in using a given behavioral technique, the availability of certain equipment (as in the case of biofeedback), the presence of medical difficulties, the importance of immediate short-term gains in light of the patient's motivational level, and/or the patient's specific anxiety symptoms (i.e., physiologic, affective, or cognitive).

Thus far, our proposed orientation to the problem-solving model of clinical decision making emphasizes the notion that client problems are potentially caused by multiple factors and that behavioral treatment should be viewed as a strategic approach. The last key principle that we advocate concerns the therapist's willingness to recognize that clinicians from all different theoretical orientations are vulnerable to making the judgmental errors described in chapter 1. We hope that the information presented in this earlier chapter has convinced the reader that such biases do exist. We further hope that it has engendered a desire to reduce the probability of making such biased decisions. Unfortunately, one of the major conclusions from the clinical judgment literature is that simply telling clinicians about these biased heuristics and providing exhortations to stop using them is ineffective (Arkes, 1981; Nisbett & Ross, 1980). Advising therapists about such errors and urging them to cease being influenced is akin to telling depressed people to think more rationally and logically and hoping that such advice is therapeutically sufficient.

Although accepting the possibility that one can make judgmental errors in various clinical endeavors has not proven to be a sufficient deterrent, it is perhaps a necessary starting point. In our social problem-solving approach to therapy (Nezu et al., 1989), we strongly suggest that behavior therapists pause and reflect upon each situation. We have found it helpful to use the subvocal reminder to "Stop and Think!" as a cue to slow down the decision-making process. This self-statement is aimed at decreasing the likelihood that the therapist will make clinical inferences automatically.

The type of clinical reasoning we further promote is embedded in the next four problem-solving processes. Although it should be noted that the specific manner in which these processes are carried out depends on the actual clinical subproblem being addressed, undertaking them can help the clinician actively avoid making judgmental errors and can be invaluable in formulating the optimal treatment for a particular client.

Problem Definition and Formulation

Problem definition and formulation involves assessing the nature of the problem situation and identifying a realistic goal or objective toward which latter problem-solving activities can be directed. The importance of this phase for guiding these latter problem-solving processes cannot be overemphasized. A well-defined problem is likely to have a positive impact on the generation of relevant solutions, improve decision-making effectiveness, and contribute to the accuracy of solution verification. Research incorporating both cognitive/impersonal problems and interpersonally relevant problems generally supports this hypothesis (Cormier, Otani, & Cormier, 1986; Nezu & D'Zurilla, 1981a, 1981b).

On a broad level, problem definition and formulation can be thought of as an approach to behavioral assessment in which the major tasks are problem identification, target problem selection, treatment selection and design, treatment implementation, and treatment evaluation. As noted earlier, we have designated these tasks as clinical subproblems within the overall therapeutic problem. Although overall treatment goals may already have been established as a function of the identification of the patient's most important problems, each of these clinical subproblems must be idiographically defined. In other words, the therapist must identify the most important problems for *this* particular patient, with *this* particular set of presenting complaints, given *this* particular set of circumstances or conditions.

Optimal problem definition involves five specific component activities: (a) seeking all available facts and information about the problem; (b) describing these facts in clear and unambiguous terms; (c) differentiating relevant from irrelevant information and objective facts from unverified inferences, assumptions, and interpretations; (d) identifying those factors and circumstances that actually make the situation a problem; and (e) setting a series of realistic and attainable problem-solving goals (D'Zurilla & Nezu, 1982; Nezu et al., 1989). Using these guidelines is likely to decrease the occurrence of biased search strategies and the anchoring heuristic.

Generation of Alternatives

The purpose of generating alternatives is to make available as many solution ideas as possible and to maximize the likelihood that the best or most effective one(s) will be among them. Within the context of this model, an effective solution is defined as one that, in addition to achieving specified goal(s), maximizes possible positive consequences and minimizes potential negative consequences. The theoretical underpinnings of this problem-solving process are related to the *brainstorming* method of idea production (Parnes, 1967). Brainstorming is based primarily on (a) the quantity principle and (b) the deferment-of-judgment principle. According to the quantity principle, the more alternatives individuals produce, the more likely they are to arrive at the best ideas for solutions. The deferment-of-judgment principle states that more high-quality ideas can be generated if individuals defer critical evaluation of any particular alternative until after an exhaustive list of possible solutions and combinations of solutions has been compiled.

At the point of generating ideas, consideration of the value or effectiveness of the alternative should be avoided, with the one exception of the requirement that the idea be relevant to the given problem. Our criteria for defining relevancy includes two key concepts. First, an idea is considered relevant if it represents a variable that has been empirically documented to be related to a given problem, subproblem, or issue. For example, with regard to identifying those factors that may be causally related to a patient's depressive symptoms, hypotheses would be restricted to those previously identified within the literature (e.g., cognitive distortions, self-control deficiencies, lowered positive reinforcement, poor social skills, ineffective coping skills, aversive marital relationship, experience of major life changes, etc.). In the absence of these criteria, relevance requires the generation of a logically derived rationale characterized by indirect supportive evidence. Such rationales (commonly included in the introductory sections of research reports) cite previous research and/or theory indirectly supporting the proposed set of hypotheses.

In keeping with aspects of our specified problem orientation, we also advocate the use of a strategies-tactics procedure (D'Zurilla & Nezu, 1982). This approach suggests that individuals initially conceptualize general means or strategies to solve a problem and then subsequently produce various tactics or specific ways in which the strategy might be implemented. In this manner, a greater variety of ideas are produced, and these in turn can increase the generation of alternatives. For example, with regard to identifying the most appropriate method for assessing a given patient's interpersonal relationships, one strategy might be the use of behavioral observations. Tactics could include unstructured interviews, formal role-play situations, unobtrusive observations at home or at work, and observations of interactions with designated collaterals (e.g., family members, friends, or co-workers).

In general, findings from studies using a variety of different types of problems have provided substantial evidence in support of these idea-production guidelines (D'Zurilla & Nezu, 1980; Nezu & D'Zurilla, 1981b). Moreover, increasing the number of alternatives ultimately considered can serve to decrease automatic and biased judgments.

Decision Making

The goals of the decision-making process are to evaluate the available solution possibilities and to select the most effective alternative(s) for implementation. The focus during this problem-solving process is on the evaluation of alternatives with regard to their consequences. Related to this process are both causal and consequential thinking (i.e., identifying cause-effect relations and anticipating the consequences of one's actions).

To make the best decision possible, we suggest that an individual first assess the various alternatives and then choose those that have the greatest utility. Within our model, *utility* is defined as a joint function of the *likelihood* of that alternative's actually achieving a particular goal and the *value* of the alternative.[3]

The first assessment that the problem solver should make concerns likelihood, or the potential a particular alternative has for producing a particular effect. In other words, will the alternative meet the previously stated problem-solving goals? In this regard, it is important also, as an independent concern, to consider whether the alternative can be implemented in its optimal form. A given solution might be an excellent idea in theory but have practical limitations. For example, with regard to the treatment of agoraphobia (see chapter 5), therapist-assisted in vivo exposure to feared situations might be considered a potentially effective intervention. However, if the therapist does not have the time to devote to such an undertaking, this procedure should not be implemented, regardless of its potential efficacy. In addition to evaluating the effectiveness and feasibility of a given treatment approach, in determining the likelihood of a given effect, the therapist must also assess his level of competence and experience and his ability to implement that particular intervention strategy.

In making judgments about the value of an alternative, we suggest that four categories of consequences be considered: personal (effects on oneself), social (effects on others), short-term, and long-term. Personal consequences might involve the time and effort required to implement a particular alternative, personal and emotional costs versus gains, consistency of the alternative with one's ethical and moral standards, and effects on physical well-being. Specific social consequences might include effects on one's family, friends, or community. Short-term consequences refer to the immediate effects of a solution, such as the reduction in anxiety symptoms once relaxation skills are learned. Long-term consequences within this context address the important issue of maintenance of treatment effects. In other words, how long do the benefits last? Even if a treatment procedure reliably reduces distress symptoms, assessment of the likelihood of relapse also needs to be conducted. Evaluation of such consequences needs also to focus on both patient and therapist. For example, in considering the value of a therapist-assisted exposure procedure to reduce acrophobic symptoms, the clinician should consider not only the effects on the patient, but also the time and effort required to conduct such a treatment plan in its

---

[3] For a more detailed discussion of likelihood and value criteria in the decision-making process, see chapter 3.

optimal form. Because individual patients differ in their personal beliefs, goals, and commitment to change, it is impossible to develop a standard set of criteria against which to evaluate consequences for each type of clinical problem. As such, it is important for the therapist to brainstorm all the potential consequences and effects of a given alternative, especially when the situation is novel.

In evaluating the various costs and benefits associated with each alternative, the problem solver must assess the total picture rather than the valence of any specific outcome criterion. For example, a solution might be judged as extremely favorable as concerns two criteria but might be rejected because the overall expected costs outweigh the overall expected benefits. On the basis of such comparisons, the therapist should then choose those alternatives for which the expected overall outcomes most closely match the desired goals. If only a few ideas appear to be satisfactory, then the problem solver may need to engage again in the previous problem-solving processes.

Research assessing the effectiveness of training in this decision-making paradigm has generally provided supportive evidence (Cormier et al., 1986; Nezu & D'Zurilla, 1979, 1981a; Nezu & Ronan, 1987). Carefully articulating the criteria by which clinical decisions are made can also serve to prevent potential errors in judgment.

Solution Implementation and Verification

The major function of solution implementation and verification is to compare anticipated and actual consequences of an implemented solution. Even though a problem may appear to be solved, the effectiveness of the alternative implemented and the appropriateness of the decision to use it have not yet been established. By carrying out the alternative (or, in certain cases, by making a clinical decision or choice), it is possible to evaluate that solution's effectiveness or accuracy.

The manner in which the match between anticipated and actual outcomes takes place is best articulated by *self-control theory* (Kanfer, 1970; see also *control* or *cybernetics theory*, Carver & Scheier, 1982). This theory involves four key components: performance, self-monitoring, self-evaluation, and self-reinforcement. Within a general problem-solving framework, this procedure therefore encompasses (a) implementation of the solution response, (b) observation of the actual consequences that occur after carrying out the solution, (c) evaluation of the effectiveness of the solution, and (d) self-reinforcement when the problem is resolved (D'Zurilla & Nezu, 1982). These key operations can serve the problem-solving therapist as a basis for extrapolation in evaluating the effectiveness of critical clinical decisions.

The performance step of this process involves the actual implementation of the solution. However, depending upon the nature of the problem, at times implementing the solution does not necessarily involve an overt behavioral response. It may represent making a decision or identifying a particular choice. Within the clinical decision-making model, for example, problem-solving can be used to help identify and select important patient target behaviors. Implementation of the solution in this case does not require any response beyond verification.

The second step in this process, monitoring, involves observing the effects of the implemented solution. This observation entails measurement of the solution outcome at varying levels, not simply attendance to global consequences. In order to obtain accurate information concerning the outcome, it is necessary at times to include an objective recording procedure. A clinical example would be periodic measurement of a patient's behavior or symptom change in order to assess the outcome of a particular treatment procedure.

In the evaluation step, the problem solver compares the observed outcome with the desired outcome, as specified during the problem definition and formulation process. If this match is satisfactory (i.e., the discrepancy between the expected outcome and the actual outcome is low), the clinician moves to the last step, reinforcement. This last step may seem superfluous (i.e., the clinician may view patient improvement as sufficient reward). However, we recommend that the therapist at least covertly acknowledge certain positive self-statements concerning her efforts. We strongly suggest that such self-reinforcement be directed toward the therapist's efforts at effective clinical decision making, rather than toward the patient's improvement per se. Acknowledging the processes underlying clinical success also reduces the risk of future biases based on overconfidence. In other words, the clinician should say, for example, "I helped this phobic patient through sound clinical decision making" versus "I'm good with phobics."

If the match between the observed outcome and the problem-solving goal(s) is not satisfactory, the problem solver needs to discover the source of this discrepancy. The actual difficulties may involve suboptimal performance of the solution response, misapplication of certain aspects of the problem-solving processes, or both. In any case, the therapist has the option to return to one or more of the previous problem-solving operations to identify a more effective solution plan. It is possible that the problem(s) were not adequately defined and formulated or that various mediating factors were not previously identified. In addition, it is possible that insufficient ideas were initially generated or that the consequences of the solution were not evaluated accurately. In essence, a discrepancy between expected and actual outcomes highlights the need to continue to engage actively in the problem-solving processes.

If the discrepancy is due to deficient performance, the problem solver can either recycle through the problem-solving processes or attempt to improve upon solution implementation. Assessment of performance may need to focus on both the therapist and the patient. For example, if deep muscle relaxation does not appear to be effective in reducing a patient's anxiety symptoms, the therapist should assess whether or not the patient is implementing this solution correctly but should also evaluate whether or not he has adequately trained the patient in these skills.

SUMMARY

We have briefly described a general model of problem solving. This model entails five processes: problem orientation, problem definition and formulation, generation of alternatives, decision making, and solution implementation and verification. Problem orientation is characterized as one's overall general set or approach to problems in living. Aspects of this orientation specific to the behavior therapist as problem solver were highlighted. In general, these aspects involve the therapist's world view or philosophical perspective concerning normal and abnormal behavior. In particular, we advocated adoption of a world view that emphasizes the concept of multiple causation, that is, that the pathogenesis of similar problems is potentially varied and that the particular path for a given patient needs to be assessed idiographically. Our orientation further implies that behavior therapy be viewed as a strategic approach, rather than as a set of tactics.

We also argued that simple knowledge of the various judgmental errors to which clinicians are prone is insufficient to de-bias them. Rather, engaging in specific problem-solving procedures in addressing a multitude of clinical tasks may minimize the influence of such inferential errors. However, knowledge of these "bad habits" is viewed as an important initial step towards using any formal model of clinical decision making. In concert with our version of such a model, we further advocated the use of the heuristic "Stop and Think!" The specific type of clinical thinking to be done is reflected in the remaining four problem-solving processes.

These four major problem-solving processes provide very specific goal-directed guidelines for individuals in general (and therapists in particular) to use in attempting to solve problems of all types, including those encountered within the clinical arena. The specific cognitive-behavioral activities associated with each of these four processes are summarized in Table 2.1. Each of these tasks was described as making a unique contribution to the overall goal of problem-solving. In addition, the dynamic and synergistic nature of problem-solving was underscored. Effective application of these problem-solving processes across a multitude of clinical tasks reflects the essence of our clinical decision-making model. How this application is to be accomplished is detailed in the next chapter.

Table 2.1 Activities Associated with Four Major Problem-solving Processes

PROBLEM DEFINITION AND FORMULATION

1. Gather all available facts about the problem.
2. Describe these facts in clear and unambiguous terms.
3. Differentiate between facts and assumptions.
4. Identify those factors that make the situation a problem.
5. Set a series of realistic problem-solving goals.

GENERATION OF ALTERNATIVES

1. Generate as many alternative solutions as possible.
2. Defer critical judgment.
3. Generate alternative strategies first, then think of as many tactics for each strategy as possible.

DECISION MAKING

1. Evaluate each alternative by rating (a) the likelihood that the alternative, if implemented optimally, will achieve the desired goals and (b) the value of the alternative in terms of personal, social, long-term, and short-term consequences.
2. Choose the alternative(s) that have the highest utility.

SOLUTION IMPLEMENTATION AND VERIFICATION

1. Carry out the chosen plan.
2. Monitor the effects of the implemented solution.
3. Compare or match the predicted and actual effects.
4. Self-reinforce if the match is satisfactory; recycle through the process if the match is unsatisfactory.

References

American Psychological Association. (1981). *Ethical principles of psychologists.* Washington, DC: Author.

Arkes, H. R. (1981). Impediments to accurate clinical judgment and possible ways to minimize their impact. *Journal of Consulting and Clinical Psychology, 49,* 323–330.

Bellack, A. S., & Hersen, M. (1985). General considerations. In M. Hersen & A. S. Bellack (Eds.), *Handbook of clinical behavior therapy with adults.* New York: Plenum.

Blalock, H. M. (1961). *Causal inference in nonexperimental research.* Chapel Hill, NC: University of North Carolina Press.

Campbell, D. T., & Fiske, D. W. (1959). Convergent and discriminant validation by the multitrait-multimethod matrix. *Psychological Bulletin, 56,* 81–105.

Carver, C. S., & Scheier, M. F. (1982). Control theory: A useful conceptual framework for personality—Social, clinical, and health psychology. *Psychological Bulletin, 92,* 111–135.

Cook, T. D. (1985). Post-positivist critical multiplism. In L. Shotland & M. M. Marks (Eds.), *Social science and social policy.* Beverly Hills, CA: Sage.

Cormier, W. H., Otani, A., & Cormier, S. (1986). The effects of problem-solving training on two problem-solving tasks. *Cognitive Therapy and Research, 10,* 95–108.

Craighead, W. E. (1980). Away from a unitary model of depression. *Behavior Therapy, 11,* 112–118.

D'Zurilla, T. J., & Goldfried, M. R. (1971). Problem solving and behavior modification. *Journal of Abnormal Psychology, 78,* 107–126.

D'Zurilla, T. J., & Nezu, A. M. (1980). A study of the generation-of-alternatives process in social problem solving. *Cognitive Therapy and Research, 4,* 67–72.

D'Zurilla, T. J., & Nezu, A. M. (1982). Social problem solving in adults. In P. C. Kendall (Ed.), *Advances in cognitive-behavioral research and therapy* (Vol. 1). New York: Academic.

Evans, I. M. (1985). Building systems models as a strategy for target behavior selection in clinical assessment. *Behavioral Assessment, 7,* 21–32.

Evans, I. M. (1986). Response structure and the triple-response-mode concept. In R. O. Nelson & S. C. Hayes (Eds.), *Conceptual foundations of behavioral assessment.* New York: Guilford.

Glass, G. V., McGaw, B., & Smith, M. L. (1981). *Meta-analysis in social research.* Beverly Hills, CA: Sage.

Haley, J. (1976). *Problem-solving therapy.* San Francisco: Jossey-Bass.

Hersen, M. (1981). Complex problems require complex solutions. *Behavior Therapy, 12,* 15–29.

Kanfer, F. H. (1970). Self-regulation: Research, issues and speculations. In C. Neuringer & J. L. Michael (Eds.), *Behavior modification in clinical psychology.* New York: Appleton-Century-Crofts.

Kanfer, F. H. (1985). Target selection for clinical change programs. *Behavioral Assessment, 7,* 7–20.

Kanfer, F. H., & Busemeyer, J. (1982). The use of problem-solving and decision-making in behavior therapy. *Clinical Psychology Review, 2,* 239–266.

Kazdin, A. E. (1985). Selection of target behaviors: The relationship of the treatment focus to clinical dysfunction. *Behavioral Assessment, 7,* 33–48.

56   Chapter 2

Nelson, R. O., & Hayes, S. C. (1986). The nature of behavioral assessment. In R. O. Nelson & S. C. Hayes (Eds.), *Conceptual foundations of behavioral assessment.* New York: Guilford.

Nezu, A. M., & D'Zurilla, T. J. (1979). An experimental evaluation of the decision-making process in social problem solving. *Cognitive Therapy and Research, 3,* 269–277.

Nezu, A. M., & D'Zurilla, T. J. (1981a). Effects of problem definition and formulation on decision making in the social problem-solving process. *Behavior Therapy, 12,* 100–106.

Nezu, A. M., & D'Zurilla, T. J. (1981b). Effects of problem definition and formulation on the generation of alternatives in the social problem-solving process. *Cognitive Therapy and Research, 5,* 265–271.

Nezu, A. M., & D'Zurilla, T. J. (in press). Social problem solving and negative affective states. In P. C. Kendall & D. Watson (Eds.), *Anxiety and depression: Distinctive and overlapping features.* New York: Academic.

Nezu, A. M., Nezu, C. M., & Perri, M. G. (1988, September). *Clinical decision making in behavior therapy: A problem-solving perspective.* Workshop presented at the World Congress of Behaviour Therapy, Edinburgh, Scotland.

Nezu, A. M., Nezu, C. M., & Perri, M. G. (1989). *Problem-solving therapy for depression: Theory, research, and clinical guidelines.* New York: Wiley.

Nezu, A. M., Nezu, C. M., & Perri, M. G. (in press). Psychotherapy for adults within a problem-solving framework: Focus on depression. *Journal of Cognitive Psychotherapy.*

Nezu, A. M., Petronko, M. R., & Nezu, C. M. (1982, November). *Cognitive, behavioral, or cognitive-behavioral strategies? Using a problem-solving paradigm for clinical decision making in behavior therapy.* Paper presented at the annual convention of the Association for Advancement of Behavior Therapy, Los Angeles.

Nezu, A. M., & Ronan, G. F. (1987). Social problem solving and depression: Deficits in generating alternatives and decision making. *The Southern Psychologist, 3,* 29–34.

Nisbett, R. E., & Ross, L. (1980). *Human inference: Strategies and shortcomings of social judgment.* Englewood Cliffs, NJ: Prentice-Hall.

Parnes, S. J. (1967). *Creative behavior handbook.* New York: Scribner's.

Pepper, S. C. (1942). *World hypotheses.* Berkeley: University of California Press.

Popper, K. R. (1968). *The logic of scientific discovery.* New York: Harper.

Spivack, G., Platt, J. J., & Shure, M. B. (1976). *The problem-solving approach to adjustment.* San Francisco: Jossey-Bass.

Shadish, W. R. (1986). Planned critical multiplism: Some elaborations. *Behavioral Assessment, 8,* 75–103.

Urban, H. B., & Ford, D. H. (1971). Some historical and conceptual perspectives on psychotherapy and behavior change. In A. E. Bergin & S. L. Garfield (Eds.), *Handbook of psychotherapy and behavior change* (Vol. 1). New York: Wiley.

Voeltz, L. M., & Evans, I. M. (1982). The assessment of behavioral interrelationships in child behavior therapy. *Behavioral Assessment, 4,* 131–165.

Chapter 3

Clinical Decision Making in the Practice of Behavior Therapy

INTRODUCTION

Behavior therapy, as a treatment enterprise, encompasses several major clinical tasks. These can be classified into four main stages of therapy: (a) screening and problem identification, (b) problem analysis and selection of focal target problems, (c) treatment design, and (d) evaluation of treatment effects (Haynes, 1986; Kanfer & Grimm, 1980; Nelson & Hayes, 1986). Within each of these treatment stages, the therapist continually encounters a plethora of clinical decisions, ranging from "Should I treat this patient?" to "What measures should I use to evaluate the effects of therapy?" As noted previously, the effectiveness and validity of the decisions made in one stage greatly affect other treatment stages. Successful completion of such clinical tasks, then, is predicated on accurate choices and the minimization of judgmental errors (Nezu, Nezu, & Perri, 1988).

In this chapter, we will describe our model of clinical decision making and judgment and demonstrate how the behavior therapist can use the problem-solving processes described in chapter 2 (problem orientation, problem definition and formulation, generation of alternatives, decision making, and solution implementation and verification) to make more effective decisions and thereby accomplish each of these major clinical tasks. In essence, we advocate the application of all five problem-solving processes across each of the four major therapeutic stages. Following discussion of the application of these problem-solving processes, we will draw implications for theory, research, and training.

STAGE I: SCREENING AND PROBLEM IDENTIFICATION

The screening and problem identification stage of therapy involves obtaining a broad-based overview of the nature of the patient's problem(s). The behavior therapist's overriding goal at this point is to be able to answer the general question, "Given this particular patient, as well as the specific nature of the presenting problems described and goals desired, will I be able to help?" Obviously, any attempt to answer this self-inquiry would be premature before first answering several additional questions. However, it is important not to assume automatically that every patient who comes to treatment can be helped (an error of overconfidence). Based on information gathered during this initial screening phase, the therapist can begin to answer this question and make informed and deliberate decisions. Several obstacles or impediments may impinge on these decisions. We will label these *initiation difficulties* because their presence may serve to impede the initiation of further assessment and formal treatment. Specifically, these initiation difficulties involve the appropriateness of behavior therapy, therapist-related factors, and client-related variables.

Appropriateness of Behavior Therapy

One important screening decision involves the suitability of a behavioral treatment approach for a given patient. We are definitely not advocating that only certain types of patients (or problems) be handled via a behavioral orientation. Rather, we suggest that decisions be made concerning (a) the appropriateness of any psychosocial treatment being considered for implementation; (b) alternative treatments that may be more cost-effective; and (c) the advisability of providing therapeutic intervention at all, given the severity and/or nature of the problems involved.

With the first two decisions in mind, we often refer obese patients for a medical checkup before suggesting that they undertake a behavioral program involving reduced caloric intake and increased caloric expenditure (see chapter 6). Doing so ensures that the treatment will be safe and rules out the possibility that any medical problems might preclude such an approach. With regard to the third decision, we recall a case in which parents came to therapy because their child forgot to do her homework on an average of once a month. Offering normative information allayed the parents' concerns. Indeed, in cases in which the "problem" behavior differs little from a normal response, the only therapeutic intervention required may be the provision of such information.

Therapist-related Factors

A second set of potential impediments to goal achievement that should be addressed during this initial stage of therapy relates specifically to the therapist. An initial self-assessment of one's competence or experience with a particular clinical problem is important. For example, the therapist with little or no background in addictive behaviors who interviews a client having severe difficulties with alcohol should clearly undergo such a self-evaluation. We do not recommend that therapists practice only within a restrictive specialty. However, we suggest that a clinician is ethically bound to assess whether or not he can in fact be as helpful to a particular client as another therapist with more specialized training. Another competence issue can emerge when a patient's presenting problems involve moral or religious dilemmas; such a client may be best served by a member of the clergy.

Other ethical considerations exist that might impinge on the clinician's decision making at this point. Goals specified by a patient that are inconsistent with either the particular therapist's values or those values represented by society should serve as a cue for the therapist to "Stop and Think!" (see chapter 2). One example would involve the client who wishes to continue physically abusing her child. A situation in which the client is an agency or company seeking to gain aversive control over students, patients, or employees may also present such a conflict.

Another therapist-related factor concerns emotional reactions to the patient. We are not necessarily invoking the psychodynamic construct of countertransference at this point. Rather, we perceive that the patient and/or his presenting problems may serve as discriminative stimuli for the therapist (who is only human) and may elicit emotional responses. Examples may involve racial, cultural, or religious differences between the therapist and patient that engender an affective response on the clinician's part. Such reactions can be either prejudicial or overly solicitous in nature. In either case, they can impede goal attainment. Other emotional reactions may involve jealousy (e.g., the patient is a multimillionaire complaining about lack of achievement), anger (e.g., the client has been accused of murder), arousal (e.g., the patient is sexually provocative), fear (e.g., the patient has been physically harmful to others), or sympathy (e.g., the patient is a victim of gang rape). Again, we do not suggest that a therapist's strong emotional reactions automatically preclude successful treatment. However, they can serve as impediments.

Client-related Variables

A third general category of potential impediments that can be identified during this screening phase involves the client. One major factor concerns the level of client motivation or cooperation. If, for example, the client comes to treatment because of a court mandate and is generally uncooperative, the therapist must determine whether this circumstance is a major obstacle to successful treatment. Another example might concern one partner in a distressed marital dyad who is unwilling to participate in conjoint therapy. Another client-related issue, not often discussed within the behavioral literature, involves a client's ability to pay for services. If a patient has limited funds to support long-term behavioral treatment, the therapist needs to ask, in light of the patient's resources, "Can I help this patient achieve the desired goals?"

This list is far from exhaustive, especially in light of the differences among patients, therapists, and patient-therapist combinations. Because of the uncertainty engendered by such circumstances, it is important for the therapist to "keep her eyes and ears open." Doing so is analogous to the problem orientation variable of being sensitive to the existence of problems (see D'Zurilla, 1986; Nezu, Nezu, & Perri, 1989). If such initial impediments exist, the therapist's goal-related self-question then becomes "Given these particular impediments, will I be able to help this patient achieve his goals?" Applying the various problem-solving processes can help answer this question.

Applying the Decision-making Model to the Screening and Problem Identification Stage

Upon recognizing at this early stage that an obstacle to successful treatment exists, the therapist should begin to define and formulate the specific nature of any initiation difficulties. Doing so entails gathering relevant information, separating facts from assumptions, identifying the specific nature of the problem, using unambiguous language, and delineating a goal to direct further problem-solving efforts. One goal at this point involves asking questions to help minimize the impact of particular initiation problems. Examples could include the following: "How can I, as the therapist, help this client become more motivated to participate actively in therapy?"; "How can I overcome feelings of anger towards this patient in order to minimize their influence on treatment?"; and "How can I help this patient, who is seeking a more satisfying marital relationship, when her husband refuses to enter conjoint therapy?"

At times, several initiation problems may exist, in which case the therapist needs to articulate multiple goal statements. If several difficulties are apparent, efforts should also be made to determine whether they are interrelated. Goal statements more consistent with such an analysis would then need to be delineated. For example, it is possible that a patient who initially appears uncooperative is displaying counterproductive behavior because he is fearful that change will not occur regardless of treatment or therapist. In such a case, the therapist's goal should be to address both the patient's participation difficulties and his fears.

We recommend that the therapist continue to engage in the remaining problem-solving processes for each goal statement identified. Brainstorming principles can be used to generate alternative strategies geared to overcome initiation difficulties. In addition, they can help in developing the criteria by which to evaluate the utility of possible solutions and in making decisions regarding such screening choices as whether or not to refer a patient to another professional. The consequences of a given solution should then be evaluated according to their likelihood and value. A choice based on a systematic cost-benefit analysis can then be made concerning the optimal solution. After an alternative is implemented, actual consequences should be evaluated as to how closely they match predicted consequences. Recycling through the various problem-solving processes may be required if a significant discrepancy occurs. If the discrepancy between the predicted and actual outcomes is small, exiting this therapeutic stage and moving on to the next (problem analysis and selection of focal problem targets) would be appropriate.

The more severe or difficult the initiation problem, the more strongly we recommend that the therapist formally and systematically engage in the problem-solving processes. With less severe impediments (e.g., the patient's schedule is erratic, making appointment times uncertain), going through the decision-making model systematically may be costly and contribute little toward utility. However, we suggest that even a "quick run through" may minimize biased clinical judgments, regardless of how minor the initiation difficulty appears to be.

It is important to note that the decision-making model should incorporate the patient's input as much as possible. Depending on the nature of the difficulty, attempts to define the initiation problem can be conducted in conjunction with the patient. Such collaboration would include discussing goal statements, generating possible alternative solutions, making decisions, and evaluating the consequences of solutions.

A systematic application of the model to the decisions involved in this initial phase of therapy is illustrated by the following clinical example.

> After conducting two sessions, Dr. Jones identifies an initiation problem concerning her treatment of John Brown. John appears to be somewhat uncooperative and unmotivated to participate actively in therapy. This state is evidenced by "I don't know" answers to most questions, incompletion of a brief demographic questionnaire, missed payment, and late arrival for sessions. To understand the nature of this impediment better, Dr. Jones outlines the problem and asks for John's feedback. His reply is "I don't know; I think I want some help."
>
> At this point, the therapist poses the following goal-oriented question to herself: "How can I get John to become more motivated and actively involved in treatment?" Using brainstorming principles, Dr. Jones identifies several initial alternative strategies: increasing the reinforcing properties of the treatment process, conducting structured testing in session, ignoring the problem, discontinuing treatment, attempting to obtain minor clinical changes as a means of demonstrating the feasibility of treatment, improving the therapist-patient relationship, and using paradoxical intention strategies (i.e., conveying the attitude that John is supposed to remain uncooperative; see Kanfer & Schefft, 1988, for more potential strategies to enhance client motivation).
>
> Dr. Jones then identifies possible tactics under the first strategy (increasing reinforcing properties): offering refreshments, breaking down the task of completing the questionnaire into smaller steps, playing John's choice of music in the background, focusing initially on superficial areas chosen by John (e.g., movies, sports), discussing potential positive consequences of change, having John complete the questionnaire during the session, charging a lower fee per session, and watching films together. She then generates tactics for the remaining strategies and attempts to combine various alternatives to produce novel solutions.
>
> Dr. Jones next evaluates the utility of each of the various tactics generated according to the criteria specified in our model: the likelihood of the alternative's achieving the prob-

lem-solving goal; the likelihood of the alternative's being optimally implemented; and the value of the alternative in terms of personal, social, short-term, and long-term consequences. She uses a simple rating system (+3 = very positive and -3 = very negative) to rate each alternative according to these criteria, then chooses the alternative or group of alternatives that has the highest overall ratings.

In completing this task, Dr. Jones decides on three tactics: outlining the positive consequences associated with change, having John fill out the questionnaire during the session, and structuring initial treatment to require less active participation on John's part.

After implementing these alternatives, Dr. Jones monitors their effects. She notes any increase in the frequency of John's on-time arrivals, any increase in the frequency of payment for sessions, and any decrease in the frequency of "I don't know" answers. If Dr. Jones observes positive changes, treatment can proceed to the next stage. If no changes have occurred (or if they confirm the patient's lack of motivation), Dr. Jones may want to recycle through the model to identify more effective alternatives. If repeated attempts end in failure, it would be appropriate at this point for Dr. Jones to refer John to another therapist, thus terminating therapy.

One final point regarding initiation difficulties: We have continually emphasized the changeable nature of the therapeutic enterprise. We should therefore point out that initiation difficulties are not always identifiable during the first few sessions. It is possible that certain events occur or pieces of information emerge later to change the therapist's "game plan." In other words, some of these problems can and do occur throughout the various stages of therapy. We suggest that a procedure similar to the one just described be applied whenever such difficulties arise.

STAGE II: PROBLEM ANALYSIS AND SELECTION OF FOCAL TARGET PROBLEMS

Assuming either that no initiation problems have been identified or that those present have been solved, treatment then proceeds to the next stage, problem analysis and selection of focal target problems. During this stage, the therapist attempts to obtain a detailed understanding of the patient's problems, as well as those factors or variables that are etiologically or functionally related to them. Specific, albeit tentative, goals for treatment must also be identified. Basically, the problem for the therapist at this point can be represented by the following set of goal-related questions: "What is the specific nature of this patient's difficulties?"; "What are the factors or circumstances that have resulted in these problems?"; and "What are the specific treatment goals?"

We have suggested that, during the first stage of therapy, screening and problem identification, the therapist needs to obtain only a general picture of the patient's difficulties to make a determination concerning the initiation of further assessment and/or formal treatment. During the problem analysis stage, a more in-depth analysis takes place. The initial global assessment has provided clues that will enable the therapist to specify treatment goals and to design an effective, idiographic treatment plan. However, at this juncture the potential for a variety of judgmental errors is high. Depending upon the nature of presenting problems, the therapist's preferred theory, comparisons between the current patient and the therapist's most recent patients, and so forth, the clinician can make representativeness, availability, and anchoring errors. These inferential errors can, along with preconceived notions, lead to biased search strategies, which in turn can lead to ineffective problem analysis. Further, inappropriate target behaviors might be selected, resulting in ineffective treatment. In essence, relying on informal rather than formal decision-making procedures to understand and identify the patient's salient problems can lead to ineffective therapy.

Applying the Decision-making Model to the Problem Analysis Stage: Problem Orientation

To assess the specific nature of the patient's problems, the therapist must engage in the problem definition and formulation process. Initially, this process involves gathering information about the problems as comprehensively as possible. However, the actual areas of assessment and the methods incorporated to conduct this assessment depend heavily upon the therapist's overall conceptualization about the proper content of this search. In other words, the therapist's problem orientation greatly affects the manner in which problems are defined and analyzed.

We suggest that the proper *problem space* from which to identify client difficulties is not one designated on the basis of judgmental errors (see chapter 1 for relevant examples). The concept of problem space within the context of assessment refers to the universe of possible problems or difficulties that a patient may be experiencing. Such problems may be construed in psychological (e.g., low self-esteem), biological (e.g., hypertension), social (e.g., lack of support from peer group), and/or environmental (e.g., overcrowding) terms. The problem space inherent in our model is expansive, based as it is on evidence provided by the individual case, but restricted somewhat by relevant empirical findings. To distinguish this approach from one addressing only target behaviors, we adopt the terms *focal problems* or *focal problem areas*. These terms reflect the patient's idiosyncratic impediments to goal attainment at the time of initial therapeutic contact. We view the monosymptomatic patient or unitary target behavior as a misrepresentation of clinical reality and, as noted in chapter 2, advocate a multiple causality framework.

The manner in which problem areas interact with one another to engender the patient's current complaints is a key component of effective behavioral analysis. A general systems framework is helpful in understanding such interactions. According to Kanfer (1985), a systems approach

> views living systems as intricately relating environmental, psychological and biological events in a continuously changing flux, with adjustmental reactions aimed at maintaining a steady-state. The focus is on the current state of the system . . . this approach has been characterized as relatively ahistorical. It is the functional relationships among components rather than their development which is emphasized. . . . Target selection within this approach emphasizes intervening on those component processes or behaviors that hold a key position and can affect other events in a network-like system. . . . Targets may be environmental inputs, cognitive mechanisms or behavioral sequences. Preference is given to those elements which promise to alter the system balance most quickly and widely. (pp. 11–12)

Our systems approach deviates from Kanfer's (1985) definition in two minor ways. Although we agree with Kanfer's emphasis on interventions designed to achieve future goals, we believe that developmental antecedents are also important. Significant historical events, or distal causes, can provide an understanding of the manner in which current problems have developed. At times, treatment strategies, although focused on future goals, may need to be applied differentially depending upon idiographic variations in patients' developmental histories.

Our recent first trip to Great Britain provides a nonclinical example of this assertion: In Britain, vehicles are driven on the left-hand side of the road and are operated from a driving position on the right. In the United States, where we learned to drive, this situation is, of course, exactly the opposite. In attempting to cope with this major difference, we realized that our previous driving experience could be both an advantage and a disadvantage. On the positive side, our previous experience gave us the advantage of adapting rather more quickly to the new situation than might the British individual learning to drive for the first time. However, as a function of this same learning history, our habits (e.g., reaching to the right to turn on windshield wipers, shift gears, adjust the mirror, etc.) served at times to interfere with our learning new behaviors. This prior learning history would be important to note in designing an optimal training program for driving, whether such a program were conducted formally (i.e., driver's school) or whether it focused on self-teaching.

The second minor deviation from Kanfer's (1985) definition of the systems approach involves our emphasis on program design. Rather than relying (or hoping) that when certain problem areas change they will automatically have the desired impact on other focal problem areas, we recommend identifying several problems for which several treatment strategies can be implemented. In essence, we suggest that the overall set of problems be attacked from a number of different vantage points. Doing so increases the likelihood of maintenance and generalization and is conceptually consistent with research showing dysynchrony among various response modes (e.g., that changes in affect may not be correlated highly with changes in behavior; Lang, 1968).

Consistent with Kanfer's (1985) conceptualization of the proper problem space, we also emphasize identifying those areas that will have a clinically significant impact on patient goal attainment. The most relevant arena for change consists of variables that can help the client move towards her goal state. This view is somewhat in contrast with a treatment approach involving only removal of hypothesized causative factors. For example, cognitive restructuring procedures might be used to ameliorate those cognitive distortions identified as functionally related to a patient's depression. Conceptually, this procedure is based on the assumption that cognitive distortions caused the depression. Treatment, then, is designed to remove or alleviate such etiologic factors. The present model would augment cognitive restructuring procedures with treatment geared towards increasing the patient's adaptability to novel, stressful life situations. Coping skills training or social problem-solving therapy may be important alternatives to consider later on in the decision-making process (Nezu et al., 1989). In this light, the emphasis is on increasing future functioning in addition to helping the client overcome identified obstacles to goal attainment (see Kanfer, 1985).

In summary, we suggest that the arena in which to search for relevant problems be expanded beyond unitary target behaviors. Instead, the therapist needs to identify *all* focal problem areas that may be causally related to the patient's presenting complaints. These problem areas are embedded within a greater systems model incorporating a wide variety of possible variables. According to the criteria of relevancy described in chapter 2, the boundaries of this system are drawn by the empirical findings relating to a given disorder or problem. Such an approach further implies that treatment be focused on strategies that increase the probability that the client will actually achieve his goals, even if those strategies do not directly relate to the removal of features presumed to cause the patient's problems.

In general, we suggest that this orientation can minimize judgmental errors by increasing the therapist's adaptive flexibility during the assessment process. More specifically, this orientation implies an expansive search for potentially relevant causal factors, rather than the automatic and restrictive targeting of behavioral responses. The omission of formal decision analysis makes the clinician vulnerable to errors of availability, representativeness, and anchoring. As Barrios (1988) notes,

> All too often the sole reason for our selecting a particular behavior as the focus of treatment has been convenience. The target behavior has been one that could be easily operationalized, easily measured, and easily interpreted via visual inspection. Such a behavior has all too often been an inadequate representation of the client's concerns, and in those cases where it has not been a trivialization of the client's concerns, it has all too often been an incomplete representation of those concerns. That is, even in those cases where the isolated target behavior has been a relevant feature of the client's difficulties, it has not been the *embodiment* [italics added] of the client's difficulties. (pp. 10–11)

We suggest, then, that the remaining four problem-solving processes be conducted in concert with this particular orientation.

Applying the Decision-making Model to the Problem Analysis Stage: Problem Definition and Formulation

As delineated in chapter 2, the major activities included in the process of problem definition and formulation are gathering all relevant information about the problem(s), separating facts from assumptions, identifying features that actually contribute to the problem situation (i.e., those factors that are causally linked to the patient's complaints), and identifying realistic problem-solving goals. To further minimize biases inherent in this process, the therapist should use unambiguous and concrete language to describe such information.

In terms of gathering information about the client's difficulties, the therapist is confronted with two specific clinical questions: "Which areas of the patient's life space should be assessed?" and "Which assessment procedures should be used to conduct this assessment?" Although these questions are interrelated, the clinician should exercise care not to let the answer to the first dictate the answer to the second. Due to the potential for availability and representativeness errors, it may be easier to identify assessment procedures that are similar in modality to the problem area being measured. For example, if the presenting complaints involve depressive symptoms, the therapist must guard against using only measures (whether self-report or clinician-rated) geared to assess the severity of depressive affect. Other assessment procedures (e.g., role plays, behavioral observation, count of missed work days, perceptions of family members) might also be important in minimizing the potential for monomethod bias and for accurately evaluating treatment effects. As such, the clinician may need to apply the overall decision-making model to identify the optimal assessment tools. This search is restricted both by the types of assessment procedures available and by the relevancy criteria concerning the specific nature of the patient's problems. Table 3.1 provides an overview of the important steps in this process. Because a description of the various types of behavioral assessment procedures and techniques is beyond the scope of this book, we refer the reader to the excellent compendiums by Barlow (1981); Ciminero, Calhoun, and Adams (1977); and Hersen and Bellack (1988).

With regard to which specific problem areas should be assessed, we suggest that the next level of assessment after screening be a broad-based investigation of possible difficulties that the patient is currently experiencing in a variety of life areas. Although the following list contains items that may overlap and is certainly not exhaustive, we recommend that assessment focus on the following general areas:

Table 3.1 Application of the Problem-solving Processes for Identifying and Selecting Assessment Methods

PROBLEM ORIENTATION

1. Adopt multimethod approach: For each focal area, use various assessment methods to increase the reliability, validity, and utility of information obtained.

2. Adopt strategic approach: Generate various strategies or general approaches concerning possible assessment procedures. Examples include role plays, observational methods, interviews, self-report inventories, and so on.

PROBLEM DEFINITION AND FORMULATION

1. Identify any potential problems involved in conducting assessment: Examples might include the client's language difficulties, cognitive/intellectual impairments, or unresponsiveness, as well as the therapist's lack of resources.

2. If no such problems exist, state goal(s): Ask the question "Which assessment procedures should I incorporate to maximize the chances of obtaining valid, reliable, and comprehensive information about this client?"

3. If certain problems are identified, state goal(s) as including any impediments: For example, ask the question "How can I obtain valid, reliable, and comprehensive data about this client given that she is developmentally disabled?"

GENERATION OF ALTERNATIVES

1. For each life area previously identified as problematic, generate as many strategies as possible: Different focal problem areas (both personal and environmental) should be considered in producing this list. For example, if one focal area involves interpersonal problems, potential assessment methods might include self-report inventories, interview procedures with client, interview procedures with relevant collaterals, behavioral observation, and structured role plays.

2. For each strategy, generate as many tactics as possible: Possible tactics for the previously mentioned strategy of collateral interviews might include in-session or telephone interviews with family members, friends, or co-workers. Combine various tactics across strategies to produce novel approaches (e.g., family members complete self-report inventories).

DECISION MAKING

1. For each tactic, evaluate the potential effects according to the following criteria.

   Likelihood

   a. Is this assessment procedure likely to produce reliable, valid, and comprehensive information about this particular life area/focal problem? (Base this evaluation on data provided by the empirical literature—e.g.,

Table 3.1 *(cont'd)*

use data concerning reported reliability and validity of a particular self-report measure.)

b. Can the therapist and/or patient carry out this procedure optimally?

Value

a. How much time is involved?

b. How much effort needs to be expended by the therapist? By the patient?

c. Is this procedure consistent with the morals, values, and ethics of the therapist? Of the patient?

d. What is the emotional impact (cost versus gain) on the therapist? On the patient?

e. Is there any physical danger to the patient? To the therapist?

f. What are the effects, if any, on other people involved (i.e., family, friends, community)?

g. What are the short-term effects?

h. What are the long-term effects?

2. Based on these ratings, choose the alternative(s) that have the highest utility.

SOLUTION IMPLEMENTATION AND VERIFICATION

1. Implement assessment procedure(s) as optimally as possible.

2. Monitor the effects (i.e., is the assessment procedure generating reliable and valid information about this particular focal problem?).

3. Compare predicted consequences with actual effects.

4. If the match is satisfactory (i.e., goals are attained), exit from the decision-making model.

5. If the match is unsatisfactory, assess whether this discrepancy is due to misapplication of the problem-solving processes, suboptimal implementation of the assessment procedure, or both. Recycle through the processes to identify the presence of certain problems (e.g., low client motivation impeding completion of various inventories), then attempt to correct them.

6. Recycle through the problem-solving processes until goal(s) are achieved.

---

interpersonal relationships (marital, family, social, and work) career/work, finances, sex, physical health, education, recreation/leisure, religion/moral values, and personal goal attainment. The therapist should attempt to address each of these areas to obtain as comprehensive a picture of the patient as possible, as well as to avoid making biased choices. Addressing each of these life areas helps the clinician to avoid neglecting potentially important information. This broad-based approach also provides data concerning the client's strengths (i.e., those areas of life that are not problematic). These areas can be capitalized upon at a later point in therapy, if appropriate, to increase motivation or to help transfer effective skills in one life area to another.

During the screening and problem identification stage and the initial phases of the problem analysis stage, the therapist adopts a "wide-band scanning approach" to identify potential problem areas. The clinician's next task is to conduct a functional analysis on a more micro-level for each of those life areas that are identified by either the patient or therapist as problematic. At this point, the therapist begins to focus in greater detail on specific difficulties, giving attention to those factors or variables that describe the client's problems across a variety of response modalities (behavioral, cognitive, affective), as well as those variables that are causally or functionally related to these maladaptive responses.

Figure 3.1 depicts a three-dimensional framework that can aid the therapist in conducting this microanalytic assessment. (Note that it also provides guidelines concerning selection of treatment goals and therapeutic evaluation targets.) The first dimension involves *focal problem areas.* These areas concern both the person (behavioral, affective, cognitive, and biological variables) and the environment (physical and social variables). The second dimension involves *temporal considerations,* that is, whether aspects of the six focal problem areas pertain to the patient's current state or whether they are viewed within the context of the patient's developmental history. The third dimension involves actual and perceptual *data sources.* Information in the actual category includes factual data directly supported by well-validated sources. Perceptual data involve the client's own appraisal of the nature of these variables. These two classes of information are included to highlight the potential for discrepancies evidenced by the patient, as well as those possibly produced by the clinician's biased judgment. An example of the former would be the discrepancy between a patient's verbalizations "I'm no good; I can't do anything right; I'm never going to make anything of myself" and actual data that indicate above-average grades in school and consistent career promotions. This type of discrepancy provides important clinical information about how the patient's belief systems may impinge on her problems.

As noted, clinical bias may also result in discrepancy. For example, the clinician may appraise (and consequently label) the patient as anxious based on information presented in a somewhat biased and/or self-selected form (e.g., data obtained through verbal self-report

Figure 3.1 Three-dimensional Framework for Assessment, Treatment, and Therapy Evaluation

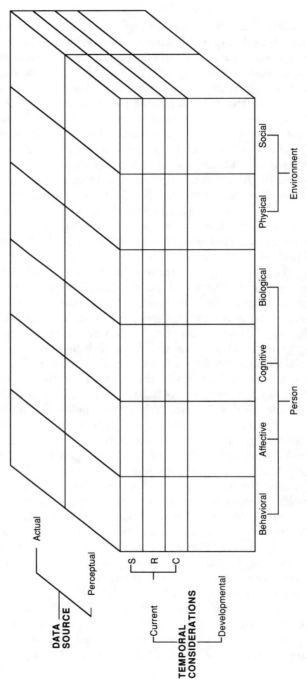

during an interview). However, on the basis of several self-report inventories, the clinician may find that the patient's level of anxiety does not appear to deviate significantly from the norm. Locating such a discrepancy can signal the therapist to rethink using a treatment design based on an anxiety-reduction paradigm.

Within a systems approach to behavioral analysis, a fourth level of assessment can be identified. This concerns the function or type of relationship that each of these variables serves with regard to the identified problem area. As depicted in Figure 3.1, across each of the six focal areas within the patient's current state of functioning, each aspect of a particular variable can be identified as a stimulus (S), response (R), or consequence (C). Figure 3.2 provides an example in which various cognitive variables are viewed within these categories. It can be argued that a consequence can actually serve as a discriminative stimulus for another response (which can act as a stimulus for a third response, etc.). However, depending upon where one delimits the stimulus-response-consequence unit within a behavioral chain, it is useful to identify the presenting problem as the response. Assessment can then be geared towards analyzing which variables, within this

Figure 3.2 Cognitive Variables in a Client's Current Functioning as Stimulus, Response, or Consequence

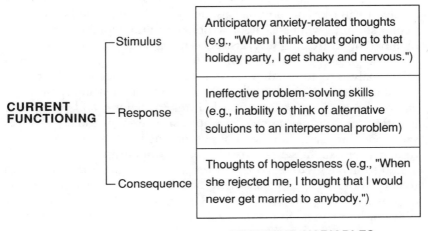

COGNITIVE VARIABLES

three-dimensional model, actually serve as antecedents and consequences of the response.

To conduct such an analysis, the clinician can use the *SORKC formula* to summarize the relationships among these variables, where *S* = stimulus (individual or environmental antecedents), *O* = organismic variables that might mediate the stimulus (e.g., biological, emotional, or cognitive state of the individual), *R* = response, *K* = ratio of consequence frequency to response, and *C* = consequence. This formula was first proposed by Kanfer and Phillips (1970) as a way to summarize the major variables that influence the probability that a response will occur. According to problem-solving terminology, this sequence identifies variables that serve as major impediments to goal attainment at the time of the initial therapeutic contact. The real value of depicting this sequence in such a manner lies in its provision of invaluable information concerning potential focal problems. Depending upon the specific nature of a case, hypothetical interventions can be developed to address each of the variables within the chain. In other words, treatment can focus on changing aspects of the stimulus, organism, response, consequence, and/or the operant relationship between the response and consequence.

It is likely that, instead of the simple, unidirectional relationships among these variables depicted in a standard SORKC formula, many variables relate reciprocally to create a "vicious cycle." In other words, a particular consequence may not only increase the likelihood that a behavior will reoccur, but may also increase the likelihood that a particular stimulus will be elicited.[1] Optimal treatment gains can thus be obtained by addressing several aspects of this chain simultaneously.

A hypothetical example of such a behavioral chain involves a microanalysis of John's depressive reaction. John becomes depressed (response) when he is alone in his bedroom (stimulus) and feels somewhat tired and focused on past failures, rejections, and feelings of isolation (organismic state). The depressive reaction usually involves sad mood; increased fatigue; thoughts of loneliness, hopelessness, and despair; and slight sensations of anxiety (topography of response). When John begins to feel such depression, it becomes difficult for him to get out of bed and engage in any activity that would counteract the depressive feelings (consequence). Often, when friends call to cheer him up, he focuses on his internal state and refuses to interact with

---

[1] The transactional model of stress proposed by Lazarus (see Lazarus & Folkman, 1984) is one example of how variables relate in this reciprocal fashion.

them. This behavior usually aggravates his friends, who then cease calling him (social consequence). This pattern has occurred frequently during the past 3 months (ratio of consequence to response).

In terms of potential treatment alternatives, intervention strategies can be identified to address each of the variables within this behavioral chain. For example, attempts can be made to (a) decrease the amount of time John spends in isolation (focus on stimulus), (b) provide training in self-control and self-monitoring skills in order to redirect his selective attention toward negative events (focus on organism), (c) teach John relaxation skills to counteract feelings of depression when he is alone (focus on response), (d) teach him problem-solving skills to increase or facilitate his ability to identify alternative ways to react in response to depressive feelings (focus on consequence), and/or (e) increase the frequency of pleasurable activities when he initially becomes sad (focus on ratio of consequence to response).

In order to be able to identify those variables that may potentially influence the probability that a particular problem will continue (i.e., causal and maintaining factors), a clinician should possess a working knowledge of the various theories, models, and research findings concerning that disorder. This nomothetical information then serves as a potential data base from which to assess the idiographic applicability of the model, theory, or analysis to the patient's problems. In utilizing the literature, the therapist must avoid focusing on a preferred theory or set of data. Biased search strategies can also occur with regard to selected readings. Assessing potential variables across all six focal areas therefore becomes particularly important as a means of minimizing judgmental errors during the problem analysis phase. In this manner, the clinician can obtain both confirming and disconfirming evidence concerning those variables that may be causally related to identified patient problems.

Another useful set of guidelines within this assessment framework is provided by Kanfer and colleagues (Kanfer & Grimm, 1977; Kanfer & Schefft, 1988). These investigators have delineated categories that describe process and event variables cutting across a wide range of nonpsychotic adult disorders. They suggest that most adult presenting problems fall into one or more of the following five groups: behavioral deficits, behavioral excesses, inappropriate environmental stimulus control, inappropriate self-generated stimulus control, and inappropriate reinforcement contingencies. Table 3.2 lists possible variables within each category. The authors do not suggest that this list is exhaustive or applicable to every psychological problem. However, they do

Table 3.2 Categories of Potential Focal Problems

BEHAVIORAL DEFICITS

1. Lack of knowledge for effective action
2. Lack of skills for maintaining social interactions
3. Limited or defective self-regulatory skills
4. Lack of appropriate self-evaluation and self-reinforcement
5. Deficits in self-monitoring
6. Deficits in self-control
7. Low level of satisfaction due to a restricted range of reinforcers
8. Deficits in cognitive and motor behaviors needed to meet daily living requirements

BEHAVIORAL EXCESSES

1. Excessive anxiety
2. Excessive self-observation

INAPPROPRIATE ENVIRONMENTAL STIMULUS CONTROL

1. Inappropriate or socially unacceptable affective responses
2. Milieu restrictions on pursuit of goals
3. Failure to meet environmental demands

INAPPROPRIATE SELF-GENERATED STIMULUS CONTROL

1. Inappropriate self-labeling
2. Inappropriate cognitive cueing
3. Mislabeling internal cues

INAPPROPRIATE REINFORCEMENT CONTINGENCIES

1. Lack of support for appropriate behaviors
2. Social support for undesirable behaviors
3. Excessive environmental support
4. Noncontingent reinforcement

Note. From *Guiding the Process of Therapeutic Change* (pp. 194–198), by F.H. Kanfer and B.K. Schefft, 1988, Champaign, IL: Research Press. Adapted by permission.

point out that addressing each of these areas across various psychological difficulties increases the scope and range of potentially important data.

Another method of categorizing problems or patient complaints is represented by psychiatric diagnoses delineated in the most recent version of the *Diagnostic and Statistical Manual of Mental Disorders* (DSM-III-R; American Psychiatric Association, 1987). Although it is beyond the scope of this book to debate the merits or limitations of such taxonomic systems (see Haynes & O'Brien, 1988; Hersen, 1988), we would like to highlight two important points. On the one hand, we believe that diagnostic classifications can provide useful guidelines for understanding response constellations and response covariations (Kazdin, 1982b). The term *response covariation* refers to the correlation among various responses that tend to be reliable over time. Understanding the types of covariations that occur within a particular diagnostic category can facilitate the identification of those variables that might be causally or functionally related to the patient's difficulties within our three-dimensional framework of assessment (see Figure 3.1). Such diagnostic categories also serve as useful constructs under which various research findings can be subsumed and guide the potential idiographic application of this nomothetic data base. This time- and labor-saving procedure avoids "reinventing the wheel" with each new client. Without such nomothetic data, the clinician would have to develop the field of psychology from the beginning.

On the other hand, diagnostic categories can entice the user to engage in availability and representativeness heuristics, which can then lead to substantial judgmental errors. If, via these two judgmental heuristics, certain patient complaints automatically access a particular diagnostic schema, the probability increases that the clinician will also engage in biased search strategies and the anchoring heuristic. Unless a formal decision analysis is conducted along the lines previously described, problem analysis, selection of focal problem targets, and treatment design can become highly compromised. In this light, we advocate the use of taxonomic systems such as the DSM-III-R only as an initial step towards identifying the potential focal problem areas idiographically relevant to a given patient.

Thus far, we have suggested that, during this stage of therapy, the clinician apply the problem definition and formulation process in the following manner: (a) gather data across a wide range of life areas (interpersonal relationships, career/work, finances, sex, physical health, education, recreation/leisure, religion/moral values, and personal goal attainment); (b) identify, by applying the entire decision-making model, the appropriate assessment procedures (i.e., tools or techniques) that will aid in this search; (c) when developing hypotheses about the patient's difficulties, gather data within the three-dimensional framework to obtain confirming and disconfirming evidence; and (d) utilize the SORKC formula to gain an understanding of how these variables relate functionally or causally. This process is the basis for formulating hypotheses about how the patient's problems were first initiated and how they are currently being maintained.

As a final step during the problem analysis phase, we have found it particularly useful to depict this formulation by constructing a Clinical Pathogenesis Map (CPM; see Figure 3.3). Such a map delineates the major elements hypothetically contributing to the initiation and maintenance of the patient's problems. Sharing the CPM with the patient may be useful as a means of education and motivation enhancement (although this may not always be the case). When this formulation is shared, the patient serves as a source of feedback concerning the potential validity of the problem conceptualization. Moreover, the CPM provides an important basis upon which to design treatment and offers a concrete statement of our hypotheses against which to test alternative hypotheses. Like our three-dimensional assessment grid (see Figure 3.1) it is a means of determining whether vital information may have been overlooked.

Important information not obtained during the initial assessment sessions needs to be incorporated within the existing CPM. In this case, the original CPM can serve as a working, idiographic model of a patient's difficulties and a framework upon which to add new data. At this point, the therapist asks the question "How does this new development fit into my existing formulation?" At times, the CPM may need substantial revision, or a new CPM may need to be constructed, in order to represent more accurately the patient's difficulties. As emphasized throughout our discussion, the therapist needs to be quite flexible to address adequately the various exigencies that often occur during therapy.

The hypothetical CPM illustrated in Figure 3.3 has been constructed around the problem of depression. Note that, in addition to focusing on the patient's current dysfunctional system, the CPM delineates distal and proximal causal variables. Also note the reciprocal nature of the relationships among the elements within the CPM. As shown, the consequences of depression (e.g., rejection by friends) can engender increased depression, reinforce the patient's irrational cognitions, and initiate a vicious cycle (see Nezu et al., 1989).

After developing an individualized CPM, the therapist can then move on to the next problem-solving processes, namely, generation of alternatives and decision making. These processes center on selecting focal problem areas that can be targeted for change.

Figure 3.3 Example Clinical Pathogenesis Map (CPM)

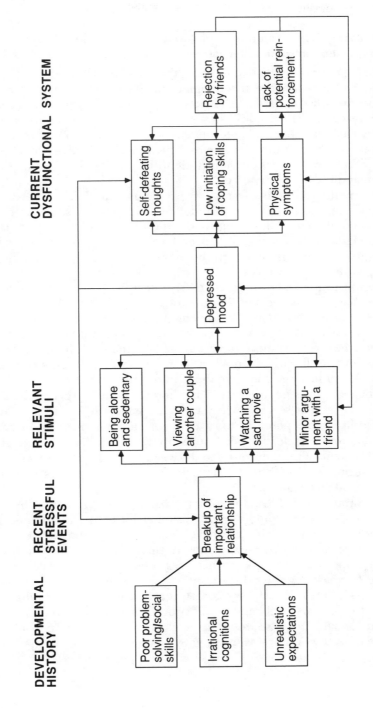

Note. This CPM depicts variables hypothesized to be involved in the initiation and maintenance of a client's depressed mood.

Applying the Decision-making Model to the Problem Analysis Stage: Generation of Alternatives and Decision Making

During the problem analysis stage, the clinician utilizes the focal problem areas within the three-dimensional model (see Figure 3.1) to develop a list of possible target problems. More specifically, using brainstorming principles, the therapist now generates a list of those variables that appear, based on a SORKC analysis, to be functionally related to the identified problems. This list is restricted by the relevancy criteria to those areas previously identified during the problem definition and formulation process.

In attempting to select target problems, the clinician then applies the various decision-making guidelines to identify those variables most in need of change. In doing so, the therapist should consider criteria associated with the likelihood and value of therapeutic change as regards a specific target problem. Because even patients who experience similar problems can differ vastly in their CPM profiles, the therapist will need to augment these criteria with a consideration of all possible consequences of therapeutic change. Table 3.3 lists questions the therapist should ask in assessing these matters.

Using these criteria (and any additional ones unique to a particular case), the therapist should create a cost-benefit profile for each problem area on the list of potential targets. Those rated highly (i.e., those assessed as having a high likelihood of positive effects and a low degree of negative effects) should then be chosen as initial target areas. Again, our bias is that several highly rated areas be selected as a means of maximizing the potential for overall goal attainment. In addition, this evaluation and selection procedure should be conducted in concert with the patient. The therapist should weight the client's answers to the questions listed in Table 3.3 heavily in any attempt to evaluate and select potential target areas.

Simultaneously with identifying focal target problems, the therapist and patient should develop a similar list to articulate those goals that the patient may initially have come to therapy to reach (e.g., to be less depressed) and those subgoals the therapist has identified based on the problem analysis (e.g., to increase problem-solving and coping skills and decrease cognitive distortions).

As is the case in selecting focal target problems, the therapist should use the various problem-solving processes to identify realistic therapeutic goals. Doing so would involve generating a list of possible goals and objectives via brainstorming; evaluating and rating each potential

Table 3.3   Decision-making Criteria for Evaluating the Consequences of Therapeutic Change

LIKELIHOOD CRITERIA

1. What is the likelihood that this particular target problem is amenable to behaviorally oriented treatment?

2. What is the likelihood that this target problem is amenable to the treatment the particular therapist can provide?

3. What is the likelihood that the treatment necessary to effect change for this problem is available?

4. What is the likelihood that any treatment designed to ameliorate this problem will be effective?

5. What is the likelihood that this problem can be resolved?

6. What is the likelihood that addressing this problem will achieve the patient's overall goal(s)?

VALUE CRITERIA

Personal consequences

1. How much time and other resources (e.g., money) will be involved in resolving this problem?

2. How much effort will be required by the patient to ameliorate this problem? By the therapist?

3. What will the emotional cost or gain of addressing this problem be for the patient? For the therapist?

4. Is resolving this problem consistent with the morals, values, and ethics of the patient? Of the therapist?

5. What are the physical side effects associated with resolving this problem (i.e., is the problem life-threatening)? Concerning the patient? Concerning the therapist?

6. What impact will addressing this problem have on the patient's personal growth?

7. What are the effects of resolving this problem on other patient problem areas?

Social consequences

1. What effects would ameliorating this problem have on the patient's family? On friends? On the community?

2. Is resolving this problem consistent with the values of others?

3. Will addressing this problem engender support or antagonism from others?

Table 3.3 *(cont'd)*

Short-term consequences

1. Will resolving this problem have a positive or negative effect on the patient's motivation?

2. Will resolving this problem have an immediate positive or negative impact on the patient's other problems?

3. Are there any immediate iatrogenic effects, even though long-term consequences are predicted to be positive?

Long-term consequences

1. Will the long-term consequences of resolving this problem be to achieve the patient's goal(s)?

2. Will ameliorating this problem prevent or minimize the need for future psychological intervention?

---

idea along the major decision-making criteria; and selecting, in conjunction with the patient, those goals that appear to have the greatest utility (highest likelihood and value ratings). The questions presented in Table 3.3 for evaluating the consequences of change with regard to potential target problems may be readily adapted for judging the utility of potential goals.

We have found it useful to construct a Goal Attainment Map (GAM; see Figure 3.4) similar to the CPM to provide a visual representation of where the client is currently and where she wants to go. The GAM includes treatment subgoals and ultimate goals, as well as intervention strategies identified during the treatment design stage, that would facilitate goal attainment. However, before the therapist specifies target problem areas and potential goals, he performs the last problem-solving process, solution implementation and verification.

Applying the Decision-making Model to the Problem Analysis Stage: Solution Implementation and Verification

Construction of a patient's CPM represents the implementation component of this problem-solving process. During this operation, the clinician monitors the effects of treatment decisions to compare predicted consequences with actual effects. With regard to the verification aspect, three levels of monitoring help guide this evaluation process. One level involves feedback from the patient. Although mutual

Figure 3.4 Example Goal Attainment Map (GAM)

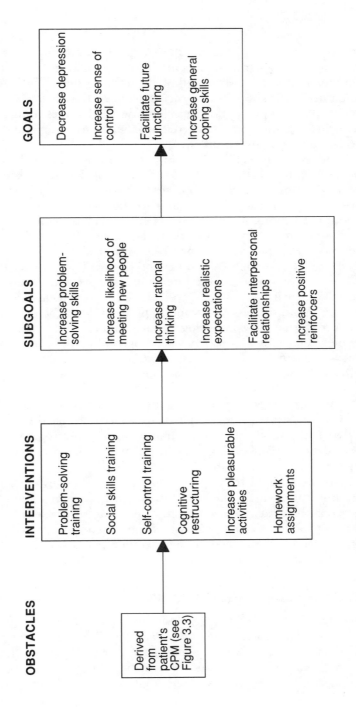

OBSTACLES	INTERVENTIONS	SUBGOALS	GOALS
Derived from patient's CPM (see Figure 3.3)	Problem-solving training Social skills training Self-control training Cognitive restructuring Increase pleasurable activities Homework assignments	Increase problem-solving skills Increase likelihood of meeting new people Increase rational thinking Increase realistic expectations Facilitate interpersonal relationships Increase positive reinforcers	Decrease depression Increase sense of control Facilitate future functioning Increase general coping skills

Note. This GAM illustrates goals, subgoals, and interventions involved in a treatment plan for an individual with depressed mood.

discussions concerning the case should have been conducted before this point, at this time a formal presentation of the CPM and GAM (without the intervention analysis) should be made in order to elicit feedback from the client, especially in terms of goals. Although it can be argued that the patient's perceptions may be biased and the resulting feedback inconclusive, without mutual agreement between therapist and patient, successful treatment is unlikely.

The second level of monitoring, suggested by the work of Turkat and colleagues (Meyer & Turkat, 1979; Turkat & Maisto, 1985), regards testing specific hypotheses derived from a behavioral case formulation approach. According to the case formulation model, several predictions about current or future behavior can be made on the basis of one's problem analysis. For example, if a CPM analysis suggests that a patient's major presenting problem involves anxiety related to interpersonal difficulties and fears of rejection, the therapist can outline certain predictive statements. One prediction might be that the patient will have high scores on self-report measures of social avoidance and distress. A second hypothesis might be that, during a structured role play involving a party situation (i.e., meeting new people), the client will display visible signs of anxiety and will report distress. Confirmations and disconfirmations of these predictions can help the therapist begin to evaluate the veracity of the original problem analysis.

The third level of monitoring involves assessing the actual effects of treatment strategies identified on the basis of the particular problem analysis. Although this particular monitoring step is removed from actual decisions concerning target problem selection, it does provide an important source of feedback.

On the basis of these three modes of monitoring, the therapist continues to evaluate the match between predictions about clinical decisions and actual consequences. The therapist recycles through the various problem-solving processes if the match is unsatisfactory or, if the match is good, proceeds to the next therapeutic stage, designing an idiographic treatment program.

STAGE III: TREATMENT DESIGN

This stage of therapy involves designing an overall treatment plan to assist the client in achieving her goals, as specified during the previous stage. Part of this treatment plan is geared toward helping the patient overcome those impediments to goal achievement outlined in the CPM (see Figure 3.3). In addition to generating an overall treatment plan, the therapist must identify certain treatment components, as well as any differential training methods that might be necessary to implement the plan optimally.

During this stage, the main clinical question is "Given these particular goals and focal target problems, what kind of intervention plan is necessary to proceed in a timely and cost-effective manner?" If the therapist has applied the various problem-solving processes in conducting the previous therapeutic stages, the probability of further judgmental errors and biased decision making in designing a treatment plan should be low. For example, if the decision-making model has engendered an accurate picture of the patient's difficulties, it is unlikely that a treatment plan will be proposed to change the "wrong" behaviors. Further, the therapist will probably be more aware of any patient, therapist, or environmental variables that could moderate the efficacy of a given treatment strategy.

However, the design of an optimal treatment plan still requires continual clinical decisions, even in the rare cases in which interventions run smoothly. Which treatment strategies to implement becomes a crucial question for the problem-solving therapist. Even though accurate problem analysis and goal specification provide clues for the therapist in selecting treatment approaches, the potential for making judgmental errors still remains high. Representativeness and availability errors are possible depending upon the nature of the client's problems, the diagnosis, the therapist's preferred treatment approach, and/or a wide variety of additional factors (see chapter 1). Often the treatment of choice is inadvertently based on judgmental errors rather than formal decision analysis. For example, the recent successful use of a certain treatment technique may influence the therapist to use the same treatment approach for the next patient who complains of similar symptoms.

Further, if the patient's presenting problems are thought to be easily amenable to treatment, the therapist may decide to employ a particular intervention before a comprehensive decision analysis is completed. Yet other initiation difficulties exist concerning the timing of treatment. For instance, although relaxation training may be an effective treatment alternative for an individual suffering from severe phobic symptoms, it may be necessary for the therapist to engage first in various cognitive strategies to decrease the patient's depressive symptoms (which emanate from his perceptions of helplessness). At times, only after depression lifts can phobia be optimally treated. In order to minimize these types of errors, we again advocate the use of a formal decision-making approach.

Applying the Decision-making Model to the Treatment Design Stage: Problem Orientation

Problem-orientation aspects of the treatment design stage of therapy involve the assumptions that (a) treatment be based on the idiographic application of nomothetic principles, (b) behavioral treatment be viewed as a strategic approach to clinical intervention, (c) multiple problems may require multiple treatment procedures; and (d) the treatment plan be designed not only to help the patient overcome the impediments to goal attainment outlined in the problem analysis but also to include strategies to increase overall capacity to cope with future stress. We believe that designing treatment programs with this set in mind helps minimize potential inferential errors and increase the probability of overall goal attainment.

Nomothetic Application of Idiographic Principles

The rationale for an idiographic application of nomothetic principles is twofold. First, a treatment plan should be tailor-made to fit the factors associated with a particular case, including the nature of the patient's problems; her strengths and weaknesses (e.g., cognitive/intellectual functioning, physical health); her age, gender, culture, and socioeconomic status; and the degree of environmental support (both physical and social) currently available. Even if an effective treatment can be easily identified, these additional factors may suggest that the treatment be applied differentially. For example, an exposure paradigm to reduce phobic symptoms might initially be identified as efficacious. However, for a patient with a history of heart failure, another procedure might be safer. At the very least, the therapist would need to deliberate upon the implementation of such an approach with this patient as compared to another patient without medical complications. In general, the therapist does not simply assess whether a given treatment strategy will be effective for a given disorder or set of problems. Rather, he assesses whether that particular intervention will be effective for the particular patient experiencing a certain set of symptoms or problems. Instead of treating a disorder, we advocate treating the person.

A second justification for this idiographic approach involves the variety of effective treatment strategies available under the general umbrella of cognitive-behavioral approaches. Although the technology has not yet produced a "cookbook" from which a therapist can readily choose the optimal treatment approach for any given disorder, a substantial amount of research has underscored the effectiveness of certain treatment strategies for certain problems. Examples would include systematic densensitization for some anxiety disorders, response prevention for obsessive-compulsive problems, cognitive restructuring for depression, sensate focus for sexual dysfunctions, and parent training for certain family problems. Although these strategies are not the only approaches that can be used to treat these difficulties, they represent an impressive pool of options. As such, behavior therapy does not represent an omnibus approach whereby the same treatment strategy is used regardless of the disorder or other contributing factors. Instead, it represents a broad array of empirically based procedures that can be chosen on the basis of the unique characteristics of the client. When designing optimal intervention plans, the behavior therapist therefore needs to be vigilant in utilizing the broad spectrum of potential treatment strategies rather than focusing on only those that are preferred, come easily to mind, or are assumed to be effective based on previous experience.

Behavior Therapy as a Strategic Approach to Treatment

As delineated in chapter 2, perceiving behavioral interventions in terms of strategies decreases errors of availability and representativeness. For example, if a patient's presenting complaints include symptoms of anxiety, the technique-oriented therapist may think automatically of relaxation training as the treatment of choice. On the other hand, viewing behavior therapy as a strategic approach allows the clinician to consider a wide variety of different tactics belonging under the general category of anxiety management approaches.

In our work with professionals untrained in behavioral therapy, we have encountered many who, being familiar with the overall effectiveness of this approach, have recommended that a particular patient can use "a little behavioral treatment." This somewhat naive recommendation, although made with good intentions, emanates from the perspective that behavior therapy consists of a "bag of tricks." It is unfortunately possible that many failures in behavior therapy are a function of misapplying these "tricks."

Multiple Problems, Multiple Interventions

Throughout these first three chapters, we have strongly advocated a multivariate understanding of a patient's problems, as well as the notion that an overall treatment plan should incorporate intervention components addressing several different target problems either simultaneously or sequentially. We will not belabor this point except to say that a unidimensional search for effective interventions is unlikely to result in satisfactory patient goal attainment. However, it should also be underscored that a multivariate approach need not be implemented in every clinical situation. Factors such as time, expense, and availability of resources might make a comprehensive treatment package too costly. Decision making regarding treatment design should take into account the benefits and costs of any treatment approach, whether it is multidimensional or not. Based upon such a decision analysis, an overall treatment plan can be formulated; at times, this may include only a single intervention.

Inclusion of Future-oriented Intervention Components

In addition to designing intervention strategies to ameliorate causally related variables or overcome impediments to goal achievement, the therapist should also include strategies that address generalized coping skills. These future-oriented components enhance goal attainment (Kanfer & Schefft, 1988), promote maintenance and generalization of treatment effects, and increase the client's abilities to cope with subsequent problems or stressful circumstances. Including such components is analogous to teaching writing and communication skills to psychology students not because deficits in these areas would prevent them from becoming psychologists, but because such skills would augment their abilities, thus increasing future life satisfaction (e.g., job satisfaction, feelings of self-efficacy, etc.).

With regard to therapy, such skills might include problem-solving training (Nezu et al., 1989), relapse prevention techniques (Marlatt & Gordon, 1985), stress management strategies (D'Zurilla & Nezu, chapter 13), and self-control or management skills (Kanfer & Schefft, 1987). These generic approaches can address specific target problem areas; however, they should also be applied to achieve a broader purpose. For example, in Michael G. Perri's program for the treatment of obesity (see chapter 6), problem-solving training is included to help patients identify and implement alternative ways to deal with situations conducive to overeating. Application of these general skills to a wider variety of problems in living is also emphasized as a means of increasing overall coping ability. Such enhanced capacities can help minimize the future emotional distress that can serve to moderate previously acquired weight management skills (Kirschenbaum, 1987).

After considering these four problem orientation aspects, the clinician continues to move through the decision-making model. Because much of the information necessary to design a treatment plan has already been obtained during the stage of problem analysis and selection of focal target problems, the clinician can go on to generate alternatives. However, we will again emphasize the notion that such movement within the overall model does not always flow in an uninterrupted, unidirectional manner. It is possible that, even after a carefully constructed CPM has been developed, new exigencies in the patient's life occur. An unexpected layoff due to a corporate takeover or the accidental death of a family member can have a great impact on the patient's life and goals. Beyond these major life events, more subtle changes can occur to affect the therapist's plan. Many patients who initially appear quite motivated for therapy may become more hesitant as they get closer to their goal state. At the very least, such situations require a detour from the proposed CPM and GAM. Again, the therapist needs to be sensitive to such occurrences in order to devise an optimal treatment plan.

Applying the Decision-making Model to the Treatment Design Stage: Generation of Alternatives

This problem-solving process involves generating a list of potentially effective treatment ideas, given the previously constructed CPM and list of therapeutic goals. In addition to adhering to the two general brainstorming principles (i.e., quantity and deferment of judgment), the therapist should apply the strategies-tactics approach to idea production. A list of strategies or general approaches for each focal problem area located on the CPM should be generated first. Then, for each strategy, a list of specific treatment tactics should be developed. The therapist can then review these lists to determine whether various ideas across strategies can be combined to enhance overall treatment effectiveness.

In addition to generating different tactics under the same general strategy (e.g., the tactics thought stopping vs. relaxation training under the strategy of anxiety reduction), the therapist should also generate different methods for implementing each tactic. Depending upon various client-related factors (e.g., cognitive ability), a given tactic may need to be implemented differentially. For example, teaching relaxation skills to a 13-year-old is likely to be substantially different from teaching the same skills to a 33-year-old. In the former case, more therapist modeling may need to be included, whereas in the latter case simple didactics may be sufficient.

Table 3.4 illustrates the relationship among strategies, tactics, and methods by showing how the therapist might conceptualize these aspects in order to treat a patient with depressed mood (see the example CPM and GAM presented in Figures 3.3 and 3.4, respectively). After

Table 3.4   A Partial List of Strategies, Tactics, and Methods for Treating Depressed Mood

Overall Goal: To decrease depressive symptoms

POTENTIAL STRATEGIES

1. Decrease self-defeating thoughts
2. Increase rational thinking
3. Increase problem-solving skills
4. Increase pleasurable activities
5. Decrease unpleasurable activities
6. Increase tolerance to negative memories
7. Increase tolerance to negative visual images
8. Facilitate existing interpersonal relationships
9. Increase new relationships
10. Increase amount of time spent with others
11. Increase self-control skills
12. Decrease negative attributional style
13. Decrease cognitive distortions
14. Refer patient to physician for medication

POTENTIAL TACTICS

—Under strategy 1 (decrease self-defeating thoughts)

1. Cognitive restructuring
2. Systematic rational restructuring
3. Thought stopping
4. Hypnosis
5. Bibliotherapy
6. Values clarification
7. Implosive therapy
8. Covert desensitization
9. Covert stimulus control
10. Positive mood induction
11. Systematic desensitization
12. Problem-solving therapy
13. Induction of positive self-statements
14. Meditation

15. Encouragement of religious beliefs
16. Reinforcement for positive self-statements
17. Punishment for negative self-statements
18. Use of unconditional positive regard

POTENTIAL METHODS
  —For conducting tactic 1 (cognitive restructuring)
1. Bibliotherapy
2. Modeling
3. Mild refutation
4. Overt confrontation
5. Didactics
6. Relevant homework assignments
7. Use of family members to serve as adjunct therapists
8. Use of friends to serve as adjunct therapists
9. Visualization
10. Use of diagrams and pictures
11. Use of cartoons/humorous material
12. Reversed advocacy role plays

---

constructing such a list of potential treatment ideas, the therapist can begin the next problem-solving process, decision making.

Applying the Decision-making Model to the Treatment Design Stage: Decision Making

Before selecting any particular components of a treatment plan, the therapist must evaluate each tactic according to the various decision-making criteria delineated in the following discussion.[2] One of the advantages of viewing the therapeutic enterprise as part of a greater systems approach is especially apparent during this process. Specifically we previously emphasized that a patient's problems cannot be perceived in isolation from individual situational factors, environmental variables (social and physical), and various other client-related factors.

---

[2] A variation of this approach is to generate strategies first and then evaluate their utility before generating tactics. Afterwards, tactics are generated for only those strategies that were rated highly and chosen for implementation. This variation may be more cost-effective in certain cases.

These factors serve as potential mediators of the effectiveness of any treatment approach. Identifying these variables during the problem analysis stage helps the therapist better evaluate their impact. The iatrogenic or side effects of a treatment may also be better assessed prior to treatment implementation. For example, confrontational cognitive restructuring procedures should be avoided with a borderline patient early in therapy because they may elicit increased emotionality, possibly leading to premature termination. In addition, being aware of the potential interactions between the patient's changed behavior and the social environment is imperative when designing treatment plans. For example, increase in a client's assertiveness may engender loss of reinforcement from her spouse, which may lead to marital distress. Operating on a framework that focuses only on a unidimensional, single target behavior may seriously impede treatment gains and may result in poor overall goal attainment.

On the basis of the following decision criteria, the therapist rates each tactic in relation to the identified goal it addresses.

Likelihood of Treatment Effects

1. What is the likelihood that this particular intervention will achieve the specified goal(s)?

To answer this question adequately, the therapist needs to be familiar with the empirical literature on the effectiveness of a given treatment technique for a given problem. Interventions shown to be effective for a particular problem should be rated more highly than the therapist's preferred mode of treatment. However, even though the efficacy of various interventions is increasingly being documented (see Part II of this volume), many problems exist for which behavioral strategies have not been developed or evaluated. If this is the case, innovative application of known behavioral strategies (and possibly those outside the traditional behavioral realm) becomes the therapist's task. As is consistent with the overall philosophy of this book, such novel applications should be made only after conducting a comprehensive problem analysis and a formal decision analysis that incorporates all utility criteria.

Moreover, although the potential efficacy of an intervention strategy might be high, the patient at hand might be quite different from the population with whom empirical research has been conducted. Thus the idiographic application of such nomothetic data necessitates asking further questions concerning various systems issues that may be involved. Inexperienced behavior therapists, eager to apply documented treatments, are particularly susceptible to this judgmental error. The warning to "look before you leap," although trite and perhaps somewhat condescending, may in fact be important to remember.

2. What is the likelihood that this particular therapist can optimally implement this particular treatment approach?

This evaluation involves an assessment of a clinician's ability to apply a particular approach. It is unlikely that all behavior therapists are expert, or even competent, in all behavioral strategies. As new techniques or novel applications of established techniques become available, it becomes incumbent upon the concerned clinician to keep up with the field. Active participation in related workshops, continuing education courses, and professional conferences serve this purpose. We also recommend developing local peer-supervision groups. However, it is ethically imperative to assess objectively one's own ability to implement a particular treatment approach in evaluating the overall likelihood of goal attainment.

3. What is the likelihood that the client will be able to carry out a particular strategy in an optimal fashion?

Many behavioral strategies require participation by the client beyond session attendance. Homework assignments designed to obtain assessment data or to provide practice in various strategies are common in behavioral programs. Several client-related factors may moderate the likelihood that participation or adherence will be high. One important variable involves the patient's level of motivation or resistance to the specific treatment plan. Although continual collaboration between the therapist and client concerning specification of goals, identification of problem areas, and selection of treatment approaches can enhance motivation, the therapist must also monitor the patient's cooperation throughout treatment.

Other client-related factors that can moderate the effectiveness of treatment involve various personal resources (both strengths and weaknesses), including time, money, cognitive ability, special skills, education, and physical health. Limited resources or deficits in any of these areas need to be considered potential problems in addition to those specified in the CPM.

4. What is the likelihood that collateral or paraprofessional therapists will be able to implement a particular strategy in an optimal way?

If treatment involves others who might serve as adjunct treatment providers, it is important to assess their ability to carry out treatment competently and cooperatively. Such individuals might include institutional staff, parents or caregivers, spouses or family members, and therapists-in-training. The competence of such adjunct behavior change agents is an important factor in predicting treatment outcomes. Unfortunately, according to Haynes (1986), one disadvantage of behavioral approaches "is that they sometimes erroneously appear simple to apply. As a result, individuals with insufficient training sometimes apply behavioral intervention programs without adequate understanding of their controlling parameters" (p. 413).

In addition, depending upon the nature of their investment, certain adjunct therapists might even act as treatment saboteurs. For example, the spouse of an individual coming to treatment for weight management might be jealous because the spouse is losing weight or afraid that this newly attractive person might end the relationship. In such a case, the spouse as adjunct therapist may "forget" to help take data or "inadvertently" purchase forbidden foods, stating that "the kids and I shouldn't be made to suffer!"

5. What is the likelihood that this treatment approach will contribute to the client's ability to cope more effectively with future problems or stressful situations?

An underlying assumption of behavioral approaches involves having clients learn new behaviors that are more adaptive and functional than their old ones. As such, treatment should not simply involve amelioration of the presenting problem. Rather, it should additionally incorporate means by which the client can learn to prevent such problems from occurring in the future. For example, psychopharmacological interventions may alleviate distressing symptoms, but they contribute little to the patient's overall learning process. If the client learns nothing new to guide future adaptive functioning, the probability that he will need therapy again remains high. Although various behavioral strategies may be useful in ameliorating distressing symptoms, unless such strategies are applied in a self-management modality or implemented in conjunction with other, more generalizable skills, their utility is limited. A treatment plan should incorporate components that facilitate overall life satisfaction.

Value of Treatment Effects

Personal consequences

1. How much time and other resources are required to implement the treatment?

An analysis of this type is pertinent to both therapist and patient. For the clinician, one time consideration might be the degree to which time outside of sessions is required to implement a program. An in vivo exposure paradigm, for example, may require considerable amounts of the therapist's time in order to be effective. Additional time might also be necessary to train and/or supervise adjunct therapists involved in implementing a comprehensive token economy.

For the client, time and financial cost may also be important factors. Most clients would prefer treatments that involve the least amount of time and cost the least amount of money. Such considerations can seriously affect the success of a given treatment approach. Too much time spent in treatment, as perceived by the client, may engender premature termination.

2. How much effort is involved in implementing the treatment approach?

The amount of effort required to carry out an intervention plan must be considered. Interventions that exceed the therapist's or client's available resources may be doomed to failure. For example, a treatment plan that requires an excessive amount of effort and that takes time away from the client's spouse, family, or job may engender negative side effects that ultimately impinge on overall goal attainment.

3. What emotional cost or gain would result if this treatment were implemented?

This criterion focuses on the affective responses that might occur as a function of a given treatment approach. As such, it involves the particular client's ability to tolerate immediate negative effects in the process of reaching a long-term positive goal. For example, training parents to use an extinction paradigm to reduce tantrum behavior in their 6-year-old son may produce immediate negative responses when the child's behavior initially escalates (especially if the behavior occurs in public places). Different parents have different levels of tolerance for such immediate negative effects.

4. Is use of this intervention consistent with morals, values, and ethics?

Again, this question is relevant for both therapist and client. Clinicians need to be particularly aware of attempts to foist their own values on a client or to implement plans that may be in marked disagreement with the patient's wishes. A divarication in values may exist when, for example, a therapist recommends the use of reinforcement procedures to a parent who believes that "my child should want to clean her room and do her homework." Other conflicts in values may occur when issues of sexuality, religion, or culture arise. For example, within certain ethnic cultures, encouraging a young adult to be assertive would be in direct conflict with cultural mores. Treatments inconsistent with a client's values are unlikely to be successful.

5. What are the physical side effects of the treatment?

The therapist should always take into account any physical side effects the treatment may cause. A given treatment approach may have highly rated long-term effects but, given the overall nature of the client's problem, have questionable immediate consequences. For example, in vivo exposure for acrophobia may have positive long-term effects (e.g., symptom reduction), but for a certain patient may represent a potential short-term risk if a sudden increase in anxiety leads to motoric panic and the patient's falling off a ladder. Another related concern involves the iatrogenic effects of treatment. For instance, a weight reduction program incorporating exercise might pose a health risk for someone with cardiac difficulties; similarly, a massed practice procedure would be an unwise course for someone with the goal of smoking reduction. Needless to say, this criterion becomes an essential consideration when the treatment might in some way engender harm to self or others (e.g., suicide).

6. What is the impact of this treatment on related problem areas?

This issue concerns the potential positive effects of a given intervention on several focal problem areas, as well as the possible negative effects of treatment on other areas of the client's life. An example of simultaneous positive effects might involve the use of relaxation training to address both a client's social evaluative anxiety and his insomnia. Further, such training may be helpful as a general means of stress management and as a basic skill to use during later systematic desensitization.

A potential negative effect of treatment might occur when teaching a patient to become more assertive with her employer if the boss is in fact unreceptive (or even antagonistic) toward such behavior. Similarly, in work with children it is often advisable, in addition to programming for a decrease in negative behavior (e.g., use of extinction for temper tantrums), to include a component to increase positive behavior (e.g., use of social skills training to increase the quality of interpersonal interactions). Otherwise, the child might adopt an alternative negative behavior as a means of obtaining social reinforcement (e.g., use of aggressive behavior to elicit attention from others). Finally, as discussed in the chapter on personality disorders (chapter 9), interventions to increase competency in patients with generalized, dependent interpersonal patterns may engender increased anxiety along with skill acquisition.

Social consequences

1. What are the effects of a particular treatment alternative on the client's family and on others who have an influence on the client's life?

Because many behavioral programs emphasize the importance of social variables in the etiology of psychological problems and view client change outside the therapist's office as a sine qua non of treatment effectiveness, it is essential to consider various social impact criteria. The focus of the first part of this particular question is on the client's immediate family (spouse, parents, children, siblings). Although, as previously discussed, the family may be able to carry out a treatment plan, additional consequences also need to be considered. For example, teaching parents to change one child's maladaptive behavior may engender behavior problems in another child if that child is ignored. Or encouraging a client to go back to school in order to satisfy career desires may elicit a negative response from her husband or children, whose lives will most likely be significantly affected.

In essence, the therapist needs to consider whether family support is available, directly or indirectly, to help implement the treatment plan and to enhance the generalization and maintenance of treatment gains. In other words, will this treatment result in an increase or decrease in the family's social reinforcement of the client? Similar questions should be asked with regard to others who influence the client's social environment. Specifically, these include friends, neighbors, and social and work acquaintances, as well as the community as a whole.

Short-term consequences

1. What are the immediate effects of implementing this treatment approach?

The immediate and short-range effects of a treatment approach should be evaluated with regard to each of the criteria contained in both the likelihood and value categories.

Long-term consequences

1. What are the long-term consequences of this treatment approach?

The long-term effects of a given intervention also should be evaluated with regard to both likelihood and value criteria.

It is obvious that a preferred treatment approach would be one that is both very effective in reaching the client's goals and highly likely to be implemented optimally. It should have results that are mostly posi-

tive as regards both personal and social consequences. It should cost
very little in terms of time, money, and effort, and should have wide-
reaching and far-reaching positive consequences. It should not only
ameliorate the distress associated with the patient's presenting
problems, but also enhance the overall quality of his life. Further, it
should engender positive reinforcement from all quarters of the social
environment and be consistent with the client's and therapist's morals,
values, and ethics. Given the current state of behavior therapy (and
psychotherapy in general), it is unlikely that any treatment package can
meet all such criteria. However, the responsibility of the behavior
therapist is to approximate such a treatment plan as closely as possible,
given a particular client with particular problems and unique life circumstances.

Using the preceding decision-making criteria is a major step
towards reaching this goal. In applying these criteria, the therapist
should rate each treatment tactic. Figure 3.5 contains a decision-making
form to facilitate these ratings. We do not suggest that a negative rating
on any of these criteria (with the exception of serious physical side
effects) renders a given treatment alternative ineffective. Rather, the
existence of a negative rating serves two purposes. First, a high frequency of negative ratings across various criteria would likely place an
alternative low on a list of choices, thus helping the clinician make a
better treatment choice. Second, evaluating each alternative in this
manner aids the therapist in identifying those factors that might
mediate successful treatment. In other words, pinpointing negative
aspects helps the therapist anticipate possible difficulties in treatment
implementation and/or maintenance and generalization of positive
treatment effects.

It is also important to note that, if a given treatment alternative
receives a high general rating but is evaluated as having potentially
negative effects, the therapist need not necessarily discard the treatment idea. Instead, he can engage in the problem-solving processes
once again to identify the means by which to modify the treatment plan
to enhance positive effects and minimize negative ones.

Based on the results of the original decision analysis and any
further problem solving, the therapist then chooses the most promising
treatment alternative. Again, our bias is to include several alternatives
within an overall treatment package to enhance maintenance and
generalization effects and to facilitate multiple goal attainment. The
clinician then moves on to the next step in the decision-making model,
solution implementation and verification.

Figure 3.5 Form for Evaluating the Effects of Various Treatment Alternatives

Rating Scale:
Positive (+1 to +3)
Neutral (0)
Negative (-1 to -3)

Target Problem: _____

Goal(s): _____

TREATMENT ALTERNATIVES	Likelihood of achieving goals	Likelihood of optimal implementation	Overall goal attainment	Time resources	Effort	Emotional effects	Morals, values, and ethics	Physical side effects	Impact on other problems	Other personal effects	Effects on family	Other social effects	Short-term effects	Long-term effects	Other	Other	Other	TOTAL SCORE

Applying the Decision-making Model to the Treatment Design Stage: Solution Implementation and Verification

Before formal treatment is actually initiated, the therapist should attempt to verify the choices made during the decision-making process by obtaining the client's feedback.[3] Even though the therapist is still in the "design stage," evaluation of these choices at this juncture can prevent possible treatment failure. Implementing the solution at this point involves completion of the GAM (see Figure 3.4 for an example). Solution verification involves evaluating the match between expected and actual outcomes.

To obtain the client's feedback, the therapist first completes the GAM by listing those selected treatment approaches that serve as pathways toward goal attainment. Discussing the GAM with the client provides immediate feedback concerning several of the therapist's initial treatment choices. For example, parents may suggest that an intervention based on a reinforcement paradigm does not seem to be consistent with their values because it involves "bribing" their child. Based on such feedback, the therapist can discard the alternative or attempt to resolve this difficulty to increase the potential for a successful treatment outcome.

On the basis of this initial feedback, the therapist then attempts to match predicted and actual effects of the treatment decisions. If the match is satisfactory up to this point, the clinician is ready to implement treatment. If the match is unsatisfactory, he needs to recycle through the various problem-solving processes as a means of identifying the source of the discrepancy and then attempt to rectify it. If such attempts do not lead to a satisfactory resolution, then it is possible that the patient should be referred to another professional. Referral may be the best choice when the therapist's goals or treatment decisions differ substantially from those of the client and this impasse cannot be resolved.

STAGE IV: TREATMENT IMPLEMENTATION AND EVALUATION

The treatment implementation and evaluation stage of the overall therapeutic process is similar to the solution implementation and verification process within our decision-making model. Both opera-

---

[3] Feedback can also be obtained through peer-supervision groups, in which other professionals informally evaluate a therapist's treatment plan for a particular client. Such a review can serve as a form of "quality assurance" similar to that utilized by hospitals and mental health centers.

tions involve actual implementation of a solution (i.e., treatment plan), collection of information as a means of monitoring the effects of the solution (i.e., process and outcome data), comparison of predicted and actual consequences of implemented solutions, changing the treatment plan if the match is unsatisfactory, and exiting from the problem-solving process if the match is satisfactory (i.e., mutual termination of therapy).

However, in order to engage in the entire clinical decision-making model, we suggest that all five problem-solving processes be applied within the context of this last stage of therapy. Rather than going through each of these processes again, at this point we will highlight several decisions involved in implementing and evaluating treatment. For each of these decisions, we again strongly recommend at least a "quick run through" of the model to maximize effective decision making and minimize the potential for judgmental errors. If possible, a more formal analysis should be conducted.

As a brief illustration of the application of the decision-making model to this therapeutic stage, consider the issue of selecting problem areas to be assessed as a means of evaluating treatment success. Consistent with assertions associated with other therapeutic stages, the problem orientation relevant here is characterized by a multivariate perspective involving a broad-based evaluation of a range of focal problem areas (e.g., reduction in distress symptoms, increase in coping skills, improvement in interpersonal relationships, increase in self-esteem, etc.). The problem definition and formulation process involves identifying those assessment areas relevant to the treatment implemented. For example, if the chosen treatment plan involves relaxation training to reduce anxiety symptoms, then potential assessment areas might include physiological and subjective feelings of anxiety and acquisition of self-controlled relaxation skills. A list of possible assessment procedures (e.g., self-report inventories, simulated role plays, clinician ratings) to measure these two areas can be generated according to brainstorming principles. Use of the decision-making criteria aids in selecting the appropriate evaluation procedures. Implementing the solution at this point involves administration of the chosen assessment protocol; verification entails evaluation of the effects of this assessment process (e.g., whether the evaluation data are forthcoming and meaningful).

Timetable for Implementing Various Treatment Components

Especially in those cases in which the optimal treatment plan incorporates several different intervention tactics, the therapist must develop a tentative schedule indicating when each component should be implemented. Tactics can be implemented simultaneously or sequentially, depending upon the client, therapist, and environmental factors described throughout this chapter. For example, if a client appears to be wavering in her motivation concerning therapy, it might be important to implement a treatment for a relatively simple problem as a means of enhancing motivation. Or, if a severe anxiety problem tends to inhibit the patient's ability to engage in any form of social skills training to improve interpersonal relationships, a treatment for reducing physical anxiety symptoms should be implemented first.

A second time-related issue involves the number of sessions sufficient to assess whether a particular treatment plan can, in fact, be successful. Knowledge of the empirical literature is helpful, but, once again, a number of mitigating circumstances may moderate the success of treatment with any given client (e.g., severity of symptoms, lack of social support to engage in therapy). Whether the treatment is brief or extends over a period of years, the therapist needs to continually monitor whether therapeutic movement is on course.

This brings us to a third time-related concern, that is, when to begin gathering information to aid in the verification operation. Our bias is to suggest that information gathering begin immediately. Such verification does not necessarily require formal behavioral assessment procedures. However, at the very least, the therapist should elicit direct verbal feedback concerning treatment outcome almost immediately after treatment is begun. We further recommend that assessment be conducted repeatedly throughout actual treatment implementation.

Selection of Assessment Tools and Areas to Be Evaluated

Even in the situation in which a single behavioral target is the focus of treatment, it is crucial to include multiple assessment procedures, as well as to evaluate changes across a variety of areas outside of the targeted problem. The first case involves inclusion of several different types of measures to monitor changes across a variety of response modalities. For example, if depression is a major patient problem, rather than administering only a self-report inventory (e.g., Beck Depression Inventory; Beck, Ward, Mendelsohn, Mock, & Erbaugh, 1961), the therapist can also complete a clinician-rated instrument (e.g., Hamilton Rating Scale for Depression; Hamilton, 1960). Using a range of assessments ensures the reliability of measured therapeutic changes.

The second case involves including measures unrelated to the target problem to evaluate the potential for various negative or positive side effects. Such assessments are crucial to monitor the effects of change in a targeted behavior on the remainder of the system. This type of evaluation should also be undertaken to identify any newly emerging difficulties. Otherwise, the probability of successful treatment is lowered. In addition, this kind of information helps the therapist to determine whether any problems have been overlooked during the previous stages of therapy. For example, eliciting feedback from clients undergoing parent training may result in a therapist's changing the problem formulation from one emphasizing inappropriate external contingencies to one focusing on the parents' unrealistic expectations.

Of related concern is selection of the type of assessment tools to use when conducting these process and outcome evaluations. One alternative is to include those measures incorporated during the problem analysis phase as pretest and posttest measures. However, depending upon the nature of the assessments actually used, additional measures should be identified. For example, the therapist may want to select certain assessment tools to avoid measurement error due to practice or social desirability effects.

In general, we offer the following recommendations regarding the choice of assessment tools: (a) include several measures for each target problem area; (b) select measures that are sensitive to the intervention being implemented; (c) select psychometrically sound measures; (d) if available and of high quality, choose less obtrusive and inconvenient measures; (e) include measures that assess areas not necessarily targeted for intervention; (f) include measures that vary in the source of the data (e.g., client's self-report, family observation, in-session observation); and (g) focus on both outcome and process data (e.g., assess changes in both anxiety levels and in hypothesized controlling variables such as cognitive distortions or deficiencies in coping skills). It should be noted that anecdotal patient feedback, although not entirely data based, can indicate those interventions that have been the most salient in the patient's reeducation process. This information can be useful for future decision making regarding the match between patient characteristics and treatment choices.

Related to assessment at this stage of therapy is the use of single-case experimental designs as a framework by which to structure the verification process. The various design models can help identify specific assessment methods, structure the timing of treatment implementation, and plan the timing of data collection concerning treatment evaluation. Discussion of the advantages and disadvantages of the various procedures is far beyond the scope of this book. The reader is referred to Barlow, Hayes, and Nelson (1984) and Kazdin (1982a) for two excellent sources concerning single-case research designs. However, it should be pointed out that these designs generally require a fair amount of experimental control, such that exigencies that occur in treatment may actually render the validity of such approaches tentative. Such designs also tend to lend themselves best to situations in which problems are more circumscribed and conducive to operant procedures. We recommend that the therapist view such procedures as one viable alternative to aid in the verification process and choose whether to incorporate a particular N of 1 methodology on the basis of a formal decision analysis given a particular clinical case, rather than attempting to fit the case into such a design regardless of mitigating circumstances.

Termination, Troubleshooting, and Follow-up

Throughout the verification process, the therapist continues to be confronted with numerous decisions (e.g., "Is therapy working?"; "Should additional treatment approaches be added to enhance motivation?"; "Is the client making sufficient progress?"; "Have any other problems been overlooked?"; and "Has treatment thus far created any additional problems?"). If the answer to any of these questions suggests a change in the therapeutic game plan, the clinician should recycle through the various problem-solving processes to identify and address these impediments to overall goal attainment. Table 3.5 contains a list of questions the clinician should ask if treatment appears to be ineffective.

If the comparison between the actual effects and the predicted consequences appears to be satisfactory, the therapist's next decision involves termination of treatment. Appropriate termination involves a mutual agreement between the client and therapist that the previously specified goals have been satisfactorily reached. Not only have the presenting problems been solved, but positive consequences have been maximized and negative effects have been minimized. Under these circumstances, both parties would likely be satisfied, especially if treatment has been running smoothly and in a timely fashion.

The manner in which this aspect of treatment is handled is one of the therapist's last clinical decisions. Even though (or perhaps because) treatment has been effective, certain clients are afraid to end treatment for fear of symptom or problem recurrence. Although an emphasis has been placed on including treatment components designed to facilitate general coping, some patients may continue to be somewhat hesitant. Therefore, the therapist needs to plan, via use of the decision-making model, the optimal method of terminating treatment for a given patient. By this time, the clinician will have a detailed understanding of

Table 3.5 Problem-solving Questions the Therapist Should Ask If Treatment Appears Ineffective

1. Is psychotherapy/behavior therapy appropriate for this patient?
2. Did I overlook any related problems?
3. Is this client motivated to change?
4. Is this client afraid to change?
5. Have I overlooked any negative consequences?
6. Is this treatment generally effective for this problem?
7. Am I implementing this intervention properly?
8. Does the patient understand this treatment?
9. Does the patient agree with the use of this treatment?
10. Is treatment too costly?
11. Is treatment taking too long?
12. Is there adequate social support for this client?
13. Was the problem analysis accurate?
14. Does this treatment incur any negative effects of which I am unaware?
15. Does this treatment conflict with the client's values?
16. Does the patient have unrealistic goals or expectations concerning therapy? Concerning this treatment?
17. Is the patient completing homework assignments?
18. Is the client optimally practicing the technique(s) that are part of treatment (e.g., relaxation skills)?
19. Are any of the client's family members sabotaging this treatment approach?
20. Should I use a different treatment approach?
21. Should I change the method of using this treatment approach?
22. Am I sensitive to the patient's feelings?
23. Is the implementation of this approach too mechanistic?
24. Is the use of this treatment premature?
25. Does this patient view me as invested in his treatment?
26. Does this patient trust me as her therapist?
27. Have I identified the most salient reinforcers for this patient?
28. Are there conflicting problems or variables that serve to maintain the patient's difficulties, thereby controverting a successful outcome?
29. Should I terminate treatment?
30. Should I get opinions from other professionals?

a particular client and will be able to predict his reaction to termination. Alternative ways to structure the termination phase include (a) gradually increasing the time between sessions to allow increased independence from the therapist; (b) scheduling future "booster" sessions; (c) scheduling future evaluation or follow-up sessions; (d) structuring future informal contacts (e.g., limited telephone calls or letters); and (e) helping the patient conceptualize the termination process as an experience involving both success and conflict, but nonetheless being an opportunity to employ newly acquired coping skills (i.e., terminating treatment can become yet another problem to solve). In general, we recommend that termination not be abrupt or unexpected. Otherwise, treatment gains accrued to this point may be compromised.

SUMMARY

In this chapter, we have conceptualized the overall therapeutic enterprise as a series of clinical decisions that need to be made effectively for treatment to be successful. Therapy was described as encompassing several major clinical tasks. These tasks can be grouped according to four stages: screening and problem identification; problem analysis and selection of focal target problems; treatment design; and treatment implementation and evaluation.

Within each of these four stages, we strongly advocated applying all five problem-solving processes—problem orientation, problem definition and formulation, generation of alternatives, decision making, and solution implementation and verification—as a way to minimize potential judgmental errors and to facilitate overall patient goal attainment. More specifically, to increase both the reliability and validity of the numerous clinical decisions inherent within the treatment process, we argued that the therapist should actively and formally engage in the overall decision-making model for each decision encountered. Figure 3.6 provides a flow chart depicting this application across the major decision points occurring during the course of therapy.

Within the first stage of therapy, screening and problem identification, we discussed possible initiation difficulties that may seriously impede continued assessment and eventual treatment implementation. Such problems involve decisions concerning the impact of a variety of client- and therapist-related factors, as well as the appropriateness of psychological interventions given the specific nature of the patient's complaints.

Application of the decision-making model during the second stage of therapy, problem analysis and selection of focal target problems, was discussed as a function of (a) obtaining a comprehensive understanding of the nature of the client's problems, (b) identifying those factors or variables that are causally or functionally related to these problems, and (c) delineating a series of realistic goals and subgoals for treatment. To assist in these tasks, we advocated the use of a three-dimensional framework to guide the therapist in gathering data across six focal problem areas (behavioral, affective, cognitive, biological, physical environmental, and social environmental variables), two temporal domains (current and developmental), and two data sources (actual and perceptual). This broad-based assessment across a variety of potentially important areas is consistent with the philosophy emphasizing multiple causality and the adoption of a systems approach.

With regard to the client's current functioning, we stressed that the therapist should identify the functional relationships among those variables located within each of the six focal areas. In other words, by using the SORKC formula, the therapist describes which variables serve as stimuli, responses, or consequences concerning the patient's major problems. Nomothetic information gleaned from the empirical literature was identified as one major source to help guide this idiographic problem analysis.

We also described the use of the CPM (see Figure 3.3) as a means of graphically depicting the therapist's overall conceptualization of the client's problems. The purpose of the CPM is to delineate the therapist's clinical hypotheses regarding the major elements contributing to the initiation and maintenance of the patient's problems. As a useful check, we further suggested that the therapist compare the constructed CPM with a three-dimensional framework of assessment, treatment, and therapy evaluation (see Figure 3.1) to identify influential variables that may have been overlooked. We additionally proposed mutual collaboration between the therapist and client throughout this process.

In terms of selecting target problem areas (as well as identifying goals), we advocated the use of the problem-solving process involving generation of alternatives. A variety of decision-making criteria were also included by which the therapist can rate the overall utility of any of these targets. These criteria regard both the likelihood and value of certain effects, given the selection of a particular problem. Three levels of evaluation data were identified to aid in conducting the solution implementation and verification process: client feedback, clinical hypothesis testing, and actual treatment effects. Based on a comparison between the actual and predicted consequences of these choices, the

Figure 3.6 Flow Chart for the Clinical Decision-making Model

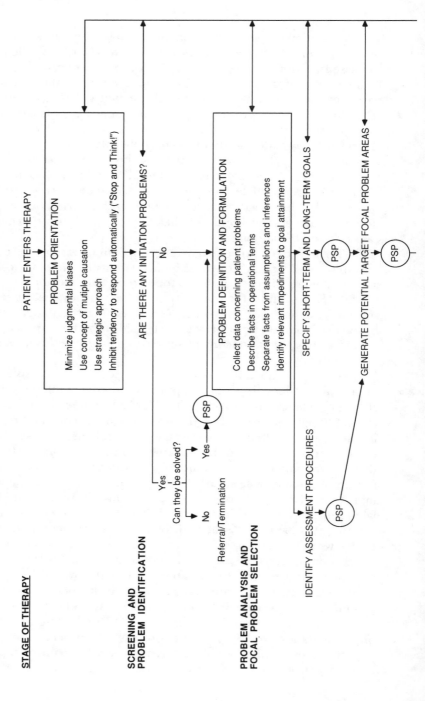

STAGE OF THERAPY

PATIENT ENTERS THERAPY

PROBLEM ORIENTATION

Minimize judgmental biases
Use concept of mutiple causation
Use strategic approach
Inhibit tendency to respond automatically ("Stop and Think!")

ARE THERE ANY INITIATION PROBLEMS?

SCREENING AND
PROBLEM IDENTIFICATION

Can they be solved?

Yes

No

Yes

No

Referral/Termination

PSP

PROBLEM DEFINITION AND FORMULATION

Collect data concerning patient problems
Describe facts in operational terms
Separate facts from assumptions and inferences
Identify relevant impediments to goal attainment

PROBLEM ANALYSIS AND
FOCAL PROBLEM SELECTION

IDENTIFY ASSESSMENT PROCEDURES

PSP

SPECIFY SHORT-TERM AND LONG-TERM GOALS

PSP

GENERATE POTENTIAL TARGET FOCAL PROBLEM AREAS

PSP

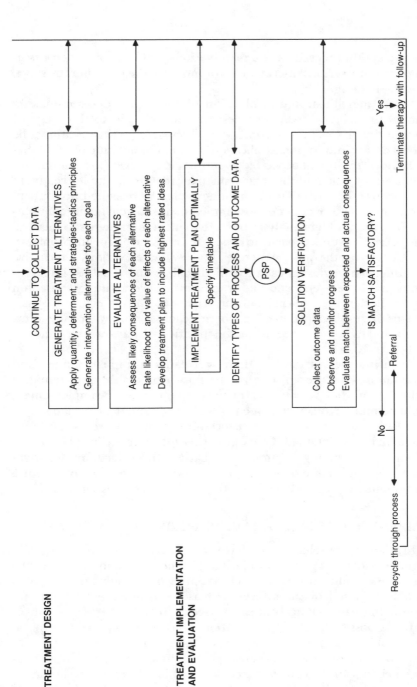

TREATMENT DESIGN

CONTINUE TO COLLECT DATA

GENERATE TREATMENT ALTERNATIVES

Apply quantity, deferment, and strategies-tactics principles

Generate intervention alternatives for each goal

EVALUATE ALTERNATIVES

Assess likely consequences of each alternative

Rate likelihood and value of effects of each alternative

Develop treatment plan to include highest rated ideas

IMPLEMENT TREATMENT PLAN OPTIMALLY

Specify timetable

IDENTIFY TYPES OF PROCESS AND OUTCOME DATA

PSP

TREATMENT IMPLEMENTATION AND EVALUATION

SOLUTION VERIFICATION

Collect outcome data

Observe and monitor progress

Evaluate match between expected and actual consequences

IS MATCH SATISFACTORY?

No

Referral

Yes

Terminate therapy with follow-up

Recycle through process

Note. PSP = Problem-solving process.

therapist either recycles through the various problem-solving processes to rectify any serious discrepancies or moves to the next therapy stage, treatment design.

We then illustrated application of the entire decision-making model to facilitate treatment design. Also relevant to this stage of therapy, four specific assertions were discussed: (a) that treatment be based on the idiographic application of nomothetic principles; (b) that behavioral treatment be viewed as a strategic approach to clinical intervention; (c) that multiple problems may require multiple treatment procedures; and (d) that the treatment plan be designed not only to help the patient overcome those impediments to goal attainment outlined in the problem analysis, but also to include strategies to increase the patient's overall capacity to cope with future stressful life problems.

After the therapist generates and evaluates various alternative treatment strategies for each specified goal, he chooses those interventions that have been rated highly in terms of overall utility. Based on these choices, the clinician can construct a GAM (see Figure 3.4) as a means of graphically depicting where a client is now, where she wants to go, and hypotheses regarding the specific pathways by which she can get there.

During the last stage of therapy, treatment implementation and evaluation, the therapist must develop a timetable or a tentative schedule of when various treatment components will be implemented, either simultaneously or sequentially. In addition, the clinician selects particular assessment tools or procedures by which process and outcome data are obtained. One of the therapist's final clinical decisions involves terminating treatment. For each of these decisions, we advocated the application of all five problem-solving processes to minimize judgmental errors and maximize the utility of resulting choices.

IMPLICATIONS FOR BEHAVIOR THERAPY

Throughout this chapter, we have repeatedly suggested the use of a problem-solving approach to facilitate clinical decision making in the practice of behavior therapy. This approach highlights the potential problems posed by the inferential biases and judgmental errors inherent in various clinical endeavors (see chapter 1). More important, it offers a possible prescriptive solution. As such, it has several implications for clinical practice, research, and training.

First, use of a decision-making model based on a problem-solving perspective can help practicing clinicians utilize the empirical literature in a more meaningful manner. Nonacademically affiliated therapists have often questioned the utility of various research findings and have been left wondering what to do with certain difficult cases not specifically addressed in the literature. Although research has documented the efficacy of a wide variety of behaviorally oriented intervention strategies, often the gap is wide between the specific population focused upon by a research study and the patient at hand. Use of a problem-solving approach in clinical decision making can provide specific guidelines concerning how best to conduct an idiographic application of empirically based nomothetic information. Although we concede that behavioral therapy will always involve art as well as science, the decision-making model described here stresses the empirical nature of clinical practice and places more weight on the scientific side of the scale regarding the practice of behavioral approaches.

Second, because this clinical decision-making model has not yet been subjected to extensive empirical study, implications for research are enormous. Investigations need to be conducted to determine whether this model does, in fact, facilitate clinical decision making in the practice of behavior therapy. Also, inherent in our model are various assumptions concerning the relation between behavioral assessment and treatment. One assumption is that accurate problem analysis and selection of target problems have a significant impact on the likelihood of treatment success. It is possible that, regardless of the problems targeted for intervention, goal attainment will not be affected. Further, inaccurate selection of treatment plans may also have little impact on goal attainment. Although the link between assessment and treatment selection is a sine qua non of the behavioral approach, this relationship has been the focus of few empirical investigations (Nelson & Hayes, 1986).

Third, with regard to professional training, we would hope to see formal teaching of methods to enhance clinical decision-making skills become part of a student's graduate education in mental health and related areas. Proposals to increase or enhance graduate level statistics and research design courses as a means of minimizing judgmental errors in clinical situations are, we believe, missing the point. Such courses provide a strong and necessary basis from which to draw upon; however, clinically related seminars specifically focusing on decision-making skills are imperative. The model described here offers one potential approach to address the complex processes embedded in such clinical judgment and decision making.

Finally, as is consistent with a problem-solving philosophy, it is important to gather information concerning the effectiveness and utility of the proposed model. The validity of this approach awaits future empirical scrutiny and investigation. In attempting to solve the problem of judgmental errors in the practice of behavior therapy, the present model represents our best solution. Future attempts to address this important concern may provide for either variations of this model or for its refutation. In the meantime, we hope the model engenders interest, curiosity, and a desire to invest more theoretical and empirical attention in the area of clinical decision making and behavior therapy than has heretofore been afforded.

References

American Psychiatric Association. (1987). *Diagnostic and statistical manual of mental disorders* (3rd ed. rev.). Washington, DC: Author.

Barlow, D. H., Hayes, S. C., & Nelson, R. O. (1984). *The scientist-practitioner: Research and accountability in clinical and educational settings*. New York: Pergamon.

Barlow, M. (1981). Complex problems require complex solutions. *Behavior Therapy, 12,* 15–29.

Barrios, B. A. (1988). On the changing nature of behavioral assessment. In A. S. Bellack & M. Hersen (Eds.), *Behavioral assessment: A practical handbook* (3rd ed.). New York: Pergamon.

Beck, A. T., Ward, C. H., Mendelsohn, M., Mock, J., & Erbaugh, J. (1961). An inventory for measuring depression. *Archives of General Psychiatry, 5,* 562–571.

Ciminero, A. R., Calhoun, K. S., & Adams, H. E. (Eds.). (1977). *Handbook of behavioral assessment*. New York: Wiley.

D'Zurilla, T. J. (1986). *Problem-solving therapy: A social competence approach to clinical intervention*. New York: Springer.

Hamilton, M. (1960). A rating scale for depression. *Journal of Neurology, Neurosurgery and Psychiatry, 23,* 56–62.

Haynes, S. N. (1986). The design of intervention programs. In R. O. Nelson & S. C. Hayes (Eds.), *Conceptual foundations of behavioral assessment*. New York: Guilford.

Haynes, S. N., & O'Brien, W. H. (1988). The Gordian Knot of DSM-III-R use: Integrating principles of behavior classification and complex causal models. *Behavioral Assessment, 10,* 95–105.

Hersen, M. (1988). Behavioral assessment and psychiatric diagnosis. *Behavioral Assessment, 10,* 107–121.

Hersen, M., & Bellack, A. S. (Eds.). (1988). *Behavioral assessment: A practical handbook* (3rd ed.). New York: Pergamon.

Kanfer, F. H. (1985). Target selection for clinical change programs. *Behavioral Assessment, 7,* 7–20.

Kanfer, F. H., & Grimm, L. G. (1977). Behavior analysis: Selecting target behaviors in the interview. *Behavior Modification, 1,* 7–28.

Kanfer, F. H., & Grimm, L. G. (1980). Managing clinical change. A process model of therapy. *Behavior Modification, 4,* 419–444.

Kanfer, F. H., & Phillips, J. S. (1970). *Learning foundations of behavior therapy*. New York: Wiley.

Kanfer, F. H., & Schefft, B. K. (1987). Self-management therapy in clinical practice. In N. S. Jacobson (Ed.), *Psychotherapists in clinical practice: Cognitive and behavioral perspectives.* New York: Guilford.

Kanfer, F. H., & Schefft, B. K. (1988). *Guiding the process of therapeutic change.* Champaign, IL: Research Press.

Kazdin, A. E. (1982a). *Single-case research design: Methods for clinical and applied settings.* New York: Oxford University Press.

Kazdin, A. E. (1982b). Symptom substitution, generalization, and response covariation: Implications for psychotherapy outcome. *Psychological Bulletin, 91,* 349–365.

Kirschenbaum, D. S. (1987). Self-regulatory failure: A review with clinical implications. *Clinical Psychology Review, 7,* 77–104.

Lang, P. J. (1968). Fear reduction and fear behavior: Problems in treating a construct. In J. M. Schlien (Ed.), *Research in psychotherapy* (Vol. 3). Washington, DC: American Psychological Association.

Lazarus, R. S., & Folkman, S. (1984). *Stress, appraisal, and coping.* New York: Springer.

Marlatt, G. A., & Gordon, J. R. (Eds.). (1985). *Relapse prevention: Maintenance strategies in the treatment of addictive behaviors.* New York: Guilford.

Meyer, V., & Turkat, I. D. (1979). Behavioral analysis of clinical cases. *Behavioral Assessment, 1,* 259–270.

Nelson, R. O., & Hayes, S. C. (1986). The nature of behavioral assessment. In R. O. Nelson & S. C. Hayes (Eds.), *Conceptual foundations of behavioral assessment.* New York: Guilford.

Nezu, A. M., Nezu, C. M., & Perri, M. G. (1988, September).*Clinical decision making in behavior therapy: A problem-solving perspective.* Workshop presented at the World Congress of Behaviour Therapy, Edinburgh, Scotland.

Nezu, A. M., Nezu, C. M., & Perri, M. G. (1989). *Problem-solving therapy for depression: Theory, research, and clinical guidelines.* New York: Wiley.

Turkat, I. D., & Maisto, S. A. (1985). Personality disorders: Application of the experimental method to the formulation and modification of personality disorders. In D. H. Barlow (Ed.), *Clinical handbook of psychological disorders: A step-by-step treatment manual.* New York: Guilford.

Part II

Clinical Applications

Chapter 4

Unipolar Depression

Christine M. Nezu
Arthur M. Nezu

INTRODUCTION

The ubiquity of depression would seem to be universally accepted. The psychiatric diagnosis of major depressive disorder reflects one of the most significant mental health problems facing our nation (Nezu, Nezu, & Perri, 1989). For example, 1 out of every 5 women will experience depression of clinical proportions during her lifetime; the probabilities for men are about 1 in 10 (Secunda, Friedman, & Schuyler, 1973). The magnitude of the personal costs of the disorder is represented by the significant number of depressed individuals who commit suicide—approximately 15 percent (Copas & Robin, 1982). On a broader societal level, the cost of depression related to decreased work productivity and the provision of health care has been estimated to be close to $11 billion each year (Craighead, Kennedy, Raczynski, & Dow, 1984). Clearly, depression continues to represent a serious and significant personal and social mental health problem.

However, unlike many of the disorders addressed in this book, a tremendous amount of research has been conducted during the past two decades on various aspects of depression, including etiological, prevalence, and treatment considerations. The majority of empirical research addressing psychosocial aspects of depression has largely been conducted from those residing within the cognitive-behavioral camp (Nezu, Nezu, & Perri, 1989). For example, researchers have delineated several major psychological models based upon behavioral and cognitive formulations that attempt to account for the etiology of depression and to suggest interventions for its treatment. A behavioral model articulated by Lewinsohn (1974), equates depression with a pervasive reduction in an individual's rate of positive reinforcement, often caused by deficient social skills or the reduced effectiveness of the person's instrumental activity. In the revised learned helplessness framework, causal attributions concerning a lack of control over negative outcomes are posited as the major determinants of a person's affective reactions (Abramson, Seligman, & Teasdale, 1978). Beck's (Beck, Rush, Shaw, & Emery, 1979) cognitive model suggests that depression is a consequence of distorted cognitive schemata that predispose an individual to negative views of the self, the surrounding world, and the future. The position based on self-control theory (Kanfer & Hagerman, 1981; Rehm, 1977) considers depression to result from deficits in self-monitoring, self-evaluation, and self-reinforcement. Finally, in an attempt to integrate some of these approaches, we have recently described a model of depression based on a problem-solving formulation (Nezu, 1987; Nezu, Nezu, & Perri, 1989). According to this model, deficits in one's ability to cope effectively with stressful stimuli (both intrapersonal and interpersonal) serve as one important vulnerability factor for unipolar depression.

Although treatment programs emanating from each of these theoretical frameworks have proven empirically to be therapeutically effective in reducing depressive symptomatology (see edited books by Beckham & Leber, 1985, and Clarkin & Glazer, 1981, for recent summaries of such research), it is unlikely that any one intervention approach would be optimally effective for every depressed individual (Craighead, 1980; Nezu, Nezu, & Perri, 1989). As emphasized in Part I of this book, individuals experiencing similar distress symptomatology (in this case, depression) are likely to vary greatly with regard to predisposing, precipitating, and maintaining variables. Moreover, the life circumstances of depressed individuals concerning both personal and social assets and deficits are also likely to differ substantially.

For this reason, some researchers have been urging that depression be viewed within a more pluralistic framework (Craighead, 1980; Liberman, 1981; Nezu, 1987). Adherents of this view see the pathogenesis of depression as multiple in nature, finding that theories based on a unitary model, as a function of their narrow focus, fall short of clinical reality and that various depression-associated characteristics or components vary from patient to patient. Moreover, such components, which need to be assessed for each unique case, then serve as the basis for treatment decisions. In other words, behavioral assessment aims initially to identify those variables that are causally related to an individual's experience of depression. On the basis of this functional analysis, specific treatment strategies are chosen to address goals uniquely relevant to a given patient (e.g., to decrease cognitive distortions, to increase social skills, to increase reinforcement, etc.). In this manner, the content of cognitive-behavioral treatment for depression can be quite heterogeneous across a population of depressed individuals (Nezu, Nezu, & Perri, 1988; Nezu, Petronko, & Nezu, 1982).

As the reader can readily observe, a pluralistic framework concerning depression is consistent philosophically with the clinical decision-making model delineated in chapter 3. No single theoretical model predominates as a means of guiding treatment decisions; rather, each depressed patient is perceived as being both homogeneous (e.g., having sad mood, feelings of hopelessness) and heterogeneous (e.g., possessing differing life circumstances) with other depressed individuals.

In the present chapter, we will first discuss various issues regarding cognitive-behavioral therapy of unipolar depression, applying certain aspects of the clinical decision-making model. Our discussion will focus on the first three of the four treatment stages: screening and problem evaluation, problem analysis and selection of focal target problems, and treatment design.[1] Following discussion of these issues, we will then offer a clinical case example that illustrates the application of several important aspects of the decision-making model.

APPLYING THE CLINICAL DECISION-MAKING MODEL

Regardless of the demonstrated efficacy of several cognitive-behavioral treatment strategies for depression, each patient who enters the clinician's office presenting depressive symptoms represents a unique case. Because of the diversity among individuals across a wide range of influential variables (e.g., age, sex, marital status, socioeconomic level, previous depressive episodes, severity of depression, presence of suicidal ideation, etc.), the clinician will likely engage continually in decision making concerning a number of assessment and treatment issues across the four stages of therapy.

In this section, we will consider the first three stages of therapy in terms of several important clinical issues associated with decision errors.

---

[1] The literature on various cognitive and behavioral strategies for depression is replete with detailed descriptions of the fourth stage of therapy: treatment implementation and evaluation (e.g., Beck et al., 1979, on cognitive therapy; Lewinsohn, Antonuccio, Steinmutz, & Teri, 1984, on behavior therapy; Nezu, Nezu, & Perri, 1989, on problem-solving therapy). For this reason, we refer the reader to these sources for further study. Additional discussion of the four stages of therapy can be found in chapter 3.

This compilation of issues is not meant to be exhaustive or necessarily exclusive to the treatment of depression. However, the issues do represent salient clinical problems that could seriously affect the success of any treatment endeavor. In keeping with the overall philosophy outlined in Part I, we strongly advocate applying the five problem-solving processes (see Figure 2.1) where relevant as a means of effectively addressing each of these issues.

Screening and Problem Identification

During the initial stage of screening and problem identification, three major clinical decision-making issues can be identified: accurate differential diagnosis, depression-related suicide, and depression-related motivational problems. These issues represent significant initiation problems and will be discussed in turn.

Diagnostic Issues

Many books or comprehensive chapters on the topic of depression begin by discussing the difficulties associated with operationally defining the construct itself:

> Depression has proven to be remarkably difficult to define. Dozens of different definitions all purportedly describe the same phenomenon. In some, depression simply refers to the common feeling of sadness, but in others depression may refer to an abnormal mood state, a symptom, a clinical syndrome, or even a disease process. (Nezu, Nezu, & Perri, 1989, p. 4)

The most commonly accepted definition of depression is likely to be found within the recently revised *Diagnostic and Statistical Manual of Mental Disorders* (DSM-III-R, American Psychiatric Association, 1987). Table 4.1 lists the symptoms, as specified by the DSM-III-R, that are necessary criteria for the diagnosis of major depressive disorder.

In addition to these *inclusion criteria,* there are also *exclusion criteria.* The diagnosis of major depression is inappropriate if depressive symptoms are associated with an identified organic factor or if they are part of a normal reaction to the loss of a loved one. Moreover, the diagnosis is inappropriate if the disturbance is superimposed on schizophrenic, schizophreniform, or delusional disorders, or if the criteria for schizoaffective disorder are met. Adequate knowledge and understanding of these diagnostic decision rules help in conducting a differential diagnosis. In other words, to be able to state with any degree of accuracy that an individual is suffering from major depression, as

Table 4.1 Symptoms Constituting the Diagnosis of Major Depressive Disorder

1. Depressed or sad mood
2. Markedly diminished interest or pleasure in all, or almost all, activities
3. Significant weight loss or weight gain when not dieting
4. Insomnia or hypersomnia
5. Psychomotor agitation or retardation
6. Fatigue or lack of energy
7. Feelings of worthlessness; excessive or inappropriate guilt
8. Diminished ability to think or concentrate; indecisiveness
9. Recurrent thoughts of death or suicidal ideation

Note. From *Diagnostic and Statistical Manual of Mental Disorders* (3rd ed. rev., p. 222), by the American Psychiatric Association, 1987, Washington, DC: Author.

distinct from schizoaffective disorder or a grief reaction, the clinician must be familiar with both inclusion *and* exclusion criteria.

Although such global knowledge aids the diagnostic process substantially, there are considerable complications concerning the transition between accurate diagnosis and treatment design. These include the aforementioned variability in how depression is viewed (i.e., as a symptom, syndrome, or disease process) and the relation between depression and other medical and psychological disorders.

The following example will illustrate the complexities of this transition.

Alice G., a potential client, comes to the therapist's office, stating that lately she has been "feeling down in the dumps" and tired. In response to several preliminary questions, Alice further says that she has not been sleeping or eating well lately and has been worried about what the future may bring. The clinician, being aware of the necessity for conducting a differential diagnosis, may inquire about other aspects of Alice's life in an attempt to rule out other major diagnoses (e.g., schizoaffective disorder). Additionally, to obtain quantitative validation, the clinician may even administer a self-report inventory of depression such as the Beck Depression Inventory (BDI; Beck, Ward, Mendelsohn, Mock, & Erbaugh, 1961). On the basis of this information (i.e., a differential diagnosis and a

BDI score of 29), the therapist then draws two conclusions: (a) that Alice is suffering from major depressive disorder and (b) that, given the wide use of and empirical support for cognitive therapy (or any other single strategy), such an approach is indicated as the treatment of choice for Alice.

The therapist's decisions concerning Alice are similar to those made by many of the students-in-training whom we have supervised. Much to their surprise, their clients, like Alice, often terminate therapy prematurely, not because the chosen therapy was ineffective per se, but because it may have been inappropriate for them. Possible reasons for this poor match may include inaccurate diagnosis, incomplete assessment of important maintaining variables, inattention to the client's inability to understand the rationale for treatment, presence of medical complications, and/or suboptimal implementation of the quickly chosen strategy due to lack of training or experience with that technique. The point to emphasize here is the need to guard against decision errors such as the representativeness and availability heuristics, which can lead to biased search strategies (see chapter 1).

If the clinician treats the presenting complaint "I've been feeling down lately" (a symptom) as equal to major depressive disorder (a clinical construct or syndrome) on the basis of their similarity (i.e., the representativeness error), then inaccurate diagnoses and/or poor treatment decisions are likely to follow. Moreover, inattention to both medical and psychological disorders in which depression is but one of several characteristic symptoms can also engender treatment disasters. The clinician must be aware of the wide range of medical or physical problems associated with a high risk for affective symptoms, among them endocrine, vitamin and mineral, infectious, neurological, collagen, cardiovascular, malignant, and metabolic disorders (Kathol, 1985; Klerman, 1987). Moreover, depressive reactions appear to be among the potential side effects of various pharmacologic agents, such as antihypertensives, antiparkinsonian agents, certain hormones, corticosteroids, and antituberculosis and anticancer drugs (Klerman, 1987). Additionally, feelings of dysphoria often coexist both with other Axis I (Lehmann, 1985) and Axis II (Millon & Kotik, 1985) disorders.

The ubiquity of depression as a symptom complicates the entire diagnostic enterprise. This concern, together with the popularity of various cognitive-behavioral theories and therapies of depression, suggests that what may be perceived initially as a relatively straightforward therapeutic process (i.e., a patient presents with dysphoric feelings, is therefore depressed, and is thus a good candidate for X form of cognitive-behavior therapy for depression) would, in reality, prove particularly complex.

This emphasis on diagnostic accuracy does not mean that, once a diagnosis of depression is confirmed, treatment decisions are simple. Rather, one essential first step towards effective behavior therapy for a depressed client is the identification of all influential factors that either serve as predisposing, precipitating, or maintaining variables in the depression. Such information is likely to have a great impact on the clinician's decision-making process. One example involves the important distinction between bipolar and unipolar depression (i.e., the former has been found to be quite amenable to treatment with drugs such as lithium).

The five problem-solving processes involved in the decision-making model can readily serve as a means of guiding the diagnostic procedure. For example, the clinician's problem orientation should emphasize an acknowledgment of the complexity of the diagnostic process and include a willingness to adopt a pluralistic framework. The problem definition and formulation process would entail a comprehensive assessment of those variables that would affect a valid diagnosis, including the use of a variety of assessment procedures (e.g., interview, self-report questionnaires, simulated role plays) that evaluate not only the presence and severity of depressive symptoms, but also the presence of those characteristics that would suggest other diagnostic entities (e.g., presence of delusions, recent medical problems, severe interpersonal difficulties). On the basis of such assessment, the clinician can engage in the generation of alternatives and the decision-making processes. Continual monitoring and evaluation of the accuracy of the diagnosis (i.e., avoidance of the anchoring heuristic) would be a major element of the solution implementation and verification process.

Using the diagnosis as an initial indicator, the clinician may need to problem solve the following questions: "Does this client require additional specific testing (neurological or psychological)?"; "Should the client be referred for psychiatric or medical evaluation?"; "Does the client require hospitalization?"; and "Should the client be referred to another therapist with expertise in this area?" Essentially, depending upon the outcome of the diagnostic process, the behavior therapist needs to answer the following basic question: "Is behavior therapy appropriate for this client at this particular time?" This question should be asked even if the diagnosis is clearly one of unipolar depression because medication may be required for severe neurovegetative symptoms, such as sleep disturbances, lack of energy, and eating problems (Hollon, Spoden, & Chaster, 1986; Nezu, Nezu, & Perri,

1989). Use of the decision-making model would be geared to aid in solving this initiation problem.

Presence of Suicide Potential

Many suicides occur in individuals suffering from depression (Boyer & Guthrie, 1985). Therefore, assessment of the presence, severity, and lethality of suicidal ideation and intent is an essential clinical task that must be accomplished prior to the initiation of any behavioral treatment for depression (Nezu, Nezu, & Perri, 1989). Because a detailed discussion of suicide assessment and treatment is beyond the scope of this chapter, we refer the reader elsewhere (Boyer & Guthrie, 1985; Hankoff, 1982; Linehan, 1981). Suffice it to state the rather obvious fact that inattention to a depressed patient's suicidal risk can have potentially disastrous effects. Standardized self-report inventories can aid in the assessment of suicidal intent and ideation; these include the Scale for Suicidal Ideation (Beck, Kovacs, & Weissman, 1979), the Hopelessness Scale (Beck, Weissman, Lester, & Trexler, 1974), the Time Questionnaire (Yufit & Benzies, 1979), and the Suicide Intent Scale (Beck, Schuyler, & Herman, 1974).

If suicidal intent is present, we again advocate the use of the clinical decision-making model as a means for determining a specific course of action. Although the literature offers many recommendations (see earlier citations), individuals may differ concerning a wide variety of factors, such as availability of family and/or social support. The clinician needs to make decisions specifically in the context of the unique life circumstances of the patient at hand. For example, helping the client to increase his social support base is a common treatment recommendation (e.g., Boyer & Guthrie, 1985; Kiev, 1975; Wekstein, 1979). However, the therapist must conduct a thorough decision analysis before incorporating this alternative as a fixed part of suicide treatment. The availability, quality, and accessibility of such support for the particular client will determine whether or not this suggestion is viable.

Another example of the application of problem-solving principles involves the recommendation that the therapist offer to provide support to the client by, for example, increasing the number of therapy sessions per week or having the client call in between sessions. The decision-making model can help the clinician assess her actual ability to provide these extra services and thus determine the advisability of such treatment suggestions.

Although the exact effects of the clinician's mood state on the clinical decision-making process have not been extensively explored, research concerning the effects of mood on judgment per se underscores the potential biasing consequences of affect for recall, learning, and decision making (Salovey & Turk, 1988). Because, as compared to other psychological difficulties that a behavior therapist might confront, the question of suicide is literally a life-and-death matter, the clinician's affective reaction (e.g., anxiety, fear, sadness) to such a serious problem needs to be self-monitored and viewed as a potential mediating factor. Again, as a function of its underlying systematic and comprehensive nature, the decision-making model would appear to be a particularly good framework within which to address this treatment issue.

It may also be of interest that clinical recommendations for the treatment of suicide often include the need for the therapist and patient to engage in mutual problem-solving strategies as a means of identifying alternative courses of action (e.g., Kiev, 1975; Linehan, 1981). In addition, more recently, theories of suicidal ideation have begun to identify deficits in social problem-solving skills as one important vulnerability factor (Bonner & Rich, 1988; Schotte & Clum, 1982, 1987).

Depression-related Motivational Problems

In addition to diagnostic issues and the question of suicide potential, a third possible initiation difficulty involves the client's motivation to engage actively in treatment. Although the issue of client motivation is not unique to depressed persons nor to the early stages of treatment (Kanfer & Schefft, 1988), the definition of depression inherently includes symptoms of hopelessness, lethargy, and decreased participation in normally reinforcing activities. Although the individual's seeking of treatment may reflect an intent to change, his depressive features may require special focus early in treatment as a means of facilitating adherence to therapeutic strategies that will be implemented later.

Application of the clinical decision-making model would entail using each of the five problem-solving processes in helping such clients to overcome their motivational difficulties (see chapter 3 for a detailed example). An appropriate problem orientation at this point includes the desire to provide a therapeutic medium for increasing the patient's sense of hope, rather than chalking up motivational problems to severe resistance. The problem definition and formulation process requires a thorough analysis of the various parameters involved in the initiation problem. Next, the clinician generates alternatives to enhance motivation. (Kanfer and Schefft, 1988, have already provided a list of such alternatives, as contained in Table 4.2.) On the basis of the specific problem analysis previously conducted, the therapist then engages in the decision-making process, delineating and weighing the various

Table 4.2 Possible Strategies to Enhance Client Motivation

1. Disrupt automatic responding.
2. Encourage use of self-regulation skills.
3. Make small demands.
5. Involve tasks that are not associated with fear of failure.
6. Associate outcome with previous reinforcers.
7. Reattribute causes.
8. Use role plays.
9. Work toward self-generated goals.
10. Use "provocative strategies" (e.g., paradoxical intention).
11. Encourage positive self-reinforcement.
12. Record progress.
13. Use environmental cues.
14. Require a prior commitment.
15. Promote a facilitative environment.
16. Make therapeutic contracts.
17. Use the therapeutic alliance.
18. Encourage the client to dream new dreams.

Note. From *Guiding the Process of Therapeutic Change* (pp. 138–139), by F. H. Kanfer and B. K. Schefft, 1988, Champaign, IL: Research Press. Adapted by permission.

consequences associated with each of the alternatives relevant to the particular client. Following this decision analysis, the therapist undertakes the process of solution implementation and verification. Because issues of motivation, compliance, and adherence are relevant throughout the course of treatment, continual monitoring and evaluation of the treatment plan is imperative.

Problem Analysis and Selection of Focal Target Problems

As delineated in chapter 3, the major clinical task during the stage of treatment involving problem analysis and selection of focal target problems is obtaining a detailed understanding and working knowledge of the patient's problems, as well as of the factors or variables etiologically or functionally related to those problems. In addition, the therapist and client together begin to articulate specific treatment goals and objectives. To accomplish these tasks via the clinical decision-making model requires application of each of the five problem-solving processes.

Major concerns relevant to each of these processes are discussed in the following pages.

Problem Orientation

We will not belabor the need to view depression from a pluralistic framework because we have already argued (convincingly, we hope) the utility of approaching *all* psychological disorders from such a vantage point. However, a pluralistic approach requires a comprehensive search for factors that potentially affect the presence and severity of the client's difficulties. Such an orientation helps the clinician avoid judgmental errors such as the availability, representativeness, and anchoring heuristics when evaluating the patient's problems.

Problem Definition and Formulation

After confidently arriving at a differential diagnosis of nonpsychotic unipolar depression, the therapist often finds it useful to obtain a quantitative assessment of the severity of the patient's depressive symptoms. This evaluation not only offers a means of normative comparison concerning a global classification of severity (i.e., mild, moderate, or severe), but also provides a useful baseline against which future scores can be compared in an assessment of therapeutic progress. Table 4.3 lists various assessment procedures, including clinician-rated and self-report measures, that can be helpful in this process.

To gather information about the nature of the client's depression, we recommend using the following procedures, outlined in more detail in chapter 3.

1. Survey the general life areas within which problems exist, either as contributors to the onset of the depression (e.g., severe relationship difficulties, work problems) or as consequences of the depression (e.g., decrease in leisure activities, low rate of instrumental activities geared toward personal goal attainment).

2. Using the three-dimensional framework (see Figure 3.1), conduct a microanalysis to obtain a detailed and comprehensive understanding of the specific nature of the client's problems.

3. Apply the SORKC formula to identify both global and specific behavioral chains as a means of pinpointing impediments to the client's goal attainment (see Figure 3.2).

To accomplish the first goal, the therapist can conduct a semistructured clinical interview to survey the client's functioning across a range of life areas. As an assessment adjunct (and as a potential primary evaluation measure), we recommend the use of Lazarus's (1980) Multimodal

Table 4.3 Standardized Assessment Procedures Concerning Depression-associated Characteristics

Focal area	Construct	Assessment procedure	Description
BEHAVIOR	Activities	Pleasant Events Schedule (MacPhillamy & Lewinsohn, 1982)	Self-report checklist of common pleasurable activities
		Unpleasant Events Schedule (Lewinsohn & Talkington, 1979)	Self-report checklist of common aversive events
	Social skills	Interpersonal Events Schedule (Youngren & Lewinsohn, 1980)	Self-report measure of interpersonal dysfunctions
		Rathus Assertiveness Schedule (Rathus, 1973)	Self-report inventory of assertive behavior
	Coping skills	Ways of Coping Checklist (Folkman & Lazarus, 1980)	Self-report measure of coping responses to a stressful event
		Coping Responses Inventory (Billings & Moos, 1981)	Self-report measure of coping responses to a stressful event
		Coping Strategies Scale (Beckham & Adams, 1984)	Self-report inventory of coping responses specific to depression
	Problem-solving skills	Means-End Problem-Solving Procedure (Platt & Spivack, 1975)	Paper-and-pencil measure of responses to a series of hypothetical problems
		Problem-Solving Inventory (Heppner & Petersen, 1982)	Self-report measure of problem-solving self-appraisal
		Social Problem-Solving Inventory (D'Zurilla & Nezu, 1988)	Self-report measure of problem-solving ability based on a five-component model
		Problem Inventory for College Students (Fisher-Beckfield & McFall, 1982)	Simulated audiotaped role-play measure of behavioral competence (problem solving)
		Problem-Solving Self-Monitoring Method (D'Zurilla, 1986)	Self-report measure of problem-solving responses to real-life situations
COGNITION	Causal attributions	Attributional Style Questionnaire (Peterson et al., 1982)	Self-report ratings of causal beliefs concerning 12 hypothetical situations
	Cognitive distortions	Cognitive Bias Questionnaire (Hammen & Krantz, 1976)	Paper-and-pencil measure of depressive negative thinking
		Automatic Thoughts Questionnaire (Hollon & Kendall, 1980)	Self-report measure of dysfunctional thoughts

Focal area	Construct	Assessment procedure	Description
	Cognitive distortions (cont'd)	Irrational Beliefs Test (Jones, 1969)	Self-report measure of irrational beliefs based on Ellis's RET model
		Dysfunctional Attitude Scale (Weissman, 1978)	Self-report measure of depressive cognitions
	Self-control	Self-Control Questionnaire (Rehm et al., 1981)	Self-report measure of attitudes and beliefs about self-control behaviors
		Self-Control Schedule (Rosenbaum, 1980)	Self-report measure of self-control behaviors
AFFECT	Depressive affect/severity	Beck Depression Inventory (Beck et al., 1961)	Self-report measure of severity of symptoms
		MMPI Depression Scale (Dempsey, 1964)	Self-report measure of depressive symptoms—one of the clinical scales from the MMPI
		Zung Self-Rating Depression Scale (Zung, 1965)	Self-report measure of depressive symptoms
		Depression Adjective Checklist (Lubin, 1965)	Self-report inventory of negative mood
		Schedule for Affective Disorders and Schizophrenia (Endicott & Spitzer, 1978)	Semistructured interview guide to aid in quantifying depressive symptoms
		Hamilton Rating Scale for Depression (Hamilton, 1960)	Clinician-rated scale to assess severity of depressive symptoms
		Carroll Rating Scale for Depression (Carroll et al., 1981)	Self-report inventory based on the Hamilton Rating Scale for Depression
ENVIRON-MENTAL FACTORS	Stressful events	Life Experiences Survey (Sarason et al., 1978)	Self-report measure of the occurrence and impact of various major life events
		Hassles Scale (Kanner et al., 1981)	Self-report inventory of the occurrence of daily "hassles"
		Mooney Problem Checklist (Mooney & Gordon, 1950)	Self-report checklist of current problems
		Personal Problems Checklist (Schinka, 1986)	Self-report checklist of current problems
		Problem Check List (Nezu, 1986a)	Self-report measure of the frequency of problems encountered across various areas of living

Life History Questionnaire, a general instrument that elicits both demographic information and data on various psychological variables (thoughts, feelings, behaviors). In addition, there are several checklists that can help reveal the nature and frequency of problems that the patient is currently experiencing (see Table 4.3 under the category pertaining to environmental factors). Because of time constraints and other clinical realities (e.g., a patient's limited motivation to complete a large number of inventories), the therapist should use the decision-making model to identify those measures that would have the greatest utility with regard to a specific case (see Table 3.1 for a summary of this process).

With regard to the content of data specific to depression that constitutes the focus of the second and third goals, the therapist should look to the literature for nomothetically driven constructs as represented by the cognitive-behavioral models of depression briefly described earlier in this chapter. In other words, the various theories of depression highlight several psychosocial variables thought to increase one's risk for a depressive episode. These include decreased reinforcement, poor social skills, inadequate coping ability, cognitive distortions, deficient self-regulatory skills, ineffective problem-solving ability, and negative causal attributions. Although not all depressed individuals can be unilaterally characterized by these vulnerability factors (Nezu, Nezu, & Perri, 1989), all have been empirically linked to unipolar depression. More important, therapeutic strategies aimed at counteracting these risk factors have demonstrated strong clinical utility as a means of reducing severity of depression.

For example, investigations have suggested that treatment strategies designed to increase pleasant or reinforcing activities can help to alleviate depression (Lewinsohn, Weinstein, & Alper, 1970; Zeiss, Lewinsohn, & Munoz, 1979). Cognitively based interventions (Rush, Beck, Kovacs, & Hollon, 1977; Sacco & Beck, 1985), as well as self-control procedures (Fuchs & Rehm, 1977; Rehm, Fuchs, Roth, Kornblith, & Romano, 1979), have likewise proven effective for depression reduction. In addition, providing social skills training to individuals with unipolar depression has proven to be an efficacious approach (Hersen, Bellack, & Himmelhoch, 1980). Finally, training depressed individuals in social problem-solving skills has been found to be a fruitful treatment model (Hussian & Lawrence, 1981; Nezu, 1986b; Nezu & Perri, in press).

In this light, the vulnerability factors mentioned earlier can serve as a group of important focal target areas to assess for every depressed client. An identified deficit in any of these skill areas can then be listed as one of several possible major targets; the articulated goal would specify changes regarding this vulnerability factor. As an adjunct to the clinical interview, in vivo observations, daily logs, simulated role plays, and self-report inventories can yield relevant information concerning these risk factors. Table 4.3 includes a list of standardized assessment tools addressing these variables; they are categorized according to the focal problem areas included in the three-dimensional framework of assessment mentioned earlier in this chapter.[2] The clinician's actual choice of assessment procedures should be based on a decision analysis that follows the decision-making model (see Table 3.1).

Using the information gleaned from this comprehensive process, the therapist can then construct a Clinical Pathogenesis Map (CPM). The CPM graphically depicts the clinical hypotheses concerning the major variables that idiographically contribute to the initiation and maintenance of a particular patient's depressive symptoms. The CPM helps to lay the foundation for an overall treatment plan. It can also serve as one important stimulus for the client's feedback concerning agreement or disagreement with the therapist's overall conceptualization. Figure 3.3 depicts a hypothetical CPM relevant to depression (see also Figure 4.1, on p. 147).

Generation of Alternatives and Decision Making

During the problem analysis stage of treatment, the therapist applies the two problem-solving processes involving generation of alternatives and decision making in order to select problems that will be targeted for intervention and to identify a set of realistic therapeutic goals. Use of brainstorming principles within the generation of alternatives process results in a comprehensive list of target problems and therapeutic goals. The clinician then conducts a decision analysis by evaluating the value and likelihood of each alternative idea (see chapter 3 for specific criteria relevant to this clinical task). Those focal target problems and treatment goals that have the highest utility then become the ones to include within the overall treatment plan. Using the results of this process, the therapist can then begin to construct the Goal Attainment Map (GAM; see Figure 3.4), a graphic representation of the

---

[2] The focal area concerning biological/medical variables was omitted here because a detailed discussion encompassing such standardized measurement procedures is beyond the scope of this chapter. Moreover, it is highly unlikely that the behavior therapist would conduct such as assessment. Rather, referral to the appropriate professional (e.g., neurologist or psychiatrist) would be more appropriate. Interested readers are directed to Koslow and Gaist (1987) and Stokes (1987) for descriptions of biologically oriented evaluations.

overall recommended treatment plan showing which clinical techniques are proposed for which treatment subgoals and objectives. (However, only after the specific interventions are identified during the next
therapeutic stage can the GAM be fully completed.)

From the empirically derived nomothetic data available in the
literature, a pool of potentially relevant treatment goals and objectives
for depressed individuals can be identified. Table 4.4 presents a list of
possible therapeutic goals. As emphasized throughout Part I, as part of
the underlying philosophy of multiple causality, patients experiencing
similar difficulties can be characterized with completely different
CPMs. for this reason, this list should be viewed only within the context
of *possible* treatment goals for a given depressed client. The empirical
literature suggests that attainment of these therapeutic objectives will
lead to a reduction in depression.

Solution Implementation and Verification

Application of the solution implementation and verification problem-solving process during the problem analysis stage of therapy entails
constructing a CPM and attempting to verify the validity and utility of
the choices made concerning focal target problems and therapeutic
goals. Verification would involve discussion with the depressed client,
as well as the testing of specific hypotheses emanating from a behavioral
case formulation approach (Meyer & Turkat, 1979). For example, on
the basis of initial information gleaned from intake interviews, it appeared that Joe, a 39-year-old client, was depressed in part because of
an unsatisfactory marital relationship. The therapist verified her
hypothesis by asking Joe to complete a marital distress inventory (e.g.,
the Marital Satisfaction Inventory; Snyder, 1979) and by having his
spouse, Janet, come to treatment to provide adjunctive information
about him. The results of this verification effort suggested that it was
valid to identify Joe's marital relationship as a focal target problem.
Subsequent treatment incorporated strategies to improve Joe's marriage, thus helping to alleviate his initial complaint of depression.

Treatment Design

During the treatment design stage of therapy, the clinician attempts to
design an overall treatment plan that will idiographically help the client
to attain the goals delineated during the problem analysis stage. In
essence, treatment is geared to address those impediments to goal
attainment outlined within the client's individualized CPM. As part of
the overall treatment plan, specific therapeutic components must be
identified and chosen. It might also be necessary to identify differential

Table 4.4 Possible General Therapeutic Goals for a Depressed Client Based on Nomothetic Data

1. Increase pleasant activities.
2. Decrease unpleasant activities.
3. Increase future expectation of positive outcomes.
4. Increase focus on positive rather than negative events.
5. Increase coping abilities.
6. Increase problem-solving ability.
7. Increase assertive behavior.
8. Increase time management skills.
9. Increase communication skills.
10. Facilitate marital relationship.
11. Facilitate various interpersonal relationships.
12. Decrease negative automatic thoughts.
13. Decrease negative self-evaluations.
14. Decrease negative ruminations.
15. Decrease associated anxiety.
16. Reduce unrealistically high expectations.
17. Increase positive self-reinforcement.
18. Decrease self-punishment.
19. Increase cognitive flexibility and perspective taking.
20. Facilitate positive orientation to problems in living.
21. Decrease cognitive distortions.
22. Decrease errors in logic.
23. Decrease irrational thinking.
24. Decrease self-blame.
25. Decrease negative attributions.
26. Decrease stress.
27. Increase social skills.
28. Decrease importance of unattainable goals.
29. Increase tolerance of negative images and memories.

training or treatment procedures if problems exist that would inhibit optimal implementation of a given strategy. Use of the clinical decision-making model can help the therapist achieve these particular objectives.

Problem Orientation

As discussed in detail in chapter 3, the particular mind-set that we advocate adopting for this stage of treatment incorporates the following principles.

1. Behavioral treatment should be based on the idiographic application of nomothetically driven constructs.
2. Treatment should be viewed as a strategic (versus technical) approach to psychotherapy.
3. Complex clinical disorders may require multiple treatment interventions.
4. Treatment should not only aim to overcome the specific impediments to goal attainment identified during the problem analysis stage, but should also include a plan for increasing the patient's overall capacity to cope in the future.

Concerning the treatment of depression, the first principle addresses the clinician's need, when designing a treatment plan, to consider comprehensively the wide range of characteristics (e.g., age, sex, symptom severity, presence of suicidal ideation, etc.) and life circumstances (e.g., marital status, socioeconomic level) unique to a particular client, rather than "jumping in" with a specific treatment intervention.

The second principle concerns the need to distinguish between general therapeutic strategies versus specific intervention tactics. A wide variety of different methods may be geared to achieve the same therapeutic goal. For example, to help the depressed client cease thinking illogically, the therapist can choose from a number of different techniques: direct refutation, cognitive restructuring, systematic rational restructuring, reverse advocacy role plays, paradoxical intention, reinforcement of rational statements, attributional retraining, and so forth. Although there may be some overlap among these techniques, each is implemented differently; one may be more appropriate than another for a given depressed client, depending on individual circumstances.

The third principle concerns the idea that multiple treatment techniques may be required to address multiple depression-related target problem areas. For example, a comprehensive assessment of Clare, a 33-year-old patient, revealed that her depression was related in part to unsatisfying interpersonal relationships. This problem appeared to be a function of both deficient social skills and severe negative self-evaluations related to most social situations, including her place of work. As is consistent with this third orientation principle, Clare's therapeutic plan incorporated interventions aimed at both target problems (i.e., assertiveness and communication training to remediate social skills deficits, along with cognitive procedures to overcome negative self-appraisal).

The final orientation principle, that of including future-oriented intervention components, is illustrated by the case of Tony, a 56-year-old client whose beliefs about and perceptions of stressful life situations could be characterized as classic examples of a negative attributional style. This hypothesis was confirmed by Tony's answers to a self-report inventory (e.g., the Attributional Style Questionnaire; Peterson, Semmel, von Baeyer, Abramson, and Seligman, 1982), as well as by his behavior during numerous therapy sessions. Tony tended to attribute negative events to internal, stable, and global causes. Moreover, his responses on other inventories suggested that he had also experienced a large number of recent stressful problems. As such, Tony's overall treatment plan included two major goals: (a) to reverse his negative attributional beliefs and (b) to increase his coping abilities as a means of decreasing both the incidence and stressful impact of negative events in the future. The therapist predicted initially that changing Tony's negative attributional style would produce positive effects in the short run, but would be insufficient with regard to long-term effects (see Nezu, Kalmar, Ronan, & Clavijo, 1986). Making the coping skills component an important part of Tony's overall therapeutic plan served to facilitate maintenance of treatment gains over time.

Generation of Alternatives

Because much of the information necessary to generate potential intervention strategies has already been obtained during the problem analysis stage of treatment, the clinician is largely able to bypass the problem definition and formulation process. In generating a list of possible treatment procedures for a certain goal or objective, the behavior therapist should use the three brainstorming principles: quantity, deferment of judgment, and strategies-tactics. An example of such a list relevant to depression has already been generated in Table 3.4.[3]

---

[3] Familiarity with these cognitive-behavioral strategies is assumed. More detailed clinical explanations of these approaches can be found in Beckham and Leber (1985), Clarkin and Glazer (1981), Nezu, Nezu, & Perri (1989), and Rehm (1981). For information concerning marital and family approaches for depression, see Haas, Clarkin, and Glick (1985). A chapter by Noll, Davis, and DeLeon-Jones (1985) provides an excellent comprehensive overview of psychopharmacological treatments for depression.

Decision Making

After listing the possible intervention tactics for each major therapeutic goal, the clinician should then assess the utility of each alternative according to the various decision-making criteria set forth in Table 4.5.

In line with the underlying emphasis of behavior therapy on empirical scrutiny, the most important criteria involves the following question: "What is the likelihood that this particular intervention will achieve the specific goal?" To answer this question adequately, the therapist should be familiar with the research literature concerning the efficacy of a given approach for the treatment of depression. Many of the clinical strategies mentioned throughout this chapter have been documented to be effective in reducing depressive symptoms and therefore can be rated highly with regard to this criterion. However, research in this area has not been so comprehensive that all strategies have been tested across a wide range of depressed individuals varying in population characteristics.

An example concerns problem-solving therapy, which has been found to be an effective treatment model for depressed geriatric inpatients (Hussian & Lawrence, 1981), community outpatient volunteers diagnosed with unipolar depression (Nezu, 1986b; Nezu & Perri, in press), and depressed Veterans Administration inpatients (Nezu, Mahoney et al., 1989). However, the model has not been tested with regard to depressed persons who are also acutely suicidal, economically disadvantaged, or concomitantly diagnosed with an Axis II disorder. This does not mean that problem-solving therapy would not be effective for individuals in these latter groups; however, if the patient at hand is from such a group, then problem-solving therapy would be rated as potentially less effective than if the patient were from one of the populations with whom the therapy has been tested. Similarly, cognitive-behavioral treatment approaches that have been tested only with college populations should be rated as potentially less effective than those that have been successfully applied to a clinically depressed population.

In addition to considering the documented efficacy of a specific treatment, the clinician needs to take into account various idiosyncratic characteristics of a given depressed patient. The utility and ultimate effectiveness of a specific treatment approach for a particular patient, then, depends on the application of a variety of additional decision-making criteria. (These criteria, discussed in detail in chapter 3, are summarized in Table 4.5 for the reader's convenience.)

Table 4.5   Decision-making Criteria for Evaluating Alternative Treatment
Strategies

LIKELIHOOD OF TREATMENT EFFECTS

1. What is the likelihood that this particular intervention will achieve the specified goal(s)?

2. What is the likelihood that this particular therapist can optimally implement this particular treatment approach?

3. What is the likelihood that the client will be able to carry out a particular strategy in an optimal fashion?

4. What is the likelihood that collateral or paraprofessional therapists will be able to implement a particular strategy in an optimal way?

5. What is the likelihood that this treatment approach will contribute to the client's ability to cope more effectively with future problems or stressful situations?

VALUE OF TREATMENT EFFECTS

Personal Consequences
1. How much time and other resources are required to implement the treatment?

2. How much effort is involved in implementing the treatment approach?

3. What emotional cost or gain would result if this treatment were implemented?

4. Is use of this intervention consistent with morals, values, and ethics?

5. What are the physical side effects of the treatment?

6. What is the impact of this treatment on related problem areas?

Social Consequences
1. What are the effects of a particular treatment alternative on the client's family and on others who have an influence on the client's life?

Short-term Consequences
1. What are the immediate effects of implementing this treatment approach?

Long-term Consequences
1. What are the long-term consequences of this treatment approach?

On the basis of the results of this evaluation process, the clinician then chooses the alternative(s) predicted to be the most effective for the particular patient in achieving a certain goal or goals. As in Part I, we advocate that several alternative interventions be implemented simultaneously for each therapeutic goal as a means of enhancing maintenance and generalization.

Solution Implementation and Verification

Because, according to the decision-making model, solution implementation and verification involves continued planning, the process at this treatment stage involves completion of a patient's GAM and not formal treatment implementation per se. The GAM is then shared with the client as one important way to verify the products of the clinical decision-making model thus far (i.e., the chosen treatment plan). Depending upon the outcome of this discussion, the therapist either is ready to begin formal treatment or needs to recycle through the decision-making model to identify a more acceptable treatment approach.

Treatment Implementation and Evaluation

We began this chapter by stating that we would not focus on the treatment implementation and evaluation stage of therapy because the literature offers excellent resources on the various cognitive-behavioral interventions. Nonetheless, it is imperative to remember that implementation of a particular treatment strategy rarely runs smoothly. The programs described in the empirical literature represent focused therapeutic protocols necessary to test adequately a particular hypothesis, usually one addressing efficacy issues. They do not necessarily reflect the actual application of a particular treatment approach in the typical clinical setting (e.g., outpatient clinic or private office). Therefore, use of the decision-making model is required in order to facilitate ultimate goal attainment.

For example, in the case of Carol Ann, a 25-year-old client with mild to moderate mental retardation and an Axis I diagnosis of dysthymic disorder, a comprehensive decision analysis pointed to assertiveness training as one means of improving her interpersonal skills and thus her overall social relationships. However, in part because of Carol Ann's limited cognitive abilities, her therapist could not implement the standard assertiveness training designed for nonretarded persons and typically described in the literature. Carol Ann's assertiveness training took longer and required additional problem-solving efforts to identify alternative training approaches (e.g., use of videotapes, pictures, simulated role plays with dolls).

A second example involves the case of Julia, a 54-year-old depressed woman whose GAM included problem-solving therapy as a means of improving her overall coping abilities. When Julia was asked to begin generating various coping solutions to a recent stressful situation, it became apparent that she experienced substantial difficulties in producing ideas by brainstorming. The therapist did not conclude that this difficulty rendered problem-solving therapy ineffective for Julia but rather, in keeping with the decision-making model, identified it as another obstacle to overcome. By invoking the model to address this concern, the therapist generated several strategies that helped Julia use the brainstorming process successfully. These strategies included visualization and thinking about how certain role models may have handled the problem situation (see Nezu, Nezu, & Perri, 1989).

The identification of potentially effective treatment strategies via a comprehensive decision analysis does not guarantee successful implementation or goal attainment. Continued evaluation (i.e., verification) of the short- and long-term effects of a given intervention is needed as a means of monitoring treatment utility. Obstacles that appear during this stage of treatment can be addressed via the decision-making model.

CLINICAL CASE EXAMPLE

To highlight several of the points made thus far, we present the following case example.

> Fred A., a 67-year-old white male, initially scheduled an appointment for help concerning feelings of depression. He was accompanied at the first interview by both his wife and his 32-year-old son. Fred described his depression problem as having occurred over the past 2 years. His complaints included intense worry, ruminations, feelings of guilt, sad mood, and negative self-evaluations; he also experienced poor sleep, paranoid-type thinking (e.g., "Everyone at work is watching me"), anhedonia, and social withdrawal. Fred had asked his internist for medication to help with his "nerves," and the physician had suggested a psychiatric/psychological evaluation. Fred believed that medication might help because he had experienced similar symptoms approximately 2 years earlier and a prescribed neuroleptic medication seemed to have alleviated the symptoms. Fred had also participated briefly in psychotherapy, but had stopped because "it didn't do any good."
>
> Fred's son, Marc, appeared quite concerned that his father would not be able to enjoy his upcoming retirement fully and had supported the physician's suggestion for a psychiatric evaluation. Fred's wife, June, expressed concern that her husband had seemed especially "nervous" and in "bad spirits,"

although she described him historically as being "a nervous type of guy." June had insisted on an evaluation after discovering that Fred had, on numerous occasions, taken several drinks at a local bar before returning home from work. This behavior was extremely unusual: As June stated, "You could set your clock by Fred's routines—he has walked in the door at 5:35 p.m. for the last 30 years."

Issues in Screening and Problem Identification

This case description reminds us again of the complexities involved in conducting a behavioral assessment to develop effective treatment recommendations. To begin with, the basic question of whether or not the patient is an appropriate candidate for psychotherapeutic treatment represents an initial problem to be solved. Fred's age alone (67 years) implies a host of possible explanations for the existence of depressive symptomatology that might be unrelated to psychosocial issues. Various toxic, metabolic, or endrocrine disorders could also explain such symptoms. Yet there is some evidence that, if any of these conditions were found to exist, psychosocial factors (e.g., fear about the impending retirement) might also contribute to the patient's distress. Moreover, even if all possible medical or biological etiologies were ruled out, the following question would remain: "How willing would Fred be to engage in psychotherapy, given his own bias, based upon a negative past experience?"

Fred's complaints of distress appeared significant, and, although intervention of some type was surely indicated to help alleviate his difficulties, a plethora of questions needed to be answered before an empirically based treatment could be initiated.

Assessment of depression, as with the other disorders described in this book, should involve an examination of multiple etiological contributions to the patient's distress: genetic/biological vulnerability factors; previous developmental characteristics; social learning history; environmental factors; current problems in the form of minor and major life stress; and current depressive symptoms involving cognitive, affective, physical, and social systems spheres. Fred's case exemplifies the need to explore all of these areas fully. For example, the diagnosis of depression itself appeared uncertain because features of an anxiety disorder were also present. Fred's intense worry, anxious rumination, history of possible ritualistic behavior, and requests for "some pills to calm my nerves" required further investigation as to the presence of a primary anxiety disturbance.

After further assessment through various self-report inventories; a brief neuropsychological screening; social, developmental, and medical history; and physical examination (including laboratory tests), it was concluded that the diagnosis of major depressive disorder did correspond most closely to Fred's complaints and experiences. His history also indicated a chronic and habituated pattern of coping with increased anxiety through avoidance behavior and confinement to "safe" activities. For example, the patient tearfully described his military experience, stating that it had been the first time he had ever left his immediate neighborhood. He had found the separation from his family intolerable and, upon his return, vowed never again to leave his neighborhood. He had met and married June after his return to his community, had secured a carpentry job with the local municipal system, and had remained there for the last 40 years.

Fred's overall constellation of symptoms, then, was consistent with a diagnosis of major depression, even though his anxiety symptoms were also intense enough to require treatment. Moreover, there is much overlap clinically between these two affective constructs (Nezu & D'Zurilla, in press). What is most important within the clinical decision-making model, though, is not solely the accuracy of a differential diagnosis. Rather, it is the identification and functional analysis of those problem areas in need of treatment, regardless of the diagnosis itself.

Issues in Problem Analysis and Selection of Focal Target Problems

Having established that Fred was a suitable candidate for psychological intervention, the therapist next faced the task of selecting target problem areas. Developing a treatment approach for this patient might not appear initially to represent a major difficulty. The biologically oriented psychiatrist, for example, might have begun considering the most appropriate medication alternatives as soon as the diagnosis of depression was made. The cognitive therapist might have targeted the patient's irrational fears of self-evaluation, as well as any attributions of negative, global, and stable self-blame he displayed when discussing work-related difficulties. The family therapist might have focused on the transition to retirement faced by Fred and his family. Indeed, finding an intervention among the many possibilities would not present a major problem. However, developing a tailor-made program for optimal treatment of an individual is more demanding. Doing so means conducting a comprehensive assessment of the unique characteristics of the patient at hand, rather than simply prescribing a treatment for a "disease" without considering individual factors.

As discussed throughout this volume, a more objective problem orientation for the clinician often involves understanding that the most salient target areas for intervention are not those that are most familiar to behavior therapists, but those that appear most immediately distressing to the patient. Fred's case provides an illustration. During the initial interview, the client had described his wife, June, as a "doll" and "the sweetest person around," denying any marital problems and talking only about work-related difficulties. However, during later sessions, it was disclosed that June's sister had moved into the family home several years previously and that her presence infringed on the patient's time alone with his wife. In reaction to this intrusion, Fred often retreated to his room, engaging in isolated activities and spending evenings in jealous and angry ruminations about his sister-in-law. In the course of therapy, one strategic intervention focused on building Fred's assertiveness skills so that he could appropriately discuss these family issues. The patient himself, however, had not identified this family problem as an area in need of intervention during the initial sessions.

In addition, a patient's own learned methods of coping in general with distress can often influence him to request a certain type of help. Thus Fred's request for medication may have represented the continuation of a pattern of avoidance of current difficulties, as exemplified by his increased frequency of drinking, staying away from home, recent absenteeism at work, and spending long periods of time alone in his room.

Because discussions of professional biases concerning various diagnostic categories, preference for theoretical explanations of pathology, and approaches to treatment appear elsewhere in this book, we will not belabor this point here. However, Fred's case does highlight the need to overcome biases concerning various patient characteristics. For example, Fred's age (67 years) and socioeconomic status (high school equivalency diploma, union laborer) might inadvertently suggest to some clinicians—as well as to the patient—a decreased emphasis on the exploration of certain assessment areas. One such area is that of sexual functioning. Fred and his wife had experienced a significant decrease in sexual activity over the past year; nevertheless, when the therapist explored this area with several rudimentary questions during the initial interview, the patient had responded, "That stuff is OK." During subsequent sessions, however, when the area was explored in more detail, Fred confessed that he had been uncomfortable talking about sexual issues with a younger, female therapist. Moreover, with his wife present at the first interview, he did not want to say anything that might cause her embarrassment. The patient did subsequently reveal that, following his first bout with depression 2 years earlier, he and his wife had experienced difficulty resuming their previous frequency of sexual activity. In addition, the presence of Fred's sister-in-law in the home made finding time together especially difficult.

The loss of sexual intimacy appeared to contribute significantly to Fred's depressive symptoms. However, given his initial reluctance to discuss this matter, it would likely not have been a therapeutic focus if the clinician had assumed at the outset that further exploration of the issue was unnecessary because of the patient's age (see chapter 8 for further discussion of issues in the treatment of sexual dysfunction).

Finally, Fred's limited education, preference for medication, hesitancy in self-disclosure, and limited ability to express himself verbally might have biased the therapist against most dialectically oriented therapies. This assumption would have been unfortunate in that Fred was capable of displaying warmth and sensitivity, a desire to relate to others, and a propensity to learn about himself if one related to him in down-to-earth language.

To learn more about the patient's functioning across a wide range of areas, the therapist sought more specific information in the following domains.

Medical/Biological Factors

Details about Fred's family revealed a history of alcoholism and depression with regard to his father. Physical and neurological examinations ruled out any organic explanation for the depressive symptoms. In light of the patient's age, it was important also to rule out progressive or acute brain dysfunctions, as well as metabolic or toxic conditions. A brief neuropsychological screening yielded results indicating that cognitive functioning was mostly normal, although a decrease in performance was noted when the patient became nervous about giving a correct answer. Patience and encouragement on the part of the examiner resulted in increased performance when Fred was asked to add numbers and recall sequenced digits.

Fred did reveal some neurovegetative signs of depression, such as decreased energy and sleep problems. Appetite, however, appeared normal and stable.

Psychosocial Functioning

Assessment in the psychosocial area was broad based and addressed various cognitive components, perceptions of control, feelings of helplessness, behavioral characteristics, and self-regulation skills. In the clinician's view, rigid adherence to only one of the treatment models associated with these depression-related variables would decrease the effectiveness of further decision making.

Fred revealed very low self-esteem, irrational cognitions regarding his ability to meet the expectations of others, and feelings of being undeserving of his wife and children. He also exhibited an almost catastrophic guilt over making even minor mistakes. For example, he described staying away from work for 3 days because he had accidentally set off a new alarm system. He could not return to work, he stated, "because I felt like I made such a damn fool of myself." He perceived that he had no right to become angry at his wife, relatives, or co-workers, and he frequently became tearful when discussing his feelings toward his family. He described a day-to-day existence that included almost constant fears of criticism and rejection, fear of experiencing another clinical depression, fear of humiliating or hurting his family by his "emotional weakness," and increasing periods of isolation to avoid these outcomes. He began to smoke cigarettes after a 10-year abstinence and would have a few drinks on the way home "in order to relax me and help me hide how I was feeling from my wife." The patient's symptoms continued to worsen in that his preoccupation with hiding his feelings of sadness and fear and his increased alcohol consumption actually began to impair his memory for certain tasks at work, causing him even more concern over his abilities.

Behavioral Observations

Information gleaned from both in-session therapist observation and self-reports of behavior indicated that Fred experienced a heightened and intense state of arousal across many situations. The predominant variable common to most of these situations involved any perceived threat of evaluative criticism. He reported experiencing a dry mouth, sweaty palms, an accelerated heart rate, flushed sensations, and a "hot" face, along with increased worry that others would notice these reactions. This increase in arousal was, indeed, easily observable during sessions and was accompanied by the patient's frequently excusing himself, stumbling over words, and giving explanations or apologies for his feelings.

In addition, Fred described avoidant behavior that appeared to reduce his anxiety significantly but that simultaneously resulted in a loss of various reinforcing activities. For example, he described how much he would enjoy visiting a vacation home owned by his son and daughter-in-law. However, he rarely made such visits because he avoided asking his wife to plan a weekend trip without her sister's accompanying them.

At work, Fred served as the foreman in charge of stock inventory. He would often go through a day feeling angry and depressed because he would avoid confronting workers who had not returned tools at the appropriate time. It appeared that he was afraid that they might view him as unfair or "too picky."

Plans for Fred's upcoming retirement were also an object of avoidance because he anticipated a confrontation with his wife regarding a decision about whether his sister-in-law would continue to live with them. The patient made frequent statements such as "I guess I'll just cross that bridge when I come to it" and, as a result, viewed his future with a sense of futility and hopelessness. He focused blame for this difficult situation upon himself; continued avoidance of the topic provided some temporary relief in that his relationship with his wife was at least superficially pleasant.

Despite initial inhibitions to talk about himself, Fred was observed during the assessment sessions to be especially cooperative and motivated to attend. He generally arrived on time and used a fair portion of the session to air feelings of resentment, anger, and hopelessness. Although these moments were frequently accompanied by apologies and self-criticism, he described a sense of relief at being able to discuss these issues in a confidential environment.

Measures

To obtain information that would corroborate data gathered during interviews with Fred, as well as to provide for a treatment evaluation protocol, the therapist administered several measures. These included a Multimodal Life History Questionnaire (Lazarus, 1980), the Beck Depression Inventory (Beck et al., 1961), the Hamilton Rating Scale for Depression (Hamilton, 1960), a self-report anxiety inventory (State-Trait Anxiety Inventory; Spielberger, Gorsuch, & Lushene, 1970), the Social Problem-Solving Inventory (D'Zurilla & Nezu, 1988), and a measure of assertiveness (Rathus, 1973).

Clinical Pathogenesis Map

A CPM was constructed next to represent the major variables hypothesized to be involved in the initiation and maintenance of Fred's symptoms of depression and anxiety. Although a diagnosis of major depression was generally consistent with his symptoms, his distress also included anxiety symptoms intense enough to require specific focus. In this regard, Fred exemplifies the typical case, which often necessitates repeated assessment that may lead to changes in the original treatment plan. As we have stressed, complex problems often require multiple solutions.

As shown by Fred's CPM (see Figure 4.1), his current symptoms can be seen as the cumulative result of developmental and physiological vulnerabilities, recent psychosocial stressors, the continued presence of environmental and intrapsychic triggers or stimuli, and deficient coping ability. Any one of the variables noted in the CPM could be a valid target for intervention. However, intervention focused on any solitary variable would likely be insufficient; the clinician needs to keep the entire map within view. Moreover, when focusing on any one variable as a treatment target, the clinician faces the task of choosing how to intervene, that is, which strategy to implement in order to achieve desired change. Either way, a variety of clinical decisions need to be made.

The therapist initially provided Fred with an explanation of the CPM in straightforward language that emphasized the distortions present in his self-deprecation. The therapist also engaged him in an educative discussion that gave him a basic understanding of anxiety and avoidant patterns and recommended behavioral psychotherapy, describing what would be involved in such an endeavor.

Fred was predictably more enthusiastic about attending therapy than he had initially reported, for several reasons. First, his previous experience had been what might be described as a traditional psychoanalytic experience. He reported that he had been angry and confused by the therapist, who "just sat there and listened—never told me anything or gave me any advice." It is quite likely that his experience with this therapist had heightened his evaluative anxiety and that the lack of therapeutic structure had provided him with little perception of control. Second, Fred's experience with the current therapist had informed him with data that not all therapies would be a repetition of his first therapeutic encounter. Now, in contrast, he was receiving an explanation of his difficulties, a framework for change, and a presentation consistent with his own language and vocabulary.

Selection of treatment target alternatives was pursued according to the clinical decision-making framework outlined in chapter 3. Initially, all variables included in the CPM were submitted to a cost-benefit analysis and assessed for their value as primary targets for intervention. The potential targets were rated as to (a) the likelihood that they would ameliorate Fred's distressing symptoms, (b) generalized impact upon other variables in the CPM, (c) accessibility for intervention, (d) amount

Figure 4.1 Client's Pathogenesis Map (CPM)

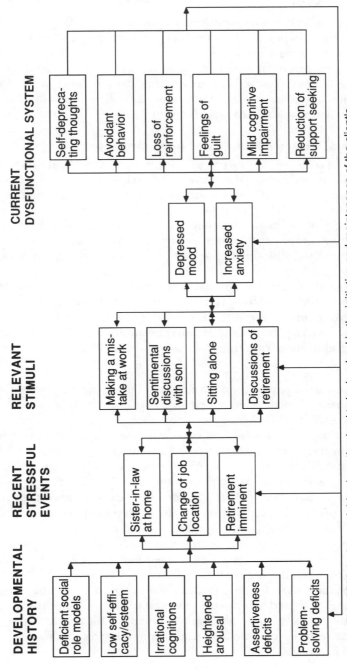

Note. This CPM depicts variables hypothesized to be involved in the initiation and maintenance of the client's presenting problems (i.e., depressed mood and anxiety). Note the reciprocal relations among the various elements.

of time and effort that would be required to modify the symptoms, (e) required expertise, (f) possibility of change, and (g) short- and long-term consequences.

The targets for intervention most highly rated focused on increasing Fred's use of social support systems, present level of reinforcing activities, and assertive communication, as well as decreasing his acute anxiety symptoms and his avoidance of problems.

Issues in Treatment Design and Implementation

Decisions concerning strategies for intervention involved first generating a list of treatment alternatives for each target problem and then evaluating the predicted treatment effects of each alternative for a particular target. For example, treatment alternatives for decreasing avoidance of problems included social problem-solving therapy, confrontative therapy techniques, family therapy sessions, a patient diary of distressing situations, group therapy for retired workers, and medication.

Once the treatment alternatives for the various intervention targets had been evaluated, the priority of interventions became yet another problem requiring the application of the decision-making model. The final treatment plan resulting from these multiple decisions is discussed in the following paragraphs.

Phase I

Individual psychotherapy aimed at equipping the patient with a more rational and challenge-oriented approach to problem solving was begun initially. It is important to note that additional decision making was necessary to establish the appropriate language to use in implementing this cognitive strategy. For example, given Fred's interpersonal inhibitions, initial use of role-play exercises was too anxiety provoking. However, analogies to familiar subjects were received well. One particular analogy that appealed to Fred concerned the fact that most professional baseball players, although considered the individuals most skilled in the sport, can rarely sustain a batting average greater than .350. Fred frequently commented on how this analogy was useful when he was being too hard on himself and "worrying about making mistakes that don't really matter."

During Phase I, equal priority was given to providing Fred with strategies designed to reduce his increased anxiety. Relaxation training was the main vehicle to achieve this purpose, although the cognitive therapy techniques were also useful for reducing anxious, as well as depressive, cognitions.

Phase II

Once Fred achieved a reduction in acute anxiety, a more rational understanding of his problems, and increased motivation to approach problems rather than avoid them, the therapist introduced the second focus of treatment, coping skills training. This approach included assertiveness training, continued social problem-solving therapy, and cognitive restructuring strategies to modify the patient's dysfunctional thinking.

Phase III

Phase III of therapy focused on increasing Fred's involvement in reinforcing activities or events; increasing his risk-taking behavior in seeking greater support and intimacy with his wife and family; and, finally, getting him to take an active role in planning his retirement.

Confirming the notion that the therapeutic game plan often changes in midstream, one major obstacle occurred midway through the first phase of treatment, when relaxation strategies failed to achieve the results predicted by the decision-making model. The patient stated that, although initial exposure to the relaxation strategies had been a pleasant experience during the sessions, he found himself overwhelmed by the task of learning these strategies and by the time investment needed for the strategies to be useful in combating the intense anxiety associated with confrontation of problems. The therapist called a brief "time out" from the original therapeutic plan to review the alternatives for reducing current distress symptoms so other important treatment variables might be addressed. After rating the other alternatives according to the decision-making criteria, the therapist consulted with a physician, who prescribed short-term medication specifically to promote relaxation.

Fred was prescribed a minimal dose of an antianxiety medication, with instructions to self-administer it on an as-needed basis, not to exceed two doses per day. This intervention was designed to assure the patient that he had a rapid remedy available to combat his fears when he would become overwhelmed by anxiety and be unable to benefit maximally from psychotherapy. Fred took one dose of the medication daily for approximately 3 days; thereafter, he reported that "just having a pill with me in my pocket" gave him enough sense of control to continue therapeutic work. He never felt the need to take the medication again.

Following the initial assessment period, Fred needed 6 months to complete the three phases of therapy described. Phase III involved several problems concerning the initiation of risk-taking behavior and in vivo practice of assertive seeking of family support. Fred had great difficulty finding enough time alone with his wife to air his feelings about their lack of privacy, to request her help in generating alternatives for coping with his sister-in-law's presence in the home, and to discuss his concerns regarding retirement. He found the alternative of a family therapy session objectionable because he feared his wife and sister-in-law might view his discussing resentments with his therapist as a betrayal.

Therapist and patient subjected this impasse to the problem-solving processes involved in the decision-making model. The result was a "prescription" for a weekend away so that Fred and June could have time alone. The patient returned from the weekend stating that the time alone had provided him with the opportunity to practice his new skills. His wife had been supportive of his concerns, and they jointly decided to ask their son to mediate a family meeting with June's sister. Time alone together became a regularly scheduled source of reinforcement for them both, resulting in a concomitant decrease in anxiety, an ability to discuss problems associated with June's sister, and a renewal of sexual intimacy. Fred was surprised initially to find how enthusiastically his family responded to his needs and how helpful his son was in assuming the role of family mediator. The family was particularly helpful in reinforcing the interpersonal risk-taking behavior that had remained so difficult to initiate. If they had taken a less supportive stance, an entirely new set of clinical problems would have emerged.

Although Fred reported significant progress, as also reflected on the measures administered at baseline and repeated at various points in therapy, the termination process itself represented a final clinical concern. Fred actually retired during the final months of therapy. Although he made this transition with a set of concrete plans, family support, and no exacerbation of symptoms, Fred would frequently state that he hoped he would continue to feel "this good" and spoke of the return of a major depression as something that he hoped would not happen, but that he had little control over.

After considering the long-term consequences of terminating therapy at a point where the patient's symptoms were alleviated, but where he assumed almost no responsibility for his wellness, the therapist recommended to Fred that he continue in treatment for several additional months in order to learn how to prevent future episodes. Thus, Phase IV was added to the treatment plan. It focused on giving the patient a greater sense of control over future episodes. Strategies included listing and identifying early warning signs or symptoms and setting forth several "plans of attack" or steps to follow in getting help. In addition, therapist and client agreed upon follow-up phone contacts, whereby Fred would assume responsibility for monitoring his wellness. This overall plan proved to be quite effective in increasing Fred's confidence in his continued ability to cope with future stressful situations.

SUMMARY

By virtue of the enormous interest on the part of behavior therapists in understanding and treating depression, several effective treatment strategies are available. Although this state of affairs should be heralded as especially positive, it also can inadvertently leave the practicing behavior therapist particularly susceptible to a variety of decision-making errors. The popularity, availability, and documented efficacy of such interventions (with certain populations) can overshadow the need to focus on the individual patient. Not all depressed persons are homogeneous with regard to the various causal variables identified by the major theoretical formulations. For example, one person may be depressed due to the manner in which she attributes the cause of a recent stressful event; another individual, equally depressed, may have become so for entirely different reasons (e.g., coping skills deficits, cognitive distortions, etc.). For this reason, we suggest that treatment design be governed by the principle of developing a tailor-made therapeutic plan based on a comprehensive assessment specific to a given patient.

An additional issue raised in this chapter concerns the difficulties inherent in the actual diagnosis of depression. Because depressive symptoms are often related to a variety of both medical and psychological disorders, the clinician needs to be particularly vigilant in conducting a comprehensive assessment before making any diagnosis.

As a means of addressing these and other clinical issues, we applied the decision-making model described in Part I to the treatment of unipolar depression from a cognitive-behavioral perspective. A case example was described in some detail to highlight important decision-making issues. In keeping with the major theme of this entire volume, we advocated that treatment for this depressed individual be based on a joint consideration of the idiosyncratic characteristics of the patient himself and of the empirically based recommendations offered within the research literature.

References

Abramson, L. Y., Seligman, M. E. P., & Teasdale, J. (1978). Learned helplessness in humans: Critique and reformulation. *Journal of Abnormal Psychology, 87,* 49–74.

American Psychiatric Association. (1987). *Diagnostic and statistical manual of mental disorders* (3rd ed. rev.). Washington, DC: Author.

Beck, A. T., Kovacs, M., & Weissman, A. (1979). Assessment of suicidal intent: The Scale for Suicidal Ideation. *Journal of Consulting and Clinical Psychology, 47,* 343–352.

Beck, A. T., Rush, A. J., Shaw, B. F., & Emery, G. (1979). *Cognitive therapy of depression: A treatment manual.* New York: Guilford.

Beck, A. T., Schuyler, D., & Herman, I. (1974). Development of suicidal intent scales. In A. T. Beck, H. L. P. Resnick, & D. J. Lettieri (Eds.), *The prediction of suicide.* Bowie, MD: Charles Press.

Beck, A. T., Ward, C. H., Mendelsohn, M., Mock, J., & Erbaugh, J. (1961). An inventory for measuring depression. *Archives of General Psychiatry, 5,* 562–571.

Beck, A. T., Weissman, A., Lester, D., & Trexler, L. (1974). The measurement of pessimism: The Hopelessness Scale. *Journal of Consulting and Clinical Psychology, 42,* 861–865.

Beckham, E. E., & Adams, R. L. (1984). Coping behavior in depression: Report on a new scale. *Behaviour Research and Therapy, 22,* 71–75.

Beckham, E. E., & Leber, W. R. (Eds.). (1985). *Handbook of depression: Treatment, assessment, and research.* Homewood, IL: Dorsey.

Billings, A. G., & Moos, R. H. (1981). The role of coping responses and social resources in attenuating the impact of stressful life events. *Journal of Behavioral Medicine, 4,* 139–157.

Bonner, R. L., & Rich, A. (1988). Negative life stress, social problem-solving self-appraisal, and hopelessness: Implications for suicide research. *Cognitive Therapy and Research, 12,* 549–556.

Boyer, J. L., & Guthrie, L. (1985). Assessment and treatment of the suicidal patient. In E. E. Beckham & W. R. Leber (Eds.), *Handbook of depression: Treatment, assessment, and research.* Homewood, IL: Dorsey.

Carroll, B. J., Feinberg, M., Smouse, P., Rawson, S., & Greden, J. (1981). The Carroll Rating Scale for Depression: I. Development, reliability and validation. *British Journal of Psychiatry, 138,* 194–200.

Clarkin, J. F., & Glazer, H. I. (Eds.). (1981). *Depression: Behavioral and directive intervention strategies.* New York: Garland.

Copas, J. B., & Robin, A. (1982). Suicide in psychiatric patients. *British Journal of Psychiatry, 141,* 503–511.

Craighead, W. E. (1980). Away from a unitary model of depression. *Behavior Therapy, 11,* 112–128.

Craighead, W. E., Kennedy, R. E., Raczynski, J. M., & Dow, M. G. (1984). Affective disorders—unipolar. In S. M. Turner & M. Hersen (Eds.), *Adult psychopathology and diagnosis.* New York: Wiley.

Dempsey, P. (1964). A unidimensional depression scale for the MMPI. *Journal of Consulting Psychology, 28,* 364–370.

D'Zurilla, T. J. (1986). *Problem-solving therapy: A social competence approach to clinical intervention.* New York: Springer.

D'Zurilla, T. J., & Nezu, A. M. (1988, November). *Development and preliminary evaluation of the Social Problem Solving Inventory (SPSI).* Paper presented at the annual meeting of the Association for Advancement of Behavior Therapy, New York.

Endicott, J., & Spitzer, R. L. (1978). A diagnostic interview: The schedule for affective disorders and schizophrenia. *Archives of General Psychiatry, 38,* 98–103.

Fisher-Beckfield, D., & McFall, R. M. (1982). Development of a competence inventory for college men and evaluation of relationships between competence and depression. *Journal of Consulting and Clinical Psychology, 50,* 697–705.

Folkman, S., & Lazarus, R. S. (1980). An analysis of coping in a middle-aged community sample. *Journal of Health and Social Behavior, 21,* 219–239.

Fuchs, C. Z., & Rehm, L. P. (1977). A self-control behavior therapy program for depression. *Journal of Consulting and Clinical Psychology, 45,* 206–215.

Haas, G. L., Clarkin, J. F., & Glick, I. D. (1985). Marital and family treatment of depression. In E. E. Beckham & W. R. Leber (Eds.), *Handbook of depression: Treatment, assessment, and research.* Homewood, IL: Dorsey.

Hamilton, M. (1960). A rating scale for depression. *Journal of Neurology, Neurosurgery and Psychiatry, 23,* 56–62.

Hammen, C. L., & Krantz, S. E. (1976). Effects of success and failure on depressive cognitions. *Journal of Abnormal Psychology, 85,* 577–586.

Hankoff, I. D. (1982). Suicide and attempted suicide. In E. S. Paykel (Ed.), *Handbook of affective disorders.* New York: Guilford.

Heppner, P. P., & Petersen, C. H. (1982). The development and implications of a personal problem solving inventory. *Journal of Counseling Psychology, 30,* 537–545.

Hersen, M., Bellack, A. S., & Himmelhoch, J. M. (1980). Treatment of unipolar depression with social skills training. *Behavior Modification, 4,* 547–556.

Hollon, S. D., & Kendall, P. C., (1980). Cognitive self- statements in depression: Development of an automatic thoughts questionnaire. *Cognitive Therapy and Research, 4,* 383–395.

Hollon, S. D., & Kendall, P. C. (1980). Cognitive self-statements in depression: Development of an automatic thoughts questionnaire. *Cognitive Therapy and Research, 4,* 383–395.

Hussian, R. A., & Lawrence, P. S. (1981). Social reinforcement of activity and problem-solving training in the treatment of depressed institutionalized elderly patients. *Cognitive Therapy and Research, 5,* 57–69.

Jones, R. G. (1969). A factored measure of Ellis' irrational belief system, with personality and maladjustment correlates. *Dissertation Abstracts International, 29,* 11–13.

Kanfer, F. H., & Hagerman, S. (1981). The role of self-regulation. In L. P. Rehm (Ed.), *Behavior therapy for depression: Present status and future directions.* New York: Academic.

Kanfer, F. H., & Schefft, B. K. (1988). *Guiding the process of therapeutic change.* Champaign, IL: Research Press.

Kanner, A. D., Coyne, J. C., Schaefer, C., & Lazarus, R. S. (1981). Comparison of two modes of stress measurement: Daily hassles and uplifts versus major life events. *Journal of Behavioral Medicine, 4,* 1–39.

Kathol, R. G. (1985). Depression associated with physical disease. In E. E. Beckham & W. R. Leber (Eds.), *Handbook of depression: Treatment, assessment, and research.* Homewood, IL: Dorsey.

Kiev, A. (1975). Psychotherapeutic strategies in the management of depressed and suicidal patients. *American Journal of Psychotherapy, 29,* 345–354.

Klerman, G. L. (1987). Depression associated with medical and neurological diseases, drugs, and alcohol. In A. J. Marsella, R. M. A. Hirschfeld, & M. M. Katz (Eds.), *The measurement of depression.* New York: Guilford.

Koslow, S. H., & Gaist, P. A. (1987). The measurement of neurotransmitters in depression. In A. J. Marsella, R. M. A. Hirschfeld, & M. M. Katz (Eds.), *The measurement of depression.* New York: Guilford.

Lazarus, A. A. (1980). *Multimodal Life History Questionnaire.* Kingston, NJ: Multimodal Publications.

Lehmann, L. (1985). The relationship of depression to other DSM-III Axis I disorders. In E. E. Beckham & W. R. Leber (Eds.), *Handbook of depression: Treatment, assessment, and research.* Homewood, IL: Dorsey.

Lewinsohn, P. M. (1974). A behavioral approach to depression. In R. J. Friedman & M. M. Katz (Eds.), *The psychology of depression: Contemporary theory and research.* New York: Winston-Wiley.

Lewinsohn, P. M., Antonuccio, D. O., Steinmutz, J. L., & Teri, L. (1984). *The coping with depression course: A psychoeducational intervention for unipolar depression.* Eugene, OR: Castalia.

Lewinsohn, P. M., & Talkington, J. (1979). Studies on the measurement of unpleasant events and relations with depression. *Applied Psychological Measurement, 3,* 83–101.

Lewinsohn, P. M., Weinstein, M., & Alper, T. (1970). A behavioral approach to the group treatment of depressed persons: A methodological contribution. *Journal of Clinical Psychology, 26,* 525–532.

Liberman, R. P. (1981). A model for individualizing treatment. In L. P. Rehm (Ed.), *Behavior therapy for depression: Present status and future directions.* New York: Academic.

Linehan, M. M. (1981). A social-behavioral analysis of suicide and parasuicide. In J. F. Clarkin & H. I. Glazer (Eds.), *Depression: Behavioral and directive intervention strategies.* New York: Garland.

Lubin, B. (1965). Adjective checklists for measurement of depression. *Archives of General Psychiatry, 12,* 57–62.

MacPhillamy, D. J., & Lewinsohn, P. M. (1982). The Pleasant Events Schedule: Studies on reliability, validity, and scale intercorrelations. *Journal of Consulting and Clinical Psychology, 50,* 363–380.

Meyer, V., & Turkat, I. D. (1979). Behavioral analysis of clinical cases. *Behavioral Assessment, 1,* 259–270.

Millon, T., & Kotik, D. (1985). The relationship of depression to disorders of personality. In E. E. Beckham & W. R. Leber (Eds.), *Handbook of depression: Treatment, assessment, and depression.* Homewood, IL: Dorsey.

Mooney, R. L., & Gordon, L. V. (1950). *Manual: The Mooney Problem Checklist.* New York: Psychological Corporation.

Nezu, A. M. (1986a). Effects of stress from current problems: Comparison to major life events. *Journal of Clinical Psychology, 42,* 847–852.

Nezu, A. M. (1986b). Efficacy of a social problem-solving therapy approach for unipolar depression. *Journal of Consulting and Clinical Psychology, 54,* 196–202.

Nezu, A. M. (1987). A problem-solving formulation of depression: A literature review and proposal of a pluralistic model. *Clinical Psychology Review, 7,* 121–144.

Nezu, A. M., & D'Zurilla, T. J. (in press). Social problem solving and negative affective conditions. In P. C. Kendall & D. Watson (Eds.), *Anxiety and depression: Distinctive and overlapping features.* New York: Academic.

Nezu, A. M., Kalmar, K., Ronan, G. F., & Clavijo, A. (1986). Attributional correlates of depression: An interactional model including problem solving. *Behavior Therapy, 17*, 50–56.

Nezu, A. M., Mahoney, D. J., Perri, M. G., Renjillian, D. A., Arean, P. A., & Joseph, T. X. (1989, August). *Effectiveness of problem-solving therapy for severely depressed hospitalized veterans.* Paper presented at the annual meeting of the American Psychological Association, New Orleans.

Nezu, A. M., Nezu, C. M., & Perri, M. G. (1988, September). *Clinical decision making in the practice of behavior therapy.* Workshop presented at the World Congress on Behaviour Therapy, Edinburgh, Scotland.

Nezu, A. M., Nezu, C. M., & Perri, M. G. (1989). *Problem-solving therapy for depression: Theory, research, and clinical guidelines.* New York: Wiley.

Nezu, A. M., & Perri. M. G. (in press). Problem-solving therapy for unipolar depression: An initial dismantling investigation. *Journal of Consulting and Clinical Psychology.*

Nezu, A. M., Petronko, M. R., & Nezu, C. M. (1982, November). *Cognitive, behavioral, or cognitive-behavioral strategies? Using a problem-solving paradigm for clinical decision making in behavior therapy.* Paper presented at the annual meeting of the Association for Advancement of Behavior Therapy, Los Angeles.

Noll, K. M., Davis, J. M., & DeLeon-Jones, F. (1985). Medication and somatic therapies in the treatment of depression. In E. E. Beckham & W. R. Leber (Eds.), *Handbook of depression: Treatment, assessment, and research.* Homewood, IL: Dorsey.

Peterson, C., Semmel, A., von Baeyer, C., Abramson, L. Y., & Seligman, M. E. P. (1982). The Attributional Style Questionnaire. *Cognitive Therapy and Research, 6,* 287–299.

Platt, J. J., & Spivack, G. (1975). *Manual for the Means-End Problem-Solving Procedure (MEPS): A measure of interpersonal cognitive problem-solving skills.* Philadelphia: Hahnemann Community Mental Health/Mental Retardation Center.

Rathus, S. A. (1973). A 30-item schedule for assessing assertive behavior. *Behavior Therapy, 4,* 398–406.

Rehm, L. P. (1977). A self-control model of depression. *Behavior Therapy, 8,* 787–804.

Rehm, L. P. (Ed.). (1981). *Behavior therapy for depression: Present status and future directions.* New York: Academic.

Rehm, L. P., Fuchs, C. Z., Roth, D., Kornblith, S., & Romano, J. M. (1979). A comparison of self-control and assertion skill treatments of depression. *Behavior Therapy, 10,* 429–442.

Rehm, L. P., Kornblith, S. J., O'Hara, M. W., Lamparski, D. M., Romano, J. M., & Volkin, J. I. (1981). An evaluation of major components in a self-control therapy program for depression. *Behavior Modification, 5,* 459–489.

Rosenbaum, M. (1980). A schedule for assessing self-control behaviors: Preliminary findings. *Behavior Therapy, 11,* 109–121.

Rush, A. J., Beck, A. T., Kovacs, M., & Hollon, S. D. (1977). Comparative efficacy of cognitive therapy versus pharmacotherapy in outpatient depressives. *Cognitive Therapy and Research, 1,* 17–37.

Sacco, W. P., & Beck, A. T. (1985). Cognitive therapy of depression. In E. E. Beckham & W. R. Leber (Eds.), *Handbook of depression: Treatment, assessment, and research.* Homewood, IL: Dorsey.

Salovey, P., & Turk, D. C. (1988). Some effects of mood on clinicians' memory. In D. C. Turk & P. Salovey (Eds.), *Reasoning, inference, and judgment in clinical psychology.* New York: Free Press.

Sarason, I. G., Johnson, J. H., & Siegel, J. M. (1978). Assessing the impact of life changes: Development of the Life Experiences Survey. *Journal of Consulting and Clinical Psychology, 46,* 932–946.

Schinka, J. A. (1986). *Personal Problems Checklist.* Odessa, FL: Psychological Assessment Resources.

Schotte, D. E., & Clum, G. A. (1982). Suicide ideation in a college population. *Journal of Consulting and Clinical Psychology, 50,* 690–696.

Schotte, D. E., & Clum, G. A. (1987). Problem-solving skills in suicidal psychiatric patients. *Journal of Consulting and Clinical Psychology, 55,* 49–54.

Secunda, R., Friedman, R. J., & Schuyler, D. (1973). *The depressive disorders.* Washington, DC: U.S. Government Printing Office.

Snyder, D. K. (1979). *Marital Satisfaction Inventory.* Los Angeles: Western Psychological Services.

Spielberger, C. D., Gorsuch, R. L., & Lushene, R. E. (1970). *Manual for the State-Trait Anxiety Inventory.* Palo Alto, CA: Consulting Psychologists Press.

Stokes, P. E. (1987). The neuroendocrine measurement of depression. In A. J. Marsella, R. M. A. Hirschfeld, & M. M. Katz (Eds.), *The measurement of depression.* New York: Guilford.

Weissman, A. N. (1978, November). *Development and validation of the Dysfunctional Attitude Scale (DAS).* Paper presented at the annual meeting of the Association for Advancement of Behavior Therapy, Chicago.

Wekstein, L. (1979). *Handbook of suicidology.* New York: Brunner/Mazel.

Youngren, M. A., & Lewinsohn, P. M. (1980). The functional relation between depression and problematic interpersonal behavior. *Journal of Abnormal Psychology, 89,* 333–341.

Yufit, R., & Benzies, B. (1979). *Preliminary manual for the Time Questionnaire: Assessing suicide potential.* Palo Alto, CA: Consulting Psychologists Press.

Zeiss, A. M., Lewinsohn, P. M., & Munoz, R. F. (1979). Nonspecific improvement effects in depression using interpersonal, cognitive, and pleasant events focused treatments. *Journal of Consulting and Clinical Psychology, 47,* 427–439.

Zung, W. W. (1965). A self-rating depression scale. *Archives of General Psychiatry, 12,* 63–70.

Chapter 5

Agoraphobia

Michael R. Petronko

INTRODUCTION

Few clinical conditions present the therapist with as formidable a task as the treatment of agoraphobia. Unlike other disorders, agoraphobia affords the clinician a problem of some magnitude even before the first session is scheduled: How and where is the housebound client to be seen? Many of the calls made to our clinic have been from individuals expressing enough discomfort at the thought of traveling to an office for a visit to make this trip a virtual impossibility without assistance. The manner in which the therapist resolves this dilemma will likely have a profound impact on the subsequent treatment's success or failure. Indeed, it may determine whether or not there is even an agoraphobic to treat.

Perhaps the complexity of agoraphobia treatment as it relates to the initial contact can best be illustrated by a personal experience I had with one of my first cases: A middle-aged man walked into our outpatient clinic without an appointment, requesting to see me. He was red-faced, perspiring, breathing rapidly, and pacing back and forth. He told me he was an agoraphobic experiencing a panic attack. At the end of an emergency session, I asked him how he had come to know of my work. The client said that he had never heard of me but instead had read my name on the clinic sign outside, which just happened to be midway between his house and his job. On this particular day, he was stuck between the two, being able neither to complete his journey to work nor to return home to safety. I had erroneously believed that his unannounced presence was due to my reputation in the field of agoraphobia treatment, but, in his state of crisis, "any port in a storm" would do. It was sheer luck that he had arrived at my office for that first meeting. What would he have done if my office hadn't been there? What would have happened if he had found a therapist with a different orientation?

The purpose of this chapter is to demonstrate the use of the clinical decision-making model discussed in chapter 3 as it applies to this and many other problems associated with the treatment of agoraphobia. Due to the inherent complexities associated with this disorder, such an approach is especially important. As Johnson (1950) has pointed out,

> Prevailing usage seems to list an experiment under the heading of problem solving rather than learning when the situation is rather complicated and the activities involved correspondingly variegated, and when the experiment is focused on the process by which the solution is first attained rather than the improvement of repeated performance of the solution. (p. 279)

The treatment of agoraphobia is always complicated and variegated and therefore seldom amenable to repeated performances that would support the use of a one-dimensional approach to treatment. Indeed, as Wolpe (1982) suggests, "The cases vary markedly in their stimulus-response structure and therefore call for varied treatments. For this reason, the recent practice of offering uniform 'packages' to all comers is deplorable" (p. 284). The application of a systematic decision-making process can allow all concerned parties to "mix and match" various therapeutic methods, creating testable strategies that will ultimately yield dynamic scripts for the client, therapist, family member, and environment.

The usefulness of this approach is evident from the very beginning of treatment. For example, should clinicians not identify the first appointment as a problem to solve and adopt a set of "Stop and Think!" (see chapter 2), it is likely that they might respond automatically with old habits and tried-and-true, but not necessarily accurate, therapeutic beliefs. One of the oldest of these beliefs is that it is the patient's responsibility to get to the office, for it is only in the sanctity of the office (clinic, hospital) that treatment can actually take place. This idea might be supported by the judgments that patients share this belief and that their ability to come represents a sign of their motivation. Further erroneous beliefs include the assumptions that those individuals who are unable to come are not motivated enough to withstand the rigors of treatment and that it is best to "weed them out now" or wait until they become sufficiently motivated. Any such assumptions would be made without the benefit of clinical information normally obtained during an interview and certainly without the assistance of formal decision-making. These beliefs do not allow therapists to focus, for example, on their own frustration or lack of motivation as an equally compelling source of "noise" in the system.

Once clinicians are able to resist the tendency to engage in negative attributional biases (i.e., patients are not motivated enough to come to the office), they must identify the salient problems involved in order to make effective clinical decisions. In solving the first problem—achieving an initial session—possible alternatives include (a) having the client come with a *safe person*, (b) arranging for the client to use medication, (c) traveling to the client's home or another *safe location*, and (d) conducting therapy over the telephone.[1] A second problem concerns identifying those factors that influence decision making. Among these many factors are (a) a patient's ability to take medication, (b) the availability of a physician to prescribe it, (c) the availability of a practice large enough to support an assistant or blocks of time during which the therapist might travel to and from a client's home, (d) the presence and cooperativeness of a safe person, and (e) the risks associated with reinforcement of dependency. The complexity of these and other initial decisions (again, all before the first interview) challenges therapists' beliefs, attitudes, and therapeutic dogma at a time when therapists may be somewhat unaware of the implications of their decisions.

Problems associated with the initial visit are only a harbinger of the unique challenges presented by agoraphobic clients. Although the literature is burgeoning with research on this condition, little guidance can be found regarding how to apply this knowledge systematically in developing treatment programs that include the patient, significant others, and the environment. The decision-making model offers a valuable means of managing treatment efforts more systematically.

APPLYING THE DECISION-MAKING MODEL

In applying the decision-making model, this chapter first examines problem orientation concerns. The next section, devoted to problem definition and formulation, discusses treatment failures, assessment tools,

---

[1] A safe person is anyone whose presence allows the client to travel to locations that would otherwise be too frightening. A safe location (usually the home or other familiar surroundings) is any location in which the client feels reasonably comfortable.

the assessment process, and the construction of treatment goals. A brief section on the generation of alternatives is followed by a discussion of decision making, including a review of relevant outcome studies, and a consideration of treatment selection and implementation concerns. A discussion of issues in solution implementation and verification completes the chapter.

Problem Orientation

To convey a sense of the problem orientation issues involved in agoraphobia, this section will provide a working definition of agoraphobia, discuss current conceptual understandings of the disorder, and point out important issues relating to treatment.

General Characteristics of Agoraphobia

Agoraphobia is easily distinguishable from other anxiety disorders by virtue of the agoraphobic's pervasive avoidance of public places, situations in which escape to safety is difficult, and/or travel without a safe person. Anxiety is increased if the individual must go somewhere at a specific time (e.g., to a doctor's appointment or on a business trip). Thus time pressure serves to prevent escape. The typical presenting complaint reflects frustration over the restrictions this condition imposes on the person's life (or on that of a loved one), as well as the insidious manner in which restrictions increase over time, rendering the individual a virtual prisoner exiled to a self-imposed sanctuary.

In other phobias, relief is possible if the phobic object is avoided; in the case of agoraphobia, life is defined in terms of degrees of safety (i.e., places or people). Thus the agoraphobic cannot easily adjust his life to accommodate his phobia (e.g., take a job with no possibility of public speaking, go on vacation but insist on a first-floor room). The extent to which the person's life is restricted defines the disorder's level of severity. This level ranges from mild (i.e., a person who enjoys a relatively normal life, albeit with elevated stress in most public situations) to severe (i.e., a person who, in spite of being housebound, is still anxious in some parts of the house). Most agoraphobic people have experienced panic attacks that follow the typical pattern of physiological arousal (racing heart, shortness of breath, etc.) accompanied by catastrophic cognitions of death or insanity and affective overload described as sheer terror (American Psychiatric Association, 1987).

It is estimated that between 2.7 and 5.8 percent of the general population experience some form of agoraphobia (Weissman, 1985). Of this number, a disproportionally high percentage, between 75

(Marks, 1970a, 1970b) and 80 percent (Chambless, 1985; Chambless & Mason, 1986), are women. It is not as yet clear why this difference exists. Explanations have included the higher incidence of mitral valve prolapse in women (Kantor, Zitrin, & Zeldis, 1980) and its proposed association with panic attacks. Biological differences such as changes in endocrine functioning (Klein, cited in Liebowitz & Klein, 1982) have also been proposed. Last, factors such as degree of entrapment perceived by married women have been offered (Chambless & Goldstein, 1980; Goldstein, 1970). Barlow and Waddell (1985) have questioned the high incidence in women by suggesting that men may not be coming in for treatment as often as women.

The onset of agoraphobia typically occurs between late adolescence and midlife (18 to 35 years), with higher distributions at ages 20 and 30 (Marks, 1970a, 1970b). Rarely can a specific traumatic event prior to the onset of agoraphobia be identified (Goldstein & Chambless, 1978). Rather, the process is gradual, with family members often being persuaded to assume more and more responsibility for performing the duties of the agoraphobic or to accompany the agoraphobic on even uneventful journeys. Given the insidious nature of the disorder, it is very common to find middle-aged people coming in for treatment long after the initial manifestation of an avoidance pattern.

Agoraphobic avoidance behavior has also been found to fluctuate. It is not uncommon to observe periods of severe restrictiveness (i.e., being housebound) followed by times of relative freedom (Chambless, 1982). Agoraphobics are also likely to manifest other phobias (Chambless, 1982) and thus should not be viewed as representing the quintessential phobia. However, this last point might be argued by those who see the disorder as being at the end of a continuum.

Agoraphobics have been found to demonstrate increased dependency and unassertiveness (Goldstein & Chambless, 1978) and to evidence interpersonal problem-solving deficits (Broadbeck & Michelson, 1987). Hafner (1982), in summarizing the family and couples literature on agoraphobia, has characterized agoraphobics as coming from families that reinforce dependency and avoidance of problems and as being more likely to choose mates who will assume these problems. Marriages of agoraphobics are seldom asymptomatic.

Conceptual Understandings of Agoraphobia

As noted earlier, agoraphobia is experienced in three dimensions: extreme behavioral avoidance (being housebound), somatic hyperarousal (elevated heart rate, blood pressure, etc.), and negative cognitions (fear of death, insanity, embarrassment, etc.). Much of the behavioral literature has attempted to support theories that focus almost exclusively on avoidance behavior. Indeed, some form of graduated in vivo exposure is often reported as the treatment of choice (Barlow & Waddell, 1985; Emmelkamp, 1982). This approach is frequently understood as an extension of Mowrer's (1960) two-factor learning theory. This theory presumes that avoidance behavior is being negatively reinforced because it allows the individual to escape feelings of fear that have been classically conditioned to various stimuli. The theory holds that, if one encourages the individual to encounter the stimuli associated with fear, the conditioned avoidance response habituates or fades via the absence of associative conditioning (a classical conditioning paradigm). From an operant perspective, exposing the individual to the feared stimuli while simultaneously blocking the avoidance response would prevent negative reinforcement from occurring, thus producing extinction.

Rachman (1983, 1984) has taken exception to these conceptualizations, arguing that they explain neither the tenacity of avoidance behavior in the absence of conditioning nor, more importantly, the presence of the agoraphobic's preoccupation with safety. In suggesting that clinicians have become closed-minded in their preoccupation with avoidance, Rachman (1984) proposes explaining the safety issue by exploring three additional theories: Mowrer's (1960) safety-signal explanation of avoidance, Seligman and Johnson's (cited in Rachman, 1983) notions of disconfirmation and avoidance behavior, and Bandura's (1977) theory of self-efficacy. Rachman suggests that, with regard to the first theory, one might capitalize on the agoraphobic's approach-to-safety behavior by placing an object of safety in the domain of the avoidance stimuli (e.g., a safe person at the next bus stop). Using the therapy-by-disconfirmation approach, he suggests that, in cases in which the patient expects to experience intolerable anxiety, disconfirmation can take the form of showing that anxiety remains within manageable levels and in most instances dissipates within a few minutes. Last, Rachman suggests that we might focus on building self-efficacy in the office setting by including participant modeling, symbolic modeling, desensitization, and so forth.

In their now-classic paper, Goldstein and Chambless (1978) proposed that the key issue for agoraphobics is *fear of fear*, not fear of open spaces. In addition to describing the central element of panic, they recognized the associated personal attributions of insanity. Thus "the panic attack is a terrifying experience which when paired with a low level of self-sufficiency, reinforces the agoraphobic person's belief that someone must take care of her or him" (p. 52). These authors go on to present an argument reflecting the individual's view of herself in panic as going crazy. If it is this state of insanity that is feared, as opposed to open spaces or distance from safe places, then *phrenophobia* (fear of going crazy) may be a more correct diagnosis.

Raimy (1975) has proposed that phrenophobia is one of the most pervasive yet intransigent of all phobias. With phrenophobia as the central ingredient, the agoraphobic can be expected to avoid situations that elicit fear; approach those things, people, or states that represent safety; or do both. This pattern would be the same for internal states and cognitions. Thus both approaches toward safety and away from danger can be understood.

It is argued here that the agoraphobic does in fact make both of these movements—and does so out of intense fear coupled with a yearning for safety. The agoraphobic can therefore be understood as an individual who lacks *personal safety*. It thus becomes the goal of behavior therapy to assist the agoraphobic in becoming a safe person (i.e., a person who can travel into dangerous places or away from safe ones with self-confidence and who can cope with whatever challenges may present themselves). One pervasive fear expressed by many patients concerns the ability to deal with the unexpected: "What would happen if . . . ?" is an often-asked question.

Although skill deficits can be identified and corrected (e.g., through relaxation training), a person needs an internalized management system to help deal with the unexpected before he can feel safe. Learning problem-solving skills can help the client establish such a system for safety management. The following case illustration serves as an appropriate example: As part of a graded-exposure exercise using participant modeling, a client and I traveled through the Lincoln Tunnel. I drove in front of him as a means of providing a safe person. The client had made remarkable progress and was prepared for both the confinement of the tunnel and the delay unexpected traffic might produce. We went back and forth several times. On the last trip, as both of us ventured into the bowels of the tunnel, I lost him. I proceeded about 100 feet and noticed an accident in progress up ahead. Everything stopped. My own anxiety elevated as I began to envision my client experiencing all manner and form of catastrophes. Mercifully, the traffic moved in about 10 minutes. On the Jersey side, we both stopped, and I asked him how he had felt. His anxiety level had not risen over 50 (on a scale of 10 to 100).

Although this client couldn't see the source of the gridlock, he had prevented his anxiety from elevating by problem solving to generate a number of potentially helpful techniques. When questioned about his experience upon exiting the tunnel, he attributed much of his success to the guideline "Stop and Think!" Doing so helped him to avoid his previously preferred patterns of behavior. In other words, he was able to identify the real solution to his problem as his ability to manage his stress, not escaping the tunnel or finding his therapist in the traffic. Once he focused on managing his stress, he was able to evoke several relaxation strategies he had learned previously to deal with other high arousal situations. Guided imagery (imagining himself on a New Jersey beach) offered him the most relaxation. He also monitored his Subjective Units of Disturbance (SUDS; Wolpe, 1982) and reminded himself that he had been able to relax during a similar experience of entrapment. He therefore allowed himself to become his own safe person.

Parenthetically, once we had finished discussing his successful exposure experience, I asked him to return to New York and continue the exposure exercise by invoking paradox. Knowing that to do so would mean we would once again experience gridlock, he exclaimed, "Are you crazy? I may be an agoraphobic, but I'm not stupid!" A good sense of humor benefits therapist and client alike. And, despite my negative fantasies, I also had survived the experience by using the same techniques my client had.

Issues in Agoraphobia Treatment

Barlow and Waddell (1985) have commented that clinicians tend to agree on the diagnosis of agoraphobia more often than they do on that for any other anxiety disorder. Why then, when attempting to examine the various stimuli associated with avoidance behavior, does Emmelkamp (1982) suggest that "an agoraphobic is not an agoraphobic is not an agoraphobic" (p. 69)? This comment probably reflects the inordinate challenges experienced by the treating clinician and how little the diagnosis reflects the range and variety of the individual's complaints.

A wide array of behavioral treatment strategies are available for the agoraphobic client. Interventions include graduated exposure in groups (Chambless & Goldstein, 1982; Goldstein & Chambless, 1978), paradoxical intention and imagery (Ascher, 1981; Michelson & Ascher, 1984), group treatment of clients and their spouses (Barlow & Waddell, 1985), couples therapy (Hafner, 1982), problem-solving training (Broadbeck & Michelson, 1987; D'Zurilla, 1985), medication plus graduated in vivo exposure (Goldstein & Munjack, 1987; Telch, Tearnan, & Taylor, 1983), flooding (Boudewyns & Shipley, 1983), self-paced graduated exposure without medication (Emmelkamp, 1982), and partner-assisted graduated exposure using self-help training manuals (Mathews, Gelder, & Johnston, 1981a, 1981b, 1981c).[2]

This list is not exhaustive; rather, it highlights the vast selection of behavioral treatments available for one diagnostic condition. Given this availability, certain clinical concerns emerge. For example, how many of these treatments are available at any given clinic? What is the likelihood that a practitioner can remain objective in determining appropriate treatment? Will the preferred treatment meet the client's needs, or the therapist's? Lazarus (1985) states, "In theory, most clinicians agree that every client is unique and treatment has to be tailored to his or her specific problems; yet in practice, the consumer is all too often fitted to preconceived treatment modes, whether or not this is what he or she requires" (p. 170). As the discussion in chapter 1 points out, clinicians are not immune to biases such as these.

Hafner (1982) has discussed the need to maintain an open mind when treating agoraphobics from a marital perspective: "First, it may be that a self-perpetuating myth has arisen, with clinicians seeing in their own patients only what has been reported by other clinicians. The more powerful the myth, the wider the clinical consensus, which in turn strengthens the myth" (p. 83). Levine and Sandeen (1985) address this concern by encouraging the use of *conceptualizations* or *psychological processes* instead of diagnoses in clinical practice. Specifically, they discuss the case of an agoraphobic to illustrate how meaningless a diagnosis can be, suggesting that, depending on whether the therapist is Pavlovian or has a social learning perspective, the person might receive treatment ranging from counterconditioning to training in safely traversing a neighborhood.

Having a reputation as a behavior therapist who specializes in agoraphobia presents its own problem orientation challenges. Therapists may profit from this reputation when they encounter a highly motivated patient who has knowledge of the treatment strategy and who requires little preparation before treatment can actually begin. They may also be cursed by this same reputation when, for example, they discover they must justify at great length why extended in vivo graduated exposure sessions were appropriate for the client's friend but are not appropriate for the client. Emmelkamp and Van Der Hout (1983) have recognized such discongruent expectations as a source of

---

[2] Comprehensive reviews on the behavioral treatment of agoraphobia have recently been published and should be consulted for a more complete understanding. See Chambless & Goldstein, 1982; Mathews et al., 1981a; Barlow & Waddell, 1985; Barlow, 1988; and Jansson & Öst, 1982.

treatment failure in agoraphobia. Being able to use the decision-making model as a guide, with an understanding of problem orientation issues as the first step, can help both clients and therapists avoid making such prejudgments.

Problem Definition and Formulation

One typically describes the purpose of behavioral assessment as providing information about an individual in order to understand the instigating and/or maintaining variables that serve to explain the existence of target behaviors. Although assessment assisted by the decision-making model and traditional behavioral assessment both address the three response systems (behavioral, physiological, cognitive), the former approach requires more comprehensive information. In order to ensure that the assessment is broad enough, it is helpful first to understand the literature on failures in behavioral treatment for agoraphobia.

Treatment Failures

One of the most detailed analyses of treatment failures in agoraphobia was conducted by Emmelkamp and Van Der Hout (1983). These investigators asked several individuals who did not accept the behavioral treatment offered to respond to a series of questions concerning their reasons for refusal. Results indicated that 7 out of 16 respondents reported being frightened by the treatment. An additional five patients resisted giving up their medication. Another major category (13 out of 16) listed the belief that they would have to overcome their fears alone as problematic. Therapist characteristics did not appear to influence patients' decision making, but Emmelkamp and Van Der Hout found secondary gain, obtained through partners who provided considerable assistance, to be extremely significant.

Dropouts from therapy were also evaluated, with 8 out of 15 responding to the questionnaire. Discomfort over having to tolerate anxiety was most often listed as a reason for terminating treatment. Another major factor reflected clients' a priori expectancies regarding treatment. Here, factors such as expecting to talk individually to a doctor and anticipating a less demanding approach were voiced as causes of attrition. The researchers summarized the dropout data by highlighting the large degree of variability presented by agoraphobics and thus the concomitant need for individualized treatment programs. This variability occurred in the following areas: initial severity of the problem, assertiveness, level of depression, marital complications, illness phobias (a preconceived belief in the validity of proneness toward illness), therapist variables (e.g., length and quality of the therapeutic relationship), and parental characteristics (e.g., controlling, overprotective, rejecting).

Emmelkamp and Van Der Hout's study of treatment failures supports the need for a behavioral assessment that evaluates not only the three major response systems, but significant additional factors in the individual's life as well.

Assessment Tools

By using Lazarus's Life History Questionnaire (Lazarus, 1976), the clinician can gain access to seven broad categories of information: behavior, affect, sensation, imagery, cognition, interpersonal, and drugs. A profile can be constructed according to the contribution each area makes towards understanding and treating the target problem. (See also the three-dimensional framework for assessment, treatment, and therapy evaluation illustrated in Figure 3.1.)

Because panic is intricately involved in a patient's experience of agoraphobia, a second useful tool is the panic disorder section of the Anxiety Disorders Interview Schedule-Revised (Di Nardo et al., 1985). This instrument gives the clinician specific information regarding the client's experience of panic and assists in determining whether the initial focus of therapy should be the treatment of panic. A revision of this measure appears in Barlow and Cerny (1988).

In order to assess the degree and extent of fear-eliciting stimuli, any variation of Wolpe and Lang's (1964, 1969) Fear Survey Schedule is recommended. An 87-item version of this schedule appears in Wolpe (1982). A factor analysis of a 22-item version of this scale was conducted by Rubin and Lawlis (1969), in which five relatively pure factors were found to account for 90 percent of the variance. Although the authors use these results to recommend a shorter version, it is possible that doing so sacrifices a certain breadth.

In keeping with a philosophy advocating comprehensive assessment, the therapist should also attempt to evaluate problems concerning assertiveness, depression, stressful life events, and catastrophic thoughts. Assertiveness may be measured by Rathus's (1973) Assertiveness Schedule, depression by the Beck Depression Inventory (Beck, Ward, Mendelsohn, Mock, & Erbaugh, 1961), and catastrophic thoughts by the Agoraphobic Cognitions Questionnaire (Chambless, Caputo, Bright, & Gallagher, 1984). Holmes and Rahe's (1967) Stressful Life Events Scale can be used to appraise the clinician of any major life changes that may have occurred during the past year.

Depending on the information gathered during the initial interview, hints of marital difficulties can be followed up by using Stuart and

Jacobson's (1987) Couple's Pre-Counseling Inventory. This question-naire requests detailed information regarding the marital relationship as both the client and spouse see it.

To measure behavioral avoidance, some public route near the therapist's office or client's house can be used to evaluate how much distress the individual experiences at various stations, as well as how far the person can proceed unassisted. Wolpe's (1982) SUDS, mentioned earlier in this chapter, is recommended for use as a distress index. The SUDS can be used throughout treatment to monitor changes in discomfort.

The Assessment Process

The decision-making model views assessment as an ongoing process involving constant feedback to adjust and refine treatment. In addition to emphasizing evaluation as an ongoing process, the therapist should stress the agoraphobic's personal ownership over the assessment process. The goal of personal safety cannot be achieved without mastery over the various assessment tools and the good sense to keep them well-honed through use. Indeed, frequent use creates the behavioral equivalent of an ongoing climate analysis. Transfer of ownership of assessment from therapist to client begins with the first contact—the telephone interview—and continues throughout the therapeutic relationship.

During the telephone interview, the therapist should convey an understanding of agoraphobia and the restrictions it has placed on the client, including the difficulty travel to the therapist's office might present. The client should be informed that she will never be asked to do something she cannot do, including coming to the therapist's office. If an office visit is impossible, the therapist can briefly describe the decision-making model over the telephone. Using the model establishes "joint ownership" over treatment and, more importantly, allows for problems to be seen objectively as challenges.

Very often, the client reports an urgency to start immediately. This tendency should be tempered to allow consideration of other important factors that may influence when and where to have the first session. For example, it may be beneficial to avoid forcing a safe person to accompany a client to the office just to satisfy the first available opening. It is preferable in such cases to allow a week or two to go by until a more mutually convenient time is available. If the individual cannot come even with the assistance of a safe person and a home visit cannot be scheduled, assigning one of Weeks' (1968, 1976) self-help books can be beneficial. Weeks has reported success with these books, and they have helped to allay fears in some of our own clients. The point is to provide information the therapist and client can use to challenge the tendency to avoid anxiety. Most often, the client will have a safe person with whom to travel, and scheduling the first visit will not present a problem.

Once the therapist and client have managed a face-to-face meeting, either at the office or another location, sessions should focus on determining the specific circumstances under which this individual can become a safe person. It is very important early on for assessment to focus on any locations or persons the client has invested with the power of safeness. To gather information about safe places, it is often helpful for the therapist and client to construct a travel map with the client's safest place (usually a house) at its center. This map can show other locations important in the client's life and include a SUDS rating for each. (When complete, this therapeutic tool looks very much like a weather map, with SUDS scores replacing temperatures.)

In conjunction with development of the travel map, the client should construct a detailed avoidance hierarchy listing at least 10 progressively more difficult situations and giving each a SUDS rating from 10 to 100. One of these situations can then be explored on an assessment field trip, in which the client is accompanied by the therapist or an assistant. The client is asked to record SUDS scores along the route. During these trips, it is extremely helpful to experience the subtle cues and nuances that are simply unavailable in the office. Such trips also establish landmarks for the travel map; once these landmarks become familiar to both therapist and client, they can become very useful. For example, in subsequent sessions, the therapist might ask the client to record SUDS scores at a specific location (e.g., at the deli on the way to the office).

The therapist should also attempt to determine how travel is influenced by the safe person and how much discomfort is experienced without the person (i.e., in essence, how much safety is provided by this individual and under what circumstances). Generally, the safe person is a husband or wife who knows about the debilitating circumstances the agoraphobic faces.

When questioning the individual as to what characteristics, if any, allow another person to be considered safe, the therapist should also explore the nature of the client's perceived lack of personal safety. Likewise, fear of fear can be explored if the anxiety appears to be generated by internal versus external stimuli. Individuals experiencing fear of fear seem to have become sensitized to internal states that precede panic. Testing with the Minnesota Multiphasic Personality

Inventory and a traditional psychological interview with a mental status examination should be undertaken if the fear and/or anxiety appears to be global or nonspecific, thus presenting as agoraphobic-like behaviors instead of true agoraphobia. Clients experiencing fear of fear may be unable to distinguish the middle ranges of SUDS ratings (e.g., from 30 to 90), feeling instead that once the level reaches 20 "It's like being on a slide." In addition, they may maintain a relentless internal vigilance for any signs that might subsequently lead to the experience of terror. Fear begets fear, ad infinitum. Obviously, it is important for the clinician to distinguish fear of fear from fear of something in the environment or fear of the inability to escape.

In exploring the parameters of safety, the clinician should also evaluate the degree of dependency evidenced by the client, as well as the characteristics of the marital relationship. As such, the therapist should determine the willingness and capacity of the safe person (Levine & Sandeen, 1985) and whether specific skills-training exercises will be needed. In some cases, for example, stress management training for the spouse or helper is useful or necessary.

Yet another important assessment concern is the individual's use and potential misuse of medication. Typically, the agoraphobic has consulted a general practitioner and received benzodiazepines. Understanding the individual's experience using medication and attitudes concerning giving it up is essential.

Other Assessment Issues

A number of general issues in assessment confront the clinician. One such issue, critical in nature, concerns the development of a therapeutic alliance. Because our society often views psychological problems as examples of personal inadequacy or "craziness," the client is likely to look for a biological etiology and subsequent medical treatment. Therefore, his beliefs may be at odds with the development of an alliance. It often makes sense to capitalize on this apparent dilemma by introducing the SUDS concept early on in the sessions and by having the client begin to evaluate situations in terms of this approach.

The assessment atmosphere needs to be frank and genuine but not prescribed. Demonstrating flexibility of thought highlights the idea that there are many means to an end. Extensive use of auxiliary reading (e.g., Weeks, 1968, 1976; literature produced by various local self-help groups) takes the mystique out of the treatment and helps the individual to feel less alone. This openness also attacks two areas that Emmelkamp and Van Der Hout (1983) describe as contributing to treatment failure: discordance of beliefs and fear of encountering anxiety.

Another important issue concerns compliance. Because the client is usually asked to complete most assessment questionnaires at home, a great deal of resistance can emerge. Discussing the importance of the evaluation may not increase compliance, however, unless both client and therapist acknowledge this situation as a real problem and use the problem-solving processes in the decision-making model to approach data collection dispassionately. Thus the question becomes how or how long, rather than whether, the data will be collected. We have found that presenting assessment forms as a component of treatment, along with the functional task of evaluating SUDS scores throughout the day, helps the client to view assessment as a meaningful part of therapy.

Finally, it is necessary at some point during the assessment process for the therapist to explain the behavioral perspective of agoraphobia and, in order to allow for informed consent, to describe in detail the procedures involved in an exposure-based treatment. The assumption that an exposure-based treatment will in fact be used might seem to indicate treatment bias. However, because of the very definition of the problem in agoraphobia (i.e., avoidance of certain public situations), it goes without saying that treatment must at some point involve some kind of in vivo exposure. A good deal of the therapeutic effort will necessarily vary according to the needs of the individual client. However, at some point, in vivo exposure will begin. Before it does, the how's, why's, and wherefore's of the procedure should be clearly delineated.

Construction of Treatment Goals

From the plethora of information made available during the assessment process, the clinician must decide what is significant enough to be classified as a problem and how these problems can be transformed into measurable treatment goals. Table 5.1 lists broad-based and specific problems relevant to the treatment of agoraphobia, along with potential treatment goals, strategies, and techniques.

Both problems and goals should be viewed not only in the context of their relationship to the individual's presenting concerns, but also with respect to their relative contributions toward realistic treatment. Therefore, multiple causation needs to be considered with regard to presenting problems, and maintenance and generalization of treatment effects need to be considered in designing treatment approaches.

The unifying theme that brings these concerns together is the client's perceived lack of personal safety, with safety being operationalized as the ability to travel freely with the knowledge that one can manage one's own avoidance behavior, aroused soma, or distressing cognitions. Both panic and avoidance behavior can be understood as

Table 5.1 Decision-making Matrix for the Behavioral Treatment of Agoraphobia

Problems	Goals	Strategies	Techniques

Problems

PANIC (Somatic)
AGORAPHOBIC AVOIDANCE (Behavioral)
UNSAFE PERSON (Cognitive)
SPECIFIC
Biological
Organic
Mitral valve prolapse
Diabetes
Hypoglycemia
Temporal lobe epilepsy
Hyperthyroidism
Hyperallergic reaction
Endocrine changes
Birth
Menopause
Menstrual cycle
Functional
Hyperventilation
Frequent urination
Chemical abuse/withdrawal
Caffeine
Nicotine
Alcohol
Cocaine
Amphetamines
LSD
Other illegal drugs
Unknown/other

Goals

BROAD (MOLAR)
Eliminate panic
Eliminate behavioral avoidance
Create safe person
MIDRANGE
Optimal biological integrity
Psychophysiological balance
Psychological well-being
Interpersonal harmony
Self-efficacy
Sociological enrichment
Behavioral mastery
SPECIFIC (MOLECULAR)
Idiographic target goals
Valium withdrawal
Unassisted travel to Acme market on Poplar Street
Traveling through Lincoln Tunnel
Standing in line
Expressing anger to husband
Dinner out with friends
Going to a movie
etc.

Strategies

MEDICAL
Specialist Consultation
Psychiatrist
Endocrinologist
Neurologist
Cardiologist
Allergist
Internist
Hospitalization
Detoxification
Surgery
EDUCATIONAL
Biblio training
Video training
Audio training
Lecture/discussion
ENVIRONMENTAL
Environmental modification
Environmental preparation
Environmental relocation
SOCIOLOGICAL
Neighborhood networking
Values clarification
Racial enlightenment
ECONOMIC
Vocational Training
PSYCHOLOGICAL
Individual therapy
Couples therapy
Family therapy

Techniques

MEDICAL
Medication
MAO inhibitors
Phenelzine
Tricyclic antidepressants
Imipramine
Pamelor
Tofranil
Benzodiazepines
Ativan
Klonopin
Beta-blockers
Inderal
Xanax
Insulin
Anticonvulsants
Other
Medical education
Disorder-specific instruction
Holistic health
Drug withdrawal
Medically assisted
Alcoholics Anonymous
Narcotics Anonymous
1-800-Cocaine
Other
BEHAVIORAL
Exposure-based treatment
Location
In vivo
In vitro
Imaginary
Stress management (cont'd)
Autogenic training
Self-hypnosis
Meditation
Cognitive restructuring
Rational-emotive training
Diet and exercise
Biofeedback
Problem-solving training
Time management
Humor
Reciprocal inhibition
Induced humor
Induced anger
Induced relaxation
Self-instructional training
Relabeling
Reframing
Paradoxical intention
Disputing irrational beliefs
Thought stopping
Challenging automatic thoughts
Safety signal training
Symbolic modeling
Vicarious modeling
Covert training
Self-efficacy training
Human rights training
Stress inoculation training
Habituation training
Anger management training
Systematic desensitization
Systematic sensitization

Psychophysiological
Autonomic arousal
Low arousal threshold
Psychological
Historical antecedents
Abused child/devalued child
Overprotected child
Personality disorders
Histrionic
Hypochondriacal
Dependent
Obsessive-compulsive
Other
Neuroticism
Psychosocial
Marital conflict
Family conflict
Negative life events
Sociological
Environment (dangerous)
Beliefs (prejudice)
Economic
Impoverished
Behavioral-Cognitive
Phrenophobia
Fear of fear
Inadequate problem-solving skills
Conditioned avoidance
Irrational beliefs
Overvalued ideations
Negative self-appraisal
Low self-esteem

Group therapy
BEHAVIORAL
Coping skills training
Skill deficit reduction
Exposure therapy
Paraprofessional training
COGNITIVE
Misconception review
Restructuring
PHYSIOLOGICAL
Increase arousal threshold
MANAGERIAL
Problem-solving training

Intensity
Graduated
Prolonged
Flooded
Duration
Self-paced
Therapist assisted
Partner assisted
Other
Direct vs. indirect
Group vs. individual
Stress management
Stress trigger analysis
Education (nature of
    stress)
Audiotape assisted
Videotape assisted
Progressive muscle
    relaxation
Guided imagery
Diaphragmatic
    breathing
Reciting mantras
Reciting religious
    phrases

Covert sensitization
Assertiveness training
Therapist techniques
Exhortation
Suggestion
Coaching
Imploring
Prompting
Refuting
Reinforcing
Participant modeling
Cheerleading
Additional adjuncts
Self-help group network
Agoraphobics Anonymous
Spouse training
Psychological
Develop therapeutic alliance
Sociological-religious
Confession/communion
Church/Temple attendance
Consciousness raising

173

threats to personal safety; therefore, their elimination constitutes a desirable treatment goal. Analysis of data should therefore be conducted in order to identify those variables which, when eliminated, supplemented, replenished, or learned, would render the agoraphobic a safe person.

As indicated in Table 5.1, the list of idiographic goals is infinite because the variability of individual circumstances is also infinite. However, goals need to address socially valid and highly specific topics. Thus travel to the local food market to purchase the weekly groceries on Thursday evening when it is crowded with less than a SUDS score of 30 may represent an important idiographic goal.

Generation of Alternatives

The purpose of this process in the decision-making model is to brainstorm to produce as complete a list of treatment alternatives as possible with which to accomplish the identified goals. The more extensive the list of alternatives, the more likely a correct solution is to be found. Based on a comprehensive literature review, Table 5.1 provides a list of potential strategies and techniques used in the treatment of agoraphobia. This list is certainly not all-inclusive, but it does indicate the range of treatment possibilities and underscore the importance of using the decision-making model to choose from among them. These techniques alone, ranging from the sublime to the questionable, should dispel the simplistic notion of "one diagnosis, one treatment." It should be understood that multiple causation may result in the identification of several treatment goals; these goals can be reached through the use of broad-based strategies, within which a virtual potpourri of techniques can be applied.

The order of presentation in each column of Table 5.1 is random and does not imply priority, nor are strategies and techniques juxtaposed to suggest that they should be matched. For example, the treatment of panic might involve the use of beta-blockers (mitral valve prolapse), progressive muscle relaxation, and/or relabeling techniques. In addition, the strategies of specialist consultation, education, and coping skills training could be employed. Indeed, when the therapist constructs such a list jointly with the client, often the most difficult task is to encourage open-mindedness in perceiving the breadth of alternatives.

Decision Making

In studying the manner in which people acquire various phobias and subsequent treatment requirements, Öst (1985) stated that "the question of whether or not it is necessary to select a treatment method according to the way a phobia has been acquired is completely lacking firm empirical knowledge" (p. 683). Although the acquisition of agoraphobia does not provide any clues as to what might constitute appropriate treatment, a review of the outcome literature can provide meaningful guidelines. Such a review is in keeping with recommendations by Nezu and Nezu (see chapter 3) to use the empirical literature as a means of evaluating treatment alternatives.

Outcome Studies

Outcome studies conducted on agoraphobia invariably compare some form of exposure-based treatment with other methods. Indeed, many clinicians have proposed some variant of graduated in vivo exposure as the treatment of choice (Chambless & Goldstein, 1982). Emmelkamp (1982) also recommends this strategy, as does Wilson (1984). It would seem, therefore, that one of the treatment alternatives sought first would involve some form of exposure. However, exposure is often cited as being at the core of "no-shows" (Barlow, 1988; Barlow & Waddell, 1985) and treatment failures (Emmelkamp & Van Der Hout, 1983).

Jacobson, Wilson, and Tupper (1988) tried to resolve this dilemma by reanalyzing the outcome research on agoraphobia conducted during the period from 1976 to 1986 in which some variant of exposure was employed. They found that just over 50 percent of the subjects improved with exposure-based treatment. However, only 25 percent of the clients were no longer agoraphobic. The authors indicated that, if no-shows were factored into this data, the statistics would be substantially lower.

Jansson and Öst (1982) critically reviewed reports of behavioral treatments for agoraphobics published from 1966 to 1980. A total of 24 outcome studies involving approximately 650 clients were classified according to whether or not they were exposure based and, if so, by whether exposure was direct (in vivo) or indirect (imaginary). Within the category of direct exposure, a theoretically based distinction was made between those treatments that sought extinction of phobic behavior and those that sought to reinforce exposure behavior. A host of therapist-assisted methods associated with extinction treatments were reviewed. Research questions varied greatly, from comparing the use of prolonged versus graded exposure to investigating treatments assisted by medication and/or different instructional methods. The overall conclusion supported improvement when direct exposure methods were used.

Reinforcement methods, generally employing successive approximation and/or self-observation, also resulted in significant improvement. Indirect exposure methods in the form of imaginal flooding or systematic desensitization did not fare as well; four of the five studies reported did not support these procedures. Similar negative findings were reported in the nonexposure-based treatments. The studies reported typically pitted one form of therapy alone (e.g., problem-solving training or self-instruction) against exposure-based treatments. In every instance, exposure was found to be superior.

In summarizing the results of this review, Jansson and Öst voiced general support for the superiority of exposure-based treatment in producing change in the target problem at posttreatment and at a 6-month follow-up. However, they acknowledged the distinction between statistical and clinical significance. Because professionally acceptable methods of measuring clinical significance were not available to the authors, they proposed the use of an independent rating scale to measure degree of avoidance or anxiety. Clinical significance was defined according to the strategy outlined by Jacobson, Follette, and Revenstorf (1984). The authors found that direct exposure procedures produced both clinical and statistical significance at posttreatment and follow-up.

Trull, Nietzel, and Main (1988) conducted a meta-analysis to evaluate the issue of clinical significance in the behavioral treatment of agoraphobia. During the period from January 1975 through March 1987, they reviewed eight journals most likely to contain behavioral outcome studies. Clinical significance was defined as client posttreatment behavior that fell within normal limits on whatever dependent measure was employed. A fear questionnaire (Marks & Mathews, 1979) was the most often-used self-report measure; therefore, it served as the criterion in the meta-analysis. In a total of 71 studies reviewed, 22 reported use of the fear questionnaire and 19 actually provided access to the raw fear questionnaire data. Thirty-nine effect sizes were calculated from these data. Via the use of self-report data at posttreatment and at follow-up, the authors concluded that clinical significance was achieved. Their analysis further supports the efficacy of exposure-based treatments.

As indicated in Table 5.1, exposure-based treatments can vary across several dimensions: direct versus indirect, prolonged versus gradual, therapist-assisted versus self-paced, and so forth. Therefore, a reasonable question concerns choosing the correct type of exposure-based treatment for a given client. Emmelkamp (1982) presented an excellent summary of variations among exposure-based in vivo treatments. In general, he advocated the use of various self-paced shaping procedures, some of which incorporate the therapist as a source of reinforcement (Emmelkamp, 1974; Emmelkamp & Ultee, 1974). In a comparison of short- versus long-term in vivo sessions, longer sessions were found to be more effective (Everaerd, Rivken, & Emmelkamp, 1973; Watson, Mullett, & Pillay, 1973). Moreover, no differences were found when comparing individual versus group-facilitated exposure treatments (Emmelkamp & Emmelkamp-Benner, 1975). A general superiority of in vivo over imaginary exposure treatments was reported (Emmelkamp & Wessels, 1975).

Various forms of medication, ranging from minor tranquilizers (e.g., benzodiazepines) to monoamine oxidase inhibitors (e.g, phenelzine), have been used either as primary treatments or as adjuncts to exposure-based treatments. Imipramine has been cited most often in the agoraphobia literature as the treatment of choice. Excellent commentary on drug treatment can be found in reviews by Barlow (1988) and Telch et al. (1983).

Space does not permit a complete review of the drug literature; however, some comments are relevant. One issue, the question of whether drug treatment should be considered alone or in combination with other behavioral treatment modalities, is imbued with much passion for clinicians. Opinions range from "under no circumstances" to "always." A critical review of the literature does not provide one with an easy answer to this question. However, central issues concerning chemotherapy are (a) whether such treatment is essential to block or diminish the experience of panic in order to accomplish exposure, (b) whether anticipatory anxiety should be chemically treated, and (c) whether it is essential to provide chemical treatment for associated symptoms such as depression or generalized anxiety. In other words, is it necessary to treat panic or agoraphobic avoidance chemically and, if so, what is the cost?

The outcome literature on drugs generally supports initial treatment gains but suggests significant relapse (Barlow, 1988; Dittrich, Houts, & Lichstein, 1983; Emmelkamp, 1982; Jansson & Öst, 1982). Therefore, one concern is that maintenance may be compromised if drugs are used. Second, all drugs produce side effects. The anticholinergic side effects are particularly troublesome, as is the motor and cognitive impairment that makes driving difficult or dangerous. (Chemically limiting the capacity of an individual to travel by car could compromise the attainment of an essential treatment goal.) Last, clients can become chemically or emotionally dependent on medication and attribute gains in treatment to it. Chemotherapy should therefore be used with a great deal of caution, only after considering a host of patient variables.

With regard to other areas that affect exposure-based treatment, Barlow, O'Brien, and Last (1984) found spouse-assisted exposure to be superior to individual self-paced exposure. Likewise, training clients prior to treatment by having them view a videotape of three successful clients describing the procedures was found to reduce dropout (Emmelkamp & Emmelkamp-Benner, 1975). The use of paradoxical intention has also been found to improve exposure compliance (Ascher, 1981).

Nonexposure methods such as reciprocal inhibition via anger induction (Goldstein, Serber, & Piaget, 1970), thought stopping (O'Brien, 1979), and communications training (Chambless, Foa, Groves, & Goldstein, 1982) have also been successful with agoraphobics. Most outcome studies in which one procedure is compared with another generally demonstrate some efficacy; however, as has been indicated previously, statistical versus clinical significance is seldom evaluated.

Jacobson et al. (1988) considered this issue, but, unlike Trull et al. (1988), they focused specifically on exposure-based interventions. These authors contacted 38 researchers who published exposure-based outcome studies on agoraphobia between 1976 and 1986. Raw data were requested so that outcomes could be reanalyzed, and 11 investigators replied. Using the Jacobson et al. (1984) criteria to measure clinical significance, the authors found a great deal of variability. No study reported recovery rates greater than 54 percent, and only 27 percent of the subjects were found to be free of all agoraphobic behavior. The authors concluded by stating that "exposure alone does not seem to be a total solution to the problem of agoraphobia" (p. 522). They indicated that involving the spouse, as Mathews et al. (1981a), Barlow and Waddell (1985), and Hafner and Ross (1983) suggest, increases clinical efficacy. Clinical efficacy is also increased by specifically focusing on the experience of panic (Clark, 1986; Barlow & Cerny, 1988). Integrative treatments involving behavioral, cognitive, physiological, and psychological components such as those recommended by Chambless, Goldstein, Gallagher, and Bright (1986) were also recommended.

Michelson, Mavissakalian, and Marchione (1988) compared three specific treatment modalities: cognitive, behavioral, and psychophysiological. A total of 88 clients were randomly assigned to one of three groups receiving treatments based on paradoxical intention, graduated in vivo exposure, or progressive muscle relaxation. Clinical ratings and self-report measures of avoidance, as well as experiences of panic, were assessed before treatment, 6 weeks into treatment, 12 weeks after treatment, and 3 months after treatment. Results demonstrated that each treatment produced beneficial effects across the major clinical domains, with no between-group differences. The essential equality of the three treatments was therefore supported; however, a significant number of dropouts occurred (15 of 88 subjects). The authors used the high dropout rate and high residual endstate functioning to suggest "the limited efficacy of unitary treatment strategies, such as graduated exposure, paradoxical intention, or relaxation training" (p. 118). They advocated combining treatments to improve generalization and maintenance.

Thus far, analysis of outcome research has been offered as a means of facilitating treatment selection. One factor influencing decision making not yet covered is social evaluation. Indeed, high dropout rates and maintenance of residual agoraphobic symptomatology may reflect a disregard for this consideration. In one investigation of the social validity issue in agoraphobia research, Norton, Allen, and Hilton (1983) performed two separate studies of nonagoraphobics' (Experiment 1) and agoraphobics' (Experiment 2) ratings of the acceptability and perceived effectiveness of five treatment approaches. These approaches included use of antidepressants, use of minor tranquilizers, relationship-building therapy, exposure-based therapy, and cognitive therapy. A 9-point Likert-type scale was used by both groups to rate the treatments. Agoraphobics rated exposure and cognitive therapies as being more acceptable than treatments based on the use of tranquilizers, antidepressants, or relationship-building skills. However, effectiveness ratings were variable, suggesting that, even if effective, treatments were not necessarily acceptable. Exposure-based treatment was rated as being most effective by both agoraphobics and nonagoraphobics. Both groups also found tranquilizers and antidepressants to be least acceptable. This research therefore supports the need for consumer participation in treatment planning.

In a replication of this study (Norton & Allen, 1985), college students were asked to rate acceptability and perceived effectiveness as before; however, individual coping styles were also considered. Results indicated that people with different coping styles and attitudes towards tranquilizers preferred different forms of treatment. Although claims for treatment effectiveness could not be made, caution regarding the matching of coping styles and beliefs with treatment programs could be supported.

In attempting to predict agoraphobia treatment outcomes with husband-wife pairs, Hafner and Ross (1983) gave additional support to the notion of matching. Interpretations of their data tend to discourage in vivo exposure for individuals who typically blame other people for their problems. Here, a more traditional form of therapy designed to establish personal ownership over problems might make more sense. The investigation also showed that the training of husbands as paraprofessional guides and as sources of reinforcement was beneficial.

In keeping with the assertion throughout this chapter that there is no such thing as a prescribed treatment program for agoraphobia, the outcome studies described did not suggest a treatment of choice, even though they did generally support some form of exposure-based intervention. Likewise, they ruled out very few behavioral procedures as being totally inappropriate. It would therefore seem advisable to develop a plan that provides the most efficacious treatment for those problems identified in the assessment phase. The decision-making model must be followed in order to produce a treatment plan that is suited to the individual in question, and as many strategies as fit the individual-environment-system complex should be used. Closely abiding by the suggestions presented in chapter 3 regarding the selection of treatment strategies and techniques will help the clinician, as will considering the options presented in Table 5.1.

Solution Implementation and Verification

Thus far in treatment, a great deal has already been accomplished. Problems have been clearly identified and understood in terms of their breadth, scope, and penetration into the individual's life. Clear measurements have been taken. A therapeutic relationship has been established, and the client has been given a significant amount of information on agoraphobia and panic from behavioral, cognitive, and psychophysiological perspectives. The client has also been brought into the process of therapy as a co-therapist. To function in the role of co-therapist, the individual must master two skills: stress management and problem solving. Stress management techniques (see Table 5.1) are necessary equipment. Problem-solving training is the executive therapeutic process involved in using this equipment. For the purposes of instruction, the client can be regarded as being similar to a graduate student undergoing clinical training, except for the fact that she is both trainee and patient.

Stress Management

Approximately 20 techniques are listed in Table 5.1 for promoting stress management. With few exceptions, it is recommended that clients be exposed to all of these major techniques during the assessment phase of treatment. Mastery on both the cognitive and physiological levels is essential. In our work, we have experienced a considerable amount of individual variability in preference and mastery. We have found, therefore, that exposing clients to muscle relaxation training, autogenic training, guided imagery, and diaphragmatic breathing, as well as to strategies designed to dispute irrational beliefs (e.g., cognitive restructuring), allows them to make individual choices. It is not our practice to use meditation, mantras, self-hypnosis, or recitation of religious phrases; however, if the client has used any of these techniques before, they are encouraged and given therapeutic credibility.

If the program involves a husband, wife, or other helper, stress management training can also be offered to these individuals. It is not uncommon to find these people experiencing a significant amount of anxiety in response to seeing their loved one in distress. It is wise to help them learn to manage their own stress to prevent treatment from being aborted through their own anxiety or intolerance.

Audiotapes such as those produced by Budzynsky (1980) and Stroebel (1978) are helpful for both client and helper in learning relaxation skills. Two excellent workbooks on relaxation training and cognitive intervention are also recommended (McKay, Davis, & Fanning, 1981; Davis, Eshelman, & McKay, 1982). It is often advisable to use some additional reading on time management (Lakeim, 1973) or assertiveness (Smith, 1975) if these are minor problems. If these issues contribute significantly to the main problem, then therapy should focus on them.

Problem-solving Training

The focus of problem-solving training is to create an executive skill with which to manage treatment. The client, spouse (if indicated), and therapist subsequently demonstrate mastery by using the skill in the development of the treatment program.[3] Thus, if the broad goal of treatment is to create a safe person, the journey towards this end must involve exposure to feared environments or experiences (internal as well as external). How to proceed on this journey is the next question.

Promoting internal safety. For people who experience what Emmelkamp (1982) calls *cardiac neurosis*—those individuals whom Barlow and Waddell (1985) call *autonomic responders*— therapy should begin by exposure to progressively more distressing experiences of arousal. This

---

[3] For a detailed discussion of problem-solving training as it relates to stress management, see chapter 13.

progressive arousal should be coupled with relaxation exercises designed to provide the client with mastery experiences. Wolpe (1982) and Emmelkamp (1982) suggest encouraging such mastery by inducing hyperventilation in the office setting (either by rapid breathing or by providing appropriate imaginal scenes). Prior to engaging in this exercise, it is obviously important to seek medical clearance. Education concerning the influence of mitral valve prolapse on the experience of panic is recommended for individuals who have this condition. Actual in vivo exposure can also serve to facilitate automatic arousal for the purpose of gaining the experience of internal mastery. I prefer to use in vitro experiences, in which objects or props in and around the office serve to elevate arousal when used in conjunction with imagined or role-played scenes. A common prop is the client's or therapist's car in the parking lot, with travel to feared places being imagined or role played.

As much time as necessary is spent until the client expresses and demonstrates an experience of personal internal safety. The key is hearing the client say that he does not like the experience but feels confident in his ability to regain control by engaging in stress management techniques.

Self-confidence can often be augmented by accumulating reminders of past achievements. Thus clients are asked to save used bridge or tunnel coupons on their car dashboards. During times of distress, these can serve as distractors; in addition, they can remind the client of recently having had the capacity to meet a challenge. It is also advisable to save data sheets from exposure sessions. Getting the person to focus on the need to collect data can help mitigate potential panic. Having a close record at hand also allows the individual to remember the previous experience of greater SUDS levels. Finally, the sheer bulk of the used pages is often interpreted by the client as proof of achievement.

Promoting external safety. Eventually, the client must be exposed to those dangerous locations or situations identified in the assessment. Doing so provides the client with an opportunity to practice mastery over stress in situations that were once avoided. Using the alternatives listed on Table 5.1 as techniques for exposure-based treatment can facilitate this process. Again, none of these alternatives should be viewed as a perfect choice. Rather, the processes of the decision-making model need to be applied to identify appropriate treatment plans for each specific client.

I have typically chosen some variation of graded in vivo exposure as one treatment component. In this type of treatment, the therapist goes on field trips with the client to tackle major avoidance stimuli (bridges, tunnels, superhighways with few exits, elevators, buses, etc.), with self-paced or partner-assisted exercises being prescribed as homework. In the therapist-assisted sessions, blocks of 2 or 3 hours are programmed to allow sufficient time for the client to experience both anxiety reduction and mastery. The avoidance hierarchy and the travel map developed during the assessment phase collectively produce a framework from which to address progressively more difficult tasks. Personal efficacy can be enhanced throughout by reinforcing the client for achievement.

Another important issue concerns the client's use of *safety signals*. These people, places, or things are associated with safety (e.g., the therapist on the opposite side of the bridge, a hospital in the neighborhood, a pleasant image). Unlike Barlow (1988), who advises the elimination of all safety signals, I recommend that the clinician make use of these potentially useful therapeutic tools. As long as the client has personal mastery over safety signals and they are not so idiosyncratic or unavailable so as to be rendered impractical, they can serve as excellent adjuncts. Many of the safety signals can be faded later as self-confidence builds. When combined with stress management techniques and problem solving, the use of such signals can help the individual experience personal safety. Indeed, Rachman (1984) advocates the use of safety signals as talismans and exploits a lesser-of-two-evils strategy with success. In using this latter strategy, the therapist might, for example, challenge the client to cross a dangerous bridge accompanied by a safe person, giving the more feared alternative of spending the night at home alone.

Actively involving the client in the process of using the decision-making model to construct an exposure-based program clearly distinguishes this approach from "canned" programs. The client should not be forced to participate in a group, collaborate with a spouse, or engage in any other form of treatment simply because it is part of a clinic's prescribed program. It is better to ask, "What can *we* do to achieve in vivo exposure" than to say, "Here is what *you* must do to achieve in vivo exposure."

Pitfalls in Using Exposure

In mapping out an exposure-based strategy for a particular client, the therapist should review potential iatrogenic effects of the treatment. Emmelkamp (1982) lists one of these as embarrassment caused by having to perform exposure exercises in the presence of neighbors or strangers. If possible, "coming out of the closet" with people who may become suspicious is quite helpful. For example, I advised one client who had to make an important court appearance to make several trips to the particular courtroom in which the proceedings were to be held. Unbeknownst to us, the courthouse was experiencing threats from a terrorist group and had alerted its security force to be particularly cautious. The guard stationed in the courtroom was becoming suspicious of my client's daily trips. The client shared the fact that his presence was part of treatment (a fact I verified), and the exposure continued without further incident. Toll takers, elevator operators, neighbors, friends, family members, and bosses can all be alerted in order to prevent negative consequences.

It is also important to distinguish between avoidance behavior and the use of safety signals. As Emmelkamp (1982) notes, clients should be cautioned against hurrying through exposure exercises, taking extra medication, carrying extra pills, and so forth. When planning out an exercise, it is actually helpful to be mindful of access to safe places or people, but such safety signals should be identified openly instead of being used as covert avoidance mechanisms. When avoidance behaviors or cognitions are identified, they often reveal the client's misconceptions about the treatment itself. Once again, it should be emphasized that the client will never be asked to do something she cannot do and that she will never be required to tolerate more distress than she can handle. Indeed, providing permission to end an exposure session without penalty is part of a self-paced, graded approach. The principle to follow is not to conduct exposure exercises as a form of negative reinforcement: In other words, it is ill-advised to escape under elevated SUDS levels. In general, it is better to stop the exposure once a preset SUDS limit has been reached.

Exposure sessions should be carefully planned in such a way as to take the individual progressively into more stressful situations. The method of increasing difficulty can vary across several dimensions, depending on the results of the assessment. For example, in the case of the individual who needed to go to the courthouse, once unassisted travel was achieved, parking the car in the nearest available space regardless of its closeness to the building became the next step. (Agoraphobics often complain of not being able to park far away because of perceived entrapment.) After receiving several parking violations, the client gradually increased the distance from the door of the courthouse until he was able to park in whatever spot was available. Riding the elevator in the courthouse and then staying in the courtroom were subsequently planned.

Many behavior therapists train family members (especially husbands) to facilitate exposure-based treatment. When providing this
type of training, the therapist must exercise a great deal of care.
Barlow's (1988) treatment program, as well as that of Mathews et al.
(1981a, 1981b, 1981c), provides useful suggestions toward this end. In
addition to training, assessing the family member's competence to serve
as a paraprofessional is essential. Observations of the client and partner
working together during in vivo exposure should therefore be included
in the assessment. Without careful evaluation of competence, not only
may the treatment be put in jeopardy, but the therapist may also risk
legal liability (Knapp & Vande Creek, 1987; Roswell, 1988).

It is important that family members function to reinforce treatment
gains rather than the client's avoidance. Training a family member to
become an active component of treatment can at times present more
risks than benefits. For example, the wife of one client was deathly
afraid of her husband's having a coronary during a panic attack. Education and assurance provided by a cardiologist did not diminish these
feelings. Although the client described his wife as a safe person, she
could not be involved in his exposure sessions because of her own
hyperarousal and threat to his ability to feel safe. The therapist needs
to conduct a cost-benefit analysis to determine the effects for a given
client (see chapter 3). If the therapist can spend only a limited amount
of time with the family, the two areas that must be covered are the
physiological mechanism of panic and the role of avoidance behavior
as a stress reducer.

A final issue with regard to the family concerns dependency. Most
agoraphobic clients evidence dependency; therefore, one is at risk of
fostering this tendency if a family member's presence is perceived as
the necessary ingredient for success. It is recommended, therefore, that
this problem and other issues be carefully evaluated before making a
final decision about involving the family.

Issues in Treatment Verification

As shown in chapter 3 (especially by the Clinical Pathogenesis Map
in Figure 3.1), use of the decision-making model demands a dynamic
interaction—a symbiosis of sorts—between behavioral assessment and
treatment. This symbiosis is especially important given the multidimensional characteristics of the agoraphobic illustrated in Table 5.1. Treatment typically involves the construction of several idiosyncratic goals,
all of which are pursued simultaneously. Each goal is operationally
defined in measurable terms. Thus verifying effectiveness would at first

appear to be a rather straightforward matter (e.g., the individual client is or is not able to drive to the Acme on First Street).

However, if one accepts the importance of achieving personal safety as the universal goal of treatment, verifying treatment effectiveness may be more difficult. How is personal safety operationally defined? As noted earlier, this question should be addressed at the beginning of treatment. In collaboration with the client, the therapist can define examples of the achievement of personal safety. In my practice, patients have typically described personal safety as involving the ability to deal with the unknown in some fashion or to give up some measure of personal vigilance. For many, personal safety is described as being able to respond to an emergency or, conversely, being able to follow through with plans to attend an event scheduled long in advance. One client described this quality as being able to go to a restaurant without first locating where the bathrooms were and determining if they were easily accessible. Another client described it as being able to respond to the demands of work without constantly trying to determine beforehand what might be expected of him on a given day and whether or not he could handle the situation. Yet another defined personal safety as the ability to drive to work without checking the traffic conditions to assess whether she should take the more direct but busier route or the less travelled but interminably longer route. Other individual definitions of personal safety might involve being able to travel as a passenger in a car with business colleagues, jog around the neighborhood, experience a skipped heartbeat, or focus on the food at a restaurant—all without feeling the need to escape. In other words, personal safety means being able to do anything and know you will be able to handle the consequences.

CONCLUSION

The central focus of agoraphobia treatment enhanced by the clinical decision-making model involves the client's acquisition of a process-oriented management system. As Table 5.1 implies, the number of decisions affecting both client and therapist are legion. If one defines management as the judicious use of resources, one may certainly make the case for management in the treatment of agoraphobia: There are simply too many decisions to make without having such a system to serve as a guide. Therefore, the decision-making model can be instrumental in helping clients, therapists, and family members work collaboratively to develop and implement effective treatment.

In addition, the decision-making model can help to emphasize the difference between process-oriented and outcome-oriented treatment. The client will need to acquire lifelong skills to maintain and generalize the newly acquired experience of personal safety. This feeling will be challenged many times after treatment. Thus teaching the individual methods as opposed to producing a single therapeutic outcome makes long-term sense. And, because significant others can be trained in these methods, they can serve as adjuncts in the quest for maintenance.

References

American Psychiatric Association. (1987). *Diagnostic and statistical manual of mental disorders* (3rd ed. rev.). Washington, DC: Author.

Ascher, L. M. (1981). Employing paradoxical intention in the treatment of agoraphobia. *Behaviour Research and Therapy, 19,* 533–542.

Bandura, A. (1977). Self-efficacy: Toward a unifying theory of behavioral change. *Psychological Review, 84,* 191–215.

Barlow, D. H. (1988). *Anxiety and its disorders: The nature and treatment of anxiety and panic.* New York: Guilford.

Barlow, D. H., & Cerny, J. A. (1988). *Psychological treatment of panic.* New York: Guilford.

Barlow, D. H., O'Brien, G. T., & Last, C. G. (1984). Couples treatment of agoraphobia. *Behavior Therapy, 15,* 41–58.

Barlow, D. H., & Waddell, M. T. (1985). Agoraphobia. In D. H. Barlow (Ed.), *Clinical handbook of psychological disorders: A step by step treatment manual.* New York: Guilford.

Beck, A. T., Ward, C. H., Mendelsohn, M., Mock, J., & Erbaugh, J. (1961). An inventory for measuring depression. *Archives of General Psychiatry, 4,* 561–571.

Boudewyns, P. A., & Shipley, R. H. (1983). *Flooding and impulsive therapy: Direct therapeutic exposure in clinical practice.* New York: Plenum.

Broadbeck, C., & Michelson, L. (1987). Problem solving and attributional styles of agoraphobics. *Cognitive Therapy and Research, 11,* 593–610.

Budzynsky, T. (1980). *Relaxation training program* [audiocassette recordings]. New York: BMA Audio Cassette Publications.

Chambless, D. L. (1982). Characteristics of agoraphobia. In D. L. Chambless & A. J. Goldstein (Eds.), *Agoraphobia: Multiple perspectives on theory and treatment.* New York: Wiley.

Chambless, D. L. (1985). The relationship of severity of agoraphobia to associated psychopathology. *Behaviour Research and Therapy, 23,* 305–310.

Chambless, D. L., Caputo, G. C., Bright P., & Gallagher, R. (1984). Assessment of fear of fear in agoraphobia: The Body Sensations Questionnaire and the Agoraphobic Cognitions Questionnaire. *Journal of Consulting and Clinical Psychology, 52,* 1090–1097.

Chambless, D. L., Foa, E. B., Groves, G. A., & Goldstein, A. J. (1982). Exposure and communications training in the treatment of agoraphobia. *Behaviour Research and Therapy, 20, 219–231.*

188   Chapter 5

Chambless, D. L., & Goldstein, A. J. (1980). Agoraphobia. In A. J. Goldstein & E. B. Foa (Eds.), *Handbook of behavioral interventions*. New York: Wiley.

Chambless, D. L., & Goldstein, A. J. (Eds.). (1982). *Agoraphobia: Multiple perspectives on theory and treatment*. New York: Wiley.

Chambless, D. L., Goldstein, A. J., Gallagher, R., & Bright, P. (1986). Integrating behavior therapy and psychotherapy in the treatment of agoraphobia. *Psychotherapy, 23*, 150–159.

Chambless, D. L., & Mason, J. (1986). Sex, sex role stereotyping and agoraphobia. *Behaviour Research and Therapy, 24*, 231–235.

Clark, D. M. (1986). A cognitive approach to panic. *Behaviour Research and Therapy, 24*, 461–470.

Davis, M., Eshelman, E. R., & McKay, M. (1982). *The relaxation and stress reduction workbook* (2nd ed.). Oakland CA: New Harbinger.

Di Nardo, P. A., Barlow, D. H., Cerny, J. A., Vermilyea, B. B., Vermilyea, J. A., Himadi, W. G., & Waddell, M. T. (1985). *Anxiety Disorders Interview Schedule-Revised* (ADIS-R). Albany, NY: Phobia and Anxiety Disorders Clinic, State University of New York at Albany.

Dittrich, J., Houts, A. C., & Lichstein, K. (1983). Panic disorder: Assessment and treatment. *Clinical Psychology Review, 3*, 215–225.

D'Zurilla, T. J. (1985). Problem-solving: Still a promising treatment strategy for agoraphobia. *Behavior Therapy, 16*, 545–550.

Emmelkamp, P. M. G. (1974). Self-observation versus flooding in the treatment of agoraphobia. *Behaviour Research and Therapy, 12*, 229–237.

Emmelkamp, P. M. G. (1982). In vivo treatment of agoraphobia. In D. L. Chambless & A. J. Goldstein (Eds.), *Agoraphobia: Multiple perspectives on theory and treatment*. New York: Wiley.

Emmelkamp, P. M. G., & Emmelkamp-Benner, A. (1975). Effects of historically portrayed modeling and group treatment on self-observation: A comparison with agoraphobics. *Behaviour Research and Therapy, 13*, 135–139.

Emmelkamp, P. M. G., & Ultee, K. A. (1974). A comparison of "successive approximation" and "self observation" in the treatment of agoraphobia. *Behavior Therapy, 5*, 606–613.

Emmelkamp, P. M. G., & Van Der Hout, A. (1983). Failure in treating agoraphobia. In E. B. Foa & P. M. G. Emmelkamp (Eds.), *Failures in behavior therapy*. New York: Wiley.

Emmelkamp, P. M. G., & Wessels, H. (1975). Flooding in imagination vs. flooding in vivo: A comparison with agoraphobics. *Behaviour Research and Therapy, 13*, 7–15.

Everaerd, W. T., Rivken, H. M., & Emmelkamp, P. M. G. (1973). A comparison of flooding and successive approximation in the treatment of agoraphobia. *Behaviour Research and Therapy, 11*, 105–117.

Goldstein, A. J. (1970). Case conference: Some aspects of agoraphobia. *Journal of Behavior Therapy and Experimental Psychiatry, 1*, 305–313.

Goldstein, A. J., & Chambless, D. L. (1978). A reanalysis of agoraphobia. *Behavior Therapy, 9*, 47–59.

Goldstein, A. J., & Munjack, D. (1987, November). *Treatment of agoraphobia: Beyond exposure*. Paper presented at the annual meeting of the Association for Advancement of Behavior Therapy, Boston.

Goldstein, A. J., Serber, M., & Piaget, G. (1970). Induced anger as a reciprocal inhibitor of fear. *Journal of Behavior Therapy and Experimental Psychiatry, 1*, 67–70.

Hafner, R. J. (1982). The marital context of the agoraphobic syndrome. In D. L. Chambless & A. J. Goldstein (Eds.), *Agoraphobia: Multiple perspectives on theory and treatment.* New York: Wiley.

Hafner, R. J., & Ross, M. W. (1983). Predicting the outcome of behavior therapy for agoraphobia. *Behaviour Research and Therapy, 21,* 375–382.

Holmes, T. H., & Rahe, R. H. (1967). The social readjustment rating scale. *Journal of Psychosomatic Research, 11,* 213–218.

Jacobson, N. S., Follette, W. C., & Revenstorf, D. (1984). Psychotherapy outcome research: Methods for reporting variability and evaluating clinical significance. *Behavior Therapy, 16,* 249–262.

Jacobson, N. S., Wilson, L., & Tupper, C. (1988). The clinical significance of treatment gains resulting from exposure-based interventions for agoraphobia: A reanalysis of outcome data. *Behavior Therapy, 19,* 539–554.

Jansson, L., & Öst, L. G. (1982). Behavioral treatments for agoraphobia: An evaluative review. *Clinical Psychology Review, 2,* 311–336.

Johnson, D. M. (1950). Problem solving and symbolic process. In C.P. Stone (Ed.), *Annual review of psychology* (Vol. 1). Palo Alto, CA: Annual Reviews, Inc.

Kantor, J. S., Zitrin, C. M., & Zeldis, S. M. (1980). Mitral valve prolapse syndrome in agoraphobic patients. *American Journal of Psychiatry, 137,* 467–469.

Knapp, S., & Vande Creek, L. (1987). The risks of working at the cutting-edge: Treatment of anxiety disorders. *The Psychotherapy Bulletin, 22* (2), *18–20.*

Lakeim, A. (1973). *How to get control of your time and your life.* New York: Signet.

Lazarus, A. A. (1976). *Multimodal behavior therapy.* New York: Springer.

Lazarus, A. A. (1985). The need for technical eclecticism: Science, breadth, depth, and specificity. In J. K. Zeig (Ed.), *The evolution of psychotherapy.* New York: Brunner/Mazel.

Levine, F. M., & Sandeen, E. (1985). *Conceptualization in psychotherapy: The models approach.* Hillsdale, NJ: Erlbaum.

Liebowitz, M. R., & Klein, D. F. (1982). Agoraphobia: Clinical features, pathophysiology, and treatment. In D. L. Chambless & A. J. Goldstein (Eds.), *Agoraphobia: Multiple perspectives on theory and treatment.* New York: Wiley.

Marks, I. M. (1970a). Agoraphobic syndrome (phobic anxiety state). *Archives of General Psychiatry, 23,* 538–553.

Marks, I. M. (1970b). The classification of phobias. *British Journal of Psychiatry, 116,* 377–386.

Marks, I. M., and Mathews, A. M. (1979). Brief standard self-rating for phobic patients. *Behaviour Research and Therapy, 17,* 263–267.

Mathews, A. M., Gelder, M. G., & Johnston, D. W. (1981a). *Agoraphobia: Nature and treatment.* New York: Guilford.

Mathews, A. M., Gelder, M. G., & Johnston, D. W. (1981b). *Programmed practice for agoraphobia: Client's manual.* London: Tavistock.

Mathews, A. M., Gelder, M. G., & Johnston, D. W. (1981c). *Programmed practice for agoraphobia: Partner's manual.* London: Tavistock.

McKay, M., Davis, M., & Fanning, P. (1981). *Thoughts and feelings: The art of cognitive stress intervention.* Richmond, CA: New Harbinger.

Michelson, L., & Ascher, L. M. (1984). Paradoxical intention: Theory, research, and clinical application with anxiety disorders. *Journal of Behavior Therapy and Experimental Psychiatry, 15,* 215–220.

Michelson, L., Mavissakalian, M., & Marchione, K. (1988). Cognitive, behavioral, and psychophysiological treatments of agoraphobia: A comparative outcome investigation. *Behavior Therapy, 19,* 97–120.

Mowrer, O. H. (1960). *Learning theory and behavior.* New York: Wiley.

Norton, G. R., & Allen, G. E. (1985). Predicting treatment preferences for agoraphobics. *Behaviour Research and Therapy, 23,* 699–701.

Norton, G. R., Allen, G. E., & Hilton, J. (1983). The social validity of treatments for agoraphobia. *Behaviour Research and Therapy, 21,* 393–399.

O'Brien, J. S. (1979). A modified thought stopping procedure for the treatment of agoraphobia. *Journal of Behavior Therapy and Experimental Psychiatry, 10,* 121–124.

Öst, L. G. (1985). Way of acquiring phobias and outcome of behavior treatment. *Behaviour Research and Therapy, 23,* 683–689.

Rachman, S. (1983). The modification of agoraphobia avoidance behavior: Some fresh possibilities. *Behaviour Research and Therapy, 21,* 567–574.

Rachman, S. (1984). Agoraphobia: A safety signal perspective. *Behaviour Research and Therapy, 22,* 59–70.

Raimy, V. (1975). *Misunderstandings of the self.* San Francisco: Jossey-Bass.

Rathus, S. A. (1973). A 30-item schedule for assessing assertive behavior. *Behavior Therapy, 4,* 398–406.

Roswell, V. (1988). Professional liability: Issues for behavior therapists in the 1980's and 1990's. *The Behavior Therapist, 11,* 163–171.

Rubin, S. E., & Lawlis, F. (1969). Factor analysis of the 122-item fear survey schedule. *Behaviour Research and Therapy, 7,* 381–386.

Smith, M. J. (1975). *When I say no I feel guilty.* New York: Dial.

Stroebel, C. (1978). *Quieting response training* [audiocassette recordings]. New York: BMA Audio Cassette Publications.

Stuart, R. B., & Jacobson, B. (1987). *Couple's Pre-Counseling Inventory.* Champaign, IL: Research Press.

Telch, M. J., Tearnan, B. H., & Taylor, C. B. (1983). Antidepressant medication in the treatment of agoraphobia: A critical review. *Behaviour Research and Therapy, 21,* 505–517.

Trull, T. J., Nietzel, M. T., & Main, A. (1988). The use of meta-analysis to assess the clinical significance of behavior therapy for agoraphobia. *Behavior Therapy, 19,* 527–538.

Watson, J. P., Mullett, G. E., & Pillay, H. (1973). The effects of prolonged exposure to phobic situations upon agoraphobic patients treated in groups. *Behaviour Research and Therapy, 11,* 531–545.

Weeks, C. (1968). *Hope and help for your nerves.* New York: Hawthorne.

Weeks, C. (1976). *Simple, effective treatment of agoraphobia.* New York: Hawthorne.

Weissman, M. M. (1985). The epidemiology of anxiety disorders: Rates, risks, and familial patterns. In A. H. Tuma & J. D. Maser (Eds.), *Anxiety and the anxiety disorders.* Hillsdale, NJ: Erlbaum.

Wilson, G. T. (1984). Fear reduction methods and the treatment of anxiety disorders. In C. M. Franks, G. T. Wilson, P. C. Kendall, & K. S. Brownell (Eds.), *Annual review of behavior therapy: Theory and practice* (Vol. 10). New York: Guilford.

Wolpe, J. (1982). *The practice of behavior therapy* (3rd ed.). New York: Pergamon.

Wolpe, J., & Lang, P. J. (1964). A fear survey schedule for use in behavior therapy. *Behaviour Research and Therapy, 2,* 27–30.

Wolpe, J., & Lang, P. J. (1969). *Fear survey schedule.* San Diego, CA: Educational and Industrial Testing Services.

Chapter 6

Obesity

Michael G. Perri

INTRODUCTION

Few problems are as common, serious, and difficult to treat as obesity. Behavior therapists who work with obese clients are confronted by an array of clinical decisions. Among these are (a) determining whether a client is a suitable candidate for behavioral treatment, (b) deciding on the best treatment strategy to meet the client's particular needs, (c) dealing with plateaus in weight loss and lack of progress during treatment, and (d) developing a long-range plan for maintaining weight loss following treatment. In this chapter, clinical decision making in the behavioral treatment of obesity is addressed from the problem-solving perspective implicit in the clinical decision-making model (see chapter 3). This vantage point serves both as a framework to guide the clinician's actions and as a technique for teaching patients how to cope with difficulties in the management of obesity.

UNDERSTANDING OBESITY AND ITS TREATMENT

This chapter will first offer an overview of the problem of obesity and discuss ways to orient clients about obesity and its treatment. Next, discussion will focus on screening and assessing clients for treatment and on additional assessment procedures necessary for a full understanding of the client's problems. Options in treatment, initial clinical decisions, and common problems in treatment implementation will then be described. Finally, a consideration of the design of a maintenance program and follow-up care completes the discussion.

Obesity: An Overview

An initial question facing the clinician is which clients are suitable for behavioral treatment. Before addressing this question, it is necessary to define obesity, to examine the rationale for attempting to treat it, and to review the contribution of biological and behavioral factors to the development and maintenance of obesity.

From a technical perspective, *obesity* refers to an excess of adipose tissue or body fat. Except in experimental settings, however, assessments of an individual's body fat are rarely made. More typically, obesity is inferred by comparing a person's actual weight with an ideal weight derived from height-weight tables such as those developed by the Metropolitan Life Insurance Company (1983). The operational definition of obesity is 20 percent or more over the ideal weight for one's height and sex (Stunkard, 1985). The degree of obesity is usually further classified as mild (20 to 39 percent overweight), moderate (40 to 100 percent overweight), and severe (greater than 100 percent overweight). In the United States, approximately 35 million adults are obese. The vast majority of these individuals (about 90 percent) fall in the mildly obese category, approximately 9 percent are moderately obese, and 1 percent or fewer are severely obese (Abraham, 1983).

Obesity is clearly a highly prevalent condition in the United States and other Western nations. The question arises, however, whether it should be treated. One might argue that obesity should not be treated at all. The available literature suggests that the chances of successful treatment are quite small (Foreyt, 1987), and the common pattern of relapse following treatment may actually exacerbate the condition by increasing the individual's degree of body fatness (Brownell, Steen, & Wilmore, 1987). Thus a case can be made that clinical efforts should be focused not on treating obesity, but on helping obese persons accept their condition.

Two major arguments favor the treatment of obesity. The first involves the negative medical consequences of obesity. A substantial body of research has linked moderate and severe obesity to decreased longevity due primarily to cardiovascular disease, diabetes, and certain types of cancer (Bray, 1986; National Institutes of Health, Consensus Development Panel on the Health Implications of Obesity, 1985). Obesity contributes to the disease process through its strong association with hypertension, hyperlipidemia, increased insulin production, and impaired glucose tolerance. Weight loss can reverse many of the disadvantages associated with obesity. Reductions in body weight correlate positively and significantly with improvements in cardiac functioning, blood pressure, glucose tolerance, and cholesterol levels (Kannel & Gordon, 1979; Kannel, Gordon, & Castelli, 1979; Sorlie, Gordon, & Kannel, 1980). Moreover, researchers have estimated that a 10 percent reduction in body weight results in a 20 percent reduction in the risk of developing coronary heart disease (Ashley & Kannel, 1974).

A second argument in favor of obesity treatment centers around the adverse psychological consequences experienced by the overweight person. Many obese people experience social discrimination and psychological distress as a direct consequence of their weight. Our culture's emphasis on slimness and prejudice against obesity exacerbate the disdain that overweight people have for their own physical appearance (Stunkard, 1976). Indeed, many obese people hate their bodies, and body image disparagement serves as an ongoing source of distress that prompts many to seek professional help in losing weight. Weight loss is associated with positive psychological changes, including improvements in self-esteem and self-confidence (Wadden & Stunkard, 1985).

Because arguments can be made both for and against the treatment of obesity, how should the clinician proceed when faced with a particular person seeking treatment? First, the clinician must be aware that obesity is a complex phenomenon with multiple interactive determinants. Genetic, physiological, social, cultural, and behavioral factors combine to cause the development and maintenance of obesity. Few of these factors are accessible to intervention, but all must be appreciated if the clinician is to have an informed view of the prospects for successful treatment. Let us consider briefly the contribution of some biological factors in the development and maintenance of obesity.

Recent research studies of adoptees and twins have elucidated the role that genetic predisposition plays in the development of obesity. The weights of adopted children tend to correspond more closely to the weights of their biological parents than to those of their adoptive parents (e.g., Stunkard, Sorensen et al., 1986). Studies of twins also show that the concordance rates for the development of obesity may be twice as high for monozygotic than for dizygotic twins (Stunkard, Foch, & Hrubec, 1986). Thus there appears to be a strong genetic predisposition to the development of obesity.

Studies of individuals attempting either to lose or gain weight indicate that it is exceedingly difficult to induce significant long-term changes in body weight (e.g., Keys, 1950; Sims, 1976). A variety of physiological mechanisms appear to counteract efforts at weight change. A number of researchers (e.g., Keesey, 1986) have suggested that each person has a biologically determined *natural* or *set point weight* that the body acts to defend. Efforts to change body weight are resisted by homeostatic mechanisms that maintain the set point weight. Many obese individuals may have a natural weight that is set at a point higher than the culturally determined ideal weight. Consequently, when they attempt to lose weight, they encounter physiological resistance.

The number and size of one's fat cells determine whether a person is obese. For the most part, the number of fat cells accumulated stabilizes before adulthood. Thereafter, excess caloric intake generally results in increased fat cell size. For some obese individuals, however, periods of excessive caloric intake can trigger the development of new fat cells. Fat cell multiplication is an irreversible process; fat cells can be shrunk but not lost. When, as a result of dieting, fat cells reach normal size or smaller, weight reduction seems to become exceedingly difficult (Bjorntorp, 1986). This effect may be due to the triggering of physiological mechanisms seeking to return the body to its set point weight. The problem for many obese individuals may be that, even though the size of their cells has been decreased to the normal range, they remain obese because of the excessive numbers of fat cells. Moreover, repeated cycles of weight loss and weight gain can result in an increased proportion of body fat, thereby further diminishing the chances of successful weight loss. Clearly, the impact of biological and physiological factors must be taken into account in treating the obese client. The clinician must recognize the existence of *multiple* biological determinants of obesity. In conceptualizing obesity from a biobehavioral perspective, the clinician can approach treatment with an appreciation of the difficulties inherent in any effort to alter body weight (Brownell & Foreyt, 1985).

Although multiple biological factors contribute to obesity, the final common pathway to its development, maintenance, and modification is ultimately behavioral. It is the behavioral act of eating that determines the amount of energy available to the body to either use or store. The question of whether the obese consume more than the non-obese is a complex issue that has not been addressed adequately in the research literature (Thompson, Jarvie, Lahey, & Cureton, 1982). Cross-sectional studies have yielded conflicting findings. Some studies indicate that the obese consume more than the non-obese; others do not (Braitman, Alden, & Stanton, 1985). It may be that excessive intake during particular developmental periods leads to an excess accumulation of fat cells, which in turn leads to a higher set point weight at a later stage in life.

The behavioral contribution to obesity is seen in terms of energy expenditure as well as consumption. The available evidence suggests that obese individuals are less physically active than the non-obese (Thompson et al., 1982). Although it is not possible to determine whether this reduced activity is a cause or a consequence of their obesity, this fact does suggest a role for physical activity in the management of obesity.

During the 1960s and 1970s, early behavioral and social psychological formulations pointed to an obese eating style and suggested that the obese person was more responsive to external cues for eating and less responsive to internal cues of hunger. We now know that this is not necessarily true (Rodin, 1981). We have learned, however, that social learning principles can be used effectively to help clients change their eating and exercise habits and lose weight.

The clinical utility of behavior therapy for obesity has been the subject of scientific scrutiny in several reviews over the past 5 years (Bennett, 1986; Brownell & Wadden, 1986; Foreyt, 1987; Jeffery, 1987). The consensus of these reviews is that (a) behavior therapy is superior to alternative treatments for mild obesity, (b) behavior therapy may or may not be potent enough to accomplish meaningful amounts of weight loss in the moderately obese client, and (c) the problem of maintenance must be addressed to improve the long-term effectiveness of behavior therapy for obesity.

Orienting Clients about Obesity and Its Treatment

Once the multiple determinants of obesity and the limitations of behavior therapy as a treatment for obesity have been clarified, how does the clinician use this information in dealing with a prospective client seeking treatment for obesity? Consider the following situation: It is early September, and a prospective client telephones inquiring about treatment for obesity.

> Client: I understand that you treat people who want to lose weight.

> Therapist: That's correct.

> Client: When can I start?

> Therapist: Right now, there is a waiting list for our clinic. Over the next 2 months, we will be evaluating people on the waiting list to determine if our program is appropriate to their needs. For those people we feel we can help, we expect to begin treatment in January.

Client: January! Are you kidding? I have my 25th high
        school reunion coming up. I need to lose 40
        pounds by November 1, or I won't be able to fit into
        the dress I plan to wear. Isn't there any way I could
        start sooner?

This conversation is not an uncommon one. It illustrates several typical aspects of many clients seeking treatment for obesity. They want immediate help, and they are concerned with achieving a quick loss. They certainly do not anticipate the need for an assessment to determine whether they are appropriate candidates for treatment. This brief conversation also underscores the importance of conducting an orientation session for clients seeking treatment for obesity.

The goals of an obesity orientation session are diverse. First, it provides an opportunity for the clinician to inhibit the *dieting response*. Too often, clients approach therapy and weight loss treatment in a mindless manner. For some, an immediate goal (e.g., an upcoming party) provides an incentive to try to lose weight, and they respond with old habits (e.g., going on a diet). In an orientation session, the therapist asks the client to take a step back to get a view of the "big picture" regarding obesity and its treatment. Clients are asked to consider the personal costs and benefits associated with a weight loss effort before committing themselves to treatment.

During an orientation session, the therapist acknowledges the distress experienced by the obese client. It is important to the development of a therapeutic relationship that the therapist convey to the client an understanding of the personal dissatisfaction associated with being a fat person in a culture that idolizes the slim. An orientation session gives the clinician an opportunity to demonstrate an empathetic understanding of the personal disappointment that accompanies repeated dieting failures and what the experience of having a weight problem is like for the obese individual.

The orientation session also permits the clinician to provide the prospective client with a sophisticated understanding of obesity. Clients need to know that it is not simply a matter of "being born fat" or "lacking willpower" that has caused them to become obese. An overview of obesity can be offered to educate the client about the contributions of both biological and behavioral factors in the development and treatment of obesity. The various approaches to weight loss can be discussed, and the desirability of matching clients to certain treatments can be highlighted. A realistic assessment of the chances of successful treatment for obesity can be described in general terms and also with reference to the particular client's chances of success.

The orientation session can be used to discuss the issues of commitment and motivation, especially the importance of a long-term commitment to behavior change and the necessity of sustaining motivation through times of difficulty. The use of a *stages of change model* can be particularly helpful in this regard (Prochaska & DiClemente, 1986). Clients can see from their own experience how their motivation for change varies during the stages of precontemplation, contemplation, action, maintenance, and relapse.

A further issue for the orientation session is the expectation of what the process of therapy is going to be like. Clients need an orientation to their role in behavioral treatment, namely, that of an active participant in the therapeutic process. The therapist can provide an overview of the specific activities expected of the client (e.g., the completion of written self-monitoring records, the establishment of a daily exercise program, etc.).

From a problem-solving perspective, the clinician can present the prospective patient with a constructive orientation to the problem of obesity. This orientation involves accepting problems, including obesity, as a normal part of living. Adopting this cognitive set helps obese individuals reject the belief that obesity is proof that they are personally deficient and minimizes the emotional reactivity associated with the problem. Also involved is the belief that one has the ability to cope with problems effectively. This is not to imply the unrealistic expectation that the obesity can be "cured," but rather to suggest that, regardless of the eventual outcome in terms of pounds lost, the individual is capable of initiating and implementing effective alternatives. The clinician can label the distress experienced by the patient as a signal that a problem exists and needs attention. Finally, it is important for both client and therapist to adopt realistic expectations concerning treatment and to recognize that time and effort are necessary for success.

At the end of an orientation session, the therapist asks the client not to make an immediate decision about undertaking a weight loss effort. Instead, the clinician suggests that the client take some time, usually a week or two, to consider the various factors reviewed in the orientation session in deciding whether the time is right to initiate a weight loss effort.

Screening and Assessing Clients for Treatment

If the client decides to pursue obesity treatment, how does the clinician decide whether the individual is an appropriate candidate for behavior therapy? There are few reliable indicators to predict outcome in obesity treatment or to match treatment to patient variables. Let us consider several factors that may promote effective decision making.

Severity of Obesity

The degree of obesity is an important consideration in deciding whether to accept a patient for behavioral treatment. The chance of a successful outcome with behavioral treatment is inversely related to the individual's degree of obesity. For the mildly obese individual, behavior therapy is clearly the treatment of choice. Not every mildly obese person will be successful in behavioral treatment, but this approach typically produces weight losses of sufficient magnitude to return the mildly obese person to the normal range for height and sex. For the moderately obese person, behavior therapy alone may or may not be sufficiently powerful to produce a clinically significant amount of weight loss, but it is certainly worth a try. For the severely obese client, there is little evidence that behavior therapy alone can be helpful. Very few treatments appear to be effective for such individuals. Alternatives that might be considered include (a) behavior therapy combined with a very low calorie diet, (b) surgery (e.g., "stomach stapling"), or (c) therapy aimed at helping patients accept their obesity.

Results of Prior Weight Loss Attempts

The number of unsuccessful previous efforts at weight reduction is negatively correlated with a successful response to treatment. The prognosis is less favorable for individuals who have an extensive history of failures in weight reduction and maintenance. With a severely obese individual who has been unsuccessful with a wide variety of treatments, serious consideration should be given to not attempting weight loss as a treatment objective. For the mildly or moderately obese individual with a history of unsuccessful responses to behavior therapy for obesity, there is little reason to expect success from a repeated effort with the same treatment approach.

Current Reasons for Wanting to Lose Weight

Especially important in terms of reasons for weight loss is whether the individual is motivated by a short-term incentive such as losing weight for a party or a long-term goal such as improving health. The problem with short-term motivating events is that the successful treatment of obesity requires long-term motivation. Consider the client whose dieting was motivated by her upcoming high school reunion. What will happen to her motivation to sustain the weight loss effort when the social event has come and gone? From clinical experience, it appears that more appropriate motivators for weight loss are long-term concerns. In addition, clients whose motivation stems from self-concern rather than solely the concern of others (e.g., spouse or physician) are likely to be more committed to making treatment a success. When the client's motivation is tied too closely to a specific short-term incentive or to external motivation, the therapist may wish to consider delaying the start of obesity treatment until such issues have been adequately addressed and the client has been appropriately oriented.

Current Commitment

The key issue here is how committed clients are to the prospective weight loss effort. It is important to determine whether they are committed to participate actively by adhering to treatment recommendations in both the short and long run. With regard to the short run, a behavioral test of commitment to treatment can be undertaken by assessing how well clients adhere to a treatment assignment over an initial 2-week period. In some programs, clients are required to demonstrate their commitment by completing self-monitoring records and by demonstrating a weight loss during a 2-week trial period (Brownell & Foreyt, 1985). Longer term commitment is more difficult to determine. One approach is to ask prospective clients to post a sum of money to be refunded in the future contingent upon attendance at treatment and follow-up sessions scheduled over a 2-year period. If clients are not willing to back up their long-term commitment to treatment by agreeing to a deposit-refund contract, it is unlikely that they are sufficiently committed to persist with treatment over the long haul.

Expectations Regarding Weight Loss Treatment

Clients' expectations regarding weight loss are often influenced by advertisements for commercial weight loss products and programs. Slogans such as "thirty pounds in 30 days" and "the easy way to lose all the weight you want to lose" fulfill the obese person's desire to lose a large amount of weight, to lose it quickly, and to lose it without effort. Thus it is important to assess the amount of weight prospective clients expect to lose, their anticipated rate of weight loss, and the degree of effort they expect to expend. For behavioral treatment, weight losses of 20 to 30 pounds accomplished at a rate of about 1 pound per week typify the modal responses of mildly and moderately obese clients. In addition, some clients have unrealistic expectations about the impact that losing weight will have on their lives. For example, some believe that losing weight will help them change their social situation dramatically. They expect to be showered with invitations to parties and social events. When they lose weight and the expected changes in their social lives do not occur, they may be disappointed and lose motivation to sustain the weight loss endeavor. Clearly, the therapist should assess clients' outcome expectations regarding weight loss and its anticipated impact on their lives.

Current Physical and Mental Health

Medical contraindications to weight loss need to be ruled out before the initiation of any treatment; prospective clients should obtain medical clearance from their physicians before participating in treatment for obesity. For a client with less than a "clean bill of health," the ongoing involvement of a physician in the treatment process may be required. For clients with psychiatric disorders requiring psychotropic medication, special consideration is needed, particularly if their medication is associated with weight gain. In such cases, stabilization of weight (i.e., preventing additional weight gain) may be a more appropriate goal than weight loss. Moreover, it may be detrimental to these clients to have them participate in a group treatment program in which the other group members find it far easier to lose weight. In such instances, it may be worthwhile to use an individual treatment approach or to refer individuals to a weight loss group designed to meet the special needs of patients on psychotropic medication.

Education

A final consideration in screening patients for obesity treatment is educational background in general and reading level in particular. Most behavioral treatment programs require clients to complete ongoing, detailed written self-monitoring records of their eating and exercise, as well as sundry other homework assignments that require reading and writing skills (e.g., food plans, shopping lists, etc.). Consequently, it is important that clients possess at a minimum eighth-grade reading and writing skills. In our program, a limited number of attempts have been made without success to tailor treatment to non-literate clients.

Additional Assessment Procedures

Following an initial orientation and screening, an additional assessment can be carried out to get a fuller picture of the relevant aspects of the client's eating and exercise behavior, as well as other psychological variables that might be pertinent to defining the clinical picture and formulating goals for treatment. When the patient returns and indicates a willingness to initiate treatment, the therapist can use a baseline assessment of the client's eating and exercise behaviors. This assessment also provides a means of cutting therapy short if initial results indicate that behavioral treatment is unlikely to succeed.

During the baseline period, patients can be asked to complete a food diary as part of a comprehensive functional analysis of their eating behavior. Failure to implement this strategy should be interpreted as a warning to reexamine their motivation and commitment to weight loss. When patients fail to complete adequate food records, the therapist should attempt to identify the source of this problem and to use the clinical decision-making model as a means of resolving it. Failing that, serious consideration should be given to terminating treatment.

In addition to the functional analysis of eating, a number of self-report instruments can be used to provide a fuller description of the client's eating behaviors and general psychological state. The Master Questionnaire (Straw et al., 1984) is one of the few instruments designed specifically to tap into variables of direct relevance to the behavioral treatment of obesity. Other instruments that may provide relevant information include two scales that are eating related and several measures that provide more global information about the psychological state of the client. The Restraint Scale (Herman & Mack, 1975) and the Binge Eating Scale (Hawkins & Clement, 1980) can provide the therapist with important information about the client's approach to eating and dieting. These instruments are particularly helpful in identifying those obese clients who are binge eaters. Other instruments worth including in an initial assessment are the Beck Depression Inventory (Beck, Ward, Mendelsohn, Mock, & Erbaugh, 1961), the State-Trait Anxiety Inventory (Spielberger, Gorsuch, & Lushene, 1979), and the Symptoms Checklist (SCL-90; Derogatis, Lipman, & Covi, 1973). These instruments provide information about distress experienced by the client and may be helpful in suggesting additional target problems to be addressed in treatment.

Treatment Options

Following the screening and assessment, the clinician and client can collaboratively consider which treatment alternatives best suit the client's needs at that particular time. In making these choices, several client-related variables need to be considered, such as motivation for change, degree of obesity, and the presence of additional addictive or psychological problems. The costs (both financial and time related) of treatment also need to be evaluated. Some of the options that are currently available are discussed in the following pages.

Weight Loss without Professional Help

We are all aware of particular individuals who have lost significant amounts of weight on their own and have maintained that weight loss for many years. Indeed, some psychologists (e.g., Schachter, 1982) believe that most people who are overweight are able to lose weight successfully on their own. When should prospective clients be encouraged to attempt weight loss without professional help? There are two circumstances in which this option might be considered. First, when clients are overweight but not obese (i.e., 10 to 19 percent over ideal body weight) and have not attempted on their own to lose weight, this option may be a viable one to consider before recommending professional help. A second instance is when clients are clinically obese but extraneous factors make professional treatment difficult to arrange (financial constraints, scheduling problems, etc.). In each of these situations, clients might be advised about appropriate self-help books related to weight loss. A follow-up appointment might be scheduled for a later date to determine the outcome of the self-control effort and to decide whether other alternatives need to be considered.

Commercial Weight Loss Programs

If the two criteria noted for self-directed efforts are met, commercial weight loss programs may also offer a viable treatment alternative. However, the therapist should caution the client to exercise care in selecting a commercial program. In particular, the client will want to do some homework to determine the program's approach to weight loss, the qualifications of the treatment providers, the costs involved, and the track record of the program.

Behavior Therapy for Obesity

In behavioral treatment, participants are taught to modify their eating and exercise habits to produce a negative energy balance and weight loss. The typical program consists of a sequence of behavioral tasks, including (a) daily self-monitoring of information related to eating (e.g., food content, calories, etc.), (b) making salient those activities that might inhibit the urge to eat, (c) using appropriate stimulus control by eating only at predetermined times and places, (d) slowing the pace of eating, (e) daily graphing of progress toward weight loss goals, (f) using self-reinforcement contingent upon successful application of program strategies, and (g) using cognitive restructuring techniques to minimize negative thoughts that interfere with weight loss progress. In addition, nutritional counseling and the development of an exercise regimen are also typically included. A variety of books and manuals are available describing the details of behavioral treatment (e.g., Brownell, 1987; Ferguson, 1976; Johnson & Stalonas, 1981; Mahoney & Mahoney, 1976; Stuart & Davis, 1972). Behavior therapy is the treatment of choice for mildly obese clients; it may also be appropriate for those moderately obese clients who do not have extensive histories of unsuccessful response to conservative treatments.

Behavior Therapy Plus Very Low Calorie Diet

The combination of behavior therapy plus modified fasting using very low calorie diets (e.g., 400 calories per day) increases the magnitude of initial weight loss accomplished in treatment (Wadden & Stunkard, 1986). This powerful treatment modality is probably most appropriate for moderately obese individuals who have been unsuccessful with conservative treatment approaches. It may also be an approach worth considering for some severely obese clients who are highly motivated to pursue a dietary approach to weight loss. Very low calorie diets are powerful interventions with potentially serious side effects (e.g., orthostatic hypotension and cardiac arrythmia). Consequently, this approach should only be used under close medical supervision.

Surgery

For the severely obese person who has been unsuccessful at losing weight in repeated efforts involving alternative approaches, surgery is an option that may be worth considering. Intestinal (jejunoileal) bypass surgery has been abandoned in favor of the safer and less drastic approaches of gastric bypass and partitioning procedures (Mason, 1981). These latter approaches (colloquially referred to as "stomach stapling") involve a reduction in the size of the stomach. Weight losses may be considerable (e.g., 40 to 60 pounds), but often patients suffer side effects such as chronic nausea, and they need to adjust to eating small meals or risk stretching the stomach and undoing the effects of surgery. Therefore, it is crucial that prospective candidates be fully aware of the risks and negative side effects associated with surgery. Moreover, they should be motivated by realistic expectations about the impact that this intervention will have on their lives.

Psychotherapy or Behavior Therapy for Other Problems

In some instances, at the conclusion of the assessment, the therapist determines that a higher priority problem than obesity exists. Treatment for such issues is appropriate when clients note that they would like to deal with smoking or drinking problems. Because both smoking and alcohol abuse generally pose a greater risk to clients than obesity, it is reasonable to deal with them first and postpone treatment for obesity. Therapists will want to discuss this alternative with their individual clients before recommending a specific course of action. Depending on their expertise, clinicians may wish to provide treatment for this other problem or make a referral to another professional to provide the treatment.

Simultaneous Treatment for Obesity and Other Problems

Other complaints that are sometimes presented by obese clients are depression and marital conflict. In such cases, it may be appropriate for clients to receive treatment for several problems simultaneously. This decision can be based on both the opinion of the therapist and the preference of the client. For clients who are in marital counseling or individual therapy for depression, treatment for obesity can be undertaken in a complementary manner.

No Treatment or Postponement of Treatment

In some cases, it may be appropriate to postpone or simply not attempt treatment for obesity. If the client is not appropriately motivated or committed, or if the scheduling or timing is not right, the therapist may wish to suggest postponing treatment rather than start an intervention with a low chance of success. Asking the client to return at a future time for reevaluation may be worthwhile.

Initial Clinical Decisions

Once therapists decide to undertake behavior therapy for obesity, they must make a number of clinical decisions regarding implementation. Some of the more salient of these are discussed as follows.

Individual versus Group Therapy

In the only controlled study to examine the comparative effectiveness of individual versus group therapy for obesity, Kingsley and Wilson (1977) found the two approaches to be equivalent at the end of an 8-week treatment phase, but the group approach resulted in better maintenance of weight loss at a 6-month follow-up. Although limited by the brevity of initial treatment (8 weeks), these findings suggest that the social support clients receive in the group format may result in better maintenance of habit changes and weight loss achieved in treatment. In addition to providing the support and encouragement of group members, the group treatment approach may serve to normalize the individuals' perceptions of their weight problem by providing exposure to other people who are struggling with similar issues. Moreover, other group members may serve as coping models, thereby providing the client with an opportunity for observational learning not available in individual therapy. The group may also facilitate problem solving by generating a greater range of creative coping alternatives. An additional advantage of the group approach is its lower cost to the patient.

There are a number of circumstances in which individual therapy may be the preferred treatment modality for obesity. First, some clients simply prefer to be seen individually rather than in groups. Second, a sufficient number of obese clients may not be available at a particular point for a therapist to offer the option of group therapy. Third, when target problems in addition to obesity (e.g., depression) need to be addressed, individual therapy may be the preferred treatment. Finally, group treatment may not be suitable for some clients; individuals who are overly disruptive, domineering, or aggressive in the group context should be seen individually so that they do not have a negative impact on other group members.

Standardized versus Individualized Treatment Presentation

Behavior therapy for obesity is often presented in a standardized fashion wherein a variety of self-management strategies are offered in a fixed sequence over the course of a predetermined number of sessions. This approach is usually associated with a group therapy format, but it may also be used in individual therapy. The advantages of the standardized format include (a) the availability of treatment manuals outlining therapeutic procedures with empirically documented utility, (b) the opportunity to expose clients to a wide variety of techniques for modifying eating and exercise behavior, and (c) the availability of an organized and logical sequence for presenting the various techniques of treatment. In addition, the use of a standardized format creates an expectation (or demand) that during each week of treatment clients will implement a change in their eating or exercise behavior. The accomplishment of such changes provides an opportunity to reinforce their progress.

The major disadvantage of the standardized approach is that it may not provide an opportunity to tailor treatment to the needs of a particular client. The individualized format, in contrast, permits the therapist to select those specific treatment procedures that are relevant to a particular client. For example, most standardized behavioral programs typically include one or more sessions devoted to teaching clients how to slow the pace of their eating, but not all clients have a problem with eating too quickly. In an individualized approach, information gathered from an assessment of the client's particular eating pattern can be used to focus on those targets that are pertinent to a given client and to exclude those that are not. Moreover, the individualized approach allows the client and therapist to address target problems not typically covered in standardized treatments (e.g., depression, marital problems, etc.). A final advantage of the individualized approach is that it permits new treatment procedures to be presented at a pace that matches the client's progress. The introduction of new self-management strategies can be slowed until the client has demonstrated mastery of the behavioral techniques covered earlier in therapy.

There is no research available to help the therapist choose between a standardized and an individualized treatment format. It would appear, however, that the individualized approach is best suited to clients who have previously dropped out or have been unsuccessful in weight loss programs using a standardized format. The standardized approach, on the other hand, may be an efficient method for treating uncomplicated cases in which the client is new to treatment.

Length of Treatment

The treatment of obesity may be conceptualized as consisting of three phases: (a) an initial intervention aimed at producing weight loss through changes in clients' eating and exercise habits, (b) a maintenance period aimed at teaching clients how to maintain habit changes and weight loss and how to cope with the problem of relapse, and (c) a follow-up phase in which clients are on their own but can easily get help if significant difficulties arise or a relapse occurs. Let us consider some issues relevant to the length of each treatment phase.

In a recent review article, Bennett (1986) analyzed the results of 105 studies of behavioral treatment for obesity and found that duration of treatment was the single factor most highly correlated with success. Experimental studies also indicate that the longer clients are in treatment, the longer they adhere to the behaviors necessary for weight loss (Perri, Nezu, Patti, & McCann, in press). In deciding on the length of the initial intervention, two factors are worth considering. The first consideration is the client's degree of obesity. Since weekly rates of weight loss in behavior therapy usually range from 1.0 to 1.5 pounds, it is clear that the typical 20-week program is best suited to the mildly obese client. Moderately obese individuals may need treatment that extends for as long as 50 or more weekly sessions. A second consideration is the client's response to treatment. If it becomes clear that the client's rate of weight loss is either slower or faster than the usual rate, the length of the initial intervention can be adjusted accordingly. Moreover, if initial treatment is not successful, the therapist and client should explore alternative treatment options (such as those described previously) rather than proceed with a treatment that is producing little or no benefit.

There is little research on the relation of maintenance program length to long-term weight loss progress. However, several studies have documented that providing clients with a year-long maintenance program consisting of biweekly contacts can help them maintain habit change and weight loss (e.g., Perri et al., 1988). Therefore, in planning treatment, the therapist can explain to the client that the chances of long-term success will be increased if the initial treatment is of sufficient length to allow meaningful weight loss and if it is followed by a maintenance program of a year or more to help sustain weight losses over the long run. No research study has formally addressed the issue of follow-up care beyond a maintenance phase in the treatment of obesity. Nonetheless, clients should be assured that help will be available to them should problems arise after the maintenance period.

Common Problems in Treatment Implementation

Almost inevitably, problems will arise during the course of behavior therapy for obesity. These problems may range from common difficulties, such as temporary plateaus in weight loss, to more serious issues, such as the occurrence of binge eating episodes and depression. The general strategy for dealing with the various difficulties is to use a problem-solving approach for coping with and overcoming obstacles to progress. Both client and therapist should view the occurrence of problems as an expected and manageable part of the treatment process. Together, they should work to recognize problems and potential obstacles. When such difficulties arise, the therapist and client should collaborate to define them carefully, generate a variety of potential solutions, decide upon a course of action, implement it, and determine whether improvement occurs. Listed in the following discussion are some common difficulties that are often encountered in the behavioral treatment of obesity. Also noted are some suggestions that therapists might consider in attempting to overcome these difficulties.

Attrition and Poor Attendance

It is quite common for obese individuals to begin a weight loss program and drop out prematurely. Research on commercial and self-help weight programs indicates that 50 to 70 percent of those who begin such programs typically drop out of treatment within 12 weeks (Volkmar, Stunkard, & Woolston, 1981). One of the major advantages of behavioral treatment is that attrition rates are relatively low. For example, in a series of long-term behavioral treatment studies (Perri, 1987), the attrition rate during an initial 20 weeks of behavioral treatment was approximately 20 percent, with an additional 10 percent dropping out over 18-month maintenance and follow-up periods. Thus more than two-thirds of obese individuals who begin behavioral treatment can be expected to complete participation over a 2-year period. The use of a deposit-refund system appears to account for the lower attrition rates of behavioral treatments versus commercial and self-help programs. Requiring participants to post a sum of money (e.g., $100) to be refunded contingent upon their attendance provides an incentive for clients to stay in treatment and discourages individuals who are not seriously motivated from starting treatment. (The deposit-refund system is also commonly used to reinforce adherence to treatment strategies as well as attendance at therapy sessions.)

A problem closely related to attrition is poor attendance at treatment sessions. Clients who frequently miss treatment sessions are at a high risk of dropping out of treatment, and it is rare that they are successful in treatment. Often, when clients miss treatment sessions, they use the time between sessions as a "holiday" from adherence. Frequently, they neglect to implement treatment strategies such as completing food diaries, and they revert to old eating patterns. It is not uncommon for them to gain weight and experience a dissonance reaction that disposes them to drop out of treatment. For example, they may say to themselves, "If I'm not going to the treatment sessions, if I'm not following treatment recommendations, and if I'm not losing weight, then I must not be serious about losing weight. If I'm not serious about losing weight, there's no use in my continuing in the treatment program." This line of thinking is then reinforced by anticipated relief from the embarrassment of having to face the therapist to explain the inconsistency of being in obesity treatment and at the same time gaining weight.

To deal with the problem of poor attendance, it is essential that at the start of treatment the therapist emphasize the importance of clients' making weight loss a high priority in their lives and committing themselves to attending all treatment sessions except in the case of emergencies. The therapist in turn must work aggressively to ensure frequent therapeutic contacts (i.e., one per week) during the initial treatment period. If clients know in advance that they will not be present at a particular session, the therapist should schedule an alternative time to prevent a 2-week interval between sessions. During initial treatment, 2 weeks is a long period of time, and the longer the interval between sessions, the greater the chances that clients will experience a problem in adherence. It is often useful to have a policy agreed upon in advance for dealing with missed sessions. Further, missed sessions should be made up as soon as possible. Occasionally, a weigh-in and a 5-minute check of progress can be used in place of a full-length session. The general strategy here is to give clients every opportunity to do well in treatment. The aggressive approach to attendance reinforces the high levels of commitment and motivation needed to make obesity treatment successful. If attendance problems persist, the therapist may need to apply the decision-making model vigorously to identify and resolve the underlying difficulties.

Poor Adherence

Adherence problems in obesity treatment can take a variety of forms. In some instances, clients are reluctant to give up old habits to try new behaviors that may seem at first uncomfortable or difficult to implement. In other instances, clients are able to initiate changes in their behavior but have difficulty maintaining the changes over time. Problem-solving training offers one of the best therapeutic strategies for dealing with adherence problems. Empirical support of its effectiveness has been documented in several obesity treatment studies (Black, 1987; Black & Sherba, 1983; Black & Threlfall, 1986; Perri et al., 1987, 1988).

In using problem solving to deal with adherence difficulties, the therapist engages the client as a collaborator in a structured effort to determine the nature of the difficulty, to generate creative solutions, and to decide upon a course of action. Often, the client will report an adherence problem at the outset of a session, but there may not be time to conduct an exhaustive assessment of the problem before the therapist must decide what to do. Thus it is important for the therapist to be prepared to conduct a relatively quick assessment of the key aspects of the adherence difficulty.

An initial issue for the therapist to consider is whether the problem is one of acquisition or maintenance. If clients have not been able to initiate a new behavior, the therapist must determine whether the problem lies in their expectancies regarding efficacy, outcome, or both.

Specifically, do they believe that they have the skill to accomplish the recommended behavioral change? If not, then the therapist needs to simplify the task into smaller behavioral changes that clients can be sure to accomplish. If clients believe they are capable of the change, the problem may lie in outcome expectancies. Clients may think they have the ability to change the behavior in question but may expect that the change will not have a positive impact on their weight problem (or will have a negative impact on some other aspect of life). In this case, the therapist's job is to conduct a cost-benefit analysis anticipating the likely consequences for staying the same versus changing.

Often, it is helpful to conclude each problem-solving effort by having the client and therapist negotiate a short-term (i.e., 1- or 2-week) contract regarding implementation of the decided-upon course of action. The client specifies the particular changes she will initiate over the course of the following week(s) and, together with the therapist, determines an operational definition of success. In some instances, a contingency contract can be used wherein the client agrees that part of a monetary deposit will be returned upon accomplishment of the behavioral change identified in the contract. Often, the simple use of a single dollar can be quite powerful. (It is not the monetary factor that holds the reinforcing power; rather, it is the dollar as a symbol of accomplishment that the client will work to achieve.) One caveat regarding the use of contracts is worth noting, however. A contract should not be forced. Instead, it should be a mutually agreed-upon procedure for helping to accomplish desired goals.

Good Adherence but Slow or No Weight Loss

In considering whether a client's rate of weight loss is too slow, the therapist needs to take into account the client's weight, the change in weight over a 2-week period, and caloric intake during that same interval. Several guidelines may be helpful as well. First, in our clinic we have observed that a self-reported daily consumption of 10 calories for each pound of body weight generally balances our average client's energy equation (i.e., results in neither a gain nor loss of weight). Thus a moderately obese 200-pound person stays the same weight at a daily intake of 2,000 calories. Since a loss of 1 pound requires a deficit of 3,500 calories, if the client reduces daily intake by 500 calories, a weight loss of 1 pound per week should occur. One week, however, is generally too brief an interval to obtain a reliable indication of weight change. A 2-week period is a preferable period for assessing weight change. If there is slow or no weight loss over this 2-week interval, a careful check should be made of the individual's self-monitoring data regarding adherence in general and caloric restriction in particular. If the self-monitoring data indicate good adherence to the behavioral strategies, then it is necessary to look more closely at the client's energy balance. First of all, are the calorie estimates accurate? A spot check by the therapist of caloric totals listed for particular foods eaten can sometimes unveil mistakes not evident to the client. In some cases, it may be helpful to recommend that the client weigh and measure foods (for a limited period of time) to improve the accuracy of calorie estimates. In addition, it may be helpful to examine the content of the client's nutritional intake, particularly if caloric intake from fats is excessive (i.e., greater than 30 percent of the total). Appropriate cuts in this regard can be taken; nutritional guidelines such as those provided in the American Diabetes Association's (1986) exchange plan may be of help to the client.

If the client's adherence is good and the therapist is confident in the accuracy of the caloric intake records, it may be that the client has an overly efficient metabolism (i.e., fewer than 10 calories per pound of body weight may balance the client's energy equation). Most moderately obese women can lose a pound per week by adhering to an intake of 1,200 to 1,300 calories per day (for men, 1,500 to 1,600 calories per day). If the client with a slow rate of weight loss is consuming more than this amount, the therapist can suggest cutting down to get into this range. If reliable eating records indicate that caloric consumption is already in this range, it is important to consider a short-term contract for *plateau breaking*. This strategy consists of three tactics to be implemented rigorously over a 2-week period: (a) exercising (walking or stationary cycling) at least 30 minutes every day, (b) limiting caloric intake to 1,000 calories per day, and (c) minimizing fat intake to no more than 25 percent of total calories consumed. It is rare for a moderately obese client to follow this approach and not lose weight. Moreover, the experience of losing weight serves to reinforce the client's adherence to a program of regular exercise combined with a low-fat, low-calorie intake.

Binge Eating

Binge eating appears to be a common problem among obese clients. Estimates of its prevalence range from 20 to 46 percent (Marcus & Wing, 1987). Binge eating is seen most often in individuals who inhibit their eating severely through dietary restraint. Such individuals are also more likely to suffer emotional distress, and, although their initial response to treatment may be similar to that of obese clients who do not binge, those who do are more likely to relapse during follow-up (Gormally, Rardin, & Black, 1980). During initial treatment, clients who are binge eaters frequently set unrealistically low limits on their caloric intake. Often, they report that they have been successful in the past by sticking to diets as low as 500 or 600 calories per day. It is important that such clients learn that, in setting such severe caloric restrictions, they are placing themselves in a state of *deprivation*, are likely to experience depressed affect, and are setting themselves up for disinhibition of their self-restraint over food. This cycle of dietary restraint, disinhibition, and depressed affect decreases the chances of achieving lasting weight loss. In working with such clients, it is important for the therapist to get them to preplan enough calories in their daily diet so that they are less likely to feel deprived. It is also helpful for them to analyze personal high-risk situations—those circumstances in which they are likely to binge. For each identified situation, the therapist can help clients generate a range of alternatives aimed at avoiding the high-risk situation or developing new responses to cope effectively in the situation without binge eating.

Intrusion of Emotional Distress

It has often been observed that dieting is accompanied by negative emotional reactions, including anxiety, depression, and irritability (Stunkard & Rush, 1974). Some researchers have speculated that this reaction is associated with efforts to maintain the body at a weight below its natural or biologically determined set point (Wadden & Stunkard, 1985). The magnitude of the negative emotional side effects of dieting may be related to the degree of caloric restriction. Negative emotional reactions generally appear to be less of a problem during behavior therapy in which clients typically consume 1,000 or more calories per day. Nonetheless, clients often report that negative emotions are obstacles to their weight loss progress. Feelings of anxiety and depression are common precipitants of overeating for many clients, even those for whom binge eating is not a usual pattern. Therefore, it is helpful for the therapist to be prepared to deal with these issues. For clients who report that they are nervous eaters (i.e., report that they eat when nervous, tense, or under stress), two strategies are often helpful: Either relaxation exercises (e.g., progressive muscle relaxation, meditation, etc.) or physical exercise can serve as substitute activities that can simultaneously lower emotional arousal and inhibit the urge to eat. For many obese clients, especially women, negative thoughts about body image serve as an ongoing source of emotional distress. Rational restructuring procedures can be used to help clients change dysfunctional or self-deprecating cognitions. For example, "I'm so fat that I'll never be able to lose this weight" can be changed to "I didn't put this weight on overnight, so I can't expect to take it off overnight—I know that it's going to take time and that gradual changes in weight are more likely to be lasting changes."

Designing a Maintenance Program and Follow-up Care

Getting clients to lose weight is only the first half of the battle in the long-term management of obesity. The second half of the battle involves equipping them to maintain their weight losses over the long run. Without a structured program, clients abandon behavioral techniques, experience relapses, and regain much of the weight they lost in treatment (Jeffery, 1987; Perri, 1987). In a review of recent behavioral treatments for obesity, Brownell and Wadden (1986) found that, during the year following treatment, clients on average regained 36 percent of the weight they lost in treatment. Moreover, studies with follow-ups of 3 to 5 years (Gotestam, 1979; Graham, Taylor, Hovell, & Siegel, 1983; Stalonas, Perri, & Kerzner, 1984) indicate that the majority of clients experience significant relapses toward pretreatment weight. The maintenance problem is clearly one of the most important issues in the behavioral treatment of obesity.

Few studies have evaluated specific methods for enhancing the durability of behavioral treatment effects. The most common weight loss maintenance strategy has been the use of *booster sessions*. The rationale for booster sessions is based on the notion that additional weight loss meetings scheduled during the follow-up period will increase adherence to treatment procedures. Although the use of boosters has intuitive appeal, empirical evidence of their effectiveness is largely negative (e.g., Ashby & Wilson, 1977; Beneke & Paulsen, 1979; Hall, Hall, Hanson, & Borden, 1974).

The traditional booster approach may have failed for two prominent reasons. First, the number of booster sessions typically used has been minimal; the use of only three or four additional meetings arbitrarily scheduled during the follow-up period may not provide clients with a sufficient amount of support and advice. Second, the content of booster sessions has generally been limited to a review of techniques already implemented in treatment. During the posttreatment period, patients may need greater amounts of advice and guidance, as well as training in skills specifically targeted to maintain the behavioral changes and weight loss accomplished in treatment. More promising findings have been obtained with multicomponent posttreatment programs that include intensive professional contact coupled with skills training directed toward the specific problem of relapse (Perri, 1987). Let us consider some of the strategies and techniques that can be used to enhance the long-term maintenance of weight loss and behavior change.

Frequent Therapist Contact

Chronic problems such as obesity may require multiple stages of treatment spanning very long periods of time. An increasing body of research indicates that maintenance of behavior change improves as contacts with professionals increase during the period following initial treatment (Brownell, Marlatt, Lichtenstein, & Wilson, 1986; Whisman, in press). When they begin a weight loss program, clients need to know that their chances of success will be enhanced by their long-term involvement in treatment. For many clients, simply knowing that continued contacts are planned may decrease their fears about being able to maintain their weight losses. As a result, they may experience an increase in self-efficacy. Moreover, continued contact with their therapists enables clients to consolidate the skills they have learned during initial treatment and extends the period of time over which they maintain vigilance and adhere to the behaviors necessary for weight loss (Bennett, 1986; Perri et al., 1988). Therefore, therapists should plan a high frequency of contacts during the maintenance phase. Scheduling sessions every other week over the course of a 1-year period has resulted in significant long-term weight loss progress in several studies (e.g., Perri et al., 1987, 1988). Posttreatment client-therapist contacts by mail and telephone have also proven beneficial to maintenance and may be viable alternative or adjunct strategies to in-person contacts (Perri, McAdoo, McAllister, Lauer, & Yancey, 1986; Perri, Shapiro, Ludwig, Twentyman, & McAdoo, 1984). Regardless of the mode, it is clear that frequent posttreatment contacts can enhance the maintenance of weight loss.

Social Support

Poor maintenance of treatment effects may be due in part to a decrease in motivation (or incentives) to sustain the behaviors necessary to continue weight loss (Bandura & Simon, 1977; Brehm & McAllister, 1980; Jeffery, 1985). After several months of restricted caloric intake, many obese clients experience a plateau in weight loss despite maintenance of low calorie intake (Bjorntorp et al., 1975). As they become aware of this exceedingly high cost-benefit ratio, clients may conclude that further progress is beyond their personal control. Consequently, they may experience a loss of motivation to sustain the weight loss endeavor, and they may resume a higher caloric intake at precisely the time when a slowed metabolic rate due to prolonged dieting predisposes them to a rapid regaining of weight (Garrow, 1986; Polivy & Herman, 1985). Several social support strategies have been successfully employed to enhance motivation and weight loss progress during the posttreatment period. For example, Perri and his colleagues (Perri et al., 1986) found that teaching clients how to use peer self-help groups as a maintenance strategy resulted in improved weight loss progress when compared with a control condition involving no further contact. Similarly, Perri et al. (1988) demonstrated the substantial benefits of a comprehensive social influence program that involved (a) instructing peers to reinforce short-term weight loss progress, (b) using a contract system that included financial incentives for maintaining habit changes and weight loss, and (c) having clients publicly model appropriate weight loss techniques. The results from these studies indicate that significant long-term benefits can be derived when the therapist devises a posttreatment program using social support. Thus, when conducting group treatments, the therapist might consider teaching group members how, as a peer self-help group, they might use social support as a maintenance strategy. When conducting individual treatment for weight loss, the therapist may also consider whether referral to programs such as Weight Watchers or Overeaters Anonymous might be a suitable means of providing the client with social support during the posttreatment period.

Relapse Prevention Training

Providing frequent therapist contacts and a high degree of social support may help clients to sustain the behavioral changes begun during the initial treatment period, but an effective maintenance program must also equip clients with a new set of abilities—the skills to anticipate, avoid, and cope with those circumstances that increase the risk of their experiencing a relapse (Marlatt & Gordon, 1985). Marlatt and colleagues' relapse prevention model provides the most comprehensive and conceptually sophisticated approach to understanding and dealing with the maintenance problem in addictive behaviors. Let us consider its applicability to an obese person who has successfully lost weight during therapy: Sometime after treatment, the person will face a situation in which he will be tempted to exceed a prescribed calorie goal or deviate from the techniques taught in treatment. If the individual does not have the skills to negotiate this high-risk situation, he may have a slip, or lapse in self-control. Moreover, if the individual interprets the lapse as evidence that he is a failure at self-control, he is likely to experience a sense of hopelessness and a decrease in self-efficacy. The initial slip becomes the start of a full-blown relapse. The individual then abandons the habits acquired in treatment, returns to previous eating patterns, and regains weight (Brownell et al., 1986). If, on the other hand, the person is equipped to face the high-risk situation with an effective coping response, he is likely to experience an increased sense of self-efficacy and to maintain the positive changes accomplished in treatment. Empirical support of the relapse prevention approach as an effective maintenance strategy has been demonstrated in several obesity treatment studies (Perri et al., 1984; Rosenthal & Marx, 1979).

Marlatt and Gordon (1985) have recommended several specific strategies to prevent or minimize relapse following treatment. First, clients need to be trained to recognize and identify those situations that pose a high risk for relapse. This goal can be accomplished by asking clients to review their self-monitoring records for specific situations in which they experienced lapses during the initial treatment period. Clients can also be asked to write autobiographical statements about past weight losses and the situations in which they experienced slips and relapses. Second, clients can receive instruction in treating high-risk situations as challenges to be negotiated. Toward this end, 5 to 10 maintenance sessions can be devoted to training clients in how to use problem solving as a means of generating coping strategies for high-risk situations. Third, clients need practice in coping with actual high-risk situations: During the course of the maintenance period, they will face a variety of challenging situations that can be used toward this end. Finally, clients need to be trained in cognitive strategies to cope with the guilt feelings and sense of failure associated with lapses. During the posttreatment period, virtually all clients will experience some form of lapse. The therapist can prepare them with appropriate coping techniques to view the occurrence of a slip as a learning experience—a single independent event to be avoided in the future by the use of an appropriate coping response.

Exercise

A final intervention that may be especially relevant for the maintenance phase is a general change in life-style. In changing their eating habits, many clients feel that they are giving up an important source of satisfaction (and positive affective change). The development of an adaptive substitute behavior or alternative source of satisfaction may help them maintain changes accomplished in treatment (Perri, 1985). In this regard, exercise can play a special role in the management of obesity. Exercise increases energy expenditure, counteracts the slowing of metabolism that accompanies dieting, and may actually lower the set point for body weight (Keesey, 1986; Stern & Lowney, 1986; Thompson et al., 1982). Psychologically, exercise serves as a cue to maintain moderate caloric intake and improves one's mood and self-concept (Folkins & Sime, 1981). Furthermore, exercise is one of the few factors associated with long-term maintenance of weight loss (e.g., Katahn, Pleas, Thackery, & Wallston, 1982; Stalonas et al., 1984). In a recent study, Perri et al. (1988) compared the effectiveness of four maintenance programs for obesity. The only program that produced a significant additional weight loss during the period following initial treatment was a maintenance program that included therapist contact combined with high-frequency exercise and social support.

Several recommendations are worth considering in designing an exercise program for the obese client (Brownell & Foreyt, 1985). First, if clients have not already begun an exercise program as part of initial treatment, they should start with modest amounts of a simple aerobic activity, namely, walking. Most participants can easily accomplish a 20-minute walk. Second, clients should be encouraged to increase life-style activities as a means of supplementing their basic walking program. They can be encouraged to park a distance from their destination, use steps rather than elevators, and substitute a 5-minute walk for a coffee break. Third, behavioral principles can be used to increase exercise levels. These include the monitoring of exercise time for feedback and reinforcement, the use of stimulus control to increase environmental cues for exercise, and rational restructuring to counter negative thoughts about exercise. Fourth, the social aspects of exercise should be emphasized. Clients should be encouraged to meet with others for walking and to join walking clubs and fitness programs sponsored by local organizations such as the YMCA. Being part of a special exercise program and having a particular facility available can enhance long-term adherence and help to make exercise part of a new, healthier life-style.

Follow-up Care

Finally, the therapist needs to address the tertiary phase of obesity treatment. What happens after the maintenance phase ends? The client and therapist need to decide whether additional support is needed or whether the client is ready to go it alone. Some clients want to stay involved with a formal source of support. Groups such as Weight Watchers, TOPS, or Overeaters Anonymous may be appropriate for this purpose. If clients decide to try their wings and go it alone, they should be provided with a way to get help if problems arise or a relapse occurs. The availability of telephone contacts with the therapist, additional therapy sessions, and a refresher course in behavior therapy may be necessary for the successful long-term management of obesity. The therapist and client can also engage in brainstorming to identify additional strategies that might enhance long-term progress.

SUMMARY

Obesity is a common, complex, and difficult problem to treat. Behavior therapists who work with obese clients are confronted by a challenging array of clinical decisions. Before attempting to treat obese clients, the behavior therapist must be aware of the limitations imposed by the interaction of biological and behavioral factors. Awareness of the biobehavioral formulation of obesity enables the clinician to provide prospective clients with an informed understanding of obesity and the implications for its treatment.

Before initiating treatment, the therapist can use an obesity orientation session to acknowledge the distress experienced by the obese client and to provide the individual with a sophisticated understanding of obesity and its treatment. The orientation session can be used to inhibit the individual's impulse to begin a diet by encouraging the client to take time to consider the high degree of commitment and motivation needed for a serious, long-term weight loss effort.

An initial question facing the clinician is whether behavioral treatment is suitable for the particular client. The degree of obesity is an important consideration in this regard. For the mildly obese individual, behavior therapy is clearly the treatment of choice. For the moderately obese person, behavior therapy may need to be combined with more aggressive modalities, such as the use of a very low calorie diet. There is little evidence that behavior therapy can benefit the severely obese client. For such individuals, the therapist may need to engage in brainstorming to consider and decide upon appropriate alternatives.

Other considerations in determining the suitability of behavior therapy include the results of prior weight loss attempts. There is little reason to expect that clients who have previously failed to lose weight with behavior therapy will be successful in repeated efforts. Current reasons for wanting to lose weight, commitment to a long-term treatment effort, and expectations regarding weight loss are additional factors that need to be considered in determining the appropriateness of behavioral treatment.

Following initial orientation and preliminary screening, the clinician must decide how to carry out a further psychological assessment in order to match the client to the most suitable form of treatment and to determine appropriate targets for change. Assessment will often include baseline data derived from a functional analysis of the client's eating and exercise behavior, as well as information about other areas of the client's psychological functioning, which may be derived from a battery of self-report instruments.

Once such an assessment is completed, the clinician and client can decide which treatment alternatives best suit the client's particular needs. Among the various options that might be considered are (a) having the client attempt weight loss without professional help, (b) referring the client to a commercial weight loss program, (c) initiating behavior therapy for obesity, (d) combining behavior therapy with the use of a very low calorie diet, (e) considering whether surgery is a reasonable alternative, (f) undertaking psychological treatment for a problem other than obesity, (g) beginning simultaneous treatment for obesity and other problems, (h) postponing treatment, and (i) deciding not to initiate treatment for obesity.

Once behavior therapy has been chosen, the therapist must make a number of decisions about the implementation of treatment. Specifically, the clinician must judge whether the client will benefit more from individual or group treatment and whether it will be more efficacious to follow a standardized treatment regimen or one tailored to the needs of the particular client. In addition, the therapist must make some preliminary decisions about the length of the initial stage of treatment as well as the maintenance stage.

Once therapy is underway, both the client and the therapist should be prepared to view the occurrence of problems as an expected and manageable part of the treatment process. Among the common problems that occur during the course of behavior therapy for obesity are dropping out of treatment, poor attendance at treatment sessions, inadequate adherence to treatment strategies, good adherence but slow or no weight loss, binge eating episodes, and emotional distress. Working collaboratively, the client and therapist should seek to define problems carefully, generate a variety of potential solutions, decide on a course of action, implement it, and determine whether improvement occurs.

As therapy progresses beyond the initial phase, the clinician must be prepared to make decisions about the long-term aspects of obesity treatment. In particular, the therapist will need to design a strategy for maintaining behavior change and weight loss. Several key elements seem to be important to the development of a successful maintenance program: (a) scheduling frequent client-therapist contacts during the posttreatment period, (b) providing a high degree of social support to help clients sustain the changes accomplished in treatment, (c) training clients in the necessary cognitive and behavioral skills to negotiate potential setbacks and obstacles to continued success, and (d) developing a high-frequency exercise regimen as an integral part of a healthier life-style.

A final set of decisions for the therapist involves the provision of follow-up care. After the conclusion of a maintenance program, the client and therapist must decide whether additional support is needed and how the client can receive additional help if difficult problems arise or a relapse occurs. Continued problem solving, whether through telephone contacts with the therapist or additional treatment sessions, may be necessary for the successful long-term management of obesity.

References

Abraham, S. (1983). *Obese and overweight adults in the United States* (National Center for Health Statistics, Vital and Health Statistics Series 11, No. 230; DHHS Pub. No. 83–1680). Washington, DC: U.S. Government Printing Office.

American Diabetes Association. (1986). *Exchange lists for meal planning* (2nd ed.). New York: Author.

Ashby, W. A., & Wilson, G. T. (1977). Behavior therapy for obesity: Booster sessions and long-term maintenance of weight. *Behaviour Research and Therapy, 14,* 451–464.

Ashley, F. W., & Kannel, W. B. (1974). Relation of weight changes to changes in atherogenic traits: The Framingham Study. *Journal of Chronic Diseases, 27,* 103–114.

Bandura, A., & Simon, K. M. (1977). The role of proximal intentions in self-regulation of refractory behavior. *Cognitive Therapy and Research, 1,* 177–193.

Beck, A. T., Ward, C. H., Mendelsohn, M., Mock, J., & Erbaugh, J. (1961). An inventory for measuring depression. *Archives of General Psychiatry, 4,* 561–571.

Beneke, W. M., & Paulsen, B. K. (1979). Long-term efficacy of behavior modification weight loss programs: A comparison of two follow-up maintenance strategies. *Behavior Therapy, 10,* 8–13.

Bennett, G. A. (1986). Behavior therapy for obesity: A quantitative review of selected treatment characteristics on outcome. *Behavior Therapy, 17,* 554–562.

Bjorntorp, P. (1986). Fat cells and obesity. In K. D. Brownell & J. P. Foreyt (Eds.), *Handbook of eating disorders: Physiology, psychology, and treatment of obesity, anorexia, and bulimia.* New York: Basic.

Bjorntorp, P., Carlgren, G., Isaksson, B., Krotkiewski, M., Larsson, B., & Sjostrom, L. (1975). Effect of an energy-reduced dietary regimen in relation to adipose tissue cellularity in obese women. *American Journal of Clinical Nutrition, 28,* 445–452.

Black, D. R. (1987). A minimal intervention program and a problem-solving program for weight control. *Cognitive Therapy and Research, 11,* 107–120.

Black, D. R., & Sherba, D. S. (1983). Contracting to problem solve versus contracting to practice behavioral weight loss skills. *Behavior Therapy, 14,* 100–109.

Black, D. R., & Threlfall, W. E. (1986). A stepped approach to weight control: A minimal intervention and a bibliotherapy problem solving program. *Behavior Therapy, 17,* 144–157.

Braitman, L. E., Alden, E. V., & Stanton, J. L. (1985). Obesity and caloric intake: The National Health and Nutrition Examination Survey of 1971–1975 (HANES I). *Journal of Chronic Diseases, 38,* 727–732.

Bray, G. A. (1986). Effects of obesity on health and happiness. In K. D. Brownell & J. P. Foreyt (Eds.), *Handbook of eating disorders: Physiology, psychology, and treatment of obesity, anorexia, and bulimia.* New York: Basic.

Brehm, S., & McAllister, D. A. (1980). Social psychological perspective on the maintenance of therapeutic change. In P. Karoly & J. J. Steffen (Eds.), *Improving the long-term effects of psychotherapy.* New York: Gardner.

Brownell, K. D. (1987). *The LEARN program for weight control.* Unpublished manuscript, University of Pennsylvania, Philadelphia.

Brownell, K. D., & Foreyt, J. P. (1985). Obesity. In D. H. Barlow (Ed.), *Clinical handbook of psychological disorders.* New York: Guilford.

Brownell, K. D., Marlatt, G. A., Lichtenstein, E., & Wilson, G. T. (1986). Understanding and preventing relapse. *American Psychologist, 41,* 765–782.

Brownell, K. D., Steen, S. N., & Wilmore, J. H. (1987). Weight regulation practices in athletes: Analysis of metabolic and health effects. *Medicine and Science in Sports and Exercise, 19,* 546–556.

Brownell, K. D., & Wadden, T. A. (1986). Behavior therapy for obesity: Modern approaches and better results. In K. D. Brownell & J. P. Foreyt (Eds.), *Handbook of eating disorders: Physiology, psychology, and treatment of obesity, anorexia, and bulimia.* New York: Basic.

Derogatis, L. R., Lipman, R. S., & Covi, L. (1973). SCL-90: An outpatient psychiatric rating scale—Preliminary report. *Psychopharmacology Bulletin, 9,* 13–27.

Ferguson, J. M. (1976). *Habits not diets: The real way to weight control.* Palo Alto, CA: Bull.

Folkins, C. H., & Sime, W. E. (1981). Physical fitness training and mental health. *American Psychologist, 36,* 373–389.

Foreyt, J. P. (1987). Issues in the assessment and treatment of obesity. *Journal of Consulting and Clinical Psychology, 55,* 677–684.

Garrow, J. S. (1986). Physiological aspects of obesity. In K. D. Brownell & J. P. Foreyt (Eds.), *Handbook of eating disorders: Physiology, psychology, and treatment of obesity, anorexia, and bulimia.* New York: Basic.

Gormally, J., Rardin, D., & Black, S. (1980). Correlates of successful response to a behavioral weight control clinic. *Journal of Counseling Psychology, 27,* 179–191.

Gotestam, K. G. (1979). A three-year follow-up of behavioral treatment for obesity. *Addictive Behaviors, 4,* 179–183.

Graham, L. E., II, Taylor, C. B., Hovell, M. F., & Siegel, W. (1983). Five year follow-up to a behavioral weight loss program. *Journal of Consulting and Clinical Psychology, 51,* 322–323.

Hall, S. M., Hall, R. G., Hanson, R. W., & Borden, B. L. (1974). Permanence of two self-managed treatments of overweight. *Journal of Consulting and Clinical Psychology, 42,* 781–786.

Hawkins, R. C., & Clement, P. F. (1980). Development and construct validation of a self-report measure of binge-eating tendencies. *Addictive Behaviors, 5,* 219–226.

Herman, C. P., & Mack, D. (1975). Restrained and unrestrained eating. *Journal of Personality, 43,* 647–660.

Jeffery, R. W. (1985). Monetary contracts for weight loss. In J. Hirsch & T. B. Van Itallie (Eds.), *Recent advances in obesity research* (Vol. 4). London: John Libbey.

Jeffery, R. W. (1987). Behavioral treatment of obesity. *Annals of Behavioral Medicine, 9,* 20–24.

Johnson, W. G., & Stalonas, P. M. (1981). *Weight no longer.* Gretna, LA: Pelican.

Kannel, W. B., & Gordon, T. (1979). Obesity and some physiological and medical concomitants: The Framingham Study. In G. A. Bray (Ed.), *Obesity in America* (NIH Pub. No. 79–359). Washington, DC: U. S. Government Printing Office.

Kannel, W. B., Gordon, T., & Castelli, W. P. (1979). Obesity, lipids, and glucose tolerance: The Framingham Study. *American Journal of Clinical Nutrition, 32,* 1238–1246.

Katahn, M., Pleas, J., Thackery, M., & Wallston, K. A. (1982). Relationship of eating and activity reports to follow-up weight maintenance in massive obesity. *Behavior Therapy, 13,* 521–528.

Keesey, R. E. (1986). A set-point theory of obesity. In K. D. Brownell & J. P. Foreyt (Eds.), *Handbook of eating disorders: Physiology, psychology, and treatment of obesity, anorexia, and bulimia.* New York: Basic.

Keys, A. (1950). *The biology of human starvation.* Minneapolis: University of Minnesota Press.

Kingsley, R. G., & Wilson, G. T. (1977). Behavior therapy for obesity: A comparative investigation of long-term efficacy. *Journal of Consulting and Clinical Psychology, 45,* 288–298.

Mahoney, M. J., & Mahoney, B. K. (1976). *Permanent weight control: A total solution to the dieter's dilemma.* New York: Norton.

Marcus, M. D., & Wing, R. R. (1987). Binge eating among the obese. *Annals of Behavioral Medicine, 9,* 23–27.

Marlatt, G. A., & Gordon, J. R. (1985). *Relapse prevention training: Maintenance strategies in the management of addictive behaviors.* New York: Guilford.

Mason, E. E. (1981). *Surgical treatment of obesity.* Philadelphia: Saunders.

Metropolitan Life Insurance Company. (1983). *Metropolitan height and weight tables.* New York: Author.

National Institutes of Health, Consensus Development Panel on the Health Implications of Obesity. (1985). Health implications of obesity: National Institutes of Health Consensus Development Conference statement. *Annals of Internal Medicine, 103,* 1073–1077.

Perri, M. G. (1985). Self-change strategies for the control of smoking, obesity, and problem drinking. In S. Shiffman & T. A. Wills (Eds.), *Coping and substance use.* New York: Academic.

Perri, M. G. (1987). Maintenance strategies for the management of obesity. In W. G. Johnson (Ed.), *Advances in eating disorders: Vol. 1. Treating and preventing obesity.* Greenwich, CT: JAI.

Perri, M. G., McAdoo, W. G., McAllister, D. A., Lauer, J. B., Jordan, R. C., Yancey, D. Z., & Nezu, A. M. (1987). Effects of peer support and therapist contact on long-term weight loss. *Journal of Consulting and Clinical Psychology, 55,* 615–617.

Perri, M. G., McAdoo, W. G., McAllister, D. A., Lauer, J. B., & Yancey, D. Z. (1986). Enhancing the efficacy of behavior therapy for obesity: Effects of aerobic exercise and a multicomponent maintenance program. *Journal of Consulting and Clinical Psychology, 54,* 670–675.

Perri, M. G., McAllister, D. A., Gange, J. J., Jordan, R. C., McAdoo, W. G., & Nezu, A. M. (1988). Effects of four maintenance programs on the long-term management of obesity. *Journal of Consulting and Clinical Psychology, 56,* 529–534.

Perri, M. G., Nezu, A. M., Patti, E. T., & McCann, K. D. (in press). Effect of length of treatment on weight loss. *Journal of Consulting and Clinical Psychology.*

Perri, M. G., Shapiro, R. M., Ludwig, W. W., Twentyman, C. T., & McAdoo, W. G. (1984). Maintenance strategies for the treatment of obesity: An evaluation of relapse prevention training and posttreatment contact by mail and telephone. *Journal of Consulting and Clinical Psychology, 52,* 404–413.

Polivy, J., & Herman, C. P. (1985). Dieting and binging: A causal analysis. *American Psychologist, 40,* 193–201.

Prochaska, J. O., & DiClemente, C. C. (1986). Toward a comprehensive model of change. In W. R. Miller & N. Heather (Eds.), *Treating addictive behaviors.* New York: Plenum.

Rodin, J. (1981). The current status of the internal external obesity hypothesis. *American Psychologist, 36,* 361–372.

Rosenthal, B. S., & Marx, R. D. (1979, December). *A comparison of standard behavioral and relapse prevention weight reduction programs.* Paper presented at the annual meeting of the Association for Advancement of Behavior Therapy, San Francisco.

Schachter, S. (1982). Recidivism and self-cure of smoking and obesity. *American Psychologist, 37,* 436–444.

Sims, E. A. H. (1976). Experimental obesity, dietary-induced thermogenesis, and their clinical implications. *Clinics in Endocrinology and Metabolism, 5,* 377–395.

Sorlie, P., Gordon, T., & Kannel, W. B. (1980). Body build and mortality: The Framingham Study. *Journal of the American Medical Association, 243,* 1828–1831.

Spielberger, C. D., Gorsuch, R. L., & Lushene, R. E. (1979). *Manual for the State-Trait Anxiety Inventory.* Palo Alto, CA: Consulting Psychologists Press.

Stalonas, P. M., Perri, M. G., & Kerzner, A. B. (1984). Do behavioral treatments of obesity last? A five year follow-up investigation. *Addictive Behaviors, 9,* 175–184.

Stern, J. S., & Lowney, P. (1986). Obesity: The role of physical activity. In K. D. Brownell & J. P. Foreyt (Eds.), *Handbook of eating disorders: Physiology, psychology, and treatment of obesity, anorexia, and bulimia.* New York: Basic.

Straw, M. K., Straw, R. B., Mahoney, M. J., Rogers, T., Mahoney, B. K., Craighead, L. W., & Stunkard, A. J. (1984). The Master Questionnaire: Preliminary report of an obesity assessment device. *Addictive Behaviors, 9,* 1–10.

Stuart, R. B., & Davis, B. (1972). *Slim chance in a fat world.* Champaign, IL: Research Press.

Stunkard, A. J. (1976). *The pain of obesity.* Palo Alto, CA: Bull.

Stunkard, A. J. (1985). Obesity. In R. E. Hales & A. E. Frances (Eds.), *Psychiatric update: APA annual review* (Vol. 4). Washington, DC: American Psychiatric Press.

Stunkard, A. J., Foch, T. T., & Hrubec, Z. (1986). A twin study of human obesity. *Journal of the American Medical Association, 256,* 51–54.

Stunkard, A. J., & Rush, J. (1974). Dieting and depression reexamined: A critical review of untoward responses during weight reduction for obesity. *Annals of Internal Medicine, 81,* 526–533.

Stunkard, A. J., Sorensen, T. I. A., Hanis, C., Teasdale, T. W., Chakraborty, R., Schull, W. H., & Schulsinger, F. (1986). An adoption study of human obesity. *New England Journal of Medicine, 314,* 193–198.

Thompson, J. K., Jarvie, G. J., Lahey, B. B., & Cureton, K. H. (1982). Exercise and obesity: Etiology, physiology, and intervention. *Psychological Bulletin, 91,* 55–79.

Volkmar, F. R., Stunkard, A. J., & Woolston, J. (1981). High attrition rates in commercial weight loss programs. *Archives of Internal Medicine, 141,* 426–428.

Wadden, T. A., & Stunkard, A. J. (1985). Social and psychological consequences of obesity. *Annals of Internal Medicine, 103,* 1062–1067.

Wadden, T. A., & Stunkard, A. J. (1986). Controlled trial of very low calorie diet, behavior therapy and their combination in the treatment of obesity. *Journal of Consulting and Clinical Psychology, 54,* 482–488.

Whisman, M. A. (in press). Efficacy of booster session maintenance programs in behavior therapy: Review and methodological critique. *Clinical Psychology Review.*

Chapter 7

Marital Distress

Mark A. Whisman
Neil S. Jacobson

INTRODUCTION

Since studies on the application of behavior exchange principles to marital problems first appeared in the late 1960s (Stuart, 1969), researchers have been developing, evaluating, and refining a treatment program for distressed married couples based upon social-psychological exchange theories and learning principles derived from social and experimental psychology. As the number of factors found to differentiate happy from unhappy couples has increased, research clinicians have expanded upon and developed new techniques for the treatment of marital distress. The treatment, originally known as *behavioral marital therapy* but which we have come to call *social-learning cognitive marital therapy* (SLC) to reflect these recent clinical innovations, has been evaluated in a number of controlled studies and is not only the most thoroughly researched approach to marital therapy, but also the only approach having a substantial body of experimental research (recently reviewed by Baucom & Hoffman, 1986, and Hahlweg & Markman, 1988). However, as new techniques have been proposed to deal with the problems couples encounter, the marital therapist is faced with an ever-increasing proliferation of treatment strategies. These may present a confusing picture for even the most seasoned therapist.

Preparation of this chapter was supported by National Research Service Award #5F31MH09684-02 and Grant #5RO1MH33838-08 from the National Institute of Mental Health, awarded to Mark A. Whisman and Neil S. Jacobson, respectively.

With few exceptions (e.g., Follingstad, 1988; Olson & Kleim, 1985), there has been little effort to describe how clinical decisions are made and even less effort to match client characteristics with intervention strategies, although such matching has been identified as essential (Beach & O'Leary, 1985; Hahlweg & Markman, 1988; Margolin, 1983b). In this chapter, we present a problem-solving approach to implementing marital therapy treatment strategies. This approach, which is based on the clinical decision-making model proposed in chapter 3, is designed to aid the practicing clinician in matching client characteristics with treatment strategies. Because it is not the purpose of the chapter to offer a comprehensive review of our approach to therapy, we will attempt to provide references to sources that give more details about particular treatment strategies.

APPLYING THE CLINICAL DECISION-MAKING MODEL

The following discussion will examine the application of the clinical decision-making model in SLC marital therapy, especially as it relates to problem orientation issues, problem definition and formulation, generation of alternatives, decision making, and solution implementation and verification.

Problem Orientation

Behavioral research on marital exchange has elucidated a number of parameters that differentiate happy from unhappy couples; all of these research findings have contributed to the treatment (and underlying theoretical model) of marital distress. These studies have shown that distressed couples reward each other less and punish each other more frequently and reciprocally (e.g., Birchler, Weiss, & Vincent, 1975; Gottman, 1979; Jacobson, Follette, & McDonald, 1982; Levenson & Gottman, 1983; Margolin, 1981; Margolin & Wampold, 1981; Vincent, Weiss, & Birchler, 1975), are more emotionally reactive to immediate relationship events (e.g., Jacobson et al., 1982), and disagree significantly more often about what events occur in the relationship (e.g., Jacobson & Moore, 1981) than do their nondistressed counterparts. That is, distressed couples seem to rely upon aversive behavior control techniques and appear deficient in a number of skills necessary for the effective functioning of a relationship (Weiss, 1980). Furthermore, compared with nondistressed couples, distressed couples endorse more unrealistic beliefs and expectations regarding marital relationships (Eidelson & Epstein, 1982). They also make more destructive attributions for each other's negative behaviors and less benign attributions for each other's positive behaviors (e.g., Fincham, 1985; Fincham, Beach, & Baucom, 1987; Fincham, Beach, & Nelson, 1987; Fincham & O'Leary, 1983; Holtzworth-Munroe & Jacobson, 1985; Jacobson, Mc-Donald, Follette, & Berley, 1985).

Because so many variables have been found to differentiate happily married from distressed couples, marital therapy is often a multi-faceted endeavor. In choosing the appropriate treatment strategy, the therapist needs to exercise care in determining the extent to which the above factors are contributing to the couple's dissatisfaction with the relationship, as well as in selecting treatment alternatives.

Problem Definition and Formulation

Before therapy is undertaken, it must be determined that marital therapy is the appropriate mode of intervention. The SLC approach to working with couples is a suitable treatment for most marital problems, although there are some exceptions. First, if at least one partner is unwilling to commit to working on the relationship and would rather end it, separation and divorce therapy (e.g., Rice & Rice, 1986) may be the treatment of choice. Second, if spouses are physically abusive towards each another, individual therapy for anger management may be necessary before marital therapy can proceed. Third, if the couple's goal is to lessen one partner's serious individual emotional problems (which are unrelated to the marriage), individual therapy may be indicated. Elsewhere (Jacobson, Holtzworth-Munroe, & Schmaling, 1989) we have reviewed studies showing that marital therapy is an effective form of treatment for several psychiatric disorders, including depression, agoraphobia, and alcoholism, when the individual's prob-lem is a consequence of, or is being maintained by, relationship problems. In addition, marital therapy has been shown to result in decreases in individual psychopathology secondary to the presenting problem of marital distress (Snyder & Wills, 1989; Whisman, Schmal-ing, & Jacobson, 1988). However, in determining the appropriateness of marital therapy, it is critical that the therapist thoroughly assess the role of the relationship in the cause or maintenance of the problem behavior because marital therapy is unlikely to be beneficial if the individual's psychopathology is unrelated to marital distress. For ex-ample, marital therapy has been shown to be an effective form of treatment for depression when the couple is maritally distressed but has little impact on depression in couples who are happily married (Whis-man, Jacobson, Fruzzetti, Schmaling, & Dobson, 1988).

If it is determined that marital therapy is indicated, the next stage of treatment involves identifying the variables contributing to marital problems; only then can the appropriate therapeutic interventions be selected. In the assessment of the marital relationship, the focus is on current environmental variables rather than historical events. Because we believe that marital distress is a multidimensional construct, we employ several strategies in our initial assessment, including interviewing couples about their relationship, having them complete a number of subjective reports of attitudes and degree of satisfaction with the relationship, and conducting overt behavioral observation of their interactions. Each of these strategies will be described in turn. (For additional information on assessment, see Jacobson & Margolin, 1979, and Margolin, Michelli, & Jacobson, 1988).

Initial Intake

The first two or three treatment sessions are devoted to assessment and evaluation. We first seek to get each person's perspective on the major problems in the relationship, including when the problem first occurred and any steps the partners have taken to overcome it. We also try to assess the relationship's strengths. Gathering information through a developmental history about how the partners first met, what attracted them to each other, and what their early relationship was like is one way of assessing these strengths (Jacobson & Margolin, 1979). Creating a developmental history also shifts the couple's attention from their current problems to more positive times. Furthermore, collecting a developmental history provides important diagnostic information. Couples who have had a strong early relationship with marital problems developing in recent years may have entirely different experiences and expectations regarding marriage than those couples who have had a long history of marital problems and who have married out of loneliness, to escape from their parents, or because of unplanned pregnancy.

In addition to interviewing the partners conjointly, we routinely meet with each partner individually to explore individual histories, prior therapy experience, current and past involvements in extramarital affairs, and sexual satisfaction and adjustment. We routinely assess the number and depth of interpersonal relationships prior to marriage because this history may provide important information about beliefs and experiences with interpersonal relationships. Because they may not have been exposed to experiences that would counter the idealized, "Hollywood" picture of close relationships, individuals who have had few serious relationships before marriage may be more prone to hold

unrealistic expectations about marriage, as are individuals who have
had many short-term relationships (i.e., individuals who are looking for
the perfect spouse or relationship).

Assessment Instruments

During the first phase of therapy (either before therapy begins or
between the first and second sessions), couples are asked to complete a
number of self-report questionnaires at home. As the constructs
proposed by SLC therapists to account for marital distress have increased in number, so have the number and methods of assessing
marital dysfunction.

To determine the degree of marital distress a couple is experiencing, as well as to target areas for intervention, one or more of the
following questionnaires are routinely given. The Dyadic Adjustment
Scale (Spanier, 1976), a 32-item questionnaire, is one of the most
popular measures of overall satisfaction. The Areas of Change Questionnaire (AOC; Margolin, Talovic, & Weinstein, 1983; Weiss &
Birchler, 1975) is a 34-item questionnaire that directly assesses the
spouses' presenting complaints by asking respondents to indicate
whether they want their partners to increase, decrease, or not change
the rate of certain behaviors. More recently, Snyder (1979) has
developed the 280-item Marital Satisfaction Inventory (MSI), which
includes a validity scale, a global satisfaction scale, and scales assessing
satisfaction with (a) affective communication, (b) problem-solving communication, (c) time together, (d) discussions of finances, (e) sexual
experiences, (f) childrearing practices, and (g) relationship with
children, in addition to attitudes and experiences towards (h) role
orientation and (i) family history of distress. Elsewhere (Jacobson,
Follette, & Elwood, 1984), it has been suggested that, for effective
treatment planning, couples should be categorized according to type of
presenting problem or relationship type: The MSI is a good overall
measure for suggesting specific foci for treatment. Snyder and Smith
(1986) have derived a classification system of marital relationships from
spouses' profiles on the MSI; future research is needed to determine if
their classification system can be replicated and if the profile types can
be matched with specific treatment interventions.

To determine the behavioral transactions that occur between
spouses in the natural environment (and thereby to determine the
extent to which the partners deliver reinforcing and punishing behaviors to each other), couples are commonly asked to complete the
Spouse Observation Checklist (SOC; Weiss & Perry, 1979), a 408-item
instrument consisting of 12 behavioral categories, such as sex,

household management, and communication. The SOC is routinely used in one of two ways. First, each spouse can daily check off which items occurred during the preceding 24 hours and then rate overall satisfaction for the day. This method allows the therapist to determine the overall rate of pleasing-to-displeasing behaviors, as well as to identify behaviors that discriminate between satisfying and unsatisfying days. Second, each spouse can complete the SOC once and rate how often each behavior occurs in general within the relationship, as well as how positive or negative each spouse feels when the partner engages in the behavior. This information allows the therapist to identify positively valenced items that are occurring at a low frequency and negatively valenced items that are occurring at a high frequency.

It is also important to assess what spouses think about their marriage and their partners. The 40-item Relationship Beliefs Inventory (RBI; Eidelson & Epstein, 1982; Epstein & Eidelson, 1981) was developed to identify five common marital beliefs proposed as having a negative impact on marital functioning: (a) Disagreements are destructive, (b) Spouses should know each other's feelings without asking, (c) Relationships cannot be changed, (d) A perfect sex life is necessary in marriage, and (e) Differences between the sexes cause marital conflict. Similarly, several measures have been developed to assess how spouses interpret their partners' positive and negative relationship behaviors (e.g., Fincham, Beach, and Nelson, 1987; Holtzworth-Munroe & Jacobson, 1985). Most of these measures of attributional style present several hypothetical or real partner behaviors and ask spouses to write down the major cause for the behavior, as well as to rate the cause in terms of causal judgments (e.g., the degree to which the cause of the behavior is internal, stable, and global) and the behavior in terms of responsibility judgments (e.g., the intent, motivation, and blameworthiness of the spouse's behavior).

Finally, because couples who are physically abusive towards each other pose additional concerns in therapy, it is important to assess the existence and degree of marital violence within the relationship. A frequently used assessment instrument in this area is the Conflict Tactics Scale (Strauss, 1979), which asks partners to rate the frequency with which they and their spouse engaged in specific psychologically and physically abusive behaviors during the preceding year and to indicate whether these behaviors have ever occurred in their relationship.

Behavioral Observation

Behavioral observation has come to be viewed as one of the hallmarks of behavior therapy. Many treatment interventions for distressed couples have come from videotaping distressed and nondistressed couples engaged in conflict resolution tasks and then coding and analyzing these tapes with complex interactional coding systems. (For a recent review of research on the relationship between marital interaction and marital satisfaction, see Boland & Follingstad, 1987.) Although important to the development of theories and treatments of marital distress, these complex coding systems are of limited use to the practicing clinician. However, clinicians can gain valuable information about how couples interact (rather than how they say they interact) through direct observation. For example, saying to the couple, "Attempt to resolve this problem here, in front of me, as you would if you were at home by yourself" can provide the therapist with important information about the spouses' idiosyncratic ways of communicating with each other. Such information enables the therapist to tailor the interventions described below to each particular couple. Furthermore, observing the couple (either directly in the session or at home by audiotaping) as they acquire communication skills and providing feedback about their performance are critical components of successful skill acquisition.

Generation of Alternatives

Once a thorough assessment of the couple has been undertaken and the problems defined and formulated, the next step involves identifying intervention strategies to meet the particular needs of the couple. For each problem identified, a number of treatment strategies are generated; these are to be integrated later into a cohesive treatment plan. The core component of SLC marital therapy is a treatment manual published by Jacobson and Margolin (1979) and supplemented by a variety of more recent clinical innovations (e.g., Berley & Jacobson, 1984; Jacobson, 1983a, 1983b, 1984, 1989; Jacobson & Holtzworth-Munroe, 1986; Schindler & Vollmer, 1984; Weiss, 1980, 1984; Whisman & Jacobson, in press). What follows is a list of marital problems matched to treatment interventions.

Inadequate Levels of Pleasurable Exchanges

A common complaint raised by distressed couples is that they do not enjoy each other's company and that their relationship is no longer "exciting" or "fun." It is important to elicit further information from the couple to determine the exact nature of this problem. Usually, one of two processes has occurred. First, the couple may continue to engage in the exact same behaviors that initially attracted them to each other, but over time these behaviors have become routinized and boring, and the couple may be experiencing *reinforcement erosion*. For example, one couple's entire social life consisted of going out to dinner and a movie, whereas another couple socialized with the same group of people year after year. Both of these couples wanted a change in their routine. Second, it may be that, because of some life transition, new behaviors need to be added to the couple's repertoire of activities, but they have not yet adjusted to the change. For example, Jim and Tracy enjoyed doing many activities together as a couple and had a happy marriage until their child was born. Caring for their daughter involved many new activities, and they had not adapted to their growing family by incorporating new ways of spending quality time together. Similarly, another couple recently moved to Seattle from Indiana, where they had both grown up in the same small town. Consequently, many of their social activities revolved around their extended families. Upon arriving in Seattle, they found that they did not know what to do with each other when not in the presence of their extended families, and they were becoming increasingly distressed. Couples encounter similar problems along with other life transitions, such as job or school changes, having children move away from or back home, births, and deaths.

Behavior exchange procedures have been developed to overcome couples' low rates of reinforcing behaviors, or, alternatively, high rates of aversive behaviors. These procedures are designed to teach partners to pinpoint particular behaviors they could perform to improve each other's satisfaction with the relationship. There are several methods for increasing positive exchanges. First, each partner can be asked to generate a list of activities that he thinks would increase the other's satisfaction (e.g., bringing home flowers, greeting the spouse the end of the day with a smile and a kiss, giving compliments) and then to increase the frequency of these behaviors. This strategy is particularly helpful if the couple previously engaged in enjoyable activities in which they are no longer participating. Alternatively, spouses can fill out the SOC, rating the frequency of occurrence and the impact of their partners' behaviors. The therapist can then work with the couple to generate a list of infrequently occurring positive behaviors and frequently occurring negative behaviors. Over the course of several weeks, spouses can be asked to concentrate on increasing the occurrence of positive behaviors and decreasing the occurrence of negative behaviors. This strategy is particularly helpful for couples who have a history of not being able to please each other (e.g., "I have never known what she wants from me" or "He never tells me what he likes") or for couples who are undergoing some major life transition during which they do not feel capable of pleasing each other. With both of these interventions, spouses are asked to focus on maximizing the partner's satisfaction each day, with behavior changes occurring at the giver's initiative. When changes are perceived as coming from the giver's (rather than the therapist's or receiver's) initiative, and therefore as being internally motivated, they are likely to be favorably evaluated by the receiver (Jacobson, 1984). An additional strategy may involve each partner's providing information about behaviors that would enhance satisfaction; the partner's spouse is then free to choose which behaviors to perform, with the goal of pleasing the partner remaining in effect.

Some spouses have difficulty increasing their level of pleasurable exchanges, stating that they must first feel loving to act loving. For these couples, challenging this belief through the use of an analogy has been helpful. Doing nice things for one's partner towards the goal of improving the relationship can be compared to exercising towards the goal of better health: On any given day, an individual on an exercise program may not feel like exercising (particularly if her chosen mode of exercise involves outdoor running, and it is cold and dark outside), yet, if she is sincere in her goal, she will exercise anyway. Furthermore, she may find that once she begins to exercise, she begins to enjoy it. Similarly, on any given day, an individual may not feel like doing nice things for his partner (particularly if she is sullen, irritable, or withdrawn), yet if he is sincere in his goal, he will do them anyway and may find that he enjoys his partner more after he has done something for her. However, it is important to stipulate that neither spouse should do anything for the other person that would later be resented.

Communication Problems

Poor communication is not only the most frequently reported problem of couples seeking therapy (Geiss & O'Leary, 1981), but also one of the few problems that have consistently been associated with global marital distress (e.g., Gottman, 1979) and daily changes in marital satisfaction (e.g., Jacobson & Moore, 1981). Common complaints that suggest the need for working on the couple's communication include "He never tells me how he feels," "I can never tell what she is thinking," "We only seem to communicate on a superficial level," or "He never listens to what I have to say." High scores (high distress) on the MSI scale of affective communication are also a good indicator of communication problems in the relationship.

To assess communication difficulties thoroughly, it is important to explore spouses' explanations for the problem. Communication problems are usually due to one of two factors: Either spouses lack the skills necessary to communicate effectively with each other, or they have the requisite skills but do not emit them. Concerning the latter, Birchler et al. (1975) and Vincent et al. (1975) have shown that distressed spouses are able to interact separately in a constructive manner when involved in a conflict discussion with a stranger (but not with their spouse) and, moreover, are able to alter their communication style with their partners simply by following the experimenter's instruction to do so (Vincent, Friedman, Nugent, & Messerly, 1979). Weiss (1980, 1984) has noted that behaviorally oriented therapies often adopt the skill deficit hypothesis of communication problems by restricting themselves to providing training in skills and techniques. The common belief is that, by practicing these skills under the direction of the therapist, spouses will experience positive consequences and that this experience will lead to a higher frequency of these constructive behaviors, which in turn will be followed by a desirable cognitive change. However, spouses' causal attributions may impede changes in behavior. For this reason, after spouses have described their perceptions of the communication problem, they are each asked why they think they are having this problem or what is keeping them from communicating better with each other. If they answer that they are not communicating better because they have never been good at communicating or because they just don't know how, training in communication skills may be all that is necessary to overcome their problems. However, if some belief is blocking their communication, cognitive restructuring may be necessary before partners can communicate well with each other. Each of these interventions will be described in turn.

Our approach to communication training involves three components: (a) didactic instructions from the therapist, (b) practice by the couple both within and between sessions, and (c) the therapist's feedback regarding the practice session. The communication process is first broken down into expressive and receptive roles. Skills associated with the expressive role include using *I statements* (e.g., "I really enjoy the book that I have been reading") and linking events with emotions (e.g., "When you give me a kiss when I come home from work, I feel loved and cared for"), whereas skills associated with the receptive role include positive nonverbal listening skills (e.g., making eye contact, sitting quietly, nodding) and the effective art of paraphrasing. The therapist first models and role plays these skills and then allows the couple to practice the skills during the session, with the therapist providing feedback about their performance. Teaching couples how to paraphrase statements made by their partners gains particular importance from research showing that, compared with happily married couples, distressed couples have greater difficulty decoding each other's nonverbal behaviors (e.g., Noller, 1980). This finding may help explain why distressed spouses rate statements made by their partners as having a less positive impact, even though the two groups do not differ in the intent of such statements (Gottman, 1979; Gottman et al., 1976). Helping couples improve their ability to communicate feelings towards each other, as well as to paraphrase the impact of each other's statements, helps them acquire the skills necessary to bring together the intent behind a speaker's message and the impact it has on the listener. Furthermore, encouraging spouses to discuss their thoughts and feelings openly with their partners has the added benefit of increasing relationship intimacy (Margolin, 1983a).

If a communication problem is determined to be partly due to some belief about the spouse or the relationship, or if the partners seem to be having difficulty acquiring communication skills, changing their attributions or expectations about their communication may be necessary. Epstein (1982) has provided some guidelines for helping couples change their beliefs; these guidelines are based upon Beck's approach to challenging unrealistic expectations (Beck, Rush, Shaw, & Emery, 1979). First, the belief is translated into operational terms. For example, a belief of a husband who does not talk to his wife about his feelings because he is afraid that he will be ridiculed could be operationalized as "My wife will laugh and treat me like a child if I tell her about my fears about spending time alone with our daughter." Using earlier experiences, the therapist and couple can then examine specific evidence consistent or inconsistent with the cognition. Alternatively, the husband can test the belief by engaging in the behavior and observing his wife's reaction. By discussing the feared response in front of his wife, he challenges her indirectly (or, if necessary, directly) to behave in a manner that will disconfirm his negative expectation. If the husband does engage in the behavior and his wife's reaction is the predicted (negative) response, then changing her behavior (through training in communication skills) is indicated. If the partner's reaction is contrary to predictions, then the faulty cognition can be discarded. For some couples, changing beliefs that prevent them from communicating with each other may be sufficient to overcome their communication problems (for example, challenging the belief that they should know what the other one is feeling without asking). For other couples, training in communication skills may still be necessary, even after cognitions have been changed.

Problems with Conflict Resolution

Some couples can communicate clearly with each other regarding activities and feelings about topics internal and external to the relationship but have difficulty negotiating resolutions to problems that they are experiencing. These couples may be identified by complaints such as the following: "When we disagree about something, we argue and get angry and won't talk to each other. This seems to happen over and over, and we never seem to be able to get anywhere." These couples may also be identified by high scores (high distress) on the problem-solving communication scale of the MSI. To identify particular areas of weakness in a couple's problem-solving abilities, it is often helpful to ask both partners to spend 5 to 10 minutes attempting to resolve a moderate-sized problem in their relationship in front of the therapist.

Under the SLC approach to problem-solving training, therapists teach the couple how to solve their own problems (and thereby become their own therapists), rather than try to mediate all problems that the couple is experiencing. Couples are first given a problem-solving manual to read at home (see Jacobson & Margolin, 1979, pp. 215–251), and then the format is worked on both within and between sessions. Couples are first taught how to define a problem (i.e., by starting with a statement of appreciation; following it with a clear delineation of the problem in specific, behavioral terms; and finishing up with an expression of how the person feels when the problem behavior occurs). Following problem definition, couples brainstorm possible solutions, evaluate the appropriateness of each solution, and come up with a final change agreement. In learning the problem-solving format, couples work on small relationship problems first, and then, when they have mastered the requisite skills, move on to major relationship problems. Thus the format teaches the couple how to solve their problems and actually assists them in solving several problems.

We have also begun to incorporate strategies designed to change interactional themes underlying couples' disagreements (Jacobson, 1989). Couples frequently continue to experience recurrent, rapidly escalating arguments even after they have mastered communication and problem-solving skills. For many of these couples, we have found the following strategies (based in part upon the works of Greenberg & Johnson, 1988, and Wile, 1981) to be helpful. Couples are first asked to discuss an unresolved argument within the session. Once both partners are involved in the argument, the therapist interrupts the interaction and attempts to elicit the thoughts and feelings of each partner in front of the other partner in order to help both spouses make more sense of what is occurring between them. For many couples, these arguments revolve around a general theme, which is often based upon differences in the amount of closeness and intimacy each spouse desires. The theme is characterized by one partner's wanting more intimacy and the other partner's wanting less. At the thematic level, the therapist can help the couple identify this recurring pattern and the role each partner plays in it. At home, the couple can monitor these interactions to gain a greater understanding of the pattern. Finally, spouses can brainstorm alternative ways of interacting with each other around this theme (cf. Jacobson, 1989, and Whisman and Jacobson, in press).

Unrealistic Expectations or Related Cognitive Factors

Throughout this chapter, we have interspersed discussion of cognitive interventions. This approach reflects our tendency to use cognitive interventions throughout therapy (but see Baucom & Lester, 1986, for an alternative perspective). In addition to the previously mentioned interventions, several other cognitive techniques may be helpful in treating couples. These techniques, described below, would probably be used in conjunction with the aforementioned techniques in skill acquisition.

Studies have shown that spouses' extreme and unrealistic expectations of what relationships should be like are often related to marital discord (Epstein & Eidelson, 1981). If it is determined that one or both partners endorse unrealistic beliefs about the spouse or the marriage, the general therapeutic task is for the therapist and couple collaboratively to identify problematic thinking patterns and to substitute more realistic adaptive thoughts. For example, partners who believe that any amount of disagreement is always destructive can be taught problem-solving skills that facilitate conflict resolution without aversive consequences. Following problem-solving training, the inappropriateness of this belief can be pointed out. Epstein (1982) has a number of other suggestions for modifying unrealistic expectations. In addition to common unrealistic beliefs like those assessed by the RBI, therapists need to watch for, and actively challenge, more idiosyncratic beliefs, such as "My marriage should always be full of the same (passionate) loving feelings I had during dating," "My spouse should be interested in everything I do," and so forth.

One particularly important cognitive component of marital therapy is illustrated by Doherty's (1981a) model, in which attributions about the cause of marital problems interact with expectations about the degree to which the couple believe they can solve their problems. Couples presenting for marital therapy rarely perceive the relationship as the cause of their problems. More often, they blame the other partner for the problems in the relationship and have efficacy expectations about their ability to solve their problems that are either high (exhibited in persistent problem-solving attempts focused on changing the spouse) or low (exhibited in apathy, passivity, demoralization, and resentment at the partner for causing the unsolvable problems). In the SLC approach, it is critical that, from very early on, spouses understand that changes can occur in their relationship (high efficacy expectations) but that the focus of the behavior change is on each partner's unique contribution to the problems (self-focus). Jacobson and Margolin (1979) have proposed a number of strategies for creating and maintaining positive expectancies (including therapist enthusiasm, summarizing outcome research that supports the efficacy of the SLC approach, and beginning with interventions that produce rapid change) and for collaboration and self-focus (including conceptualizing marital problems in relationship terms that imply mutual responsibility and attaining a bilateral commitment for collaboration and compromise).

Another important cognitive intervention involves *reframing* or *relabeling,* a technique designed to provide couples with alternative explanations for their marital problems. Distressed spouses often impute negative intent to their partner's behavior, thereby causing blaming and escalation of conflict. During therapy, the therapist should seek to stop couples when they do this and should try to provide a positive (or at least benign) explanation for the behavior. For example, every time Jamey did something nice for Bill, he would withdraw and avoid her because he believed that she was being nice to try to manipulate him into doing something for her. The therapist relabeled Jamey's behaviors as acts of affection and caring; Bill could then enjoy the things she did for him rather than blame her for being manipulative. Similarly, a wife's complaint that her husband didn't value her viewpoint because he constantly interrupted her was relabeled by the therapist as a deficit in the husband's communication skills.

Schindler and Vollmer (1984) have proposed that couples should also be taught how to conduct cognitive restructuring on their own because, if spouses can learn to evaluate their partners' behavior more benignly, they will be less likely to respond aversively. For example, Terry and John had a recurrent problem when they were reunited at the end of an 8- to 10-hour workday. Terry arrived home tired, wanting to relax and unwind, and found John's questions about her day intrusive: She then became angry at John, who sullenly withdrew. With the help of their therapist, Terry was able to relabel the situation at home while it was occurring and to view John's questions as signs that he was glad to see her. This cognitive restructuring led to a more successful and positive interaction. This strategy can also help spouses move away from global and stable causal attributions about their partners' negative behavior (cf. Doherty, 1981b).

Sexual Problems

Sexual problems are frequently encountered with distressed couples and often fail to improve following therapy unless they become a direct focus of intervention (Melman & Jacobson, 1983).[1] Although sexual dysfunctions are often one of the presenting problems, such problems more often center around lack of desire or dissatisfaction with the quantity or quality of sexual activity. High scores on the MSI sexual satisfaction scale may also suggest the need for interventions in the couple's sexual relationship. Additional information about the sexual relationship can be attained through questionnaires such as the Sexual Interaction Inventory (LoPiccolo & Steger, 1974).

If the couple has a sexual dysfunction, techniques pioneered by Masters and Johnson (1970) may be helpful. However, if the couple is dissatisfied with the quantity or quality of sexual activity, then a number of strategies can be employed. Several suggestions for particular problems are given in the following discussion; the interested reader is referred to Barbach (1984) for elaboration on these and additional suggestions. Incidentally, we often instruct couples to read the Barbach book as an adjunct to therapy. For couples who are not sure how to please each other, sensate focus exercises, designed to let the other know what feels good, may be beneficial. Fantasy exercises, designed to provide information regarding sexual preferences and the conditions that enhance sexual satisfaction, may also be helpful. For couples who are bored with their sexual relationship, experimenting with different positions and locations for sexual intercourse may be helpful, as well as sharing fantasies regarding ideal sexual experiences. Some spouses may be reluctant to talk about trying new sexual experiences because they are afraid their partner or the therapist will think they are "strange" or "weird." In this situation, the therapist can set the stage before asking each partner for suggestions by first suggesting several alternative experiences for the couple, thereby giving the couple per-

---

[1] For a more complete discussion of sexual dysfunctions and the relationship of the clinical decision-making model to their treatment, see chapter 8.

mission to expand the range of their sexual repertoire. Explicit agree-
ments regarding the rituals of initiation and refusal may be necessary
for couples who frequently disagree about these areas of their sexuality.
Finally, for some couples, education about birth control and the sexual
response may be necessary if it is determined that anxiety about becoming pregnant or achieving orgasm is preventing the partners from
enjoying each other.

In addition to problems with the sexual relationship, many couples
complain about lack of general affection. For these couples, increasing
the frequency of affectionate behaviors (kisses, hugs, cuddling, back
rubs, etc.) may be as important as modifying their sexual behavior, if
not more so. Many couples need help in discriminating between affectionate (nonsexual) behaviors and signs of affection that are precursors
to sexual activity. Spouses frequently state that they are not affectionate
with their partners because the partners assume that any affectionate
behavior is a sexual overture. For such couples, assistance in making
this distinction is an important first step in increasing the frequency of
both affectionate and sexual behaviors.

Decision Making

Once the therapist has made a thorough assessment of the couple's
presenting problems and has generated a number of alternative interventions designed to treat these problems, she develops a treatment
plan. In forming the treatment plan, it is important to match treatment
strategies with the idiosyncratic needs of a particular couple and to
inhibit the tendency to respond automatically to a given class of
problems (e.g., communication problems) as though they served the
same function for each couple. In addition, it is important to graduate
the skills to be covered with the couple into steps that they can easily
learn. Although the interventions discussed earlier have been
presented in a sequential format, the therapist may want to be working
on more than one problem at a time in forming the treatment plan.
However, the order of the listed interventions is not arbitrary: Some
couples must acquire skills or behaviors at one stage before they can
complete the next stage. For example, many couples, particularly those
who question the utility of therapy, may need to see quick changes in
their relationship to stay in therapy. For such couples, increasing their
pleasurable exchanges immediately makes their relationship more
satisfying and strengthens their commitment to make more difficult
changes later on. Similarly, the acquisition of basic communication skills
is necessary before problem-solving training can be effectively imple-

mented, and changes in other areas of a couple's relationship may be necessary before they are willing to work on their sexual relationship. If two partners are in crisis or dealing with major relationship problems, beginning therapy with communication and problem-solving training may be necessary to help them through a particularly stressful period, with the other interventions following. In contrast, if a couple has a history of marital problems, addressing problems in the sequence provided may be most beneficial.

After formulating a treatment plan, the therapist presents it to the couple, usually during the third or fourth therapy session. Included in this treatment plan are a presentation of the couple's strengths and weaknesses, an explanation and rationale for each treatment chosen, and a discussion of the predicted outcome of each intervention. The couple provides feedback about the treatment plan, and any necessary modifications are incorporated. However, if one or both spouses completely disagree with the therapist's treatment plan and the philosophical underpinnings of the program, and if they refuse to suspend this judgment and act as if they agree with the therapist's presentation, referring the couple to another therapist with a different orientation may be indicated. Once the couple and the therapist agree upon the optimal plan, a commitment is made whereby each spouse agrees to complete homework assignments and work collaboratively with the other person.

In addition to incorporating their reactions to the treatment plan, the partners are actively involved in planning their treatment throughout therapy. Each session begins with the therapist's setting an agenda with the collaboration of the couple. This agenda usually involves reviewing previous homework, presenting new material, and making a new homework assignment. We routinely ask couples (particularly during the latter stages of therapy) for their input in deciding the content of sessions and upcoming homework assignments.

Solution Implementation and Verification

Throughout the course of therapy, it is important to ascertain if the treatment, or problem solution, is having the intended impact upon each spouse and upon the entire relationship. One way to gain this information is to check out the couple's reactions. Elsewhere (Jacobson, Berley, Melman, Elwood, & Phelps, 1985) we have labeled this process taking each spouse's *affective temperature*. In doing so, the therapist periodically asks each spouse to ascertain the other's degree of emotional involvement and reactions to changes occurring in therapy. Because behaviors and changes that appear positive to the therapist may not be evaluated positively by the couple (Floyd & Markman, 1983), it is particularly important during treatment for the therapist to check out his own interpretations of marital interactions with those of the couple (i.e., distinguishing between the therapist's objective value of behaviors and the couple's subjective experience of these same behaviors) and to compare his and the couple's perceptions of change. In addition, although we have presented assessment and treatment as two distinct entities, we must point out that this distinction is arbitrary. Throughout the course of therapy, the effective therapist is continually altering the case conceptualization (and subsequently altering the treatment plan) in response to new information regarding presenting problems and the addition of emergent problems.

Another way to determine whether the choice of interventions is having the desired impact on the spouse's satisfaction is to use direct measurement. From the first session through the end of therapy, spouses are asked daily to rate their satisfaction with themselves, their marriage, and eleven relationship domains (e.g., affection, consideration, communication) on a 10-point Likert scale. Therapists either call the couple the night before the session to get these ratings or ask the couple to bring them in. The ratings are then averaged for the week, and each weekly average is plotted on a chart. This technique enables the therapist to determine whether strategies designed to improve a particular relationship domain are having their intended impact (e.g. whether techniques designed to improve communication are increasing marital happiness). These graphs may also be shown to the couple during the course of therapy to provide them with visual feedback regarding the progress they are making. In addition to these daily marital happiness ratings, therapists may want to readminister some of the initial questionnaires (such as the AOC or the MSI) during the course of therapy to determine whether the couple's satisfaction has changed on these measures and to identify areas with which spouses are still dissatisfied.

If it is determined that chosen interventions are not having their intended impact, then the therapist must remain flexible to alter the treatment program. Often the cause of the problem is that the particular treatment approach is not targeted toward the central part of the problem (e.g., couples may be learning communication skills when their communication problems are related to unrealistic beliefs about the communication process). Thus the therapist needs to reassess the couple's problems and generate appropriate treatment strategies. Alternatively, it may be that the couple is holding back some information from the therapist. If therapy is not progressing, and if the therapist has conducted a thorough assessment of the couple and generated appropriate treatment strategies, lack of progress may be due to one spouse's unvoiced ambivalence about remaining in the marriage. In this situation, it is often beneficial to ask both spouses about any thoughts they might be having about ending the relationship.

CONCLUSION

Although the SLC approach has been effective in alleviating marital distress in a large percentage of couples who have received this form of marital therapy (Baucom & Hoffman, 1986; Hahlweg & Markman, 1988), some couples fail to improve. We believe that part of the reason marital therapy is not successful more often is that outcome studies generally follow a very structured treatment protocol, with little tailoring of treatment interventions to the particular problems experienced by each couple. Consequently, we have started viewing our treatment interventions as modules that therapists can opt to use or not to use, according to their assessment of the particular needs of each couple. Our initial experience has been that this flexible approach enhances the efficacy of our treatment (Jacobson, Schmaling et al., 1989), and we are continuing to evaluate this approach systematically. When treatment strategies are tailored to individual client characteristics, the need for systematic research on the process of matching client characteristics with treatment strategies increases in importance. It is our hope that marital therapy researchers will continue in the quest for the development, evaluation, and optimal patterning of interventions in the treatment of marital distress. In the meantime, given the current state of knowledge regarding this problem, we suggest that the marital therapist adopt a problem-solving approach to clinical decision making similar to that outlined in this chapter and in chapter 3.

References

Barbach, L. (1984). *For each other*. New York: New American Library.

Baucom, D. H., & Hoffman, J. A. (1986). The effectiveness of marital therapy: Current status and application to the clinical setting. In N. S. Jacobson & A. S. Gurman (Eds.), *Clinical handbook of marital therapy*. New York: Guilford.

Baucom, D. H., & Lester, G. W. (1986). The usefulness of cognitive restructuring as an adjunct to behavioral marital therapy. *Behavior Therapy, 17*, 385–403.

Beach, S. R. H., & O'Leary, K. D. (1985). Current status of outcome research in marital therapy. In L. L'Abate (Ed.), *The handbook of family psychology and therapy*. Homewood, IL: Dorsey.

Beck, A. T., Rush, A. J., Shaw, B. F., & Emery, G. (1979). *Cognitive therapy of depression.* New York: Guilford.

Berley, R. A., & Jacobson, N. S. (1984). Causal attributions in intimate relationships: Toward a model of cognitive-behavioral marital therapy. In P. C. Kendall (Ed.), *Advances in cognitive-behavioral research and therapy* (Vol. 3). New York: Academic.

Birchler, G. R., Weiss, R. L., & Vincent, J. P. (1975). A multimethod analysis of social reinforcement exchange between maritally distressed and nondistressed spouse and stranger dyads. *Journal of Personality and Social Psychology, 31,* 349–360.

Boland, J. P., & Follingstad, D. R. (1987). The relationship between communication and marital satisfaction: A review. *Journal of Sex & Marital Therapy, 13,* 286–313.

Doherty, W. J. (1981a). Cognitive processes in intimate conflict: 1. Extending attribution theory. *American Journal of Family Therapy, 9,* 3–13.

Doherty, W. J. (1981b). Cognitive processes in intimate conflict: 2. Efficacy and learned helplessness. *American Journal of Family Therapy, 9,* 35–44.

Eidelson, R. J., & Epstein, N. (1982). Cognition and relationship maladjustment: Development of a measure of dysfunctional relationship belief. *Journal of Consulting and Clinical Psychology, 50,* 715–720.

Epstein, N. (1982). Cognitive therapy with couples. *American Journal of Family Therapy, 10,* 5–16.

Epstein, N., & Eidelson, R. J. (1981). Unrealistic beliefs of clinical couples: Their relationship to expectations, goals, and satisfaction. *American Journal of Family Therapy, 9,* 13–22.

Fincham, F. D. (1985). Attribution processes in distressed and nondistressed couples: 2. Responsibility for marital problems. *Journal of Abnormal Psychology, 94,* 183–190.

Fincham, F. D., Beach, S. R. H., & Baucom, D. H. (1987). Attribution processes in distressed and nondistressed couples: 4. Self-partner attribution differences. *Journal of Personality and Social Psychology, 52,* 739–748.

Fincham, F. D., Beach, S. R. H., & Nelson, G. (1987). Attribution processes in distressed and nondistressed couples: 3. Causal and responsibility attributions for spouse behavior. *Cognitive Therapy and Research, 11,* 71–86.

Fincham, F. D., & O'Leary, K. D. (1983). Causal inferences for spouse behavior in maritally distressed and nondistressed couples. *Journal of Social and Clinical Psychology, 1,* 42–57.

Floyd, F. J., & Markman, H. J. (1983). Observational biases in spouse observation: Toward a cognitive/behavioral model of marriage. *Journal of Consulting and Clinical Psychology, 51,* 450–457.

Follingstad, D. R. (1988). Marital therapy flow chart. *American Journal of Family Therapy, 16,* 36–45.

Geiss, S. K., & O'Leary, K. D. (1981). Therapist ratings of frequency and severity of marital problems: Implications for research. *Journal of Marital and Family Therapy, 7,* 515–520.

Gottman, J. M. (1979). *Marital interaction: Experimental investigations.* New York: Academic.

Gottman, J. M., Notarius, C., Markman, H. J., Bank, S., Yoppi, B., & Rubin, M. E. (1976). Behavior exchange theory and marital decision making. *Journal of Personality and Social Psychology, 34,* 14–23.

Greenberg, L. S., & Johnson, S. M. (1988). Emotionally focused therapy for couples. In N. S. Jacobson & A. S. Gurman (Eds.), *Clinical handbook of marital therapy.* New York: Guilford.

Hahlweg, K., & Markman, H. H. (1988). The effectiveness of behavioral marital therapy: Empirical status of behavioral techniques in preventing and alleviating marital distress. *Journal of Consulting and Clinical Psychology, 56,* 440–447.

Holtzworth-Munroe, A., & Jacobson, N. S. (1985). Causal attributions of married couples: When do they search for causes? What do they conclude when they do? *Journal of Personality and Social Psychology, 48,* 1399–1412.

Jacobson, N. S. (1983a). Clinical innovations in behavioral marital therapy. In K. Craig & R. J. McMahon (Eds.), *Advances in clinical behavior therapy.* New York: Brunner/Mazel.

Jacobson, N. S. (1983b). Expanding the range and applicability of behavioral marital therapy. *The Behavior Therapist, 6,* 189–191.

Jacobson, N. S. (1984). The modification of cognitive processes in behavioral marital therapy: Integrating cognitive and behavioral intervention strategies. In K. Hahlweg & N. S. Jacobson (Eds.), *Marital interaction: Analysis and modification.* New York: Guilford.

Jacobson, N. S. (1989). The politics of intimacy. *The Behavior Therapist, 12,* 29–32.

Jacobson, N. S., Berley, R. A., Melman, K. N., Elwood, R. W., & Phelps, C. (1985). Failure in behavioral marital therapy. In S. Coleman (Ed.), *Failures in family therapy.* New York: Guilford.

Jacobson, N.S., Follette, W.C., & Elwood, R.W. (1984). Outcome research on behavioral marital therapy: A methodological and conceptual reappraisal. In K. Hahlweg & N.S. Jacobson (Eds.), *Marital interaction: Analysis and modification.* New York: Guilford.

Jacobson, N. S., Follette, W. C., & McDonald, D. W. (1982). Reactivity to positive and negative behavior in distressed and nondistressed married couples. *Journal of Consulting and Clinical Psychology, 50,* 706–714.

Jacobson, N. S., & Holtzworth-Munroe, A. (1986). Marital therapy: A social learning-cognitive perspective. In N. S. Jacobson & A. S. Gurman (Eds.), *Clinical handbook of marital therapy.* New York: Guilford.

Jacobson, N. S., Holtzworth-Munroe, A., & Schmaling, K. B. (1989). Marital therapy and spouse involvement in the treatment of depression, agoraphobia, and alcoholism. *Journal of Consulting and Clinical Psychology, 57,* 5–10.

Jacobson, N. S., McDonald, D. W., Follette, W. C., & Berley, R. A. (1985). Attributional processes in distressed and nondistressed married couples. *Cognitive Therapy and Research, 9,* 35–50.

Jacobson, N. S., & Margolin, G. (1979). *Marital therapy: Strategies based on social learning and behavior exchange principles.* New York: Brunner/Mazel.

Jacobson, N. S., & Moore, D. (1981). Spouses as observers of the events in their relationship. *Journal of Consulting and Clinical Psychology, 49,* 269–277.

Jacobson, N. S., Schmaling, K. B., Holtzworth-Munroe, A., Katt, J. L., Wood, L. F., & Follette, V. M. (1989). Research-structured versus clinically flexible versions of social learning-based marital therapy. *Behavior Research and Therapy, 27,* 173–180.

Levenson, R. W., & Gottman, J. M. (1983). Marital interaction: Physiological linkage and affective exchange. *Journal of Personality and Social Psychology, 45,* 587–597.

LoPiccolo, J., & Steger, J. C. (1974). The sexual interaction inventory: A new instrument of assessment of sexual dysfunction. *Archives of Sexual Behavior, 3,* 585–595.

Margolin, G. (1981). Behavior exchange in happy and unhappy marriages: A family cycle perspective. *Behavior Therapy, 12,* 329–343.

Margolin, G. (1983a). Behavioral marital therapy: Is there a place for passion, play, and other non-negotiable dimensions? *The Behavior Therapist, 6,* 65–68.

Margolin, G. (1983b). An interactional model for the behavioral assessment of marital relationships. *Behavioral Assessment, 5,* 103–127.

Margolin, G., Michelli, J., & Jacobson, N. S. (1988). Assessment of marital dysfunction. In M. Hersen & A. S. Bellack (Eds.), *Behavioral assessment: A practical handbook* (3rd ed.). New York: Plenum.

Margolin, G., Talovic, S., & Weinstein, C. D. (1983). Areas of Change Questionnaire: A practical approach to marital assessment. *Journal of Consulting and Clinical Psychology, 51,* 920–931.

Margolin, G., & Wampold, B. E. (1981). Sequential analysis of conflict and accord in distressed and nondistressed marital partners. *Journal of Consulting and Clinical Psychology, 49,* 554–567.

Masters, W. H., & Johnson, V. E. (1970). *Human sexual inadequacy.* Boston: Little, Brown.

Melman, K. N., & Jacobson, N. S. (1983). The integration of behavioral marital therapy and sex therapy. In M. L. Aronson & L. R. Wolberg (Eds.), *Group and family therapy.* New York: Brunner/Mazel.

Noller, P. (1980). Misunderstandings in marital communication: A study of couples' nonverbal communication. *Journal of Personality and Social Psychology, 39,* 1135–1148.

Olson, K., & Kleim, D. (1985). Selecting behavioral marital interventions: An algorithm for matching couples and treatments. *Psychotherapy, 22,* 213–218.

Rice, D. G., & Rice, J. K. (1986). Separation and divorce therapy. In N. S. Jacobson & A. S. Gurman (Eds.), *Clinical handbook of marital therapy.* New York: Guilford.

Schindler, L., & Vollmer, M. (1984). Cognitive perspectives in behavioral marital therapy: Some proposals for bridging theory, research, and practice. In K. Hahlweg & N. S. Jacobson (Eds.), *Marital interaction: Analysis and modification.* New York: Guilford.

Snyder, D. K. (1979). *Marital Satisfaction Inventory.* Los Angeles: Western Psychological Services.

Snyder, D. K., & Smith, G. T. (1986). Classification of marital relationships: An empirical approach. *Journal of Marriage and the Family, 48,* 137–146.

Snyder, D. K., & Wills, R. M. (1989). Behavioral versus insight-oriented marital therapy: Effects on individual and interspousal functioning. *Journal of Consulting and Clinical Psychology, 57,* 39–46.

Spanier, G. B. (1976). Measuring dyadic adjustment: New scales for assessing the quality of marriage and similar dyads. *Journal of Marriage and the Family, 38,* 15–28.

Strauss, M. (1979). Measuring intrafamily conflict and violence: The Conflict Tactics Scales. *Journal of Marriage and the Family, 41,* 75–88.

Stuart, R. B. (1969). Operant-interpersonal treatment for marital discord. *Journal of Consulting and Clinical Psychology, 33,* 675–682.

Vincent, J. P., Friedman, L., Nugent, J., & Messerly, L. (1979). Demand characteristics in observations of marital interaction. *Journal of Consulting and Clinical Psychology, 47,* 557–566.

Vincent, J. P., Weiss, R. L., & Birchler, G. R. (1975). A behavioral analysis of problem solving in distressed and nondistressed married and stranger dyads. *Behavior Therapy, 6,* 475–487.

Weiss, R. L. (1980). Strategic behavioral marital therapy: Toward a model for assessment and intervention. In J. F. Vincent (Ed.), *Advances in family intervention, assessment and theory* (Vol. 1). Greenwich, CT: JAI.

Weiss, R. L. (1984). Cognitive and strategic interventions in behavioral marital therapy. In K. Hahlweg & N. S. Jacobson (Eds.), *Marital interaction: Analysis and modification*. New York: Guilford.

Weiss, R. L., & Birchler, G. R. (1975). *Areas of change*. Unpublished manuscript, University of Oregon, Eugene.

Weiss, R. L., & Perry, B. A. (1979). *Assessment and treatment of marital dysfunction*. Eugene: Oregon Marital Studies Program.

Whisman, M. A., & Jacobson, N. S. (in press). Brief behavioral marital therapy. In R. Wells & V. Giannetti (Eds.), *Handbook of the brief psychotherapies*. New York: Plenum.

Whisman, M. A., Jacobson, N. S., Fruzzetti, A. E., Schmaling, K. B., & Dobson, K. S. (1988, November). *Treating the couple versus the depressed spouse alone: The short- and long-term effects of cognitive behavior therapies for depression*. Paper presented at the annual meeting of the Association for Advancement of Behavior Therapy, New York.

Whisman, M. A., Schmaling, K. B., & Jacobson, N. S. (1988). *Changes in individual adjustment following marital therapy*. Manuscript submitted for publication.

Wile, D. B. (1981). *Couples therapy: A nontraditional approach*. New York: Wiley.

Chapter 8

Sexual Dysfunction

Debra L. Kaplan
Adrian Sondheimer

INTRODUCTION

Since 1966 and 1970, with the publication of Masters and Johnson's pioneering works describing the physiology of sexual functioning and the diagnosis and treatment of sexual dysfunctions, a considerable body of literature concerning sexual therapies has emerged. For a comprehensive description of the techniques and behavioral tasks pertinent to sex therapy, the reader is advised to consult other scholarly publications (Kaplan, 1974, 1979; LoPiccolo & LoPiccolo, 1978; Masters & Johnson, 1970). This chapter will focus on the application of aspects of the clinical decision-making model discussed in chapter 3 to the treatment of sexual dysfunction, as illustrated by a composite clinical case history.

APPLYING THE DECISION-MAKING MODEL

The manner in which an experienced clinician gathers information, articulates problem areas and maintaining factors, generates treatment alternatives, determines a treatment plan, and implements and evaluates that plan will be described. First, however, an issue concerning problem orientation will be addressed: the special biases that commonly surface during the treatment of sexual dysfunction.

Potential for Bias

Without question, clinicians must be aware of the unique biases that they bring to each therapeutic encounter. These prejudices are especially likely to emerge in the treatment of sexual dysfunctions because the therapist is dealing with an area of functioning that is both highly intimate and influenced by many cultural, social, religious, and ethical values.

Obvious areas of prejudice concern the treatment of groups whose sexual practices—such as fetishistic, paraphiliac, or homosexual—may not be consonant with those of the clinician. For example, a clinician who is ill at ease in the presence of male homosexuals might offer an impotent homosexual treatment that seeks to alter his sexual preference instead of focusing on the alleviation of his erectile difficulties. Similarly, clinicians often harbor judgments about the suitability of sexual activity in elderly populations, judgments that may distort their clinical work with older patients. The therapist who feels uncomfortable when considering sexual intimacies between elderly individuals might counsel a retired man with erectile difficulties to accept his symptoms as a consequence of aging rather than suggesting a comprehensive evaluation that could lead to sexual or medical therapies.

Another area of potential bias concerns the selection of treatment approaches. A naive clinician, upon learning that a sexual dysfunction exists, might immediately and mistakenly prescribe specific behavioral techniques (such as sensate focus or stop-start) without first collecting the information necessary for a comprehensive assessment of the disorder. The rote application of techniques can lead a therapist far afield from an effective treatment strategy. Thus careful attention to individual areas of bias is necessary to prevent inappropriate approaches to treatment.

Information Gathering

The information a sex therapist collects for a comprehensive assessment of all variables relevant to a case of sexual dysfunction, the armamentarium of treatment alternatives available to the therapist, and the process of choosing from among these alternatives will be addressed in the context of a specific case. The following brief vignette, derived from the case, illustrates a typical referral pathway for patients who seek treatment for sexual dysfunctions.

Upon the advice of her gynecologist, a married woman calls for treatment. She states that she suffers from painful sexual intercourse for which her physician can find no physical basis. The therapist asks whether her husband is amenable to participation with his wife in the evaluation of the reported dysfunction. She replies in the affirmative, and they arrive together for the first interview.

In the field of sexual therapy, it is generally optimal to include both members of the dyad in the evaluation phase. At times, however, extenuating circumstances make the inclusion of a partner impossible or undesirable. A man who seeks evaluation of erectile difficulties and whose wife suffers from a painful and debilitating terminal illness that precludes engagement in any form of sexual intimacy might be an example of the latter. If the husband reported his wife to be content with their lack of sexual activity and if his erectile difficulties occurred during brief, emotionally uncommitted sexual encounters with different partners and without his wife's knowledge, inclusion of the wife in the evaluation could well prove counterproductive and potentially disastrous. In this case, for the therapist to evaluate the man's erectile difficulties while excluding the wife could mean at least temporarily condoning the husband's extramarital liaisons and de-emphasizing the generally accepted tenet of the encouragement of disclosure between marital partners. Although this situation raises troubling ethical questions, many clinicians would choose to conduct the evaluation with the husband alone.

Individuals without partners also often engage the services of sex therapists. In those cases that are limited to the evaluation of a single individual, assessment and treatment alternatives are clearly modified. This chapter, however, will focus on the clinical decision-making process that evolves when a couple is available and willing to participate.

Before treatment can proceed, the therapist must obtain a complete and thorough definition of the presenting problem(s). It is important to recognize that the etiology of a specific dysfunction can have a variety of sources, including intrapsychic, interpersonal, cultural, biological, and learned factors (Kaplan, 1974). A comprehensive assessment, therefore, elicits detailed information pertaining to the marital or partnered relationship, including the couple's knowledge of the physiologic and anatomic bases underlying sexual functioning; each individual's past sexual history; cultural influences impinging on the couple; personality traits of each individual; the evolution of the sexual difficulties in the present relationship; and, finally, an explicit description of current lovemaking. The following paragraphs outline specific questions that delve more deeply into these general areas. Further elaboration occurs in a book edited by Kaplan (1983) on the evaluation of both medical and psychological aspects of sexual disorders.

When a couple arrives at the therapist's office for the first meeting, it is important to avoid availability biases (see chapter 1) by questioning any diagnostic labels and identifying exactly what happens behaviorally. In the case example to follow, the clinician initially learns that the wife is experiencing uncomfortable, even painful, intercourse. However, she also describes past symptomatology consistent with diagnoses of vaginismus and lack of sexual excitement. It emerges, moreover, that the husband has erectile difficulties, and this information necessitates an entirely new line of questioning about his specific sexual problem.

Knowledge of the evolution of the sexual problems in the couple's relationship is indispensable for a full understanding of their impairments. It is important to ascertain when and under what circumstances the sexual difficulties began and whether they had occurred in previous relationships or are specific to the current one. Moreover, the therapist should ask whether the difficulties are ongoing and unchanging or have changed over time and should assess what behaviors the couple have utilized to cope.

Similarly, the therapist must learn about the individual sexual histories of both partners in order to understand how each member of the couple arrived at the current sexual difficulties. The therapist asks questions to elicit information, cognition, attitudes, and feelings about (a) the development of secondary sexual characteristics; (b) masturbation; (c) puberty; (d) menstruation; (e) nocturnal emissions; (f) degree of sexual knowledge and methods of acquisition of this knowledge; (g) first and early sexual experiences; (h) previous sexual relationships and partners; (i) incidents of sexual molestation, abuse, rape, or incest; (j) and sexual fantasies. The Derogatis Sexual Functioning Inventory (Derogatis, 1978) provides a pencil-and-paper assessment of the nature, quality, and frequency of sexual behaviors, as well as attitudes and feelings toward these behaviors. The elucidation of sexual myths, sexual values, and intrapsychic sexual conflicts is necessary. In addition, the therapist seeks to uncover major life events that might be temporally related to the onset of the sexual dysfunction. Assessment of each individual's psychological stability, including any previous history of psychological or psychiatric treatment, is desired. Throughout these discussions, the therapist attempts to gain an understanding of each individual's personality traits.

The information gleaned from the individual sexual histories often guides the selection of treatment approaches and the process of therapy. For example, a clinician's approach to a woman's complaint of inability to attain orgasm during intercourse would be tempered by information describing orgastic experiences during previous sexual relationships. If she had been orgastic in these past relationships, the therapist would further assess the sexual technique and knowledge of her current partner, the nature and quality of her relationship with that partner, the content of distracting thoughts occurring during lovemaking, and the existence of possibly related traumatic life events. Identification of significant tensions in the current relationship resulting in the orgastic dysfunction would suggest couples therapy as the optimal treatment approach. Alternatively, if the orgastic difficulties had been present throughout the woman's previous relationships, further assessment would focus on her sexual values and intrapsychic conflicts as well as on the aforementioned variables. The therapist might uncover thoughts about sex as "dirty and perverted" occurring intrusively during penile insertion and thrusting. Therapeutic efforts would then focus on these thoughts by seeking to determine their origin and assisting in their elimination.

In a second example, a couple seeking treatment for the woman's lack of sexual excitement and a generally poor sexual relationship might divulge information about repetitive incest experiences that had occurred during her childhood and early adolescent years. In such cases, feelings of helplessness, despair, and outrage resulting from the early events are commonly retriggered when the woman and her partner engage in sexual activity. An appropriate therapeutic approach would first focus on the psychological impact of the incest experiences, later seeking gradually to introduce pleasurable sexual activity. At that time, emphasis would be placed on allowing the woman to control the extent and nature of the couple's sexual interactions.

In a final example, a man might seek treatment for erectile dysfunction shortly following the death of his beloved wife. Assessment might reveal the presence of significant depression and unresolved mourning that would likely become the focus of therapy should a medical workup prove negative.

The presentations of vaginismus and painful intercourse necessitate a description of the specific circumstances under which the woman experiences pain. The therapist asks questions that precisely locate the pain in a particular area of the vagina and situate its occurrence at a particular point in time during the sexual experience. Questions about sexual excitement, lubrication, sexual desire, orgasm, and medical problems that may be connected to the onset of sexual symptoms are included in a complete diagnostic assessment. Often the presenting problem simply masks the presence of other, more fundamental sexual difficulties. For example, specific sexual tasks prescribed for a couple with presenting complaints of lack of sexual excitement and inadequate lubrication may prove ineffective because of noncompliance over a period of several weeks. In such a case, the more fundamental problem of low sexual desire will often emerge, necessitating a shift in treatment focus away from difficulties with arousal to the factors responsible for the low desire.

With complaints of erectile dysfunction, it is imperative that the possibility of organic etiology be explored. The therapist's initial questioning attempts to elicit instances of erections that were rigid enough to permit penetration and that were maintained for a period sufficient to result in satisfactory intercourse for both partners. (The definition of "satisfactory" is obviously subjective.) Further objective information from both partners is required to quantify the time periods involved and thus to determine whether the problem is due to inadequate maintenance, unreasonable expectations, or some combination of the two.

An assessment of erectile dysfunction commonly involves eliciting information about the adequacy and maintenance of erections with the partner(s), with masturbation, during sleep, and upon awakening. A medical history, with an emphasis on the possible presence of compromising medical conditions or medications implicated in erectile dysfunction, is crucial to the evaluation. For a complete assessment, it is also important to inquire about sexual desire, premature ejaculation, and retarded ejaculation. Answers to these questions will guide the therapist in deciding whether to refer the patient to a urologist specializing in the evaluation of sexual dysfunctions. When a purely psychogenic etiology is in doubt, such a referral must be discussed with the patient and firmly encouraged. For example, if the clinician fails to elicit current instances of erection adequate for penetration, referral to a urologist is probably indicated. If the assessment also reveals a positive medical history, such as diabetes, vascular insufficiencies, or use of particular antihypertensive medications, the necessity for referral is confirmed. For further reference, Wagner and Green (1981) present a detailed discussion of the physiological and psychological aspects of erectile dysfunction.

The therapist must also assess the couple's marital relationship, both by obtaining factual answers to questions and by directly observing their interactions. The therapist explores the evolution of the relationship, the degree and types of conflict in the marriage, and whether the individuals feel positively or negatively about their relationship. Assessment inventories, including the Locke–Wallace Marriage Inventory

(Locke & Wallace, 1959), the Dyadic Adjustment Scale (Spanier, 1976), and the Marital Satisfaction Inventory (Snyder, 1979) are useful in the identification of marital difficulty or satisfaction. In this phase of assessment, the therapist seeks to ascertain whether the sexual problems are embedded within a sound relationship or whether they are symptomatic of a poor marriage with a high degree of conflict. If the relationship is solid, with little marital conflict, the sexual problems will likely become the major focus of treatment. However, in the context of severe marital distress, relationship difficulties must usually be confronted and resolved before sexual issues can be addressed effectively. If marital difficulties are present but not preeminent, resolution of sexual difficulties will often facilitate improvement of the overall couple relationship. (For a detailed description of the evaluation of the marital relationship of clients with sexual complaints, see Hof, 1987.)

Finally, the couple's current sexual functioning is assessed. Frequency of sexual encounters and patterns and methods of initiation are discussed. How successfully does the couple make time for the sexual relationship? What priority does sex have for each member of the dyad? How easily do the partners communicate about sexual issues, wishes, wants, and needs? The therapist must obtain a detailed, explicit description of the sexual encounters to evaluate the couple's sexual knowledge, technique, variety, and modes of communication.

This information is gleaned from a series of interviews involving the couple together and the partners separately. Individual interviews are useful to avoid the possible constraint caused by the presence of the partner. The members of the couple are informed beforehand that, if they so stipulate, information revealed in the individual interview will be kept confidential. Later in treatment, the therapist might perceive a sharing of information with the partner to be crucial to the therapeutic process. The matter would then be discussed privately with the partner who first divulged the material, and the formulation of a revised treatment approach would follow.

Beginning therapists often express concern about anticipated difficulties in eliciting intimate sexual information from their patients. Apart from slight initial embarrassment, most patients readily overcome their reticence when the therapist requests information in a sensitive, straightforward, and unembarrassed fashion. If a patient is unusually evasive or reserved, various psychopathologic diagnoses should be considered; often this resistance becomes the first focus of treatment.

Case History

To demonstrate certain aspects of the process of clinical decision making in sex therapy, we will outline a specific case, following the assessment guidelines previously articulated in this chapter. For purposes of illustration this case is a composite, although not atypical of the clinical complexity of patients requesting treatment for sexual dysfunction.

Janet was a 26-year-old woman enrolled in a PhD program in fine arts. Her husband, Alex, was a 28-year-old investment banker employed in a highly competitive firm. It was the first marriage for both. They had been married for 2 years and had no children; she had never been pregnant. Prior to their marriage, they had dated for 2 years.

Janet described sex as always having been uncomfortable and painful. She had not experienced sexual intercourse before meeting her husband. Before marriage, she harbored intense conflicts about intercourse related to a strict religious upbringing and to her mother's strong warnings against a possible pregnancy. During their dating years, however, Janet and Alex engaged in petting, necking, and fondling, which Janet greatly enjoyed. These experiences included kissing, caressing, and breast stimulation. Whenever genital stimulation was included, she became increasingly anxious, experiencing decreased enjoyment. It was difficult initially to determine whether the decreased enjoyment was related to Alex's awkward sexual technique or to the conflicts Janet had acquired concerning her sexual inclinations. Despite Janet's ambivalence, the couple engaged in intercourse a few months prior to their marriage. During that experience, she felt very anxious, tense, and conflicted. She did not feel sexually excited or aroused, and vaginal lubrication barely occurred. The encounter involved minimal foreplay, in contrast to the couple's previous pattern of long periods of touching and caressing. Penile penetration proved difficult and caused Janet much pain, but she "gritted her teeth and tolerated it." Thrusting was similarly painful, and she described vaginal soreness and irritation as the activity continued. She welcomed ejaculation and the cessation of intercourse.

Janet did not inform Alex of her physical and psychological discomfort. Following this experience, the couple rarely attempted intercourse because Janet manufactured plausible excuses in order to avoid painful encounters. Finding a suitable private place also proved difficult. The couple had virtually no verbal communication about sexual matters. On their rare attempts at intercourse, penile penetration became increasingly difficult, and Alex later reported feeling as if he were "pushing against a rock." Janet believed her partner to be unaware of the existence or extent of her discomfort. This perception was accurate, although Alex began to sense that something was wrong as a consequence of her excessive avoidance of sex. They also continued the pattern of very little foreplay. Although Janet enjoyed this aspect of lovemaking, she never requested more for fear of hurting Alex's feelings. Thus he eventually concluded that she simply was no longer interested in mutual touching.

Janet hoped that marriage would resolve her conflicts and difficulties. As might be expected, that hope proved unfounded. Eventually, penetration became impossible, and Alex became increasingly frustrated when his attempts at lovemaking were rejected or merely tolerated. He developed self-doubts and felt he was failing his wife. Consequently, Alex became sexually self-conscious and experienced both increased anxiety and decreased passion. In a circular process, the greater his awareness of Janet's detachment, the more he became self-conscious and removed. Eventually, one day he failed to achieve erection and became dismayed and upset; he subsequently developed a pattern of total erectile failure during their infrequent attempts at sexual intercourse. He was embarrassed and extremely distressed by his failures because he was a person accustomed to "using his will and determination to achieve success." Alex viewed his difficulties as signs of weakness and vulnerability, and he therefore found any discussion of his condition very difficult. In fact, it emerged that because of the psychological distress both were feeling about their sexual relationship, the couple had ceased all sexual intimacy during the half year prior to the first evaluation appointment. Though they clearly felt affection for each other, caressing and touching had stopped because it signaled penetration attempts to follow. It was only at this point that Janet first spoke to her gynecologist and received the referral for sex therapy.

Janet was the elder of two girls born to a middle-class Italian Catholic family. Her upbringing was strongly religious, with a serious commitment to the values of the church. She was a very good student who excelled academically, was achievement oriented, and intellectually challenged rigid doctrines. As an adult, Janet considered herself religious, was psychologically minded, and was pursuing a doctorate.

Janet began developing secondary sexual characteristics at age 11 and viewed these changes with anticipation and pleasure. Menstruation commenced at age 12 without physical or psychological difficulties. Her mother had prepared her for this developmental milestone with straightforward and competent discussion. Janet dated occasionally during high school and college and engaged in light petting and kissing. She masturbated as a teenager, reached climax manually, and enjoyed the experience. She did not engage in this practice often, feeling residual guilt, possibly from her religious training.

It was with her husband that Janet first experienced intercourse. She was not orgasmic with him, however, through either penile or digital stimulation. She felt sexual excitement and sexual desire for him, but only in situations where penile penetration was not possible. In bed, she did not experience adequate lubrication for comfortable penile insertion. Janet was wary of upsetting her husband and therefore did not articulate her sexual desires or fears. In addition, she felt that, as a man and as her husband, he should know what she liked and needed. She feared that articulating her desires would ruin the experience— that if he did not naturally engage in activities pleasurable for her, he must find them disagreeable.

Alex was the eldest of three children, the younger two being sisters. Raised as an Episcopalian with loose connections to the church, he was emotionally close to his family of origin. As a student he performed exceedingly well and had a strong internal drive to achieve. At the time of the referral, he worked long hours as an investment banker. He was wary of psychological thinking and discomfited by self-examination.

Alex's development of secondary sexual characteristics was un-eventful and taken in stride. In his teens, he experienced nocturnal emissions that he accepted comfortably. During high school he dated several girls with whom he engaged in "heavy" petting, and in college he had several sexual experiences with different women that included intercourse. The couple met while both were attending professional school, and Alex stated that Janet represented his first serious relation-ship.

Alex had masturbated regularly since puberty and was able to attain and maintain normal erections and ejaculation with masturbation. He noted nocturnal and early morning erections, and he had no partners outside his marriage. He maintained a significant level of sexual desire, had not experienced prior erectile problems, and perceived himself to be sexually knowledgeable. His medical history was unremarkable for conditions related to erectile dysfunction.

The couple professed much love for each other, describing a fun-damentally solid marriage with conflicts stemming from interactions with their families of origin. Both individuals appeared excessively involved with their families, and this involvement at times created mutual tensions. In conjoint sessions, they were respectful of each other, with a general warmth and ease of conversation that became notably absent when sexuality was the focus. At that point, communication became awkward and tension filled.

Articulation of Problem Areas and Maintaining Factors

Having accumulated this information, the therapist needed to decide which behaviors were problematic, what were likely etiologies, what treatment alternatives were available, which interventions should be selected, and how to prioritize these interventions.

The therapist followed the clinical decision-making model to facilitate these clinical decisions, concluding that Janet's presenting problem of painful intercourse could be explained both by her lack of sexual excitement and by vaginismus. Janet also had difficulty in attaining orgasm with her husband, irrespective of method. Possible factors contributing to these problems included sexual conflicts stemming from her strict religious upbringing, the influence of sexual myths (some previously identified and others likely to be mentioned during the course of therapy), difficulties with relaxation and distraction during lovemaking, previous introital pain leading to the anticipation of pain in the future, poor sexual technique stemming from her husband's limited sexual awareness, lack of mutual communication of sexual needs and wishes, a lengthy attempt at solution via sexual avoidance, and the perpetuation of unresolved marital conflicts. Contributions to Alex's erectile dysfunction possibly included the presence of spectatoring and performance anxiety; distracting thoughts during lovemaking; Janet's poor technique stemming from her lack of sexual knowledge; and the couple's unresolved marital conflicts, sexual avoidance, and impaired communication about sex. Contributing couple issues encompassed potentially different levels of sexual desire, difficulties in making time for and giving priority to the sexual relationship, marital conflicts in areas other than sexual functioning, and mutual avoidance of lovemaking.

Generating Treatment Alternatives

The evaluation of sexual dysfunction generally proceeds best when the partner of the impaired individual participates. After the assessment phase, the clinician must decide whether to meet with the impaired individual alone, with the partners separately, and/or with the couple. The choice depends on a decision analysis concerning the indicated interventions, the desires of the individuals involved, and the differing degrees of stress presented by the identified problems, as illustrated by a continued focus on the case.

If Janet were treated alone, Kegel exercises would be indicated by the diagnosis of vaginismus. The exercises would aim to give Janet the ability to voluntarily relax the muscles surrounding the vaginal opening; she would be instructed in the tightening and relaxation of these muscle groups. When sufficiently relaxed, she would attempt to insert one finger or the smallest vaginal dilator comfortably into her vagina, using her finger or the dilator to receive feedback about the degree of vaginal muscular tension. As she became more proficient at relaxing these muscles, she would attempt to insert more fingers or larger dilators, with the goal of eventually permitting comfortable penile insertion.

The therapist could also teach Janet assertiveness skills to encourage her to express her sexual needs to her husband. Progressive muscle relaxation, with or without EMG biofeedback, might improve her capacity to relax, especially during lovemaking. In addition, cognitive therapy could help to resolve possible conflicts between religious values and sexual myths on the one hand and sexual desires and inclinations on the other. For example, Janet's sexual desires appeared inhibited by her sexual myth that her partner should know what she liked sexually without guidance or instruction. This myth had fostered many assumptions about her husband's nonperformance of sexual behaviors that appealed to her, assumptions that led to her feelings of anger and hurt as well as to a lack of fulfillment of her sexual desires. Cognitive therapy would address Janet's belief system in order to encourage her to voice her sexual preferences to her husband. Educative efforts, which might include bibliotherapy, could further help by enhancing her sexual knowledge.

Were Alex to be seen alone, his erectile dysfunction could be addressed via hypnotherapy or the use of a sexual surrogate. Education regarding sexual technique, anatomy, and physiology could be provided. Distracting cognitions, such as his focus on a physically unappealing feature of his partner or recent tensions at work, could be discussed, and he could learn techniques to replace them with sexually stimulating thoughts.

Were treatment to proceed with the husband and wife as a couple, the therapist could choose to deal with marital issues, focusing on communication and negotiating skills. Another marital strategy might be to encourage the resumption of sexual intimacy within the couple's hectic life-style by identifying potential times for sexual intimacy and the factors impeding its occurrence. Were the focus on the couple's sexual problems, the general strategy might employ a graded set of sexual experiences as pioneered by Masters and Johnson (1970) and further elaborated by Kaplan (1974). These experiences begin with the pleasuring tasks of sensate focus, which involve mutual physical touch and caress in a nondemanding, relaxed atmosphere. Touch is at first restricted to nongenital areas of the body and, later, genital touching is reintroduced, with the emphasis all the while on pleasure rather than on sexual arousal. When the couple has mastered sensate focus, different behavioral treatment techniques can address specific sexual dysfunctions. The therapist could also attempt to enhance Janet's and Alex's skills in communicating about their sexuality and to increase their knowledge and technical skills regarding sexual functioning and lovemaking.

Choosing among Treatment Alternatives

Working with the husband and wife as a couple, and prescribing the preliminary sexual pleasuring experience of sensate focus, is the most clearly suggested initial approach to treatment in the case just described. The value and utility of this choice are manifold. First, Alex and Janet perceived their problems as primarily sexual, and they were seeking therapy to ameliorate these symptoms. Second, though a degree of marital conflict had emerged, it did not appear to overshadow, or to be etiologic, of their sexual problems. Rather, the couple appeared to have a sound relationship, and working with them as a unit would, it was hoped, increase their stability and mutual enjoyment. Third, they were amenable to, and desirous of, conjoint treatment. Finally, the prescription of sensate focus and the couple's handling of that task could provide useful diagnostic information about the immediate sources of their sexual difficulties, as well as indications for future treatment approaches for their individual sexual dysfunctions. In other words, the assignment of this task and observation of the couple's implementation of it might provide a basis for further problem definition.

Following the prescription of sensate focus, the couple might report that they had not performed any of the tasks assigned by the therapist; their failure to fulfill the prescription could have a number of causes. Discussion might reveal that the presence of previously suppressed significant marital tensions precluded the expression of closeness and affection. A radical revision of the treatment approach would then be required to concentrate subsequent therapeutic efforts on pervasive marital conflict. Alternatively, the couple might report that the nonperformance was linked to a squabble immediately preceding each possible occasion for sexual pleasuring, while at other times the relationship remained comfortable. If so, the therapist would direct less attention to the content of the arguments than to the revealed pattern of fighting that embodied a resistance to the performance of the sensate focus tasks. A discussion of the couple's fears and concerns about intimacy and relating to each other sexually would ensue, and the therapist would try to ascertain whether the prescribed task should be limited to a smaller behavioral step that would generate less anxiety. Another explanation for nonperformance of tasks might be difficulty in finding times in busy schedules for the pleasuring experiences. In that case, the therapist would help to identify potential times for lovemaking and foster awareness of factors that could interfere with this activity.

On the other hand, if the couple returned having performed the sensate focus tasks, the therapist would examine the occasions closely, focusing on each partner's degree of immersion and participation in the potentially pleasurable experience. If a partner reported distraction by nonsexual, nonpleasurable thoughts, both the content of the thoughts and approaches to their elimination would be discussed.

Despite the therapist's choice to focus initially on the couple, the wife's vaginismus would receive direct attention early in treatment. Kegel exercises would be described and their use encouraged. Individual sessions with Janet might be pursued if she experienced discomfort discussing or performing the exercises with her husband. However, she would soon be expected to include Alex in these efforts.

Treatment Implementation and Evaluation

The behavioral strategies of sensate focus and those prescribed for vaginismus are designed to promote relaxation and sexual pleasure for both partners. Their initial emphasis is on the evocation of sexual pleasure and not on the production of sexual arousal. These sexual experiences thus tend to decrease or eliminate performance pressure, resulting in the spontaneous return of sexual excitement for both members—that is, lubrication and excitement in the female and full erections in the male.

During treatment, the therapist also promotes the couple's reciprocal communications concerning their sexual needs and wishes and encourages the partners to give each other constructive feedback about their joint sexual experiences. When indicated, the therapist provides information concerning sexual techniques or practices and the anatomical and physiological bases of sexual functioning. The combination of improved communication about sexual matters, increased sexual knowledge, and reduction of tension concerning sexual performance is often sufficient to facilitate full erectile functioning, increased sexual excitement, and mutual sexual comfort.

Occasionally, other conflicts emerge that interfere with the proposed treatment regimen. For example, the appearance of a more severe intrapsychic or marital disturbance than was seen initially might require a shift of focus to that area. Following a positive response to this new intervention, which might entail therapeutic work with individuals or with the couple, the original approaches would be resumed.

To enhance the sexual functioning of the couple in our case history, the most effective treatments appear to employ the behavioral techniques specific to the field of sex therapy. However, it is crucial that the couple's responses to treatment interventions be monitored continually (see chapter 3), and that the treatment approach be modified in the face of patient resistance or other mitigating circumstances.

CONCLUSION

The clinical decision-making model described in Part I of this volume provides the sex therapist with a useful guide for choosing among treatment alternatives and for implementing and evaluating the outcomes of specific interventions. Moreover, as emphasized throughout this volume, it presents a welcome structure that allows for rapid changes in the approaches to sexual problems to respond to shifts in the clinical situation.

References

Derogatis, L. R. (1978). *Derogatis Sexual Functioning Inventory* (rev. ed.). Baltimore: Clinical Psychometrics Research.

Hof, L. (1987). Evaluating the marital relationship of clients with sexual complaints. In G. Weeks & L. Hof (Eds.), *Integrating sex and marital therapy*. New York: Brunner/Mazel.

Kaplan, H. S. (1974). *The new sex therapy*. New York: Brunner/Mazel.

Kaplan, H. S. (1979). *Disorders of sexual desire*. New York: Brunner/Mazel.

Kaplan, H. S. (Ed.). (1983). *The evaluation of sexual disorders: Psychological and medical aspects*. New York: Brunner/Mazel.

Locke, H. J., & Wallace, K. M. (1959). Short marital adjustment and prediction tests: Their reliability and validity. *Marriage and Family Living, 21*, 251–255.

LoPiccolo, J., & LoPiccolo, L. (Eds.). (1978). *Handbook of sex therapy*. New York: Plenum.

Masters, W. H., & Johnson, V. E. (1966). *Human sexual response*. Boston: Little, Brown.

Masters, W. H., & Johnson, V. E. (1970). *Human sexual inadequacy*. Boston: Little, Brown.

Snyder, D. K. (1979). Multidimensional assessment of marital satisfaction. *Journal of Marriage and the Family, 41*, 813–824.

Spanier, G. B. (1976). Measuring dyadic adjustments: New scales for assessing the quality of marriage and similar dyads. *Journal of Marriage and the Family, 38,* 15–28.

Wagner, G., & Green, R. (1981). *Impotence: Physiological, psychological, surgical diagnosis and treatment.* New York: Plenum.

Chapter 9

Personality Disorders

Neill S. Cohen
Christine M. Nezu

INTRODUCTION

Until the past decade, the notion of personality has been anathema to most clinicians embracing a behavioral framework of psychotherapy. However, with the support of the third edition of the *Diagnostic and Statistical Manual of Mental Disorders* (American Psychiatric Association, 1980) by many renowned behavior therapists (e.g., Barlow, 1981), the constructs of personality and personality disorder have received greater prominence. With several important caveats, the use of these constructs seems justified. For example, there is now longitudinal evidence of enduring person variables (Mischel, Shoda, & Peake, 1988; Wright & Mischel, 1987a, 1987b; Wright & Mischel, in press) and data to support the notion of cross-situational behavior. These findings, when taken together with self-efficacy theory (Bandura, 1977) and the clinical application of cognitive psychology and social cognition, suggest a distinctly behavioral conceptualization of personality disorders. In the broadest sense, the evidence does support the revised version of the *Diagnostic and Statistical Manual of Mental Disorder's* (DSM-III-R) definition as "personality traits [that] are inflexible and maladaptive and cause either significant impairment or functional distress" (American Psychiatric Association, 1987, p. 335). However, the data base also suggests a radical departure from the traditional view with regard to discrete categories of disorders, assessment of maladaptive traits, and the conceptualization of etiological and maintaining variables.

Ultimately, the utility of any theory lies in its ability to generate treatment strategies and facilitate the process of clinical improvement. We view the clinical decision-making model presented in chapter 3 as an empirical, yet necessarily flexible, means by which to achieve these goals. The complexity of treatment planning with regard to various subtypes of personality disorders requires such a model. We are often disappointed with the common trend in the behavioral literature to provide "cookbook" interventions specific to the personality disorders noted in the DSM-III-R. To do so in the absence of sound scientific evidence (Turkat & Levin, 1984) represents an implicit endorsement of this nosology and of the analytic underpinnings from which the diagnostic terms were derived. It is better, in our view, to conduct an assessment using intermediate levels of inference (Goldfried & Kent, 1972), than to invoke abstract, higher order levels of constructs that remain untestable. The three clusters of personality disorders presented in the DSM-III-R, based as they are on the more behavioral constructs "odd or eccentric," "dramatic, emotional, or erratic," and "anxious or fearful" (p. 337), seem consistent with this notion.

One hallmark of behavior therapy has been its idiographic approach toward assessment of the client's unique problem areas. Interventions are then targeted toward these problem areas. A diagnostic label, however, does not lend itself to individualized procedures. We contend that the existing data base does not justify using discrete categories of personality disorders. Moreover, our clinical experience suggests considerable overlap of dysfunctional thought patterns and problematic behaviors across various diagnostic categories. We therefore focus our application of the clinical decision-making model to the treatment of personality disorders on the use of nomothetic conceptualizations to guide idiographic assessment.

Despite this emphasis, it would be clinically naive, as well as inconsistent with recent data, to eschew certain nomothetic precepts that relate to personality disorders. Several concepts may be derived from the psychoanalytic literature that are theoretically consistent within the context of behavioral approaches, albeit seldom mentioned. Recently, a number of authors have attempted an integration of certain psychoanalytic concepts within a behavioral framework (Goldfried, 1982; Goldfried & Newman, 1986; Mahoney, 1980; Guidano & Liotti, 1983; Safran, 1984a, 1984b; Safran & Greenberg, 1986; Segal, 1988). They have significantly contributed to our current conceptualization of personality disorders.

Individuals with personality disorders can be characterized by their *adaptive inflexibility*, that is, their limited, rather rigid strategies for relating to others, achieving goals, and coping with stress. Thus assessment should emphasize the search for historic rather than situational antecedents so that enduring patterns may be understood within a learning framework.

Because of the client's adaptive inflexibility, there is an increased likelihood that the therapeutic relationship will provide a valid sample of behavior occurring in other interpersonal contexts. Core cognitive processes also manifest this cross-situational consistency (Safran, Vallis, Segal, & Shaw, 1986). In addition to employing validated measures of interpersonal functioning, the therapist seems justified in using her own reaction to the client as a means of assessment. In other words, the therapist's reaction may be representative of other people's reactions to a given client. Hypotheses gleaned in this manner may be further strengthened (or disconfirmed) by interviewing members of the client's milieu.

Clients with personality disorders often play a role in the maintenance of their problems by engaging in *vicious cycles* (Millon, 1981; Safran, 1984a, 1984b; Wachtel, 1977, 1987). They set into motion self-defeating sequences with others and seek out situations that tend to confirm their cognitive distortions. Clients entangled in these vicious cycles often are unaware of these dysfunctional interactional patterns or the core assumptions that underlie them. As a result, such clients are more likely to come to therapy with "calling card complaints," or focal problems functionally related to more central issues. (For example, the individuals who will be discussed later in this chapter did not enter treatment for problems involving relationships with others, but for complaints about procrastination, depression, and obesity.)

The assumptions that generally define a behavioral approach apply to personality disorders as well. For example, developmental histories can be conceptualized in accord with social learning theory (Bandura, 1982). However, terms such as *vicarious learning, reinforcement history,* and *efficacy expectations* should be used in place of reified, metapsychological terms derived from psychoanalytic theory. The notion of reciprocal determinism applies as well, but, as we will attempt to illustrate, is weighted more toward the individual than the environment.

As is consistent with social learning theory, performance-based procedures are generally assumed to be more effective than verbal, evocative techniques. However, a little-known tenet of this theory is that the therapeutic relationship provides a crucial setting for in vivo interventions. The earlier, situational outlook has often led to less direct interventions (e.g., instructing the client to attempt alternative interactional patterns through homework assignments involving others). Although the generalization and maintenance of interpersonal change can be enhanced by such assignments, the acquisition of new behaviors may be more directly achieved through the therapeutic relationship.

As is evident in the two case studies that will be described, assessment of clients with characterological disturbances presents the behavior therapist with a plethora of clinical problems. Assessment of such problems and hypotheses concerning the organismic variables involved in their maintenance requires a comprehensive, multifocused assessment, as described in chapter 3. Often the process focuses initially on lower order inferences and proceeds inductively to higher order inferences. As our first case illustrates, for example, procrastination may be related to cognitions centered around perfectionism, low frustration tolerance, or stimulus control difficulties. If treatment decisions based upon such lower order inferences are not complied with or are not as effective as expected, focus on a higher order inference may be justified. In some cases, procrastination may serve as a distraction (for both client and therapist) from more anxiety-laden issues. Once these more charged issues are selected as treatment targets, the focus on procrastination is shifted.

CLINICAL EXAMPLES

The two clinical case examples provided illustrate our current working definition of the term *personality disorder* and the application of the clinical decision-making model to the treatment of individuals having symptoms representative of, respectively, the anxious or fearful cluster and the dramatic, emotional, or erratic cluster noted in the DSM-III-R.

The first patient's presentation was extremely subtle, and her dysfunctional interpersonal style was not identified as a treatment consideration until the decision-making model was applied several times. In contrast, the second patient's emotional reactivity was immediately apparent, making assessment of interpersonal patterns a more obvious consideration. In spite of these obvious differences, careful assessment in each case revealed a strikingly similar core constellation of automatic thoughts. Nevertheless, the widely divergent styles of these patients dictated markedly different processes for targeting core biases in information-processing activity, assisting each in obtaining a metaperspective on these biases, and selecting techniques aimed at their modification. In both cases, however, effective treatment resulted from use of the clinical decision-making model.

Clinical Example: Ruth

Ruth, a 40-year-old divorced woman with no children, had been working as a legal aid attorney for the past 3 years and was referred by a fellow lawyer. Her presenting complaint involved work-related difficulties that had assumed crisis proportions. Specifically, she was to have written a legal brief for a case on appeal that had been due 2 months earlier. She had told her supervisor that the brief had been written when, in fact, she had not even begun to work on it. If her failure to hand in her brief were to be discovered, it would be deemed unethical conduct, and she would lose her job.

Ruth appeared quite agitated in the initial session and had a plaintive, desperate quality to her tone and expression. The problem of the overdue brief had become the focal point in her life: It interfered with her day-to-day responsibilities at work, hindered her ability to enjoy herself at home, and kept her awake at night. Ruth reported having other procrastination-related difficulties, both within and outside work. She had read that behavior therapy could be effective in treating such difficulties and therefore had sought out this type of treatment.

Initial Assessment

The initial step in the assessment process was to conduct a functional analysis of the presenting complaint. Ruth reported that she would start work every day with the resolve to complete her brief and would begin by sitting at her desk and taking care of routine phone calls and correspondence. However, these activities would consume as much as half her morning. She would then take out the relevant documents and commence work on her brief, whereupon she would experience acute anxiety, stop work, and visit with colleagues down the hall. Physiologic concomitants of the anxiety included tightening in her chest, a "nervous stomach," and tachycardia.

Following a lunch break, she would attempt to keep up with her current caseload but would experience difficulties similar to those of the morning: devoting attention to routine matters, meeting substantive challenges with intense anxiety, and reducing anxiety through socialization with colleagues. Visits to colleagues were ostensibly for professional assistance, though work was seldom accomplished. Significantly, there was no reciprocity involved in this interactional pattern; no colleague ever came to visit with Ruth or to seek out her professional advice.

It seemed, based on the foregoing, that procrastination difficulties could be functionally related to attributes of the task at hand or to certain cognitive distortions regarding the task (e.g., magnification of its complexity or perfectionistic standards), thus resulting in anxiety and avoidance behaviors. The problem also appeared related to a rather one-sided style of relating to colleagues. This interpersonal pattern, however, appeared more temporally distant from the problem behavior, suggesting that establishing a functional relationship between these two variables would involve invoking a higher order inference. Therefore, the assessment process was initially weighted towards environmental antecedents and associated beliefs and expectations related to procrastinating complex tasks. A second focus was on the high level of physiologic arousal experienced by the client, which interfered with higher order processing. As indicated, the interpersonal context in which these difficulties occurred was a third assessment consideration but was assigned lower priority, as initially suggested by the functional analysis.

A final assessment consideration involved seeking disconfirming evidence that Ruth's procrastination was a concomitant of the vegetative aspects of a clinical depression. This hypothesis was disconfirmed on the basis of a number of factors—specifically, mental status at initial session, diurnal variation or early morning awakening, and weight change. The Beck Depression Inventory (Beck, Ward, Mendelsohn, Mock, & Erbaugh, 1961) was also administered, along with a Multimodal Life History Questionnaire (Lazarus, 1980); results provided further disconfirming evidence concerning a diagnosis of major depressive disorder.

As part of the assessment procedure, Ruth was instructed in the task of self-monitoring procrastination behavior, as is consistent with a SORKC model of assessment (see chapter 3); she agreed to carry out this homework for the coming week. At this initial session, Ruth appeared to be attempting to be a "good patient," hanging on every word as the homework assignment was outlined. Based upon this observation, one clinical hypothesis at this point was that perfectionistic expectations might be operative.

Subsequent Assessment

The assessment process continued over the next few sessions, focusing on a behavioral analysis of the presenting problem, the elucidation of historical antecedents, and differential observations of Ruth's functioning, as is consistent with the three-dimensional assessment framework illustrated in Figure 3.1. Ruth's self-monitoring results revealed two major obstacles to reaching her stated treatment goals. First, she exhibited various stimulus control problems, including eating while working, failing to prioritize tasks, disorganization of desk items, and, as mentioned previously, visiting with colleagues. Second, she had automatic thoughts consistent with the clinical hypothesis of low self-efficacy and perfectionism. Moreover, there seemed to be a global, disparaging quality to these automatic thoughts. For example, the statement "I'm not up to doing this" occurred along with "I shouldn't be in this profession; I'm a failure." There also appeared to be an interpersonal context for some of the statements (e.g., "I'll never complete this on my own" and "Susan [a colleague] will think less of me").

Ruth's history revealed an overall pattern of extraordinarily high achievement punctuated by glaring failures. Her academic performance was superlative, though she would regularly receive "incompletes" in courses that involved long papers. She completed all coursework in graduate school towards a doctorate in history but withdrew from the program after being unable to finish her dissertation. She took a job on the administrative staff of a hospital, where she received a series of promotions and raises. However, she reported feeling unchallenged and mired, and, after 2 years at this job, applied to law school. She finished in the top third of her class, though she did not make law review. She interviewed at a number of firms, but the only job offer she received was from the Legal Aid Society. She had worked there for 3 years at the time of her referral for treatment.

The clinical picture of Ruth's difficulties suggested a perceived deficit involving the completion of unstructured, lengthy tasks. Early scholastic failures had served to lower her efficacy expectations concerning similar present tasks. In the absence of consistent external reinforcement—often the case in working on a dissertation or lengthy legal brief—Ruth would minimize her abilities. Finally, she would engage in avoidance behaviors such as socializing as a means of distraction. An additional maintaining variable was hypothesized to be the lack of other stimulus controls, such as organizing her office setting or taking meal breaks outside the office. Ruth's avoidance then generalized to many simpler tasks, such as writing of memoranda and correspondence. During the past 2 months of treatment, she had also fallen behind in such household responsibilities as billpaying and housecleaning.

Throughout the assessment process, there appeared a supplicating quality about Ruth's interchanges with the therapist. This quality was subtle and manifested primarily in the nature of her eye contact and intonation. Moreover, she would sit on the edge of her chair, upright and alert, whenever a comment or suggestion was made. Although the theme of cognitive behavior therapy as a collaborative effort was reiterated several times, Ruth would generate few hypotheses or interpretations without prompting. Once explicitly given the opportunity to contribute, Ruth became quite expansive and elaborative. During this initial assessment period, these aspects of her behavior did not hinder the treatment process. Further assessment of Ruth's possible interpersonal difficulties was therefore postponed and the cost-benefit decision weighted in favor of helping her experience progress in the area of procrastination.

The initial Clinical Pathogenesis Map (see Figure 3.3 for an example CPM) for the patient included complaints of procrastination, skill deficits regarding complex tasks, time management difficulties, distractibility, stimulus control problems, and possible relationship of these difficulties to the interpersonal context.

Treatment Goals and Alternatives

Alternatives for treatment were evaluated initially in terms of available strategies and tactics, and the following three goals were targeted: (a) to increase self-efficacy expectations surrounding completion of lengthy, complex tasks (stimulus variables); (b) to eliminate escape/avoidance strategies, such as eating and socializing (response variables); and (c) to decrease high levels of physiologic arousal occurring in these situations (organismic variables). Treatment strategies aimed at modifying efficacy expectations centered around Beck's cognitive restructuring approach (Beck, Rush, Emery & Shaw, 1979) and application of session work on an in vivo basis (i.e., homework). Various stimulus control strategies were also targeted to eliminate escape/avoidance, as was suggested by the assessment. Finally, relaxation training was chosen to help Ruth quickly achieve a large decrement in subjective level of distress.

Relaxation was viewed as a useful coping skill for both arousal reduction and distraction from dysfunctional thoughts. Ruth was told not to become too good at relaxing and warned that perfectionistic expectations might undermine the intent of the exercise. Instead of acknowledging the statement, Ruth appeared dismayed. Her inconsistent reaction provided an opportunity to assess "hot" cognitions in the context of the therapeutic relationship itself. She revealed her automatic thoughts as "He doesn't think I can do this right" and, after further probing, "He doesn't think I can measure up—he won't want to work with me anymore." The therapist's immediate reaction was to reassure her and then to elicit the evidence behind these cognitions. She had interpreted this humorous instruction as the therapist's "talking down" to her because she was such a pathetic person. She seemed reassured when the statement was clarified and her deficits reframed not as a lack of strengths but as her inability to take stock of them.

At this point, the clinical decision-making model was again engaged with regard to selection of target areas. On the basis of this review, the decision was made to focus more closely on Ruth's interpersonal functioning. Examination of Ruth's Multimodal Life History Questionnaire results provided guidelines for further assessment. For example, she had stated that "being old and alone" was among her five main fears. Her responses to the questionnaire further provided evidence of interpersonal-social anxiety and minimal long-term friendships. Especially significant in light of her reaction to perceived criticism from the therapist were her reported beliefs that she was "being talked about" and "being laughed at." It now seemed as though interpersonal factors related more proximally to her complaints.

Another important reason to change the focus of treatment concerned the therapist-client relationship. Ruth's subsequent perceptions of the therapist as rejecting and critical would likely undermine her success. Equally important were the therapist's own reactions to Ruth: It was easy to become irritated with her pattern of overreliance on the therapist for directions. (The therapist's own automatic thought at times was "I'm doing all the work here, and she's doing nothing.") Ruth's apparent willingness to accept all suggestions uncritically seemed alternately disingenuous and childlike. Reassurances from the therapist were beginning to be perceived as demanded rather than volunteered.[1]

Only after Ruth's overt conflict with the therapist was it decided to reevaluate the functional importance of her interpersonal patterns. Part of the sessions were therefore devoted to treatment strategies for procrastination, based upon the initial conceptualization. The remainder of the time was used to gather information that would support and better define impressions regarding her interpersonal behavior. The assessment process at this point also became an intervention strategy in that more accurate problem definition might help Ruth better understand the development of her rigid and self-defeating personal schema.

---

[1] Ruth's behavior was extremely subtle, and the clarity with which her interpersonal responses have been presented may mislead the reader. The challenge of assessing the subtlety and nuances of interpersonal deficits, and the manner of responding to a client's interpersonal "pull," has been commented on more extensively by Safran (1984b).

With continued evaluation of this new area, it became apparent that Ruth's interpersonal style was characterized by a high degree of dependency, operationalized as reliance on others for decision making, placing the wants of others before her own, and assertion deficits relating to the expression of her own wants. She described her first year in her legal aid position as her "best ever" in that a large number of new attorneys like herself had passed through an intensive orientation process together. The group had participated in both social and work-related activities. This had been the closest Ruth had come to feeling like an accepted member of a peer group. However, with the passage of time, Ruth's class of attorneys became less cohesive. She reacted to this phenomenon by attempting to maintain the status quo: trying to organize social activities, seeking to make after-work plans, and requesting assistance from colleagues on tasks that she could have completed independently.

These various attempts at maintaining a sense of relatedness initially met with some success but soon gave way to polite rebuffs. These rebuffs then led to a rigid escalation of Ruth's behavior pattern. At this point, Ruth would elicit harsh and negative reactions from her colleagues. In session, she focused on these harsh reactions without expressing any awareness of the inflexible nature of her own behavior. Because such biases surrounding self-report data have commonly been found to exist, it seemed vital at this point to an understanding of Ruth's interpersonal pattern to bring in individuals from her work and family milieu.

An incident involving rejection by a friend and colleague, Susan, provided the impetus for such a conjoint session. This meeting added information to Ruth's self-report and provided a behavioral sample of her pattern of interaction. Susan described Ruth as being "warm, giving, bright, and articulate." She felt, however, that Ruth was "suffocating," attempting to monopolize Susan's time by distracting her from her work, calling her too often at home, and too insistently trying to schedule after-work plans. Ruth became quite agitated and tearful, arguing that Susan really didn't want to spend time with her at all and that this was yet another confirmation that she was unlikable. When Susan became soothing and reassuring, Ruth immediately calmed down.

Significant information obtained from this conjoint session included Ruth's sensitivity to Susan's criticism and the manner in which she responded to it. Ruth's sorrowful reaction was reinforced by Susan's reassurance, which defused conflict in the short run. However, the long-term consequence was that Ruth was unable to learn how escalation of her dependent behavior served to push people away rather than to facilitate interpersonal relationships. Although her issues with Susan were somewhat different, Ruth's interpersonal behavior was strikingly similar to that occurring during early sessions with the therapist. This in vivo assessment confirmed that Ruth needed to learn to identify dependency behaviors, observe their impact on others, and accept (and potentially give) constructive criticism. Unfortunately, the suggestion that she experienced dependency difficulties was heard by Ruth as damning criticism. This attitude created a major obstacle to her treatment.

Problem Redefinition and Treatment Implementation

The clinical problem for the therapist thus became identifying the central assumptions that prevented Ruth from hearing, much less acting upon, criticism. The strategy that appeared to have the most positive consequences and greatest likelihood of achieving this goal was the process of *vertical exploration* (Safran et al., 1986). Vertical exploration is distinguished from *horizontal exploration,* which is an assessment of automatic thoughts conducted without regard to the degree of centrality to the individual. The former process is a strategy whereby the therapist comes to understand the client's idiosyncratic self-perceptions and is thus led to an understanding of central, higher level constructs.

The opportunity to conduct such an assessment arose when the patient's supervisor discovered that the important legal brief Ruth was to complete had not been handed in. Ruth had been told that her job was in jeopardy if the brief were not finished by a newly established deadline. The behavioral strategies targeted at procrastination difficulties had, up to this point, met with limited success (i.e., Ruth had caught up with routine chores at her home and office). Ruth followed the schedule worked out for completing briefs to a point: She had begun to complete simpler briefs on time, but, contrary to initial clinical predictions, her success in this area did not increase her efficacy with more complex tasks. Moreover, despite the stimulus control procedures suggested, she continued to socialize when it came to working on difficult briefs and would only work on these tasks when someone else was around.

Vertical exploration involved asking Ruth to imagine herself alone in her apartment, attempting to work on her current brief. She was instructed to describe any relevant thoughts and associated images. Her automatic thoughts were "I can't do this—it's too difficult for me, and I need someone's help." Ruth then began to challenge this thought spontaneously: "But of course I'm capable of doing it on my own. I'm bright, and I passed the bar exam."

Rather than employ the previous cognitive restructuring strategies to challenge automatic thoughts, the therapist encouraged Ruth to stay with the subjective experience of helplessness and continue to describe any relevant thoughts or images. This evoked the thought "I need someone to take care of me," followed by the image of herself in the second grade, struggling with homework and crying from frustration at not feeling capable of completing it. Ruth reported that her father came in and responded to her distress by doing the homework for her. She experienced powerful feelings of relief, comfort, and closeness in having her father with her at that moment.

This memory generated a discussion about her parents, who were generally undemonstrative. Attention and caregiving were seldom expressed directly; rather, they were manifested by overinvolvement in Ruth's schoolwork and social life. Her parents' pattern of behavior rigidly persisted through adolescence, early adulthood, and, apparently, to the present. Thus what appeared to be overinvolvement in the second grade became infantilizing and controlling behavior in the seventh. Ruth's parents always stressed academic achievement, fostering her competence in this area, though they displayed an utter lack of confidence regarding broader decisions, such as her choice of friends, where to attend college, and whom to date. Ruth's only sibling, an older sister, behaved toward the client in a similar vein, assuming a parental role when Ruth's parents retired to another state.

This session produced what Mahoney (1974) terms a *cognitive click*. Ruth had not heretofore linked her procrastination difficulties with her feelings of loneliness and her fantasy of being rescued. She became willing, for the first time, to discuss how these feelings cut across many situations and how they influenced her interpersonal behavior. In later sessions, as therapy focused on identifying implicit assumptions behind Ruth's dependency behaviors, her approval-seeking behavior toward the therapist lessened. This change was particularly evident when examples of the old interpersonal pattern with the therapist occurred. Ruth became increasingly proficient at identifying these behaviors, remarking, "I'm doing it again." Her increased ability to identify these behaviors nondefensively became an important source of data in the treatment evaluation process.

The tacit assumptions that emerged from these sessions regarding relationship and dependency issues included the following.

1. Relying on others to make decisions is the way to maintain a feeling of closeness.
2. Asserting my own point of view or expressing criticism will lead to abandonment.
3. Being independent means being alone and isolated.
4. Expressing my own desires leads to abandonment.
5. Worthwhile individuals are those who are strong and directive with me. Those who give me the opportunity to make decisions on my own are weak and undesirable.
6. I am unlovable because I am not desired by the right people; the right people would like me if I tried harder to show what a nice person I am.

Having the patient reevaluate these implicit rules then became the goal of treatment. The first four assumptions centered around the theme of abandonment and the necessary strivings to avoid this dreadful state. The latter two, on the other hand, involved Ruth's tendency to minimize and devalue input from individuals who demonstrated affection or respect for her.

This second theme became evident as the therapist challenged Ruth's concerns about abandonment. Ruth did, in fact, have friends throughout childhood and adolescence. Indeed, there were people who liked her at work, but she denigrated them and found them less desirable than those who excluded her. This pattern had characterized her previous marriage, as exemplified by the perception she held of her former husband as "bland" and "weak." (These perceptions were based upon his desire for collaborative decision making and his deference to her judgment in solving problems.)

Since the time of her divorce, Ruth had failed to sustain a relationship or date in the conventional sense. Her involvements were with instructors in graduate school or with employers. In each case, she initiated a relationship, attempted to cement it by having sex on the first date, and maintained the relationship via sexual encounters. More recently, she had become involved with a married supervisor at work who, after several sexual encounters, refused her overtures. She would continue to seek his advice and support, following him home on the subway in an effort to converse with him, even though the subway trip added an extra hour to her commute.

Upon understanding the connection between her current behaviors and the assumptions on which they were based, Ruth set out to test and challenge her old pattern. To help her in this effort, the therapist explained how *schema-driven experiences* could be distinguished from *data-driven experiences* (Goldfried & Robins, 1983). The former were automatic, emotional reactions based on an implicit list of personal rules, whereas the latter were based on current experience, were not automatic, and involved a more objective appraisal of events. An agenda was then collaboratively established that centered around risking abandonment (challenging the first four of the client's six assumptions). A series of graded tasks was then devised on the basis of Ruth's perceptions of difficulty, defined in terms of her efficacy and outcome expectations. These included solitary participation in various reinforcing public and private activities and completion of the complex law brief (which she finished over the course of a weekend!).

Ruth reported profound feelings of relief and satisfaction upon accomplishing these activities, in that she no longer needed to "glom onto" people in her free time. She also reported that a list of coping statements based on the most recent conceptualization of her difficulties was very helpful because "It helped me to stay in the here-and-now rather than the past."

After Ruth succeeded in feeling more comfortable about herself, the next target area involved modifying dysfunctional interpersonal patterns. Ruth continued to complete mutually generated assignments concerning interpersonal behaviors. These included expressing contrasting points of view in discussions, taking an active role in agenda-setting when making plans, making self-complimentary statements, and confronting others when appropriate.

Confrontation and the expression of anger proved to be most difficult for Ruth because her lack of assertiveness was consistent with her core assumption that desirable individuals are directive and controlling. Were Ruth to assert herself and be rejected by such an individual, it would affirm her unworthiness. Intellectually, she knew that her involvement with the supervisor at work was one-sided; her fears, however, continued to inhibit her expression of anger. Even role playing a confrontation with this individual was unsafe, accompanied as it was by automatic thoughts centered on fears of abandonment. This problem resulted in the therapist's decision to utilize an *empty chair technique* to help Ruth express her anger toward an imaginal rather than concrete target. A double session involving much encouragement and prompting enabled Ruth to unleash a vehement diatribe chastising this individual for taking advantage of her passivity and for being unavailable to her. Ruth's ability to emit this response confirmed the hypothesis that arousal had been present all along, but that its expression had been inhibited by a core fear.

The final therapeutic objective involved helping Ruth to form a satisfying, monogamous relationship. This occurred over the course of several months; during that time, Ruth's schema-driven distress would frequently reemerge. A mutual decision was made to terminate treatment at a point where the patient had begun a relationship that seemed characterized by a healthy interdependence.

Treatment Termination

Termination provided a good opportunity to assess Ruth's reaction to what she would have perceived as a frightening rejection at an earlier point in treatment. The subject of termination had first arisen indirectly at the time the patient had begun to date. At that juncture, approximately 14 months from the onset of therapy, it was suggested that sessions might become less frequent. Ruth's immediate reaction, that of perceived rejection, was indicative of earlier patterns. When the subject was broached 6 months later, her reaction was appropriate to the circumstances. Though she was tearful, as would be expected at the end of a close relationship, she was not surprised. Recent sessions had been spent helping her consolidate therapeutic gains. She did not find fault with herself or insist on continuing treatment by raising new issues. A 3-month follow-up was mutually agreed upon.

At follow-up, Ruth had not only maintained her gains, but had also continued to progress. She had expanded her social milieu by leaving her job for a more challenging and lucrative one. She had continued the relationship she had begun while engaged in therapy. All in all, self-reports indicated durable and adaptive modifications of the previously distressful self-schema.

Commentary

The case of Ruth illustrates individual schematic obstacles that can provide barriers to even the most well-documented cognitive-behavioral strategies available in the research literature. Effective clinicians, as compared to therapists who persist in applying a clinical strategy despite its lack of utility, may be no more expert in the execution of the actual technique, but they are more acutely aware of how and when to introduce this technique into the clinical process.

It should be noted that the clinical decision-making involved in this patient's treatment did not progress in a straightforward, linear fashion. Target problems were often interrelated, and treatment objectives at any given point received varying degrees of emphasis. Treatment was consistent with the decision-making model in that multiple subproblems were often focused on simultaneously. Having specified the core assumptions by which the client behaved, both client and therapist had an overarching set of testable hypotheses. Thus Ruth's independence behaviors, interpersonal skills, choice of friends, and self-schema were interdependent target areas; improvement in one area predictably affected the others.

It is also important to be aware of the tendency we have as clinicians to respond to our own "pet" theories and to apply them without the search for disconfirming evidence or alternative explanations. Many of us have experienced frustrations when working with a patient exhibiting a characterological disturbance. We have witnessed therapists who continue to hammer away at cognitions despite continued lack of patient change. In these cases, the resistant patient seems to be growing increasingly intolerant of a redundant strategy (whereas the therapist may grow increasingly intolerant of the resistant patient).

To save both the patient and therapist from such a frustrating experience, a comprehensive assessment of the client's generalized interpersonal schemata and actions may become critical. This process may necessarily lengthen the time of initial assessment and may require the patient's informed consent (due to the expectation of many patients entering treatment that cognitive-behavioral therapists focus on target symptoms only and are not concerned with "stuff from childhood"). It is crucial during the initial stages of assessment that differential diagnoses be considered. The therapist should also be willing to embrace the concept that multiple avenues of causality may contribute to the same problem. With this cognitive set, the therapist will be more likely to devise effective, creative strategies to deal with multiple targets.

The previous case description illustrates the need for continued problem redefinition on the basis of the patient's interpersonal functioning throughout the therapeutic relationship. The following clinical case introduces a patient whose chief complaints involved depression and obesity but whose initial presentation provided evidence of distressing and overt interpersonal difficulties. An argument may ensue among readers as to which existed first: generalized interpersonal difficulties, core schematic distortions, problem-solving deficits, loss of reinforcement, or high degree of emotional reactivity. Rather than debate such issues, we believe it is more important to examine the factors currently present and functionally operative upon the patient's distress.

This patient's assessment period lasted 5 weeks, with two sessions occurring per week. The resulting treatment, which lasted 6 months, was viewed as the most effective course of action. The case exemplifies how a comprehensive, prolonged assessment period, based on the use of the clinical decision-making model, may result in a less complicated, less frustrating treatment period.

Clinical Example: Maria

Maria, a 47-year-old South American woman, was originally referred for individual therapy following her participation in a behaviorally oriented weight reduction group. Her treatment in the group had recently terminated, and the group leaders provided the following summary of her treatment: During her first session in the group, Maria assumed center stage, supporting the goals of the group, praising the group leaders, and encouraging the other, more cautious group members. She completed her homework assignments and lost weight steadily over the following three sessions. As time went on, she would frequently attempt to dominate the group, although she would often state, "Now I'll stop talking because I don't want to hog the time." She appeared irritable and impatient when other group members would speak. During the fourth week, she began to cry uncontrollably as she discussed mistakes she had made and to chastise herself for her inability to control either her eating or her emotions.

The group leaders began to experience a sense of dread prior to sessions as to what mood Maria would exhibit. For example, when she secured a part-time position as an office clerk, she came to a session stating that her life was going to "turn around," that she would now have "respect." The following session, the patient described her supervisor as a "bitch" who had turned the entire office against her. During these angry outbursts, she would make frequent negative generalizations concerning other people's racial or ethnic status.

Midway through the weight program, the group therapists realized that the patient was exhibiting a significant degree of subjective distress and a pattern of behavior that frustrated and distanced those around her. Maria continually attempted to refocus the group upon her own problems, thus creating obstacles in the achievement of her own and the group's therapeutic goals. She frequently assumed the role of a victim whom no one loved or respected. She idealized one of the therapists and made frequent attempts to meet her outside of sessions without the co-therapist. When confronted regarding this behavior, Maria became enraged and referred to the therapist as a traitor.

Finally, during one of the sessions, the patient disclosed for the first time that she had been engaged in individual psychotherapy for several years and that her therapist had recently moved to another state, thus terminating her treatment. She stated that she had often become "overemotional" with her previous therapist and, even after she had made suicidal statements, he did not take her seriously. Maria's concerns thus shifted from weight loss to her ability to tolerate the upcoming end of the group, which she perceived as a major loss of support.

Maria attended the final session having achieved a total weight loss of 32 pounds, but she remained extremely depressed. At this point, the group leaders referred her to one of the authors for cognitive-behavioral treatment for depression. Their concerns focused on cognitive distortions observed in the group and on the possible need for medication because the patient had a history of impulsive behavior and a tendency to engage in excesses.

Several months passed before the patient contacted one of the authors for individual treatment. She had, over this period of time, undertaken various other treatments, including Overeaters Anonymous, group therapy for multiple addictive behaviors, and spiritualism. She had begun each new treatment with an idealized view that the new therapist would be an "expert" who would finally help her.

Problem Orientation Issues

Because her weight reduction treatment had occurred at the same health facility at which the author was located, a summary of the patient's recent history and treatment was readily available. The initial bias associated with Maria's treatment consisted of a specific referral for depression and a description of behavior consistent with a DSM-III-R diagnosis of borderline personality disorder. Anticipated difficulties traditionally associated with patients carrying such a diagnosis include frequent between-session crisis calls, self-destructive acting out behavior, parasuicidal gestures, and labile emotions. These problems needed to be reframed as possible risk factors, rather than accepted without question.

In addition, two major assumptions needed to be avoided: (a) the tendency to see target behaviors (including depression, anxiety, periodic exacerbations of bulimic behavior, loneliness, turbulent interpersonal relationships, and job dissatisfaction) as isolated difficulties and, on the other extreme, (b) the assumption that these target behaviors were the result of a single personality disorder (as in the case of more traditional psychodynamic clinical formulations). The patient, for all her subjective distress, clearly demonstrated some unique individual strengths. It was important to look at these as well as her deficits.

A plan was developed for Maria to participate in a comprehensive assessment over several sessions, with the mutual consent that, after this period of time, she would be provided with feedback and treatment recommendations. The therapist was thus framed as a consultant who would assess the patient's areas of difficulty and provide her, as a consumer, with advice concerning the most effective treatment. If the patient required alternative or adjunct treatment, it would be based upon a thorough assessment of her target complaints. Because Maria had idealistic expectations of the therapist, it seemed especially important to restructure her assumption that a referral to another therapist meant that she had failed to make the first therapist like her. Such a reframing might serve as an important therapeutic message in and of itself. At this point, a comprehensive assessment was conducted to define the patient's chief problem areas more accurately.

Problem Definition Issues

The problem definition and formulation process calls for a multivariate, broad-based approach and for a differential diagnosis. In Maria's case, it was important to rule out melancholic features suggesting a biological or genetic influence and to use various behavioral and social learning theories to compare her perceptions of her difficulties with the facts. In an attempt to gather as much information about the patient as possible, measures were administered (a) to assess the duration and intensity of current distress regarding major problems, (b) to analyze how these problems covaried or were discrepant, and (c) to obtain a history of salient early learning experiences and emotional/cognitive development that might provide an understanding of core schemata affecting multiple problem areas.

The Multimodal Life History Questionnaire was administered and discussed, whereupon a list of the patient's most salient problems was collaboratively generated. Because Maria experienced some difficulty expressing herself in English, she authored her list in Spanish, which was then translated. The following eight problems were defined.

1. I feel ill most of the time.
2. I have reached 47 years of age without a career or a good job.
3. I am a nasty person.
4. I have no self-control.
5. I fear that I am not honest with myself.
6. I don't know how to behave with things that bother me.
7. I can't control my love of sweets.
8. When I don't like someone, I become impossible.

Other more quantitative measures revealed the following: a Beck Depression Inventory score of 34 (significantly depressed); a Hamilton Rating Scale for Depression (Hamilton, 1960) score of 26 (significantly depressed); and a State-Trait Anxiety Inventory (Spielberger, Gorsuch, & Lushene, 1970) score of 58 (significantly anxious). Results from the Social Problem Solving Inventory (D'Zurilla & Nezu, 1988) indicated severe deficits in problem orientation, problem definition, decision making, and solution verification. Although these scores and self-reports indicated deficits, the patient revealed a good degree of creativity and flexibility in generating alternative solutions to problems. Self-monitoring of bulimic episodes indicated that the patient exhibited no bulimic episodes during the 5-week assessment period. Drinking behavior involved consumption of several glasses of wine on three weekends (with meals) and one episode of inebriation when "feeling lonely."

Summary of Initial Assessment Interview Data

The patient came to treatment with a host of distress symptoms: depression, uncontrollable crying spells, feelings of low self-esteem, anxiety, anger, guilt, anhedonia, suicidal thoughts, fear of being alone, and helplessness. The patient did not exhibit a feeling of hopelessness, however, as was revealed by her low score on the Hopelessness Scale (Beck, Weissman, Lester, & Trexler, 1974). Rather, she seemed to believe that life could be better if she received the "right kind" of help. Maria also described disturbances in behavior that resulted in negative consequences for her: overeating, past binging episodes, episodic drinking, explosive angry outbursts, quitting jobs and previous therapeutic experiences, and avoiding interpersonal relationships when any conflict (real or perceived) occurred. Also present were somatic symptoms of sciatic pain and feelings of fatigue.

A summary of assessment in her major spheres of functioning follows.

Behavior.   The patient exhibited frequent crying, increased sleep, overeating, feelings of helplessness, and passive overt behavior that coexisted with angry cognitions. In addition, she often ran from jobs, personal relationships, and therapeutic experiences. She showed a tendency to disclose intimate feelings and personal experiences followed by regret for doing so and was suspicious that others would betray her. She also described negative self-labels (e.g., "I think I'm a manic-depressive"; "I must be cursed because I did something bad"). Despite verbal statements indicating disgust with her physical appearance, the patient's actual presentation indicated daily energy invested in clothing, makeup, and jewelry.

Affect. The patient appeared overtly labile, sometimes sounding enthusiastic (e.g., "This will answer my prayers") and at other times being very depressed. She exhibited continual crying and often was very angry, referring to others as insensitive or selfish and using derogatory names and racial remarks. Finally, the patient exhibited overall schemata of loneliness and incompetence despite the actual presence of many social acquaintances.

Triggers or antecedent cues to increased distress. Episodes of increased symptom intensity and presence of suicidal thoughts usually followed any perceived anger or criticism from others or fears about her own performance (anticipatory anxiety). The intensity of her response on these occasions was high and prolonged, lasting from 1 to 3 days.

Cognitions. The patient exhibited dysfunctional thinking patterns: specifically, negative, global, and stable attributions; overgeneralization; dichotomous thinking and external locus of control in interpersonal situations; and perceptions of herself as being "punished by God." She made frequent negative self-statements relative to her own cultural background and saw others as cruel and prejudiced. She described schemata of abandonment and unlovability, which, in light of her developmental history, were not completely irrational.

Developmental history. The patient was born in South America, the only child of an upper-middle-class family. She had been born with a defect that left one arm and hand slightly disfigured and weak. The patient's father abandoned the family when the patient's mother became physically ill and depressed. The patient assumed care of her mother at age 14 and, after her mother's death, lived with various relatives for brief periods of time. She described her father as strict, moralistic, and unsympathetic. Although she described herself as intelligent and as having had early success in school, she left school after her mother's death because "I couldn't face the shame of what had happened in my family."

Synthesis of the patient's developmental history and current cognitions provided an understanding of her current self-statements of poor self-control, chastisement over her own anger, and pattern of dependency. In her previous therapy, she had avoided commitment to change and elicited caretaking behavior from others, yet had never believed that she had the right to expect such attention. Selectively focused on signs of disloyalty and imminent abandonment from others, she became enraged when others did not turn out to be supportive and was angry with her own naivete in trusting them.

Environmental factors.   The patient had learned various domestic and culinary skills through her own efforts and help from friends and had managed to secure work as a cook for wealthy families in the United States. Despite her skills in this area, she viewed such employment as evidence of her inferior status, discounting the fine references she had received. Maria left most of her positions because of interpersonal difficulties with other staff or the perceived ingratitude of her employers. In fact, however, most employers had been pleased with her accomplishments and had requested that she return to work. She was currently unemployed and experienced conflict regarding the "Catch 22" of enjoying medical disability benefits but being labeled mentally ill and unable to work.

In addition, the patient had a close friend who had been diagnosed with AIDS. This situation affected her in several ways. First, she provided care and support to this friend, who was planning to return to their native country. Although she described feelings of sympathy toward this person, she believed that he was taking advantage of her and viewed his plans to return to South America as abandonment. Her friend's plans to return sparked feelings of missing South America, where Maria's background was viewed as upper class. Although she had always dreamed of returning, she believed that such a return was impossible, given her current status as a domestic in the United States (and her desire to return as a "rich lady"). This belief led to increased ruminations concerning her self-worth. In fact, her fantasies of returning to South America occurred much in the same context as previous fantasies concerning a change in jobs or therapists. A pattern of thinking emerged in which the patient would place all hope upon a given event (e.g., a new job, new social acquaintances) only to become excruciatingly disappointed and angry when she experienced even minor difficulties.

Biological factors.   Although a thorough medical examination yielded no biological etiological factors, the intensity and frequency of the patient's emotional reactions indicated a low threshold for emotional discomfort. In addition to expressing other negative self-labels, Maria stated that she was manic-depressive because of the emotional extremes she experienced. It was observed, however, that support from the therapist or a friend resulted in a rapid change of mental status.

The patient's description of her mother as depressed and "mentally ill" suggested evidence of a possible genetic predisposition towards an affective disorder. However, clear diagnosis of the mother's illness or reports of effective treatment were unavailable.

Historical environmental factors.   The patient had been married to a man who had left the marriage approximately 12 years previously when he had become aware of his homosexuality. Shortly after the end of her marriage, she had engaged in a brief affair, during which she had become pregnant. She had undergone an abortion and, later, a hysterectomy. She complained of chronic feelings of loneliness and also reported fears of homosexuality because she found erotic pictures of females sexually stimulating.

Her relationships had been markedly unstable, with accompanying lability of emotions. The patient usually terminated these relationships following an experience of intensely negative affect.

Strengths.   The patient revealed an ability to communicate with the therapist and, particularly when speaking in her native language, appeared articulate and verbally creative. She occasionally displayed a sense of humor that permitted her to distance herself from difficult issues and remain briefly objective. She was able to maintain housing over an 8-year period of time with only periodic reliance on social welfare and disability income. Although the patient described chronic suicidal feelings that became exacerbated during times of stress, she had made no suicide attempts. Finally, despite periods of anger at her previous therapist, the patient had successfully completed a weight management program and had maintained a 30-pound weight loss.

Summary of Problem Definition Issues

Target areas for intervention were the patient's distressing, dysfunctional, and habituated cognitive/emotional schemata (perceived deficits), as well as her limited skills in problem solving and assertiveness. Additional targets were her impulsive responses to negative affect. This combination of problem areas had serious aversive interpersonal consequences and served to maintain her dysfunctional cognitive-interpersonal cycle. For example, the patient would frequently engage in hostile, exaggerated responses that would antagonize others and validate perceptions of herself as "nasty" and "out of control." It became vital to collaborate with the patient to separate actual deficits from perceived deficits in order to design strategies geared toward perceptual distortions and skill deficits. However, Maria's intense perceptions of low self-efficacy, external locus of control, and pattern of dependent interpersonal behavior represented large obstacles against her working toward change in either area. In addition, it was likely that her level of anxiety might increase along with any increased competency or autonomy. Because Maria's past therapeutic relationships had revealed adaptive inflexibility (i.e., interpersonal difficulties characterized by suspicious attributions, cognitive distortions, and negative affect), the primary target of treatment involved restructuring her expectations and behaviors concerning the therapeutic relationship itself.

Other target areas were also developed. Maria's dysfunctional thinking and problem-solving deficits appeared to maintain her depressive cognitions, as did her emotional reactivity. Although the patient lacked neurovegetative signs of depression or any clear symptomatology indicating a bipolar disorder, she exhibited a significant degree of emotional sensitivity, which she and the therapist identified as a predisposition towards a "quick trigger."

Maria's interpersonal problems included hypervigilance to fears of abandonment. Although these fears had realistic roots in her early learning history, they were now functionally related to her disproportionate feelings of rage in relationships. For example, if another individual offered even a mild form of criticism, she became furious.

Generation of Treatment Strategies and Treatment Design

After identifying target areas, the therapist next attempted to develop a parsimonious yet multidimensional approach to treatment. To accomplish this task, a hierarchy of targets needed to be developed to guide the therapist in devising the most effective interventions for these major problem areas. After a review of the relevant literature concerning these chosen therapeutic targets, as well as the therapist's own areas of competence, several reasonable alternatives were considered for each major target area.

At the end of the assessment period, it was recommended that the patient continue in treatment with the present therapist. She was provided with feedback concerning both perceived and actual deficits (as well as strengths) and informed of any possible adverse effects of the therapeutic process (e.g., increased anxiety, periodic anger at the therapist, discomfort at having old beliefs challenged). These effects were described as being predictable difficulties in changing longstanding patterns. Maria's emotional reactivity remained an area of concern in that the therapist's own expertise did not include psychopharmacological treatment. For this reason, consultation with a psychiatrist knowledgeable in behavioral assessment and treatment planning was sought, and a patient interview arranged.

It is important to note that Maria's "quick trigger" was not solely a negative treatment issue. In fact, it was observed during the assessment interviews that humor helped her to distance herself from a situation in order to view an existing irony or catch herself selectively attending to information that validated negative self-views. In other words, Maria exhibited a facility for positive emotions as well.

The following treatment plan, with rationales accompanying each component, was constructed and implemented.

Phase I.   It was recommended that the patient continue in treatment with the present therapist, whom she viewed as capable of rescuing her. The patient's initial reaction to this feedback was surprise at being accepted into a therapeutic relationship and cognitive dissonance in that, according to her view, the therapist had an easy escape from the relationship by simply referring her elsewhere. The continuation of Maria's therapy provided an initial opportunity for her to test her suspicious hypotheses concerning others' intentions.

Maria was further told that the therapist's own framework of therapy was collaborative in nature and that she might experience increased anxiety and mixed feelings toward the therapist. These periodic discomforts were framed as unpleasant but predictable and especially important to report. A plan was mutually developed in case the patient felt the urge to leave treatment suddenly. (Specifically, Maria would attend a termination session if she were to choose this alternative.) In addition, patient and therapist developed a plan whereby Maria agreed to report any increase in suicidal thoughts.

Maria was provided with the therapist's conceptualization of her difficulties in layperson's language. Direct examples of her tendency to perceive prejudice or criticism from others were available because they had occurred with high frequency between her and the therapist during the assessment period. Cross-situational examples were also provided, and her perceptual distortions in this regard were explained as ways she had learned to react automatically to fear. Maria was therefore given the homework assignment to restate *You are* statements to *I want* statements whenever she experienced anger toward the therapist. For example, "You are mean because you think I'm weak or stupid" was reframed as "I want to feel more secure." This strategy facilitated Maria's exploration of her fears in pursuing personal goals and gave her the opportunity to assess required coping skills. It was explained that therapy would focus on building skills that might give her alternative ways of getting what she wanted and help her avoid looking toward the therapist for rescue.

Phase II.   The initial skill-building focus involved social problem-solving training with careful monitoring of the patient's cognitive and affective reactions to increases in her own perceived competency. Maria made many between-session phone calls at this time, and, not infrequently, a session began with her stating her anger toward the therapist for not answering a call, even when she knew the therapist had been in session with another client. Expression of anger was encouraged, but the patient was prompted to reframe accusations in terms of the needs she perceived the therapist was not meeting. Frequently, she would sob, "I need to know there is someone to take care of me the way I took care of everyone else!" Skills such as problem solving were framed as means of developing the part of herself she could count on.

Concomitantly, several sessions were devoted to assertiveness training to provide the patient with strategies to use in her own problem-solving efforts and in expressing her feelings toward the therapist. This step was particularly important in that it granted Maria permission to express her needs in the therapeutic situation. Finally, a trial of antidepressant medication was conducted to treat the patient's subjective emotionality. The problem-solving process was again employed, this time as a way of working with the patient on compliance and monitoring. The final goal of treatment was to assess the patient's ability to learn relaxation strategies, which might aid in the generalization of treatment effects and accompany a planned reduction and elimination of medication.

Evaluation of Treatment

Because initial assessment devices provided a barometer of distress, these appeared to be salient pretest and posttest measures. More important, however, was Maria's altered perception of her problems as normal and of positive changes as pleasant but far from perfect solutions. This alteration in her views indicated a more realistic appraisal of stressful situations. Maria's growing awareness that difficulties are a normal part of life became a frequent and helpful self-statement.

Although pretest and posttest measures indicated significant improvement after 4 months, it was not until the eighth month of therapy that the patient was able to maintain gains during stressful situations. As a culmination of gains and thoughtful problem solving, Maria eventually planned to return to her native country. The realistic recognition of problems she would experience in making even a positive change (e.g., facing a new situation or leaving therapy) provided the most meaningful generalization data.

SUMMARY

Maria's case is in many ways similar to the case of Ruth, presented earlier. Both patients revealed actual skill deficits that prevented them from obtaining reinforcing experiences in their environments. Both patients revealed core self-schemata that involved habituated repertoires of thinking and that appeared potently and negatively reinforced by avoidance of core fears. Both patients, after all, displayed a personality disturbance. As discussed in the beginning of this chapter, various nomothetic precepts were thus helpful in extending our assessment considerations. We attempted to use those guiding assumptions that were data-based and thus employed both the art of therapy and the decision-making model to tailor idiographic intervention.

The objective reader, viewing each patient's therapeutic experience, may observe that Maria and Ruth participated in very different treatments. Different strategies and tactics were employed at different points in the therapeutic process. Yet both individuals participated in a phenomenon conceptualized as behavior therapy. Their experiences are consistent with the philosophy we mutually embrace: combining empirically based findings from the literature within a decision-making framework in order to provide the best possible treatment. Indeed, if the treatments had been identical for both patients, we would seriously question our own biases.

Recent investigations have estimated that over 50 percent of patients seeking help from practicing clinicians exhibit the operational characteristics of a personality disorder (Turkat & Maisto, 1985). The use of the decision-making model may make the complex assessment and treatment decisions encountered with this population more manageable. We ourselves have found this model of clinical judgment particularly helpful in maintaining an idiographic, inductive approach to therapy.

References

American Psychiatric Association. (1980). *Diagnostic and statistical manual of mental disorders* (3rd ed.). Washington, DC: Author.

American Psychiatric Association. (1987). *Diagnostic and statistical manual of mental disorders* (3rd ed. rev.). Washington, DC: Author.

Bandura, A. (1977). Self-efficacy: Toward a unifying theory of behavior change. *Psychological Review, 84,* 191–215.

Bandura, A. (1982). Self-efficacy mechanism in human agency. *American Psychologist, 37,* 122–147.

Barlow, M. (1981). Complex problems require complex solutions. *Behavior Therapy, 12,* 15–29.

Beck, A. T., Rush, A. J., Shaw, B. F., & Emery, G. (1979). *Cognitive therapy of depression: A treatment manual*. New York: Guilford.

Beck, A. T., Ward, C. H., Mendelsohn, M., Mock, J., & Erbaugh, J. (1961). An inventory for measuring depression. *Archives of General Psychiatry, 5,* 562–571.

Beck, A. T., Weissman, A., Lester, D., & Trexler, L. (1974). Measurement of pessimism: The Hopelessness Scale. *Journal of Consulting and Clinical Psychology, 42,* 861–865.

D'Zurilla, T. J., & Nezu, A. M. (1988, November). *Development and preliminary evaluation of the Social Problem-Solving Inventory (SPSI)*. Paper presented at the annual meeting of the Association for Advancement of Behavior Therapy, New York.

Goldfried, M. R. (1982). *Converging themes in psychotherapy: Trends in psychodynamic, humanistic, and behavioral practice*. New York: Springer.

Goldfried, M. R., & Robins, C. (1983). Self-schema, cognitive bias, and the processing of therapeutic experiences. In P. C. Kendall (Ed.), *Advances in cognitive-behavioral research and therapy* (Vol. 2). New York: Academic.

Goldfried, M. R., & Kent, R. N. (1972). Traditional versus behavioral assessment: A comparison of methodological and theoretical assumptions. *Psychological Bulletin, 77,* 409–420.

Goldfried, M. R., & Newman, C. (1986). Psychotherapy integration: An historical perspective. In J. C. Norcross (Ed.), *Handbook of eclectic psychotherapy*. New York: Brunner/Mazel.

Guidano, V. F., & Liotti, G. (1983). *Cognitive processes and emotional disorders*. New York: Guilford.

Hamilton, M. (1960). A rating scale for depression. *Journal of Neurology, Neurosurgery and Psychiatry, 23,* 56–62.

Lazarus, A. A. (1980). *Multimodal Life History Questionnaire*. Kingston, NJ: Multimodal Publications.

Mahoney, M. J. (1974). *Cognition and behavior modification*. Cambridge, MA: Ballinger.

Mahoney, M. J. (1980). *Psychotherapy process*. New York: Plenum.

Millon, T. (1981). *Disorders of personality*. New York: Wiley.

Mischel, W. A., Shoda, Y., & Peake, P. K. (1988). The nature of adolescent competencies predicted by preschool delay of gratification. *Journal of Personality and Social Psychology, 54,* 687–696.

Safran, J. D. (1984a). Assessing the cognitive interpersonal cycle. *Cognitive Therapy and Research, 8,* 333–348.

Safran, J. D. (1984b). Some implications of Sullivan's interpersonal theory for cognitive therapy. In M. A. Reda & M. J. Mahoney (Eds.), *Cognitive psychotherapies: Recent developments in theory, research, and practice*. Cambridge, MA: Ballinger.

Safran, J. D., & Greenberg, L. S. (1986). Hot cognition and psychotherapy process: An information processing/ecological approach. In P. C. Kendall (Ed.), *Advances in cognitive-behavioral research and therapy* (Vol. 5). New York: Academic.

Safran, J. D., Vallis, T. M., Segal, Z. V., & Shaw, B. F. (1986). Assessment of core cognitive processes in cognitive therapy. *Cognitive Therapy and Research, 10,* 509–526.

Segal, Z. V. (1988). Appraisal of the self-schema construct in cognitive models of depression. *Psychological Bulletin, 103,* 147–162.

Spielberger, C. D., Gorsuch, R. L., & Lushene, R. E. (1970). *Manual for the State-Trait Anxiety Inventory*. Palo Alto, CA: Consulting Psychologists Press.

Turkat, I. D., & Levin, R. A. (1984). Formulation of personality disorders. In H. E. Adams & P. B. Sutker (Eds.), *Comprehensive handbook of psychopathology.* New York: Plenum.

Turkat, I. D., & Maisto, S. A. (1985). Personality disorders: Application of the experimental method to the formulation and modification of personality disorders. In D. H. Barlow (Ed.), *Clinical handbook of psychological disorders.* New York: Guilford.

Wachtel, P. L. (1977). *Psychoanalysis and behavior therapy.* New York: Basic.

Wachtel, P. L. (1987). *Action and insight.* New York: Guilford.

Wright, J. C., & Mischel, W. A. (1987a). Conditional analysis of dispositional constructs: The local predictability of social behavior. *Journal of Personality and Social Psychology, 11,* 1157–1189.

Wright, J. C., & Mischel, W. A. (1987b). A conditional approach to dispositional constructs: The local predictability of social behavior. *Journal of Personality and Social Psychology, 53,* 1159–1177.

Wright, J. C., & Mischel, W. A. (in press). Conditional hedges and the intuitive psychology of traits. *Journal of Personality and Social Psychology.*

Chapter 10

Chronic Combat-related Post-Traumatic Stress Disorder

John A. Fairbank

INTRODUCTION

Post-traumatic stress disorder (PTSD) is a relatively new addition to the clinical taxonomy of psychiatric disorders. It was included in the third edition of the American Psychiatric Association's *Diagnostic and Statistical Manual of Mental Disorders* (DSM-III) in 1980 on the basis of informed clinical opinion. The current definition of the disorder is based on the general hypothesis that exposure to extreme events produces in some people a specific syndrome of psychiatric symptoms. The syndrome includes symptoms of intrusive reexperiencing of the stressor event, cognitive and behavioral avoidance and emotional numbing, and increased arousal triggered by reminders of the extreme event.

The present chapter focuses on the process of clinical decision making and judgment in the behavioral assessment and treatment of PTSD in a population that has been severely affected by this disorder: Vietnam combat veterans (Kulka et al., 1988). The overarching goal of this chapter is to delineate the complex process of clinical decision making in the assessment and treatment of combat-related PTSD within the framework of the decision-making model articulated in chapter 3. Discussion will focus on the necessary steps and key principles of this approach, especially as applied to individuals who seek clinical services for PTSD. As noted throughout this book, it is important to remember that clinical decision making is a dynamic process that evolves over time. Although the problem-solving approach to clinical judgment is described in a stepwise fashion for heuristic purposes, the use of this convention does not mean that the approach unfolds in a lockstep, linear fashion.

APPLYING THE CLINICAL DECISION-MAKING MODEL

The five basic problem-solving processes involved in the decision-making model will be described and discussed in separate subsections: (a) problem orientation, (b) problem definition and formulation, (c) generation of alternatives, (d) decision making, and (e) solution implementation and verification. In addition, a case example will illustrate the utility and appropriateness of the decision-making model for assessing and treating combat-related PTSD.

Problem Orientation

Individuals react to extreme events in a variety of adaptive and pathological ways. Outcomes range from no discernible adjustment problems to clear psychopathology, including the development of severe and chronic symptoms of PTSD. Historically, clinicians have offered two basic hypotheses to explain the variability observed in the adjustment of veterans of war. The first hypothesis—the *personal characteristics argument*—maintains that psychological adjustment following exposure to extreme events is largely influenced by "person" factors such as premilitary psychosocial background characteristics and biological predisposition. The second hypothesis—the *extreme event argument*—asserts that postcombat adjustment is largely a function of the nature of the environmental stressor. Adherents of this perspective tend to argue that certain classes of extreme war events, such as surviving or participating in abusive combat violence, are sufficient to evoke significant readjustment problems in many people.

Historically, the relative influence of each of these hypotheses on the orientation of clinicians to problems of postcombat readjustment has waxed and waned. For example, during and immediately after America's involvement in the Vietnam Conflict (1964–1975), the personal characteristics explanation seemed to predominate in clinical thinking (e.g., Borus, 1973). Conversely, since the publication of the

PTSD diagnostic criteria (American Psychiatric Association, 1980), the extreme events hypothesis has exerted a stronger influence on the orientation of clinicians toward the problem of postwar readjustment.

Certainly, one's view of the relative merits of each of these (or other) hypotheses will influence one's perspective on the specific factors that relate to the development and maintenance of PTSD. At the level of assessment and treatment, the clinician's orientation regarding the relative importance of these factors will directly influence clinical judgment and decision making. Thus an awareness of one's basic assumptions about the role of person and event factors in the development and maintenance of war-related PTSD is of fundamental importance.

Fortunately, the clinical practitioner need not rely solely on theory to formulate an appropriate orientation to the problem of combat-related PTSD. A growing body of research has been devoted to investigating the qualities of the stressor event and the personal and background characteristics of the individual that influence adaptation following exposure to extreme events (e.g., Green, Lindy, Grace, & Gleser, in press). The next few paragraphs review some conceptual and empirical perspectives on the role of person and event variables in the development of various reactions to extreme stressors.

Characteristics of the Event

Characteristics of the stressor event are believed to influence patterns of postevent adjustment strongly, including the development of PTSD symptoms. As described in the revised edition of the *Diagnostic and Statistical Manual of Mental Disorders* (DSM-III-R; American Psychiatric Association, 1987),

> the essential feature of this disorder [i.e., PTSD] is the development of characteristic symptoms following a psychologically distressing event that is outside the range of usual human experience (i.e., outside the range of such common experiences as simple bereavement, chronic illness, business losses, and marital conflict). The stressor producing this syndrome would be markedly distressing to almost anyone, and is usually experienced with intense fear, terror, and helplessness. (p. 247)

Thus the two characteristics of stressor events that are necessary for a diagnosis of PTSD using these criteria are (a) severity (i.e., "a psychologically distressing event . . . usually experienced with intense fear, terror, and helplessness") and (b) unusualness (i.e., an event "outside the range of usual human experience"). The Work Group to Revise DSM-III incorporated these operational criteria for defining PTSD stressor events into the DSM-III-R on the recommendation of the APA Subcommittee on Post-Traumatic Stress Disorder (cf. Brett, Spitzer, & Williams, 1988). Thus the DSM-III-R stressor criteria for PTSD represent the current consensus opinion of clinicians with expertise in the area of traumatic stress.

Although PTSD research has focused on the effects of events that correspond to the DSM-III-R event criteria, it should be noted that events that do not meet the unusualness criterion (unemployment, acute health crises, etc.) are increasingly being acknowledged as important variables predicting psychological adaptation. Hence the relationship of more ordinary stressors to specific PTSD symptoms (e.g., intrusive reexperiencing of extreme events) is an empirical issue that deserves careful scrutiny. What are now needed to inform diagnostic decision making and treatment planning are studies that examine empirically the separate and interactive contributions of event characteristics, such as severity and unusualness, to specific PTSD symptoms and symptom classes (e.g., Breslau & Davis, 1987).

In addition to unusualness and severity, environmental stressors vary along a number of other dimensions that may influence the pattern of postevent adjustment. Such dimensions include danger (the degree to which exposure to the event entails risk of bodily injury), degree of personal involvement (the degree to which the event is personally experienced), number of persons affected, frequency (number of exposures to the event), duration (length of exposure to the event), predictability (the degree to which the stressor is anticipated), controllability (the degree to which the victim or survivor can control the onset and termination of the event), and origin (human versus natural events and, in the case of human events, whether the event was accidental or deliberate).

All of the types of events considered by the DSM-III-R to be sufficient to evoke PTSD symptoms are directly life-threatening. There is evidence, however, that some people who indirectly experience catastrophic events or their aftereffects also develop symptoms of PTSD (e.g., Amick-McMullen, Kilpatrick, & Veronen, 1989). It appears to be important, then, to consider whether most people indirectly exposed to extreme events would react with significant symptoms of distress. Clearly, we still have much to learn about the necessary and sufficient conditions for defining extreme events. Although some clinicians err in the direction of adopting criteria that are too stringent (e.g., the case of the clinician who limits trauma to events that result in personal physical injury or the mutilation or death of others), other practitioners may adopt too liberal an orientation. An example of the latter would be a clinician who makes a blanket assumption that all men and women who served with American military forces in Vietnam were, by definition, exposed to extreme events. Thus it is essential that clinicians who provide psychological health services to combat veterans be aware of their personal/professional biases regarding what constitutes an extreme event.

Characteristics of the Individual

As previously noted, characteristics of individuals exposed to extreme events are also perceived to account for some of the variability in adjustment (e.g., Mischel, 1984). The individual difference variables include survivor demographics, pre-event background and level of vulnerability, the degree of the survivor's ability to cope effectively with the stressor event or its aftereffects, and the survivor's unique perceptions of the event.

Foy, Carroll, and Donahoe (1987) recently reviewed 12 studies that examined etiological factors in combat-related PTSD in Vietnam veterans. That review and other studies in the literature (e.g., Egendorf, Kadushin, Laufer, Rothbart, & Sloan, 1981; Foy & Card, 1987; Foy, Sipprelle, Rueger, & Carroll, 1984; Frye & Stockton, 1982; Penk et al., 1981) found that combat exposure in Vietnam is the primary etiologic variable related to PTSD and that premilitary variables are more weakly associated or have no association with PTSD. The potential predisposing factors controlled for in one or another of these studies were family stability, minority status, premilitary psychosocial adjustment, family environment, war attitudes, emotional stability, age of entry into service, high school grades and school participation, alcohol and drug problems, and age at time of service (Kulka et al., 1988).

A smaller set of studies (Worthington, 1977; Nace, O'Brien, Mintz, Ream, & Meyers, 1978), however, found premilitary factors such as age at entry, education, problems with authority, and premilitary psychosocial adjustment to be more strongly linked with combat-related PTSD and other postmilitary mental health problems than was exposure to combat. Overall, findings concerning the role of background factors in the development of PTSD have been mixed, a situation that has led many to consider the interactive effects of person and event variables in the development of PTSD.

Person/Event Interaction

The intersubject variability of reactions to extreme life events has been explained in terms of the interactions of internal and external factors by means of the *diathesis-stress model* (Escobar, 1987; Keane, 1989; Meehl, 1962; Zubin & Spring, 1977). The diathesis-stress model assumes that extreme events may elicit crisis in most everyone but that, depending on the intensity of the stressor event and the individual's threshold for tolerating it, the stressor will either be contained homeostatically or lead to an episode of disorder (Zubin & Spring, 1977). Thus both characteristics of the stressor and characteristics of the individual are thought to influence the subsequent pattern of response following exposure to a stressor event. Because characteristics of both stressors and individuals differ, the resulting patterns of adjustment will differ as well (Lazarus & Folkman, 1984). To illustrate the importance of both person and event variables in understanding PTSD, some of the key findings from the recently completed National Vietnam Veterans Readjustment Study (NVVRS; Kulka et al., 1988) will be presented and discussed.

The NVVRS was designed as a multicomponent, nationally representative epidemiological study of the prevalence of PTSD and other postwar psychological problems among Vietnam theater veterans and relevant Vietnam era veteran and civilian comparison groups. NVVRS estimates of the current prevalence of PTSD indicate that 15.2 percent of all male and 8.5 percent of all female Vietnam theater veterans are current (past 6 months) cases of PTSD. This represents about 480 thousand of the estimated 3.15 million veterans who served in the Vietnam war zone.

Among both male and female theater veterans, the current PTSD prevalence is significantly higher for those with high levels of exposure to war zone stress than for those with low to moderate levels of exposure (a fourfold difference for men and sevenfold for women). Also, for both sexes, current PTSD prevalence rates for Vietnam theater veterans are consistently higher than rates for era veterans who did not serve in Vietnam (current prevalence of 2.5 percent male, 1.1 percent female) or civilian counterparts (1.2 percent male, 0.3 percent female). These rate differences are even greater when era veterans and civilians are compared with Vietnam theater veterans with the highest levels of exposure to war zone stress.

The prevalence findings thus show clearly that those who served in Vietnam are at much greater risk of having PTSD today than are their era veteran or civilian counterparts. However, comparisons of the current PTSD prevalence rates for theater and era veterans and civilian counterparts are not completely satisfying because people were not assigned at random to these groups. On the contrary, many powerful social forces operated to determine who served in the military and, within the military, who served in Vietnam. Because of this nonrandom assignment, differences that we observe today in current PTSD prevalence among the study groups may be attributable to differences in the experiences of the groups (for example, service in Vietnam), but they may also result from differences in some characteristics or experiences that Vietnam theater veterans brought with them to their military service.

To examine the contribution of premilitary characteristics to current PTSD prevalence, we began by assessing the extent to which observed differences between study groups in current PTSD prevalence could be accounted for by a large group of potential *predisposing factors* (i.e., a variety of background characteristics and mental health risk factors that might predispose a person to develop PTSD). Using multivariate techniques, we found that controlling for a large set of potential predisposing factors typically reduced the current PTSD prevalence difference among study groups (e.g., between male theater and era veterans). However, even with those factors controlled for, the current PTSD prevalence rate for theater veterans remained significantly and dramatically higher than the rates for era veterans or civilians. This finding suggests that the observed group differences in current PTSD prevalence cannot be attributed simply to the effects of background factors.

These findings also indicate an important role for the Vietnam experience in the development of PTSD in Vietnam theater veterans. To obtain a clearer understanding of the role of that experience in the current PTSD prevalence rate among male Vietnam theater veterans, we extended by one additional step the multivariate analyses that accomplished the adjustment for the potential predisposing factors. This step involved adding a war zone stress exposure variable to the predisposition adjustment models for the male theater veterans. As might be expected, exposure to extreme events in the war zone was found to be significantly and strongly related to current PTSD prevalence, independent of the effects of the premilitary characteristics.

Taken together, these results are consistent with a model of PTSD that posits a role for individual vulnerability (potentially including biological, psychological, and sociodemographic factors) and a role for exposure to environmental factors (specifically, characteristics of stressor events) in determining who among Vietnam theater veterans develops PTSD. It is clear, however, that exposure to war zone stress makes a substantial contribution to the development of PTSD in war veterans that is independent of a broad range of individual background characteristics.

These data clearly indicate that clinicians should carefully assess and consider a vast array of person and event characteristics and their interactions when formulating a perspective on the conditions that affect the expression of PTSD symptoms in a given individual. At the phenomenological level, clinicians must also continually self-monitor their preconceived judgments regarding the range of possible outcomes that follow exposure to extreme combat events. Epidemiological research with community-based samples of veterans informs us that not all individuals who were exposed to extreme events of war develop chronic PTSD, and that a majority of Vietnam veterans—nearly 85 percent—do not have PTSD today. We also know that depression, anxiety disorders, and substance abuse are present in veterans who were exposed to combat (Kulka et al., 1988). It would therefore seem important for the clinician to resist the temptation to interpret all adverse reactivity to combat trauma as the expression of PTSD. Certainly, PTSD is a prevalent disorder among the men and women who bore the brunt of combat, but it is most likely not the only possible adverse sequela to exposure to extreme events.

Problem Definition and Formulation

During the problem definition and formulation process, the therapist needs to evaluate systematically all potential problem areas and, working with the client, to develop the most effective treatment plan possible for each identified problem area. Recently, several reviewers have described multimethod, multisource approaches to the assessment of combat-related PTSD. Such assessment strategies appear to have gained wide acceptance among behavior therapists (e.g., Keane, Fairbank, Caddell, Zimering, & Bender, 1985; Lyons, Gerardi, Wolfe, & Keane, 1988; Wolfe, Keane, Lyons, & Gerardi, 1987). This approach is based on the assumption that PTSD is a complex, multidimensional disorder and that confidence in ultimate diagnostic decisions is increased when multiple indicators concur on the problems of interest. As a result, multimethod assessment of combat-related PTSD includes such varied approaches as structured clinical interviews; functional behavioral analyses of the frequency, intensity, and patterns of occurrence of specific PTSD symptoms; identification of situations antecedent and consequent to symptom onset; administration of self-report measures, clinician rating scales, and ratings of PTSD symptomatology by the primary partners of combat veterans; and psychophysiological assessment procedures.

PTSD does not appear to be the only potential outcome of exposure to extreme events in the war zone. Thus a clear challenge to clinical service providers is to devise strategies for appropriately and validly assessing other potential reactions to trauma, as well as problems that tend to co-occur with PTSD. The literature on adjustment problems among combat veterans certainly suggests that special attention should be paid to substance use and abuse (alcohol and drugs), mood disorders, and anxiety disorders. To develop meaningful individualized treatment plans, however, the clinician should avoid applying rigid, preconceived rules about the "right" problem areas to target for assessment. Such an approach could easily be counterproductive to achieving the overall goal of identifying the specific and unique problems and treatment needs of each individual.

Thus a major focus of PTSD problem definition and formulation is to identify specific problem areas, including PTSD symptoms (e.g., recurrent nightmares of combat events, intense physiological reactivity to reminders of extreme events, etc.), other associated and independent problems of clinical significance (e.g., unemployment, occupational instability, homelessness, marital and parenting difficulties, etc.), and co-occurring psychiatric disorders (e.g., substance abuse or dependence, mood disorders, anxiety disorders, etc.). For the practitioner, a key to managing this aspect of problem definition and formulation successfully is to become familiar with the range of potential adverse outcomes of exposure to extreme events and with the strategies, methods, and instruments available for assessing problems in these areas. Detailed information on specific procedures for assessing postcombat readjustment problems in Vietnam veterans is provided in comprehensive and helpful reviews by Keane, Fairbank et al. (1985), Lyons et al. (1988), and Wolfe et al. (1987). Mastery of this aspect of problem definition will increase the likelihood of obtaining information critical to the development of meaningful and effective PTSD treatment plans.

Once potential target problems have been identified through careful and comprehensive assessment, the next step in the problem definition and formulation process is to work with the patient to develop specific goals. Most treatment plans contain two types of goals: long-term and short-term. Long-term goals usually represent the ultimate outcome to be achieved by treatment. For example, an individual with chronic combat-related PTSD might desire to achieve total extinction of physiological reactivity to memories of specific combat events—a long-term goal that may require significant time and effort to achieve. Behavior therapists have long recognized that a key to the successful achievement of long-term treatment goals (often described in terms of stable symptom reduction) is the ability to develop a graduated series of challenging, but clearly attainable, short-term goals that, in principle, lead to the desired long-term goal. The identification of short-term goals is especially important in devising treatment plans for individuals with target problems of a severe and chronic nature—precisely the situation that clinicians typically encounter when treating combat-related PTSD among veterans of the United States military. Individuals who seek treatment for chronic PTSD are, understandably, often extremely eager for rapid alleviation of symptomatology; they frequently have unrealistic expectations about treatment and its effects. However, the achievement of stable PTSD symptom reduction may require an uncertain and prolonged amount of time (often months or years). Linking the measurement of treatment progress only to the attainment of long-term goals often leads to discouragement for both client and therapist and to unintended side effects, such as dropping out of treatment.

On the other hand, clearly specified short-term goals have several distinct advantages, such as permitting continual monitoring of treatment progress and fostering a sense of accomplishment and progress. Short-term goals in the treatment of PTSD should include small, but meaningful, changes in functioning that are linked to the long-term goal of PTSD symptom reduction. Thus, with a client for whom an important long-term goal is extinction of avoidance of situations that remind him of extreme events, short-term goals could include stepwise increases in the amount of time that he can talk with his spouse about aspects of traumatic events and decreases in the effort expended to avoid exposure to salient reminders of extreme events (e.g., fewer instances of programmed avoidance in daily activities, such as avoiding war movies on television or visits to a hospital ward). The key is to identify clinically meaningful behaviors such as these that are predictable short-term consequences of efficacious interventions.

Generation of Alternatives

The next problem-solving task in clinical decision making is the generation of alternatives. The clinician continues to develop an individualized treatment plan by compiling a comprehensive list of treatment alternatives for PTSD symptoms and other behaviors that have been identified as problematic and requiring treatment. The basic steps in this process are (a) the generation of a list of general treatment strategies for each problem and (b) the identification of specific techniques for each overall strategy. The primary objective at this stage is to lay the foundation for an idiographically effective treatment for PTSD by exploring the range of potential treatment options. Decisions regarding the utility, validity, and appropriateness of each option for treating this disorder as expressed in a particular individual are deferred until the next problem-solving process (decision making).

The completeness and quality of the generated list of treatment alternatives will be influenced by a variety of factors. These include the quality of the assessment of problem areas; the appropriateness of the targets selected for intervention; and the educational, training, and experiential characteristics of the clinical practitioner. Ideally, the clinician will have a working knowledge of the PTSD treatment literature and significant training and skill in implementing the various treatment strategies for PTSD.[1]

The process of generating a list of PTSD treatment alternatives will be illustrated by the following case example selected from the NVVRS (Kulka et al., 1988).

> T. L. is a 38-year-old black male living in a primarily blue-collar, working-class suburb of a major city. He has worked for a municipal airport for nearly 15 years and has been married to his second wife for more than 10 years. T. L.'s parents separated when he was 12 years old, and he and his siblings were raised by his mother in an inner-city neighborhood, which he described as "rather poor." He indicated that his relationship with his mother was good and that there was no known history of psychological disorder in his family of origin. Soon after graduating from high school in 1967, he enlisted in the United States Marine Corps.
>
> From early 1968 to 1969, T. L. served with the United States Marine Corps in the Republic of Vietnam, primarily in the vicinity of the sector that separated South from North Vietnam—the Demilitarized Zone (DMZ). He reported heavy combat exposure ("daily encounters with booby traps, a lot of

---

[1] Although a comprehensive review of treatment strategies and methods is beyond the scope of this chapter, the interested reader is referred to several recently published surveys of the PTSD treatment literature for descriptive and empirical information on specific interventions (e.g., Fairbank & Brown, 1987; Fairbank & Nicholson, 1987; Friedman, 1988).

firefights"), as well as the experience of multiple extreme events. At one point in the structured interview, T. L. described his experience in Vietnam in the following way: "It seemed like every time I turned around someone was getting shot, or had a limb blown off, or their guts hanging out. There was nothing that you could do for them." His voice fading to a barely audible whisper, T. L. described one of many specific extreme events in these words: "One time on a mission, a land mine exploded. Three guys were killed . . . blown up . . . guys on the ground, screaming."

T. L. reported that severe and persistent problems in his daily functioning began within a few months of his return from Vietnam to the United States. From 1970 to the present, he has been plagued relentlessly by symptoms of combat-related PTSD, the impact of which he has attempted to diminish through chronic alcohol abuse. He painfully acknowledged the continuing presence of distressing, intrusive memories of death and dying in the combat zone ("Sometimes my thoughts take me right back to what happened to my partners there. I wish I could have helped them."). In a voice choked with emotion, he said that he currently attempts to avoid thoughts and reminders of Vietnam, often with little success: "I try, but it's hard. In my job I deal with the public, and it seems like someone or something is always bringing it up." He also clearly described numerous discrete episodes in which memories of Vietnam overwhelmed his capacity to cope, precipitating extreme physiological reactivity, including shortness of breath and tachycardia, for which he sought medical care for "nerves." T. L. reported that these episodes were also characterized by gut-wrenching pangs of guilt, shame, and despair related to the memories of traumatic combat events.

This account of T. L.'s current functioning includes several significant problems. Regarding symptoms of PTSD, T. L. reported that he currently experiences repetitive, intrusive, and disturbing memories of extreme combat events; persistent and adverse psychophysiological arousal as a function of these memories; and severe cognitive and emotional distress in the form of guilt, shame, and despair associated with memories of Vietnam. In addition, he reported co-occurring alcohol abuse that appeared to be secondary to PTSD symptomatology. For the therapist, the first step in the generation of treatment alternatives is to identify potential general treatment strategies for the problems described in each of these areas. To counteract adverse arousal and avoidance associated with intrusive memories of extreme events in the war zone, the clinician should consider strategies that involve direct therapeutic exposure (e.g., Fairbank & Brown, 1987) and cognitive behavior therapy (e.g., Foa, Steketee, & Olasov-Rothbaum, 1989). Other interventions directed at persistent and adverse arousal could include pharmacological treatment (e.g., Friedman, 1988) and biobehavioral approaches to controlling anxiety and physiological reactivity (e.g., Gatchel, 1979). In addition, emotional processing strategies (e.g., Foa & Kozak, 1986) would appear especially relevant to the treatment of severe cognitive/emotional reactions to trauma such as the guilt and shame described by T. L.

Comprehensive treatment of an individual who seeks help for symptoms of PTSD requires that the treatment plan address comorbid disorders as well. A variety of treatment strategies should be considered for T. L.'s alcohol abuse, which appears in his case to be a problem secondary to PTSD. Potential intervention strategies might include alcohol detoxification and various regimens of abstinence therapy; controlled drinking approaches; chemotherapeutic treatments (e.g., disulfiram); relapse prevention training; and long-term social support such as that provided through Alcoholics Anonymous (O'Farrell & Langenbucher, 1985). The major point here, however, is that the need to intervene with major disorders and problems that co-occur with PTSD should be reflected in the treatment plan, a strategy that is both compatible with and necessary for good clinical management of PTSD.

The second step in the generation of alternatives is to compile a list of specific techniques within each of the broader treatment classes. Direct therapeutic exposure strategies for treating combat-related PTSD include imaginal exposure and extinction (Fairbank & Keane, 1982; Keane, Fairbank, Caddell, & Zimering, 1989), systematic desensitization (Schindler, 1980), and in vivo exposure (Williams, 1976). Cognitive behavior therapy methods for diminishing intrusive memories of extreme events could include thought stopping (Resick, Jordan, Girelli, Hutter, & Marhoefer-Dvorak, 1988) and/or therapies that focus on restructuring individual and event-specific cognitive distortions—especially attributions, expectations, and appraisals—using procedures such as covert rehearsal and guided self-dialogue (Foa et al., 1989; Resick et al., 1988).

Other interventions that specifically target reduction in psychophysiological arousal would include administration of sympathetic-acting medications, such as the benzodiazepines and beta-blockers (Friedman, 1988). Biobehavioral approaches to controlling severe arousal could include various forms of biofeedback (Gatchel, 1979) and progressive and cue-controlled relaxation training (Keane, Fairbank et al., 1985). In treatment for emotional/cognitive symptoms of guilt and shame, cognitive therapy, implemented within the context of imaginal flooding, may be employed to activate structures associated with traumatic memories and to provide corrective information about the extreme event, the individual's responses to the situation, and/or their meaning (Foa & Kozak, 1986; Foa et al., 1989).

Specific behavioral treatments for concurrent alcohol abuse could include the use of skills training, contingency management, extinction of physiological and subjective cravings for alcohol, and various forms of operant conditioning (Childress, McLellan, & O'Brien, 1985). Another approach to treating T. L.'s substance abuse would be to focus on alleviating the PTSD symptomatology that is presumed to trigger his episodes of alcohol abuse—an approach that would appear appropriate and potentially efficacious in a case where substance abuse is stimulated by adverse levels of anxiety and other forms of negative emotionality associated with PTSD.

To conclude the generation of alternatives, the clinician makes a "wish list" of potential interventions for a given individual with PTSD, for the moment deferring judgment about the feasibility of each potential option. The goal here is to design the most comprehensive and efficacious individually tailored intervention possible, irrespective of the practical constraints that will eventually shape the final treatment plan. For example, in developing an unconstrained treatment plan for T. L., the clinician might consider an enhanced regimen of direct therapeutic exposure within the context of a stable therapeutic relationship. This regimen, using multiple methods and modalities of exposure, would aim to maximize the likelihood of extinguishing T. L.'s intense physiological and emotional reactivity to memories and reminders (Fairbank & Brown, 1987; Keane, Caddell, & Zimering, 1985).

An enhanced regimen of exposure therapy for PTSD could include components of imaginal, in vivo, biblio-, audio-, and video-exposure in the context of individual and group treatment. Specifically, T. L. could be scheduled for 15 to 20 sessions of individual imagery-based implosive therapy, which would target the extinction of the adverse arousal triggered by internal and external cues associated with events that he personally experienced in combat (e.g., the death of his friends during an ambush). In vivo therapeutic exposure to feared stimuli could be accomplished through a systematic program of prolonged rides in combat helicopters with specially trained National Guard pilots;

the unconstrained treatment plan could even include a 2- to 3-week excursion to Vietnam with a therapist-led group of Vietnam veterans to visit the sites of military engagements (Largent, 1989).

The clinician could assign exposure homework, asking T. L. to listen to detailed audiotaped accounts of his own traumatic experiences, to watch videotapes of relevant documentaries and movies, and to read the published accounts of war experiences by Vietnam veterans as well as histories of the war. In addition, T. L. could be involved in weekly trauma-focused group therapy sessions that emphasize extinction of adverse arousal through prolonged discussion of the details of extreme events and the personal meaning of these events to the individual.

Decision Making

In the decision-making process, the clinician works with the patient to develop a feasible, individualized, focused, and effective treatment plan. The basic procedure at this point is to evaluate systematically the appropriateness, validity, and utility of each of the previously generated intervention possibilities for each target problem. In judging the potential utility of a specific PTSD intervention for an individual with the disorder, the clinician must carefully weigh a variety of factors.

First, the clinician should assess the likelihood that a particular PTSD treatment approach will produce the desired outcome. For example, if one treatment goal is to reduce a client's adverse physiological arousal to environmental cues associated with an extreme event, then the therapist should review all evidence that predicts whether or not various treatment options will produce this effect. Often the prediction will be based on the clinician's previous experiences in treating other individuals with a similar psychosocial history and configuration of background characteristics, PTSD symptoms, co-occurring disorders, and current life circumstances. An understanding of the relevant literature and the recommendations of knowledgeable clinical supervisors and peer consultants will also enter into the prediction.

A second major step in developing an individualized plan for treating PTSD is to estimate the feasibility of each potential treatment strategy. The goal here is to determine the likelihood that a particular treatment plan can be implemented in its optimal form with a specific individual. This judgment requires a careful analysis of potential obstacles to the implementation of each treatment strategy; these include structural and personal barriers, as well as clinical issues. Structural barriers could be any number of bureaucratic restrictions or limitations that effectively block access to treatment. Commonly reported examples include restrictive eligibility criteria (e.g., the patient lacks adequate insurance coverage), distance (e.g., the patient lives far from the treatment providers and lacks access to transportation), and the time and effort often required to implement an intervention strategy in its optimal form. Individuals are frequently reluctant to invest their often limited personal resources (time, effort, money, etc.) in the more intensive forms of behavioral treatment for PTSD, regardless of the potential for successful outcome. Consider the enhanced regimen of direct therapeutic exposure described in the previous section: It is unlikely that T. L. will be able to afford to travel to Vietnam for in vivo exposure, even if, in the clinician's opinion, this form of exposure will be the most effective. On the other hand, it may be quite feasible for him to participate in weekly sessions that employ imaginal exposure techniques and to augment these sessions with homework and occasional helicopter rides.

On the other hand, barriers to implementation of PTSD treatment sometimes originate in the perceptions and preferences of the potential treatment recipients. Such barriers may include the expressed desire of such individuals to resolve problems on their own, without assistance from clinicians. Another commonly encountered personal barrier is the perception that chronic combat-related PTSD symptoms will eventually remit with time. This perception is, unfortunately, often incorrect and can lead to the faulty conclusion that treatment of PTSD is unnecessary. Other personal barriers to participation in treatment are distrust of mental health professionals; concerns about the efficacy of behavioral interventions for PTSD; and fear of what one might learn about oneself in the process of treatment, including concerns about reexperiencing intense distress and consequently losing one's ability to cope. Additional personal barriers that are sometimes encountered include concerns about revealing classified military information in the course of treatment and about being judged by the therapist for actions that occurred under combat conditions. There are numerous potential structural and personal barriers to the implementation of each possible treatment strategy. Clearly, an essential step in formulating an effective and feasible treatment plan for combat-related PTSD is to identify, assess, and overcome these barriers.

The therapist must also take into account a substantial number of clinical issues in determining the feasibility of various treatment options for PTSD. The practitioner must consider not only the type and severity of current PTSD symptoms but also the type and severity of other significant behavior problems, including specific psychiatric disorders that may co-occur with PTSD. A specific intervention strategy in its optimal form might be quite feasible for an individual with PTSD and no other specific comorbid psychiatric disorder. However, the strategy might lose its feasibility if the individual's PTSD is accompanied by a major depressive disorder, narcotic dependence, or severe symptoms of borderline personality disorder. Certainly, the type and severity of co-occurring problems will have a great impact upon the predicted outcome of any specific intervention strategy for PTSD. For example, PTSD patients with co-occurring borderline personality disorder characterized by extremely unstable interpersonal relationships are often poor candidates for direct therapeutic exposure to psychologically painful traumatic memories, an intervention that requires a stable and trusting alliance between client and clinician over the course of treatment. Clients with PTSD and active drug or alcohol dependencies that function to restrain emotional and physiological reactivity may fail to benefit fully from emotional processing treatment strategies for PTSD.

The decision-making process additionally requires an understanding of the strengths and weaknesses of the treatment provider relative to the implementation of each intervention strategy. Relevant issues include knowledge of the complexities and subtleties of behavior therapy for PTSD, as well as competence in conducting particular procedures. Several authors have recently emphasized the importance of attending to the nuances of behavior therapy in treating combat-related PTSD, underscoring the importance of understanding the role of behavioral theories in the formulation of comprehensive treatment strategies (e.g., Boudewyns & Shipley, 1983; Foa et al., 1989; Keane, Fairbank et al., 1985; Lyons & Keane, in press). Others have stressed that behavior therapy for chronic PTSD is not simply the application of specific, validated intervention techniques, but rather involves systematic implementation of specific strategies within the context of a stable therapeutic relationship—a point that is often overlooked in descriptions of specific behavioral treatment interventions for combat-related PTSD (Fairbank & Nicholson, 1987).

Another important consideration is that certain behavioral treatment modalities for PTSD require extensive training and supervision. This factor would apply especially to the various forms of direct therapeutic exposure and extinction that have been effectively used in the treatment of chronic PTSD among combat veterans (Keane et al., 1989). Moreover, each intervention possibility must be weighed in terms of its personal consequences for the client and the clinician. Personal consequences include unintended side effects, ethical implications, level of effort required, time commitment, finances, impact on family and significant others, and emotional and physical side effects. For example, intensive interventions that place high demands on clients often produce the unintended side effect of poor treatment compliance and high dropout rates. Thus it is important to assess the likelihood that an individual will comply with each alternative treatment regimen, especially those that may require substantial commitments of time and effort on the part of both the client and the treatment provider.

Finally, deciding which PTSD treatment strategy to implement with an individual involves comparing the expected outcomes of each alternative approach for each of the short- and long-term goals that have been specified. The guiding principle is to implement the treatment strategy that appears most likely to be both efficacious and feasible for the individual. In the case of T. L., for example, the clinician should carefully examine and compare the expected clinical efficacy and feasibility of the various possible strategies for treating the target problems previously identified as requiring intervention: PTSD and alcohol abuse.

In T. L.'s case, the clinician could decide to implement a treatment plan for chronic combat-related PTSD and alcohol abuse that focuses on both problem areas concurrently. Weekly treatment sessions could be implemented on an outpatient basis and begin with the provision of a comprehensive education component on PTSD and alcohol abuse to the client and his spouse. Next, T. L. could be taught relaxation skills as a strategy to help him cope specifically with arousal associated with PTSD and generally with negative life stressors. Several sessions could also focus on the exploration of issues and the training of skills for preventing relapse into substance abuse. Once a stable therapeutic alliance between the clinician and client has been established, the clinician could consider implementing a trial of direct therapeutic exposure for combat-related PTSD, a major component of which would be systematic flooding in imagination. Given T. L.'s severe difficulty in coping with guilt and shame associated with some combat memories, the intervention should also focus on assisting the client in restructuring maladaptive cognitions (attributions, appraisals, meaning) associated with these events. Finally, the treatment plan should be developed with the participation of T. L. to ensure feasibility and to maximize the probability of compliance with the treatment regimen. Periodic reviews of treatment progress should be scheduled in advance so that changes in strategies and techniques can be made as needed.

Solution Implementation and Verification

The final problem-solving process in the decision-making model involves the implementation of the PTSD treatment plan and the systematic evaluation of its effectiveness. Certainly, the clinician's ability to verify the utility of the treatment plan depends in no small measure on the reliability and validity of the methods used to evaluate the individual's treatment progress and outcome. One approach to verifying treatment efficacy for PTSD is to assume that no single assessment method is completely error free and that verification is best accomplished with multiple measures of treatment process and outcome for each target problem. It is the confirmation of treatment progress and outcome across measures that gives the clinician a foundation for confidence in the efficacy of the implemented intervention.

For example, assessment of the efficacy of direct therapeutic exposure interventions for PTSD often includes treatment process measures such as self-monitoring of anxiety using Subjective Units of Disturbance Scale ratings (Wolpe, 1982) monitoring of psychophysiological reactivity during the course of therapy sessions (Fairbank & Keane, 1982); and motoric ratings of anxiety during treatment, recorded by independent observers (Fairbank, Gross, & Keane, 1983). Outcome measures often include reports from multiple sources on the frequency and intensity of PTSD symptoms, symptoms of other psychiatric disorders, and other problems associated with post-event readjustment (e.g., occupational status, family adjustment, and subjective well-being). Estimates of treatment efficacy outside of the treatment session may be provided by the client, the primary partner (e.g., the client's spouse), and the treating clinician. Again, because no single source of information on the effects of treatment is free from error, it is important to obtain information from multiple sources (client, clinician, and significant others) to gain a composite view of the effectiveness of the intervention.

Outcome measures for a married male Vietnam veteran in treatment for PTSD and co-occurring depression, for example, could include a structured clinical interview for specific PTSD symptomatology (e.g., the PTSD module of the Structured Clinical Interview for the DSM-III-R; Spitzer, Williams, & Gibbon, 1987). In addition, it might be helpful to obtain self-, clinician, and spouse ratings of current PTSD symptomatology on measures such as the Mississippi Scale for Combat-related PTSD (M-PTSD; Keane, Caddell, & Taylor, 1988), the clinician-administered Stress Response Rating Scale (Weiss, Horowitz, & Wilner,

1984), and a version of the M-PTSD adapted to provide information on the combat veteran's PTSD symptoms from the perspective of his primary partner (Fairbank, Marmar, & Weiss, 1988). Outcome assessment of depressed mood in this client could be ascertained by structured clinical interviews, patient-rated depression inventories such as the Beck Depression Inventory or the Zung Depression Scale (see Fairbank, Keane, & Malloy, 1983), and clinician-rated scales such as the Hamilton Depression Rating Scale (see Fairbank, Gross, & Keane, 1983).

Monitoring the efficacy of the implemented intervention is a dynamic process that continues throughout PTSD treatment (Sobell, Sobell, & Nirenberg, 1988). Monitoring provides the clinician with opportunities to detect and troubleshoot problems as they arise; revise the treatment plan with the input of the client as needed; determine when the goals of treatment have been achieved; and decide if additional treatment, aftercare/follow-up, or termination is warranted.

CONCLUSION

PTSD is a relatively new diagnosis for which assessment criteria have only recently been formally established (American Psychiatric Association, 1980). During the past decade, important gains have been made in our understanding of the prevalence, nature, assessment, and treatment of this major psychological disorder. Despite advances in PTSD research, little practical information has been made available to inform and guide the decision-making efforts of the mental health practitioners who provide most of the essential psychological services received by clients with PTSD. The present chapter has attempted to fill this void by illustrating the use of the decision-making model in managing clinical interventions for those afflicted with chronic forms of this complex and often complicated disorder.

References

American Psychiatric Association. (1980). *Diagnostic and statistical manual of mental disorders* (3rd ed.). Washington, DC: Author.

American Psychiatric Association. (1987). *Diagnostic and statistical manual of mental disorders* (3rd ed. rev.). Washington, DC: Author.

Amick-McMullen, A., Kilpatrick, D. & Veronen, L. (1989). Family survivors of homicide victims: A behavioral analysis. *The Behavior Therapist, 12,* 75–79.

Borus, J. F. (1973). Reentry: I. Adjustment issues facing the Vietnam returnee. *Archives of General Psychiatry, 28,* 501–506.

Boudewyns, P. A., & Shipley, R. H. (1983). *Flooding and implosive therapy: Direct therapeutic exposure in clinical practice.* New York: Plenum.

Breslau, N., & Davis, G. C. (1987). Posttraumatic stress disorder: The stressor criterion. *Journal of Nervous and Mental Disease, 175,* 255–264.

Brett, E. A., Spitzer, R. L., & Williams, J. B. W. (1988). DSM-III-R criteria for posttraumatic stress disorder. *American Journal of Psychiatry, 145,* 1232–1236.

Childress, A. R., McLellan, A. T., & O'Brien, C. P. (1985). Behavioral therapies for substance abuse. *The International Journal of the Addictions, 20,* 947–969.

Egendorf, A., Kadushin, C., Laufer, R. S., Rothbart, G., & Sloan, L. (1981). *Legacies of Vietnam: Comparative adjustment of veterans and their peers.* Washington, DC: U. S. Government Printing Office.

Escobar, J. I. (1987). Commentary: Posttraumatic stress disorder and the perennial stress-diathesis controversy. *Journal of Nervous and Mental Disease, 175,* 265–266.

Fairbank, J. A., & Brown, T. A. (1987). Current behavioral approaches to the treatment of posttraumatic stress disorder. *The Behavior Therapist, 10,* 57-64.

Fairbank J. A., Gross, R. T., & Keane, T. M. (1983). Treatment of posttraumatic stress disorder: Evaluating outcome with a behavioral code. *Behavior Modification, 7,* 557–568.

Fairbank, J. A., & Keane, T. M. (1982). Flooding for combat-related stress disorders: Assessment of anxiety reduction across traumatic memories. *Behavior Therapy, 13,* 499–510.

Fairbank, J. A., Keane, T. M., & Malloy, P. F. (1983). Some preliminary data on the psychological characteristics of Vietnam veterans with PTSD. *Journal of Consulting and Clinical Psychology, 51,* 912–919.

Fairbank, J. A., Marmar, C. R., & Weiss, D. S. (1988, October). *Preliminary findings of the clinical subsample of the National Vietnam Veterans Readjustment Study.* Paper presented at the annual meeting of the Society for Traumatic Stress Studies, Dallas.

Fairbank, J. A., & Nicholson, R. A. (1987). Theoretical and empirical issues in the treatment of post-traumatic stress disorder in Vietnam veterans. *Journal of Clinical Psychology, 43,* 44–55.

Foa, E. B., & Kozak, M. J. (1986). Emotional processing of fear: Exposure to corrective information. *Psychological Bulletin, 99,* 20–35.

Foa, E. B., Steketee, G., & Olasov-Rothblum, B. (1989). Behavioral/cognitive conceptualizations of post-traumatic stress disorder. *Behavior Therapy, 20,* 155–176.

Foy, D. W., & Card, J. J. (1987). Combat-related post-traumatic stress disorder etiology: Replicated findings in a national sample of Vietnam-era men. *Journal of Clinical Psychology, 43,* 28–31.

Foy, D. W., Carroll, E. M., & Donahoe, C. P. (1987). Etiological factors in the development of PTSD in a clinical sample of Vietnam combat veterans. *Journal of Clinical Psychology, 43,* 17–27.

Foy, D. W., Sipprelle, R. C., Rueger, D. B., & Carroll, E. M. (1984). Etiology of post-traumatic stress disorder in Vietnam veterans: Analysis of premilitary, military and combat exposure influences. *Journal of Consulting and Clinical Psychology, 52,* 72-87.

Friedman, M. J. (1988). Toward rational pharmacotherapy for posttraumatic stress disorder: An interim report. *The American Journal of Psychiatry, 145,* 281–285.

Frye, J. S., & Stockton, R. A. (1982). Discriminant analysis of posttraumatic stress disorder among a group of Vietnam veterans. *American Journal of Psychiatry, 139,* 52–56.

318   Chapter 10

Gatchel, R. J. (1979). Biofeedback and the treatment of fear and anxiety. In R. J. Gatchel & K. P. Price (Eds.), *Clinical applications of biofeedback: Appraisal and status.* New York: Pergamon.

Green, B. L., Lindy, J. D., Grace, M. C., & Gleser, G. C. (in press). Multiple diagnosis in post-traumatic stress disorder: The role of war stressors. *Journal of Nervous and Mental Disease.*

Keane, T. M. (1989). Post-traumatic stress disorder: Current status and future directions. *Behavior Therapy, 20,* 149–153.

Keane, T. M., Caddell, J. M., & Taylor, K. L. (1988). Mississippi Scale for Combat-related Post-Traumatic Stress Disorder: Three studies in reliability and validity. *Journal of Consulting and Clinical Psychology, 56, 85–90.*

Keane, T. M., Caddell, J. M., & Zimering, R. T. (1985). A behavioral formulation of posttraumatic stress disorder in Vietnam veterans. *The Behavior Therapist, 8,* 9–12.

Keane, T. M., Fairbank, J. A., Caddell, J. M., & Zimering, R. T. (1989). Imaginal flooding reduces symptoms of PTSD in Vietnam veterans. *Behavior Therapy, 20,* 245–260.

Keane, T. M., Fairbank, J. A., Caddell, J. M., Zimering, R. T., & Bender, M. E. (1985). A behavioral approach to assessing and treating PTSD in Vietnam veterans. In C. R. Figley (Ed.), *Trauma and its wake.* New York: Brunner/Mazel.

Kulka, R. A., Schlenger, W. E., Fairbank, J. A., Hough, R. L., Jordan, B. K., Marmar, C. R., & Weiss, D. S. (1988). *Contractual report on findings from the National Vietnam Veterans Readjustment Study. I: Executive summary, description of findings, and technical appendices.* Research Triangle Park, NC: Research Triangle Institute.

Largent, D. (1989). Contacting the past: Vietnam veterans fly back in time for stress therapy. *Evergreen, 18*(4), 8–9.

Lazarus, R. S., & Folkman, S. (1984). *Stress, appraisal, and coping.* New York: Springer.

Lyons, J. A., Gerardi, R. J., Wolfe, J., & Keane, T. M. (1988). Multidimensional assessment of combat-related PTSD: Phenomenological, psychometric, and psychophysiological considerations. *Journal of Traumatic Stress, 1,* 373–394.

Lyons, J. A., & Keane, T. M. (in press). Implosive therapy for the treatment of combat-related PTSD. *Journal of Traumatic Stress.*

Meehl, P. E. (1962). Schizotaxia, schizotypy, schizophrenia. *American Psychologist, 17,* 827–838.

Mischel, W. A. (1984). Convergences and challenges in the search for consistency. *American Psychologist, 39,* 351–364.

Nace, E. P., O'Brien, C. P., Mintz, J., Ream, N., & Meyers, A. L. (1978). Adjustment among Vietnam veteran drug users two years post-service. In C. R. Figley (Ed.), *Stress disorder among Vietnam veterans: Theory, research, and treatment.* New York: Brunner/Mazel.

O'Farrell, T. J., & Langenbucher, J. W. (1985). Alcohol abuse. In M. Hersen (Ed.), *Practice of inpatient behavior therapy: A clinical guide.* Orlando: Grune & Stratton.

Penk, W. E., Robinowitz, R., Roberts, W. R., Patterson, E. T., Dolan, M. P., & Atkins, H. G. (1981). Adjustment differences among male substance abusers varying in degree of combat experience in Vietnam. *Journal of Consulting and Clinical Psychology, 49,* 426–437.

Resick, P. A., Jordan, C. G., Girelli, S. A., Hutter, C. K., & Marhoefer-Dvorak, S. (1988). A comparative outcome study of behavioral group therapy for sexual assault victims. *Behavior Therapy, 19,* 385–401.

Schindler, F. E. (1980). Treatment by systematic desensitization of a recurring nightmare of a real life trauma. *Journal of Behavior Therapy and Experimental Psychiatry, 11*, 53–54.

Spitzer, R. L., Williams, J. B. W., & Gibbon, M. (1987). *Structured Clinical Interview for DSM-III-R, Non-patient Version* (Modified for National Vietnam Veterans Readjustment Study 4/1/87). New York: New York State Psychiatric Institute, Biometrics Research Department.

Sobell, L. C., Sobell, M. C., & Nirenberg, T. D. (1988). Behavioral assessment and treatment planning with alcohol and drug abusers: A review with an emphasis on clinical application. *Clinical Psychology Review, 8*(1), 19–54.

Weiss, D. S., Horowitz, M. J., & Wilner, N. (1984). The Strett Response Rating Scale: A clinician's measure for rating the response to serious life events. *British Journal of Clinical Psychology, 23*, 202–215.

Williams, W. (1976). Acute traumatic neurosis treated by brief intensive behavior therapy. *Journal of Behavior Therapy and Experimental Psychiatry, 7*, 43–45.

Wolfe, J., Keane, T. M., Lyons, J. A., & Gerardi, R. J. (1987). Current trends and issues in the assessment of combat-related post-traumatic stress disorder. *The Behavior Therapist, 10*, 27–32.

Wolpe, J. (1982). *The practice of behavior therapy* (3rd ed.) New York: Pergamon.

Worthington, E. R. (1977). Post-service adjustment and Vietnam era veterans. *Military Medicine, 142*, 865–866.

Zubin, J., & Spring, B. (1977). Vulnerability: A new view of schizophrenia. *Journal of Abnormal Psychology, 86*, 103–126.

Chapter 11

Child and Adolescent Therapy

Philip C. Kendall
Lynne Siqueland

INTRODUCTION

All mental health professionals are, at various times, called upon to make decisions about their clients. This chapter will examine clinical decision-making strategies and options for those who work with children and adolescents. What types of tests or assessments are needed? What forms of intervention are indicated by assessment results? Research findings concerning the most appropriate therapeutic interventions for children and adolescents with different problems are beginning to appear in the literature but are still quite limited. Clearly, the *uniformity myth* (Kendall, 1984; Kiesler, 1966)—that any one therapeutic approach is optimal for all cases—is just that, a myth. It would be an error to assume that even a skilled application of a single form of therapy is an optimal treatment for children with diverse difficulties. Conscientious therapists adjust the therapy to meet the behavioral, cognitive, emotional, and developmental needs of the individual.

We propose that therapists use the decision-making model described in chapter 3 to approach treatment planning and that they maintain flexibility in using this approach. The problem-solving therapist generates a variety of hypotheses derived from clinical experience and knowledge of the literature, systematically assesses the merits of these hypotheses in work with the individual client, and modifies and changes the strategy when necessary. In this chapter, we consider a variety of intervention strategies and their application to various problems, suggesting that careful decision making underlies effective use of interventions.

BEHAVIORAL AND COGNITIVE DIFFERENTIATION

The following discussion will outline a method for conceptualizing child and adolescent psychopathology on the basis of behavior (internalizing and externalizing behaviors) and cognitive factors (distortions and deficiencies), and will provide a framework to help the therapist plan interventions accordingly.

Behavioral Differentiation

Achenbach (1966) first proposed a distinction between *internalizing* and *externalizing* child behavior disorders based on a factor analysis of descriptions of behavior problems. This distinction was founded on information from a variety of sources: parents, teachers, and self-reports. Internalizing disorders were named for a cluster of symptoms that involved problems within the self, such as childhood depression and anxiety. Externalizing disorders, with symptoms that involved conflict with the outside world, were associated with conduct disorder, noncompliant behavior, hyperactivity, and impulsivity.

In analyzing biographical data, Achenbach also found correlates of the two groupings. When compared to internalizers, externalizers tended to show, in Achenbach's terms, poorer school performance, more previous problems, parents with more overt social problems, parents who were less concerned with their child's problems, and homes that more often lacked at least one of the biological parents. It therefore appears that the development of internalizing or externalizing behaviors is influenced by the child's socialization history. Internalizers apparently have learned to deal with their stress via internal (within-self) conflict, whereas externalizers seem to have learned to express their conflict in an aggressive or acting-out manner. Along with biographical data, information concerning internalizing or externalizing behavior can be helpful in choosing assessments, selecting target behaviors, deciding on the type and length of treatment, and so on.

Cognitive Differentiation

Kendall (1985) has proposed distinguishing between *cognitive deficiencies* and *cognitive distortions* in conceptualizing child psychopathology. *Deficiencies* refers to an absence of thinking where it would be beneficial (i.e., acting before thinking). These deficits in information processing involve a failure to engage in forethought and planning. Children and adolescents with cognitive deficiencies are loath to monitor their own performance and neglect to reflect on their own perceptions of the world. *Distortions*, on the other hand, refers to dysfunctional thinking processes, such as exaggeration of threat to the self. In distorted information processing, the individual is attending to social and environmental cues and is actively processing these data, but the processing itself is dysfunctional or "crooked."

Although some overlap exists, a distinction between cognitive deficiencies and cognitive distortions has implications for intervention procedures. For example, consider a child we will call Catherine, a 10-year-old referred for childhood depression and assessed via a variety of psychological tests and performance tasks. In general, the child's cognitive pattern was one of negative distortion. Despite her teacher's ratings, which placed her amid normal variations, Catherine self-appraised her social and academic abilities to be well below average. Similarly, her perception of her social interactions, based on her own retrospective self-assessments, was hypercritical and inaccurate. She was processing her world actively but not accurately. Therefore, an appropriate focus for treatment would be the correction of her distorted processing style.

This distinction in cognitive processing is related to the distinction between externalizing and internalizing or undercontrol and overcontrol in child behavior. For example, depressed children do not show deficiencies in thinking (Fuhrman & Kendall, 1986), although they have been found to be overly critical in evaluating themselves (Kendall, Stark, & Adam, 1989). Kendall, Stark, and Adam (1989) reported on three studies that examined the question "Cognitive deficit or cognitive distortion in childhood depression?" In Study 1, sixth graders diagnosed as depressed or nondepressed completed the Matching Familiar Figures Test (Kagan, 1966), the Children's Depression Inventory (Kovacs, 1981), and the My Standards Questionnaire (Stark, Best, & Adam, 1986). Results were consistent across raters and measures: Depression was associated with a negative style of processing self-evaluative information but was unrelated to a processing deficit. Study 2 replicated these findings and extended them to a wider age range (third to sixth graders). Study 3 tested whether the negative perceptions of depressed children were accurate or a biased distortion, as judged against teachers' observations. The results confirmed the notion that depressed children exhibit a distorted style of information processing. Other studies have shown that depressed children, like depressed adults, appear to manifest distortion in that they attribute positive events to external causes and negative events to internal causes more often than do nondepressed children (e.g., Leon, Kendall, & Garber, 1980). Distortions, not cognitive deficiencies, characterize depressed youth.

Impulsive or aggressive children often lack self-control or fail to employ verbal mediation strategies (Camp, 1977; see also Kendall & Braswell, 1985). The cognitive problem in impulsivity concerns deficient deployment of strategies and an absence of internal, self-governing self-talk that manages behavioral output. Attentional deficits are evident in impulsive children as well as in children labeled hyperactive. Indeed, a recent revision of the *Diagnostic and Statistical Manual of Mental Disorders* (DSM-III-R, American Psychiatric Association, 1987) has incorporated the label Attention Deficit Hyperactivity Disorder (ADHD), giving obvious emphasis to attentional difficulties as part of the behavioral problems of hyperactivity. Deficits in attention, problem solving, and strategy use are important components of the ADHD condition. Consider David, an impulsive 14-year-old who, initially and on prompting, would not self-appraise nor rethink social interactions. Recognizing and identifying his own and others' emotions, evaluating his social performances, and performing related cognitive activities were abilities severely lacking in his repertoire. Only after cognitive-behavioral training did David share his sense of discovery: "Hey, I never used to think about these things."

Aggressive children, such as those labeled conduct disordered or oppositional, display antisocial behavior and show both cognitive distortions and cognitive deficiencies. A number of researchers (see Kendall, 1985) have found evidence of this. Dodge and his colleagues have found that aggressive children tend to overattribute hostile intent to others (Dodge, 1980; Dodge & Frame, 1982). Lochman (1987) found that, in social interactions, aggressive boys minimized their own aggressiveness and exaggerated the aggressiveness of their peer partners more than did nonaggressive boys. Studies of the interpersonal problem-solving skills of aberrant or aggressive inner-city youth (e.g., Shure & Spivack, 1972) have shown a tendency for such children to see a limited set of alternative solutions to interpersonal problems, with the majority of the proposed solutions being aggressive in style. Spivack and Shure (1974) have referred to these children as having deficiencies in interpersonal cognitive problem solving.

One reason for the difficulty of treating aggression in children and adolescents may be that both cognitive deficiencies and cognitive distortions exist and that they interact in ways that require further intervention. Moreover, the intensity of the affective arousal associated with aggression may interfere with rational problem solving and incorrectly force the individual to confirm a distortion in processing. Thus, when agitated, aggressive youths may fail to think and hastily conclude that others are provoking them. Further investigation of the role of affect in treating aggressive young people is warranted (see Kendall, Ronan, & Epps, in press).

ASSESSMENT

As outlined in chapter 3, one of the first processes in clinical decision making is problem definition and formulation. With children and adolescents, it is especially important to perform a thorough assessment using a variety of reporting sources and a multimethod procedure. For example, the clinician must carefully evaluate the presenting problem to determine if treating the child or adolescent alone is the best approach. Often the child's difficulties are intimately linked to family problems or to school and peer difficulties. In such cases, family therapy or a school- or classroom-based intervention may be warranted. Consider the following example: A 15-year-old boy has been referred by a school counselor for possible anxiety management skills training. The reason for the referral is the prominence of problems related to school performance not in line with the boy's intellectual abilities— problems that are considered linked to anxious misperceptions. The therapist conducts an intake interview with the boy and his mother. The client is not diagnosed as having an anxiety disorder, nor does he show evidence of suspected attentional and impulse control problems. The interview does, however, reveal that the mother has been putting inordinately severe pressure on the son and that improvement would be most likely if the mother were included in the intervention. In another case, the therapist might decide to work with other therapists or agencies or to make a referral. Whatever treatment approach is ultimately chosen, a thorough assessment is an essential first step.

A variety of perspectives on a youngster's identified problem can be very enlightening at this point. Assessment of the problem as the client experiences it, as the parents experience it, and as the teacher or significant others experience it will, collectively, yield a more accurate understanding of the problem and its proper treatment. In cases of anxiety, depression, and social withdrawal, clients themselves are often the most accurate reporters. Indeed, parents and teachers may fail to recognize the problems experienced by quiet and noninterfering children. There is limited agreement among parents, teachers, and children when the target is childhood depression (Kazdin, 1988; Kendall,

Cantwell, & Kazdin, 1989). Research has suggested that children are likely to be better reporters of symptoms related to private or internal experience (see Edelbrock, Costello, Dulcan, Conover, & Kalas, 1986). By contrast, aggressive youth, often as a manifestation of their disorder, may lie or underestimate the severity of their own behavior. In such cases, laboratory or performance data along with naturally occurring frequencies noted in behavioral observation may be most informative. Impulsive children likewise often have difficulty in self-evaluation, and parents and teachers may provide more accurate assessments. In general, teachers, who may have a more thorough background regarding the behavioral norms for a particular age group, can be an excellent resource for the therapist.

One difficulty the clinical assessor faces, especially when different data sources provide divergent information, is deciding which source is accurate or correct. Different perspectives exist and are to be tolerated, but discrepant factual information calls for resolution. When striving to reconcile differences among data sources, it may be helpful to bear in mind the cognitive and behavioral distinctions discussed earlier. Hyperactive children may not be accurate self-reporters, whereas parents and teachers might offer reasoned data concerning the difficulties. On the other hand, because anxious and depressed children are most in touch with their own affect, their self-reports are valuable, perhaps even more so than parent or teacher ratings. Behavioral observations of anxiety in children, however, may override self-report data because one aspect of anxiety—trying to appear in control and unruffled while putting forth one's best social image—often interferes with accurate self-reporting. In any case, we recommend the use of a multimethod assessment including interviews, self-report inventories, symptom checklists and rating scales, and direct observation (see Kendall, 1987; Kendall, Pellegrini, & Urbain, 1981; Mash & Terdal, 1988).

INTERVENTIONS

The cognitive-behavioral intervention strategies that we will consider—contingency management, modeling, role playing, affective education, self-evaluation, training tasks, and homework—require differential use with children or adolescents who have different psychological difficulties. Each of these strategies is discussed in the following pages, along with suggestions to guide clinical practice decisions. First, it is essential that the therapist establish an open and safe environment and a caring and close relationship upon which the intervention can be based. Use of structured treatment manuals is encouraged; manuals for treating impulsive or hyperactive youngsters (Kendall, Padawer, Zupan, & Braswell, 1985) and those with anxiety disorders (Kendall, Kane, Howard, & Siqueland, 1989) are among those available.

Contingency Management

The management of contingent rewards and punishments has been a widely used and effective approach with children and adolescents. Almost all parent training programs yielding documented positive results (e.g., Forehand & McMahon, 1981; Patterson, Reid, Jones, & Conger, 1975) involve focused training and supervised practice in the deployment of contingencies. Classroom programs (e.g., O'Leary & O'Leary, 1977) and individual child programs (e.g., Kendall & Braswell, 1985) typically incorporate contingency management strategies as well. Different types of contingencies, however, may be more appropriate for some cases than for others, and therapists need to make informed decisions regarding their use.

In establishing contingencies with internalizing children—those who are anxious and depressed—it is best to focus on rewarding positive behavior and coping skills. These clients have a cognitive bias toward harsh criticism about themselves, and they fail to attend to and process positive experiences. It is wise, given this cognitive bias, to use rewards generously and to guide the processing of positive experiences. Special attention to an earned reward can counter any bias against acceptance of rewards. By rewarding successive approximations, the therapist can shape active, involved behavior. Arranging tasks to provide mastery experiences, especially in the early sessions, is desirable. In later sessions, it is beneficial to take time to help the client make sense of "praises." Time spent fostering an accurate and self-enhancing attributional style, while simultaneously discouraging the unwanted tendency to attribute negative events to internal, global, and stable characteristics of the self, will contribute meaningfully to the attainment, maintenance, and generalization of skills.

Although reinforcement is vital in working with an anxious or depressed child, *response-cost* can be the key with externalizing children. Reinforcement "pulls" for participation, encouraging the recipient to become more active and involved, and can be stimulating to a depressed child. Response-cost, where contingent loss of reward is linked to misbehavior, inhibits action and can help to slow a hyperactive or impulsive child. When response-cost is used, the child begins sessions with a set number of points or chips and loses them only by engaging in specified undesired behaviors. Aggressive young people have failed to internalize the rules that govern prosocial interactions, and their acting-out behavior necessitates contingent outcomes. Response-cost, with its inhibitive qualities, can thus augment an accepting and socially rewarding context.

The therapist must take special care to outline expectations and explain the behaviors that are related to the contingencies. A possible limitation of early behavioral contingency control programs was the failure to pay sufficient attention to the recipient's manner of processing the applied contingencies. By explaining the rules carefully, helping the child to process any contingent enactments of the rules, and discussing the proper attributions regarding misbehavior or prosocial action, the therapist can strengthen the impact of the specific contingency and prevent the child's cognitive processing from undermining or discounting it.

Modeling

Modeling is an effective intervention that helps children and adolescents acquire, inhibit, and disinhibit thoughts and actions through observing important others. Indeed, modeling is central to social cognitive theories of human behavior (Bandura, 1986). When perceived as a reasonable individual—respected, liked, and possibly even admired (and occasionally associated with positive reward)—the therapist can be a potent model for nondistorted thinking, careful reasoning, and reasonable behavior.

The therapist can also serve as a coping model not by behaving in an error-free (adjusted, nondistorted) manner, but by exhibiting misbehavior, lack of attention, and cognitive misperception while also displaying strategies to correct these difficulties. The therapist might display some of the child's own difficulties but would add a strategy for self-catching and self-correcting the difficulties. For example, to serve as a coping model for anxious children or adolescents, the therapist would become anxious, identify the feelings of anxiety, and demonstrate alternative ways to cope in anxiety-provoking situations. With depressed children, the therapist would model ways to self-disclose personal feelings and to check on the accuracy and validity of one's personal interpretations of the world. The modeled cognitive-processing style would undermine the typical distortion pattern of the depressed child.

A shared experience with the child, often outside the therapy office, can provide an occasion for modeling and a forum for discussing interpersonal interactions, expectancies, and outcomes. Catherine, the young client in our earlier illustration, shared a walk with her therapist and interacted with passersby; a simple "hello" and an exchange of glances took place. Catherine later reported that she could tell "The people didn't like me—they looked at me funny." The therapist replied that he couldn't tell whether the people liked him or not. They looked tired, they were older people, and who knows what they were thinking? After discussion, Catherine concurred that she really couldn't tell whether they liked her or not and that maybe she had been harsh with herself.

With impulsive or aggressive children, the therapist can work to overcome cognitive deficiencies by modeling coping skills and thoughtful problem solving. The therapist might choose an everyday problem that would be easy to solve and, rather than solving it automatically, break it down and think it through out loud for the child's benefit. Routine problem solving by a thoughtful, self-directive model creates a therapeutic interpersonal environment.

Modeling is an important component of child and adolescent therapy, but it should not be provided uniformly. Clinical decisions about the optimal manner of demonstration are dictated by the nature of the client's difficulties. Modeling is a valuable opportunity for children and adolescents to observe and learn; the therapist should plan demonstrations that are focused on specific cognitive and behavioral needs. As the clinical examples noted earlier have highlighted, the therapist models problem-solving strategies to overcome cognitive deficiencies, yet models of unbiased processing are needed to correct distorted thinking. Modeling can also serve as a first step toward role playing, where the child or adolescent, along with the therapist, acts out alternative solutions to the actual situations that are difficult for the client.

Role Playing

Role plays let both the therapist and the client experience how it feels to utilize each of the alternative solutions generated for a specific problem. Role plays provide opportunities for the therapist to guide the experience and to reinforce progress; this guided and reinforced practice is important in the remediation of cognitive, behavioral, and emotional difficulties. When introducing this strategy, the therapist may wish to take the lead in role playing a situation, with the child or adolescent following in a tag-along procedure (see Ollendick, 1986). While role-playing, the therapist elicits information about whether the client's feelings or thoughts are similar to or different from those of the therapist as the situation evolves. Then the child can attempt to role play a situation independently, with support and encouragement from the therapist. Role playing can start with minimally stressful situations and, as the child masters the skills, move on to situations that are progressively more stressful. The therapist can begin with imaginal scenes and then move to real-life sessions that can be arranged in the office, home, school, or community.

We have found that children can work with imaginal role plays, but developmental factors influence the use of this strategy. With younger children, who need guidance to "get into" the role play, the therapist should evoke the imaginal scene as concretely and with as much detail as possible. For instance, the therapist might say, "You are sitting in the middle of your classroom with the other kids seated around you and the teacher directly in front of you. It is third period, reading class. The teacher has just asked your friend Mary to answer a question out loud. Your teacher looks in her book at the next problem, then looks up and calls on you for the next problem." A slow pace, along with concrete details, helps children become involved in imaginal role plays.

Role plays can often be developed in a group setting. The decision to use group role plays should be guided by the nature of the specific psychological difficulties. For example, an intervention using cognitive therapy for depression would involve the testing of personal assumptions. In a group format, caution would be needed to prevent the therapist's rational analysis of a situation from being overtaken by the depressogenic views expressed by a homogeneously depressed group. Group activities can be especially appropriate for dealing with aggression. An example is the type of skit described in the perspective-taking training literature (Chandler, 1973; Little & Kendall, 1979): A skit involving a criminal, juror, and judge can be enacted and discussed, with individual feelings and perceptions being considered. Then, with the roles changed, the skit can be replayed, and clients can experience how an event unfolds from another's perspective. With groups of hyperactive, impulsive children, role playing can be difficult because of the excessive need to control behavior. A smaller group might be indicated, and a pair of therapists might be required. One group member could be asked to be vigilant for problems that arise in the group and could be equipped with a stop sign to hold up when a social problem is emerging. The first step in impulse control is recognition that a problem exists.

Affective Education

Helping clients learn about emotions is an important therapeutic intervention for children and adolescents with a variety of difficulties. As with other strategies, clinical decisions regarding treatment must be based on client-specific information. When the behavioral and cognitive distinctions noted earlier are applied, affective issues take on differential meanings. For the internalizing and cognitively distorting (e.g., depressed) child or adolescent, there is benefit in learning to process various social experiences and to recognize the different feelings that could result from those experiences. The therapist guides the client to process social experiences and their emotional consequences in a nondistorted manner.

Depressed children often have a limited vocabulary for labeling and talking about feelings; creating a *feelings dictionary* can help them build such a vocabulary. Looking at illustrations from educational materials, magazines, and books, the child can work with the therapist on labeling a variety of emotions suggested by the illustrations. A feelings dictionary can likewise be developed from selected cartoons in which the characters' thought or speech bubbles have been erased. The child is shown the cartoon's social interaction sequence and asked to identify the characters' feelings and to insert what they are thinking or saying to themselves. The feelings dictionary is also helpful in working with anxious children, though the focus for these clients is on the feelings of arousal as cues for the use of coping skills to manage anxiety. Our experience indicates that many anxious children are unaware of their anxious behaviors, both verbal and nonverbal, and that effective treatment for anxious clients (see Kendall, Howard, & Epps, 1988; Kendall, Kane et al., 1989) includes educating them about their internal and external cues for anxiety.

Externalizing, cognitively deficient children are, in many instances, acting without thinking. As part of learning how to stop and think (Kendall, 1988; see also chapter 2), these clients acquire skills in social problem solving. Reading emotional cues in others is a necessary (though not sufficient) component of effective social problem solving. Impulsive children often need to learn to identify their own emotions as well as those of others. They can then begin to focus on generating alternative solutions to problems and evaluating how they and others would feel about those solutions.[1]

With aggressive children, the task of integrating affect into treatment is more complex. When such children are taught to inhibit thoughtless behavior via practice in self-control and social problem

---

[1] For descriptions and discussions of problem-solving therapy see D'Zurilla, 1986; Nezu, Nezu, and Perri, 1989; Spivack, Platt, and Shure, 1976; Urbain and Kendall, 1980; and Weisberg et al., 1981.

solving, the treatment sessions are typically in the therapist's "safe" office. But the contexts in which they need to stop and use thoughtful problem-solving skills are emotionally charged. To facilitate the application of those skills in emotionally charged extratherapeutic settings, we suggest that the therapist create emotional arousal in the session once the skills have been acquired. The arousal is labeled as the cue for use of the problem-solving skills. When emotionally aroused and adequately prepared, the youngster can practice being in control and inhibiting thoughtless action. Therapy focuses on promoting cognitive problem-solving skills under conditions of both arousal and calm.

Self-evaluation

Skills in rational self-evaluation are important, but decisions about the type of intervention needed must be based on the behavioral and cognitive characteristics of the client. Depressed children self-evaluate excessively and need to do it less often and less critically. Hyperactive or impulsive children would benefit from adding efforts at retrospective self-evaluation to their behavior patterns.

Asking clients to evaluate their own performance after completion of therapy sessions and letting them compare their evaluation with that of the therapist can be educational and therapeutic. For depressed children, the therapist can temper the hypercritical nature of the self-evaluation. The therapist can help anxious children make their perceptions of environmental demands more realistic: One characteristic of anxiety (see Ingram & Kendall, 1987; Kendall & Ingram, 1987) is heightened self-focused attention and misperception of demands and threats (Beck & Emery, 1985) in the environment. Proper self-evaluation can help reduce the anxious person's tendency toward such misperceptions. Aggressive children tend to underestimate their own aggressiveness and exaggerate that of their peers in social interactions (Lochman, 1987). The therapist can help these children make more accurate inferences about the intentions of others and monitor their own behavior in interactions. As suggested by Dodge (1985), aggressive children incorrectly view as provocative (or intentional) situations that can accurately be described as neutral (or accidental). By combining self-evaluation with role plays, in which the aggressive child plays each role in an interaction, the therapist can address directly any misattributions of intentionality. In general, impulsive children act quickly and without stopping to reflect on their actions, showing little or no skill in self-evaluation; one task of the therapist is to teach them to evaluate their actions against their own goals and others' expectations.

Training Tasks

Appropriate training tasks, geared to individual needs, are useful at various points in therapy. Although clinical decisions determine the exact tasks, a sequential approach—in which skills are first taught on tasks that are emotionally safe and minimally cognitively challenging and then transferred to more charged and challenging tasks—is recommended for most cases. With hyperactive and aggressive children, we suggest introducing new problem-solving skills with games or simple academic tasks. The therapist can introduce new games with new rules in a way that requires the child to apply self-control and figure out what needs to be done in various situations. Later tasks can require the child to confront social interactions that were once a source of psychological difficulty. Thus the self-control skills are first taught on easy tasks and then applied to challenging social situations. The *Stop and Think Workbook* (Kendall, 1988) has been developed on the basis of these guidelines.

With both depressed and anxious children, it is best to begin identifying problems and introducing tasks in nonstressful situations. The therapist can teach children to identify feelings and plan strategies with cartoon, storybook, or hypothetical characters. We have found cartoon strips with blank thought and speech bubbles, mentioned earlier, to be useful in helping children realize that they are thinking things to themselves in challenging situations. The children can first be asked to identify what the cartoon characters might be thinking in various situations; they can then begin to discuss their own thoughts and explore how these thoughts influence their behavior and emotions. Depressed children benefit from beginning with small, manageable tasks in which they can demonstrate competence and build self-esteem (Hollon & Beck, 1979).

Homework

Assigning out-of-session tasks helps youngsters learn when and how to use the skills presented in the sessions in their day-to-day interactions. Because the term *homework* has aversive connotations, we have called these Show That I Can (STIC) tasks (see Kendall, Kane et al., 1989) to emphasize their positive qualities. STIC tasks for depressed children are small experiments that help them check the validity of their assumptions about their competence, the world, and their interpersonal interactions. With hyperactive and aggressive children, the STIC tasks emphasize the application of strategies to help clients think before acting (see Kendall, 1988; Kendall & Braswell, 1985) and carefully solve problems outside of sessions. STIC tasks for anxious youngsters call on them first to monitor their anxious thoughts and behaviors and then to alter these thoughts and plan strategies for managing difficult situations. The STIC tasks are arranged hierarchically, with movement up the hierarchy based on gains made.

CONCLUSION

Informed decision making is central to any integrative therapy. The same treatment is not appropriate for all child and adolescent clients. Indeed, to believe that any one therapy is proper for all cases would be to fall prey to the uniformity myth. Our discussion has focused on the use of several treatment strategies within a cognitive social problem-solving context and on the need to adjust these strategies through informed decisions based on behavioral and cognitive factors. It is our strong belief that to fail to treat internalizing and externalizing, distorting and deficient children differentially would be to act in an uninformed manner. Rather, the nature of the different psychopathologies dictates that informed decision making guide the application of treatment strategies.

References

Achenbach, T. M. (1966). The classification of children's psychiatric symptoms: A factor analytic study. *Psychological Monographs, 80* (Whole No. 615).

American Psychiatric Association. (1987). *Diagnostic and statistical manual of mental disorders* (3rd ed. rev.). Washington, DC: Author.

Bandura, A. (1986). *Social foundation of thought and action: A social cognitive theory.* Englewood Cliffs, NJ: Prentice-Hall.

Beck, A. T., & Emery, G. (1985). *Anxiety disorders and phobias: A cognitive perspective.* New York: Basic.

Camp, B. (1977). Verbal mediation in young aggressive boys. *Journal of Abnormal Psychology, 86,* 145–153.

Chandler, M. (1973). Egocentrism and antisocial behavior: The assessment and training of social perspective-taking skills. *Developmental Psychology, 9,* 326–337.

Dodge, K. A. (1980). Social cognition and children's aggressive behavior. *Child Development, 51,* 162–170.

Dodge, K. A. (1985). Attributional bias in aggressive children. In P. C. Kendall (Ed.), *Advances in cognitive behavioral research and therapy* (Vol. 4). New York: Academic.

Dodge, K. A., & Frame, C. L. (1982). Social cognitive biases and deficits in aggressive boys. *Child Development, 53,* 620–635.

D'Zurilla, T. J. (1986). *Problem-solving therapy.* New York: Springer.

Edelbrock, C. S., Costello, A. J., Dulcan, M. K., Conover, N. C., & Kalas, R. (1986). Parent-child agreement on child psychiatric symptoms assessed via structured interview. *Journal of Child Psychology and Psychiatry, 27,* 181–190.

Forehand, R., & McMahon, R. (1981). *Helping the noncompliant child: A clinician's guide to parent training.* New York: Guilford.

Fuhrman, M. J., & Kendall, P. C. (1986). Cognitive tempo and behavioral adjustment in children. *Cognitive Therapy and Research, 10,* 45–51.

Hollon, S. D., & Beck, A. T. (1979). Cognitive therapy of depression. In P. C. Kendall & S. D. Hollon (Eds.), *Cognitive-behavioral intervention: Theory, research and procedures.* New York: Academic.

Ingram, R. E., & Kendall, P. C. (1987). The cognitive side of anxiety. *Cognitive Therapy and Research, 11,* 523–536.

Kagan, J. (1966). Reflection-impulsivity: The generality and dynamics of conceptual tempo. *Journal of Abnormal Psychology, 71,* 17–24.

Kazdin, A. E. (1988). Childhood depression. In E. J. Mash & L. G. Terdal (Eds.), *Behavioral assessment of childhood disorders* (2nd ed.). New York: Guilford.

Kendall, P. C. (1984). Social cognition and problem-solving: A developmental and child-clinical interface. In B. Gholson and T. Rosenthal (Eds.), *Applications of cognitive developmental theory.* New York: Academic.

Kendall, P. C. (1985). Toward a cognitive-behavioral model of child psychopathology and a critique of related interventions. *Journal of Abnormal Child Psychology, 13,* 357–372.

Kendall, P. C. (1987). Ahead to basics: Assessments with children and families. *Behavioral Assessment, 9,* 321–332.

Kendall, P. C. (1988). *Stop and think workbook.* (Available from P. C. Kendall, Psychology Department, Temple University, Philadephia, PA 19122.)

Kendall, P. C., & Braswell, L. (1985). *Cognitive-behavioral therapy for impulsive children.* New York: Guilford.

Kendall, P. C., Cantwell, D., & Kazdin, A. E. (1989). Depression in children and adolescents: Assessment issues and recommendations. *Cognitive Therapy and Research, 13,* 109–146.

Kendall, P. C., Howard, B., & Epps, J. (1988). The anxious child: Cognitive-behavioral treatment strategies. *Behavior Modification, 12,* 281–310.

Kendall, P. C., & Ingram, R. E. (1987). The future for cognitive assessment of anxiety: Let's get specific. In L. Michelson & M. Ascher (Eds.), *Stress and anxiety: Cognitive-behavioral assessment and therapy.* New York: Guilford.

Kendall, P. C., Kane, M., Howard, B., & Siqueland, L. (1989). *Cognitive-behavioral therapy for anxious children: Treatment manual.* (Available from P. C. Kendall, Psychology Department, Temple University, Philadelphia, PA 19122.)

Kendall, P. C., Padawer, W., Zupan, B., & Braswell, L. (1985). *Developing self-control in children: The manual.* (Available from P. C. Kendall, Psychology Department, Temple University, Philadelphia, PA 19122.)

Kendall, P. C., Pellegrini, D., & Urbain, E. S. (1981). Approaches to assessment for cognitive-behavioral interventions with children. In P. C. Kendall & S. D. Hollon (Eds.), *Assessment strategies for cognitive-behavioral interventions.* New York: Academic.

Kendall, P. C., Ronan, K., & Epps, J. (in press). Aggression in children/adolescents: Cognitive-behavioral treatment perspectives. In D. Pepler & K. Rubin (Eds.), *Development and treatment of childhood aggression.* Hillsdale, NJ: Erlbaum.

Kendall, P. C., Stark, K. D., & Adam, T. (1989). Cognitive deficit or cognitive distortion in childhood depression? Manuscript submitted for publication.

Kiesler, D. J. (1966). Some myths of psychotherapy research and the search for a paradigm. *Psychological Bulletin, 65,* 110–136.

Kovacs, M. (1981). Rating scales to assess depression in school-aged children. *Acta Paedopsychiatrica, 46,* 305–315.

Leon, G. R., Kendall, P. C., & Garber, J. (1980). Depression in children: Parent, teacher, and child perspectives. *Journal of Abnormal Child Psychology, 8,* 221–235.

Little, V., & Kendall, P. C. (1979). Cognitive-behavioral intervention with delinquents: Problem-solving, role-taking, and self-control. In P. C. Kendall & S. D. Hollon (Eds.), *Cognitive-behavioral interventions: Theory, research and procedures.* New York: Academic.

Lochman, J. E. (1987). Self and peer perceptions and attributional biases of aggressive and non-aggressive boys in dyadic interaction. *Journal of Consulting and Clinical Psychology, 55,* 404–411.

Mash, E. J., & Terdal, L. G. (Eds.) (1988). *Behavioral assessment of childhood disorders* (2nd ed.). New York: Guilford.

Nezu, A. M., Nezu, C. M., & Perri, M. G. (1989). *Problem-solving therapy for depression: Theory, research, and clinical guidelines.* New York: Wiley.

O'Leary, K. D., & O'Leary, S. (Eds.) (1977). *Classroom management* (2nd ed.). Elmsford, NJ: Pergamon.

Ollendick, T. H. (1986). Behavior therapy with children and adolescents. In S. L. Garfield & A. E. Bergir (Eds.), *Handbook of psychotherapy and behavior change* (3rd ed.). New York: Wiley.

Patterson, G. R., Reid, J. B., Jones, R. R., & Conger, R. E. (1975). *A social learning approach to family intervention* (Vol. 1). Eugene, OR: Castalia.

Shure, M. B., & Spivack, G. (1972). Means-ends thinking, adjustment, and social class in elementary school-aged children. *Journal of Consulting and Clinical Psychology, 38,* 348–353.

Spivack, G., Platt, J. J., & Shure, M. B. (1976). *The problem-solving approach to adjustment.* San Francisco: Jossey-Bass.

Spivack, G., & Shure, M. B. (1974). *Social adjustment of young children: A cognitive approach to solving real-life problems.* San Francisco: Jossey-Bass.

Stark, K. D., Best, L. R., & Adam, T. (1986). *The My Standards Questionnaire: An investigation of its psychometric properties.* Unpublished manuscript. (Available from K. D. Stark, Department of School Psychology, University of Texas, Austin, TX 78712.)

Urbain, E. S., & Kendall, P. C. (1980). Review of social cognitive problem-solving interventions with children. *Psychological Bulletin, 88,* 109–143.

Weisberg, R. P., Gesten, E. L., Carnrike, C. L., Toro, P. A., Rapkin, B. D., Davids, E., & Cowen, E. L. (1981). Social problem-solving skills training: A competence-behavioral intervention with second to fourth grade children. *American Journal of Community Psychology, 9,* 411–423.

Chapter 12

Chronic Pain

Arlinza E. Turner

INTRODUCTION

Chronic pain is one of the most prevalent national health problems (Aronoff, 1985). Approximately 86 millon Americans suffer from chronic pain in some form, such as low back pain, headaches, or arthritis. When we consider the cost of specialized medical procedures, time lost from work, over-the-counter medications, and disability payments, the financial ramifications of this problem take on astronomical proportions; actual costs have been estimated to range between $50 and $100 billion annually (Bonica, 1985). Although this statistic highlights the significance of the problem, it may well be an underestimation; many chronic pain sufferers may never come to the attention of a reporting agency (Lipton & Marbach, 1984).

Chronic pain is often distinguished from acute pain, which is a response to a trauma and dissipates once healing has taken place. Acute pain serves the biological function of warning the body that tissue damage is present and that a change in behavior may be necessary for repair and healing to occur. Chronic pain, on the other hand, is pain that persists for 3 to 6 months or longer (Gotestam & Linton, 1985; Hendler, Long, & Wise, 1982), often in the absence of specific evidence of tissue damage. It is the latter type that is the focus of this chapter.

Given the prevalence of chronic pain and the historical attention that has been devoted to the understanding of pain (see Todd, 1985), it is alarming that pain research has been emphasized and supported primarily only during the past two decades. The bulk of the research has focused mainly on identifying characteristics of specific pain syndromes (e.g., headache and chronic low back pain); developing psychometric instruments for assessing pain; and delineating various psychological parameters associated with pain, such as cognitive and affective responses. Research has also addressed the efficacy of both medical and psychological treatments. Although research has yielded encouraging results, pain continues to be a complex phenomenon for clinicians to diagnose and track (Melzack & Wall, 1973, 1983; Roberts, 1986). One important area where confusion prevails concerns basic definitions. For example, researchers disagree on how to define pain in general and how to describe specific pain syndromes (Flor & Turk, 1984, 1989). The position that the clinician adopts in defining pain certainly has both assessment and treatment implications. Another problem involves the treatment selection process. The decision to employ a specific clinical procedure with a particular pain syndrome often appears to depend more on history and intuition than on empirical findings (Turner & Chapman, 1982). Although a number of empirically sound procedures are available for the management of chronic pain, it remains unclear how the clinician should determine which of these procedures is likely to be the most effective for a particular patient with a specific pain problem.

This chapter begins with a brief review of the various ways in which pain has been conceptualized and of their implications for the assessment and management of chronic pain. Three case presentations follow to show how the decision-making model delineated in chapter 3 can be a useful framework for clinical work in pain management.

THEORIES OF PAIN

In general, four theories of pain have been advanced: organic, operant, cognitive, and interactive. These will be briefly discussed in turn, with emphasis being given to the interactive viewpoint and to its clinical application.

Organic Theories

Organic theories of chronic pain are perhaps most notable in terms of their historical importance and their impact on patients' belief systems. All such explanations assume a purely organic etiology for pain. One particular theory proposes that pain is a specific sensation whose intensity is proportional to the extent of tissue damage (Melzack, 1973; Turk, Meichenbaum, & Genest, 1983). This *specificity theory* implies a fixed relationship between somatic pain receptors and the pain center in the brain. Stated differently, pain is experienced when a noxious stimulus is transmitted from the pain receptors along specialized peripheral nerve fibers to the spinal cord, where impulses are conducted and registered as pain.

The implications of this theory for assessment and treatment are significant, with assessment focusing simply on identifying that part of the pain pathway that is dysfunctional. Treatment, then, involves intervening on the defective area. Specific interventions might include one or a combination of procedures, such as blocking the pain pathway by surgical or pharmacological means, severing the pathway so that impulses never reach the brain, or removing parts of the brain so that pain signals can no longer be registered.

The unidimensional organic theories of pain have lost some ground during recent years as new evidence has supported the notion that pain is not a simple concept. However, it is important to recognize that such views continue to be taught in medical and graduate schools (Sternbach, 1986) and that chronic pain patients are typically quite committed to the idea that their pain is solely a function of body damage. Patients who hold this notion invariably seek interventions from the medical arena. As we shall see, this orientation has a significant impact on treatment.

Operant Theories

The distinction between acute and chronic pain is quite important in the context of operant explanations of pain. These approaches may view the emergence of pain (the acute stage) as the result of organic or tissue damage while positing a different explanation of how pain becomes chronic in nature. One such paradigm has been offered by behavioral theorists (e.g., Fordyce, 1976, 1986; Roberts, 1986). Here the emphasis is on overt pain behaviors (e.g., "doctor shopping," pain complaints, avoidance of physical activities, gesturing, grimacing, pill taking) rather than on internal states. The theory assumes that these behaviors persist because they are reinforced by the environment of the suffering person. The natural outcome of this theory is a functional analysis of behavior with an emphasis on identifying target behaviors (pain behaviors) and environmental contingencies (rewards and punishments subsequent to pain behaviors).

The goal of a behavioral program is to decrease or extinguish learned pain behaviors by altering the consequences of those behaviors while simultaneously providing positive reinforcement for increases in the patient's physical and social activities. Although its nature is often governed by the setting (i.e., inpatient vs. outpatient), such a program invariably entails instructing those in the patient's environment to extinguish pain behaviors—typically by ignoring them—and to shape more appropriate behaviors, usually through reinforcement. Because the goal requires consistent reinforcement of "nonpain" behaviors by all those in the patient's milieu, treatment may include consultations with various professionals involved with the patient, such as physicians and lawyers. It might also include vocational counseling as a means of increasing activity levels.

Cognitive Theories

Cognitive theories of chronic pain assume that factors such as attention, expectation, and negative rumination have a significant impact on a person's pain experience (Holroyd, Andrasik, & Westbrook, 1977, 1978; Turk et al., 1983). Basically, these approaches assume that, if the patient is taught to identify and understand the connection between maladaptive thought patterns and the pain experience, and then is taught either to *alter* his appraisal of the painful situation or to *divert* his attention away from the pain, the result is likely to be a decrease in the verbal report of pain and in the display of pain behaviors. A number of researchers have provided evidence in support of this position (e.g., Holroyd & Andrasik, 1981; Wernick, Jaremko, & Taylor, 1981; Worthington, 1982). However, there are as yet no clear guidelines for deciding whether to employ a cognitive procedure with a specific pain patient or for deciding whether it is preferable to divert attention or to alter self-statements regarding pain.

Interactive Theories

More comprehensive than the organic, operant, or cognitive theories are interactive explanations of chronic pain. Interactive approaches consider the relationships among physiological-biological (tissue damage), sociological, and psychological variables (Chapman & Wyckoff, 1981; Holzman & Turk, 1986; Melzack & Wall, 1965). Specifically, interactive explanations propose that it is not tissue damage alone that creates the pain syndrome. Rather, other factors such as the patient's premorbid history, problem-solving ability, and current environmental stressors might be etiologically involved. According to this orientation, any treatment aimed at extinguishing or reducing the pain experience will need to address these variables in a comprehensive manner.

Although some researchers subscribe to an interactive model, the idea that the various components are operating simultaneously and should be addressed as such remains somewhat foreign. Indeed, the variables addressed by the interactive viewpoint are complex. For example, consider a situation in which the onset of an individual's lower back pain is triggered by a fall, resulting in a pulled muscle. Even though the pain is initially caused by structural damage (the pulled muscle), other psychological and sociological factors may serve to maintain the pain experience. These factors might include increased stress, increased attention from family members, presence of disability insurance, relief from family obligations, and so forth. Suppose, on the other hand, that this individual has a reinforced dependent history characterized by poor problem-solving skills. In this case, even without identifiable physical damage, a fall might produce a very similar pain complaint. Anything that thwarts the person's dependence (e.g. decreased attention or increased social isolation) would be likely to increase the pain experience. As these two situations indicate, a quite similar pain experience may be maintained by very different constellations of interactive variables.

The evidence for an interactive model of chronic pain comes from a number of sources, including data that suggest (a) that perceptions of pain differ from person to person (e.g., Melzack, 1973); (b) that cultural factors play a significant role in how pain is perceived (e.g., Lipton & Marbach, 1984); and (c) that distraction can reduce pain perceptions (e.g., Turk et al., 1983), although secondary gain such as time away from work or financial benefits might increase this experience (Block, Kremer, & Gaylor, 1980; Roberts, 1986).

The interactive model has major implications for both the assessment and the management of chronic pain. First, it suggests that a unidimensional approach to assessment of pain is not likely to present a valid picture of the pain experience. Rather, assessment needs to be multidimensional in order to evaluate all factors potentially involved in the pain experience. Second, a patient who remains convinced that chronic pain is a symptom of an underlying organic disorder will continue to return to the health care system for help. An interactive model suggests that limiting treatment to medical approaches is not always suitable because the critical components of the pain experience may not be medically related at all. Finally, the interactive model implies that the degree of a patient's improvement may depend more on what she is willing to do to contribute to her care than on the amount of help she receives from others.

An interactive model of chronic pain assumes that a number of complex response systems involving physiological, behavioral, affective, and verbal/cognitive factors are involved in the pain experience. Therefore, an adequate assessment requires samples from all of these systems. The need for multidimensional assessment seems clear given the diversity of people who enter a pain management clinic and the similarities among their complaints. Such a clinic draws many different types of people, but invariably the presenting problem is unrelenting pain that has had and continues to have a significant impact on these persons' lives. Moreover, because of the subjective nature of the pain experience, most patients go to great lengths to convince others of the extent (i.e., the duration, intensity, location) of their pain. Whereas this information is often quite useful in making diagnoses (e.g., tension vs. migraine headache) and in evaluating treatment effectiveness, it plays a less significant role in treatment planning.

Although different patients may verbalize the same pain complaints, those complaints are frequently not the appropriate intervention targets. This situation is illustrated by two cases from our pain clinic that had superficial similarities but were, in reality, very different. Both patients entered the clinic complaining of temporomandibular joint (TMJ) syndrome of a duration of more than 5 years. Both had been referred by a dentist specifically for biofeedback treatment. The assessment included samples from the physiological, behavioral, affective, and verbal/cognitive areas. Briefly, physiological assessment involved EMG recordings plus a review of medical records and/or a telephone conversation with the referring dentists.[1]

During the initial interview phase, both patients reported high levels of pain that interfered with their lives (mainly eating). Patient A exhibited a high level of anxiety, characterized by "feelings of always being on the edge," actual avoidance behavior vis-à-vis specific family members, decreased appetite, periodic insomnia, and anhedonia. Further, she indicated that she did not know what she wanted to do in life and lacked the energy even to think about it. A Beck Depression Inventory (Beck, Ward, Mendelsohn, Mock, & Erbaugh, 1961) was administered to both patients; it revealed depressive symptomatology for Patient A, though not for Patient B. For Patient A there was also evidence of marital and family problems. Patient B, on the other hand, reported high levels of muscle tension, as evidenced by EMG recordings in the masseter muscle, as well as in the neck and shoulders.

---

[1] It is important that the physiological sample include a physical examination. The systems that should be involved, as well as the extent of that involvement, are usually indicated by the history. Because it is frequently a physician or other health professional who has referred the patient, the physiological assessment is often complete by the time the patient enters treatment.

Although they experienced the same pain complaints and had been referred by identical sources for the same treatment, these two patients ultimately received very different intervention protocols. Patient A received medication and cognitive-behavior therapy because there was clear evidence of vegetative symptoms of depression currently affecting her daily living and there were clear stressors that seemed to be caused or exacerbated by her faulty life view and her deficient coping ability. Furthermore, there was no evidence of an underlying physiological disorder such as muscle tension. Patient B, in contrast, received biofeedback training, plus education about her condition, as the primary treatment. In her case, muscle tension was apparent. Also, there was little evidence of a clinically significant negative mood state.

It is important to note that the data contributing to these treatment decisions emanated from diverse sources: interviews, medical records, physiological recordings, depression ratings, and pain ratings. The assumption underlying the interactive view, as stated previously, is that different factors may converge to produce the same chief complaint for different patients. Identifying these various factors is therefore critical in the clinical decision-making process.

ISSUES IN PROBLEM ORIENTATION

Until very recently, the management of pain has taken primarily a unidimensional approach. The general assumption was that a direct relationship existed between an underlying biological impairment and a pain sensation. The intensity and duration of pain were assumed to be correlated with the extent of tissue damage. When no such underlying organic cause could be identified, a more psychological explanation was offered. Specifically, when no organic impairment could be identified, pain then represented a more serious form of psychopathology (e.g., hypochondriasis, hysterical personality, conversion disorder). Such notions dominated our thinking for years, and their residuals continue to be quite prevalent. It is important to recognize this influence because the way in which the pain experience is conceptualized is likely to affect the manner in which the clinician carries out the assessment and, ultimately, the treatment plan and the extent of the patient's compliance. In the treatment of pain, such problem orientation issues abound. Thus discussion of these concerns from the vantage points of both the clinician and the patient seems warranted.

The Clinician's View

A singular and biased orientation on the part of the clinician can negatively affect assessment and treatment. A purely organic explanation of pain, for example, reinforces a patient's reliance on the health care system for a solution to the pain problem in the form of new treatments, new referral sources, and different trials of various medications. Furthermore, even when a clinician with an organic bias refers a patient for a more psychologically based treatment, the patient is often led to expect that something is going to change physiologically and that he will be the passive recipient of a treatment. For instance, the two patients described earlier in the chapter were referred by a dentist specifically for biofeedback training. The assumption underlying biofeedback is that a physiological disorder (muscle tension, inadequate blood flow) contributes to pain and that, given the appropriate feedback, the patient will be able to alter this physiological disorder (Turner & Chapman, 1982). Whether or not such physiological abnormalities always exist either in the etiology or the maintenance of pain is questionable (e.g., Gray, Lyle, McGuire, & Peck, 1980; Holroyd et al., 1977). Indeed, in the case of one of the patients complaining of TMJ pain, the maintaining factors were more psychological than physiological.

Orientation problems, in addition to affecting assessment and treatment, can significantly influence the way in which a problem is defined and formulated. As mentioned previously, we know that it is important to assess pain across a variety of modalities (physiological, behavioral, etc.). However, it can be difficult to determine what to assess within each of these spheres and how to interpret the results. For instance, in assessing the contributions of reinforcement to the maintenance of pain behaviors, clinicians frequently ask patients to self-monitor the amount of time they spend out of bed as an indication of pain intensity and involvement with pain. Given the evidence supporting a high co-occurrence of depressive symptoms among chronic pain sufferers (e.g., Lindsay & Wyckoff, 1981; Romano & Turner, 1985), it seems reasonable to expect that activity level could be more a function of depression than an indication of pain intensity or pain involvement (Haley, Turner, & Romano, 1985). This consideration is particularly important in light of recent research that found a decline in activity level (e.g., outdoor work, social involvement) among a group of chronic pain patients to result more from depression than from prolonged suffering (Kerns & Haythornthwaite, 1988). These authors also suggested that pain alone is not sufficient to produce depression but that other mediating factors, such as perceived loss of control and personal mastery, may be involved.

Once pain behaviors such as activity level have been assessed, the way in which the results are interpreted and employed significantly affects treatment. One interpretation of low activity level, for example, might lead directly to alteration of environmental factors that reinforce such behavior, whereas another interpretation might suggest a treatment plan that is more cognitive in nature. The patient's history often helps to develop the best focus. For example, a patient who at one time carried a great deal of responsibility and is now feeling guilty for his current lack of mobility, as characterized by numerous negative self-statements, is more likely to benefit from a treatment geared primarily toward reshaping negative cognitions than one geared toward reinforcing activity level.

Traditional psychological tests are commonly employed in the evaluation of patients with chronic pain. The bias that therapists bring to the setting is highlighted here. Again, the interpretation of the assessment results is critical. One measure that has received much attention with respect to chronic pain is the Minnesota Multiphasic Personality Inventory (MMPI). In general, this measure has proven to be a useful clinical assessment device. However, the extent of its utility in the assessment of pain is unclear. Chronic pain patients frequently exhibit a constellation of symptoms (e.g., hypochondriasis, irritability, hysteria, tension) on the MMPI. This finding seems logical given that many of these factored categories rely quite heavily on complaints of bodily symptoms and a preoccupation with self, both of which are typical of chronic pain patients. Under most circumstances, this grouping of symptoms would be pathognomonic of a longstanding characterological problem. For chronic pain patients, however, these symptoms seem often to be more a function of the pain history than personality problems (Wooley, Blackwell, & Winget, 1978). Furthermore, a change in the pain intensity is very likely to have an impact on these symptoms. Thus the utility of the MMPI might lie more in evaluating treatment effectiveness than in defining and formulating the problem.

One can easily visualize the difference in treatment if the information gathered from an MMPI is interpreted in the traditional clinical framework, instead of being regarded as a sample of the patient's involvement in the pain. A traditional approach might view pain-related symptoms as enduring traits that would likely require long-term treatment to alter.

Another instance of potential assessment bias involves clinicians' sampling of the verbal-cognitive response mode. There are a number of measures designed to assess this area, including the McGill Pain Questionnaire (Melzack, 1975), the West Haven–Yale Multidimensional Pain Inventory (Kerns, Turk, & Rudy, 1985), the Symptom Checklist-90 (Derogatis, 1977), the MMPI, and many Likert-type scales. Faced with this plethora of choices, the clinician must decide which to employ with a particular pain patient. Any selection of measures should be based on two goals: (a) to define and formulate the problem so that a treatment plan can follow and (b) to evaluate treatment effectiveness. In pain management, a measure might serve one of these purposes while having little or no utility for the other. For example, instruments that are geared toward discerning pain intensity, location, and duration are quite sensitive to the impact of treatment but have little treatment validity on their own. On the other hand, a measure such as the West Haven–Yale Pain Inventory would be quite useful in treatment planning because it can help in determining controlling variables.

One concern regarding the patient's verbal report has been its sensitivity to distortion. Because of secondary gain, a patient may exaggerate the actual pain. As a result, various devices (e.g., kinesthetic scales, pain ratings, diagrams) have been developed to counteract the problems inherent in verbal reports. Although these measures do not bypass all problems associated with self-report (Fordyce, 1983), two or more such assessment devices used simultaneously can help to collate data obtained from other sources. In addition, because pain is such a subjective response, self-report measures provide an indication of one's pain perception.

The subjective and private nature of pain, along with the lack of synchrony often observed among tissue damage, verbal report, and pain behaviors, has made pain a particularly challenging concept to assess, especially outside of the physical arena. This assessment problem significantly affects how we define and formulate problems associated with pain management.

The Patient's View

Patients also bring to the clinical setting certain orientation problems involving various images, expectations, and preconceived notions. Specifically, these issues concern how the patient understands the pain, the patient's expectations regarding treatment outcome, and the patient's expectations about the future. All of these issues have a significant impact on assessment and the efficacy of treatment.

Many patients understand their pain to be a symptom of abnormality in or damage to some structural component of the body organs and systems. They generally assume that, once the damage has been identified and treated, the pain will be ameliorated. In this view, the first, and often the only, line of defense for managing the pain is to take over-the-counter medications or to visit a physician, who may simply prescribe more potent drugs. Because medical specialists cannot always identify the specific involvement of an organ system, patients with chronic pain are likely to engage in doctor shopping. Ultimately, they may be treated by multiple specialists who may be providing different kinds of medical treatment for similar pain complaints.

Patients typically come to the attention of a pain management clinic in one of two ways. Either they are referred by a physician who has been treating the patient and has observed little or no change in the patient's verbal report of the pain, or they are self-referred. Both types of referrals tend to produce patients who have misconceptions about why they have been referred to a pain management clinic and what will happen to them once they are there. The first group, physician-referred patients, tends to be quite resistant initially. They may be maladaptively self-focused, speaking exclusively about the extent of their pain and giving the impression that they doubt that anyone could ever understand their pain experience. Many pain patients use some form of analgesics, and, although they invariably report little or no benefit from the medication, they are typically unwilling to give it up. Generally, they have been referred by a physician for what they view as a medical problem that requires a medical treatment. A referral to a pain management clinic is usually perceived as a judgment that "My case is hopeless" or "My problem is all in my head." The patient's perception is likely to lead to depression and an implicit desire to convince the therapist that she is not "mentally ill" but that the pain is real.

The self-referred group is likely to view the pain clinic as a place that possesses special techniques for assessing and treating pain. These patients often believe that new medical tests will be performed and that a medical treatment is likely to be delivered. It is not uncommon for self-referred patients to describe their current physician as inadequate and uncaring, a phenomenon quite common among chronically ill patients (Wooley et al., 1978).

If the clinician fails to address a patient's preconceived notions, whether they are about treatment or about the future of the pain and the patient's overall life-style, a resistant and noncompliant posture is likely to result. Two patients presenting with the same complaint might

have totally different treatment experiences, depending on their perceptions during earlier treatment phases. A patient who believes that
his physician has sent him to a "shrink" for what he views as a real
medical problem will certainly not benefit from a psychological approach to pain in the same way as one who believes that the pain
management clinic represents an alternative way of addressing the pain
phenomenon. Similarly, the patient who does not expect to get better
or to return to her premorbid level of functioning will be less involved
in treatment than the patient who expects to regain some control over
the problem.

Most patients do not come into pain management clinics holding
an interactive view of pain. And, of those who do, many take the
position that the physiological variables supersede and cause all other
components. It is important to educate such patients about the complex
nature of pain. Presenting chronic pain as a multidimensional construct
having psychological, physiological, and sociological components
creates a rationale for a psychological treatment without directly confronting patients' beliefs in a purely physiological etiology.

Patients typically have very strong convictions about their pain;
they are not likely to let these go easily. However, it is not always
necessary for patients to give up these beliefs in order for treatment to
proceed. Patient education is an ongoing process that may need to take
different forms. What must be addressed immediately concerns the
belief that referral to a pain management clinic represents a statement
that the pain is imaginary. Although it is important that the patient
understand the interactive view, it is equally imperative that he see his
pain as being taken seriously. It is often helpful to review past treatments with the patient, to explore specific aspects of treatment that the
patient has found either helpful or ineffective, and to offer the current
treatment as an alternative that takes into consideration a number of
different variables.

Explaining the interactive view of pain is likely to set the stage for
the patient to talk about stressful life problems that would otherwise be
ignored because they might be seen as unrelated to the pain. It may also
help the patient understand the difference between *treatment* and
management of pain, two very different goals that patients often fail to
distinguish.

It is also important for the clinician to assess the patient's internal
dialogue with respect to the pain and its treatment. Although doing so
may seem simple enough, this is not always the case. Simply asking,
"How do you feel about being here?" or "What do you expect to get out
of this?" may not constitute an adequate assessment of this most crucial

component. For many reasons, patients may not verbalize their concerns, and the clinician may need to gather data from diverse sources, such as overt behavior and collateral contact. For example, the patient who has made plans for additional medical treatment is probably not ready to make a commitment to an interactive pain management approach. A similar difficulty may exist when a patient is more interested during the first session in talking about the pain problem than in hearing what the clinician may have to offer.

CLINICAL CASES

Three cases are discussed here to illustrate the use of the clinical decision-making model. Each case has a different focus. In the first example, the focus is on developing a program for a patient whose general orientation makes treatment problematic. The second example involves several target problems, all of which seem to affect the pain; the focus here is on the use of the model as an aid to developing an overall treatment protocol when a number of problems seem relevant. The final example illustrates the use of the model with a pediatric case in which the focus is not only on treatment but also on assessment problems.

The Case of Ms. P.

Ms. P., a 74-year-old widow and the mother of two adult children, was referred to a pain management clinic by a senior citizens' support group because of her complaints of chronic chest and upper back pain with a duration of more than a year. Prior to her admission, she had seen several physicians and had gone through several medical evaluations, including an EKG. All evaluations had yielded negative results concerning any actual structural damage.

Although Ms. P. was quite focused on her pain during the initial screening, her complaints were vague. She was angry and expressed feelings of hopelessness because numerous medical personnel had attempted unsuccessfully to treat her pain. Moreover, she asked, "If they could not help, how could you?"

Six months prior to her admission to the pain management clinic, she had been on a psychiatric inpatient unit for depression, including symptoms of social isolation, difficulty in caring for herself, weight loss, and marked sleep disturbance. Treatment was largely pharmacological; within a short time, she had returned to her premorbid level of functioning. At the time of her first session at the pain clinic, Ms. P. was waiting to hear from her daughter regarding a referral to another medical specialist.

Problem Definition and Formulation

As mentioned, a medical workup of the patient was unremarkable. An attempt to have Ms. P. self-monitor the pain intensity over a 1-week period met with resistance. Specifically, in what appeared to be an effort to highlight the severity of her problem, she invariably rated her pain as being intense. The veracity of these ratings was questionable given that her activity level, assessed by verbal report, remained consistent across time, even though she described it as waxing and waning with her pain. On days when Ms. P. rated her pain as severe, she continued to engage in routine daily activities (e.g., cooking, watching television, shopping).

A conjoint interview with Ms. P. and her son revealed that the patient's current life was most notably characterized by attempts to force herself to attend meetings with other senior citizens and by waiting for her son to visit her on Friday evenings. The patient seemed invested in having her son move in with her, something that, up to the time of her admission, he had refused to do; however, to satisfy her, the son frequently stayed over on Friday evenings. Although she exhibited no vegetative signs of depression, Ms. P. described herself as depressed and engaged in mildly obsessive negative ruminations. She was also quite self-focused. In summary, the assessment involved collecting information from several different sources: physiological (e.g., review of medical records—both physical and psychiatric), verbal-cognitive (e.g., interview, pain ratings, depression ratings), and behavioral (e.g., activity level, family interactions).

On the basis of this assessment, several problems were identified. First, Ms. P. had little interest in participating in a psychological approach to pain management, as evidenced by her questionable record keeping, her plans to seek out the help of an additional medical specialist, and her general feeling that the clinic could not help. Second, Ms. P. continued to report subjective feelings of depression, which were characterized by feelings of hopelessness and negative rumination. Finally, it seemed quite apparent that the son and other family members played a significant role in helping to maintain the patient's pain complaints.

Generation of Alternatives/Decision Making

In deciding how to proceed with this patient, the clinicians generated a number of alternatives consistent with the clinical decision-making model. Some of these are listed in the following paragraphs, along with decision-making criteria that were used at a later point in the evaluation. It is important to note that the focus of this case is on the general orientation that Ms. P. brought to the clinical setting and that interfered initially with her participation in treatment.

1. Because the patient continues to show an element of depression (i.e., feelings of hopelessness, negative rumination), refer her for a treatment with little or no emphasis on the pain. That is, treat the pain as if it were a symptom of the depression.

For this patient, pain was the issue, and a referral for any other therapy was likely to encourage further resistance and reinforce the "all in your head" notion, something that was of much concern to her. Furthermore, treatment per se was not a concern. Rather, she often resisted generating ways to increase her activity level, especially as related to her senior citizen group. The patient clearly rejected this approach because she had difficulty understanding the relationship between participation in that group and enhanced ability to control her pain.

2. Refer the patient to a pain group.

Ms. P. continually verbalized that no one understood what she was experiencing. A pain management group might involve people who were experiencing similar feelings. It would also provide feedback from people who were getting better despite their pain. Such a group might also help to decrease Ms. P.'s feelings of isolation. Although this was a potentially effective treatment option, it was premature. Ms. P. was initially too negatively self-focused and too resistant to a psychological approach to participate in a pain management group.

3. Refer the patient to a medical specialist knowledgeable about the psychological management of pain.

Such a physician might conduct a thorough medical evaluation while simultaneously educating the patient concerning the etiology of her pain. Although Ms. P. was set to trust a medical specialist, any such contact would probably be of very limited duration. In addition, given her excessive self-focus, she probably would not be receptive to this approach. Furthermore, given the number of her previous medical contacts, this strategy probably had already been entertained.

4. Follow the patient's line of reasoning, that is, agree with her that we do not know how we can help. Then allow her to take the next step in her treatment.

Although this approach could certainly be offered to the patient as a thought-provoking exercise, she would probably be too self-focused to use it to her advantage. In fact, she might be likely to use it as an excuse to leave treatment.

5. Bring in the patient's significant others for a series of sessions with the primary function of education.

Family members had already supported the patient's efforts to seek out medical specialists. Furthermore, it was quite apparent from collateral contact that Ms. P.'s pain complaints and depressive symptomatology yielded much attention and support from her two children.

6. Contract with the patient for a limited period with the emphasis on assessment, support, and education.

The goal here might be twofold. First, this approach might involve continued monitoring of the patient's level of depression. Doing so would seem especially important given her recent discharge from inpatient hospitalization and her current report of depressive symptomatology. Second, the approach could help the patient problem solve other, more productive ways of keeping her children involved in her life, as well as increase her activity level. On the negative side, Ms. P. might view this approach as "therapy" and therefore resist it as an initial treatment plan.

7. Do not see the patient at this time; rather, suggest that she continue her medical evaluation elsewhere.

A critical decision concerned whether or not to continue to see this patient in the pain management clinic. There were several factors to consider. First, Ms. P. was quite vulnerable because of her recent psychiatric hospitalization. Also, she was convinced that her pain was due to physiological damage and had continued to search for medical specialists on the advice of her children. Finally, she was convinced that no one understood the extent of her pain or even cared anymore. Of these three factors, the most critical and the one that seemed most to contraindicate a psychological approach to treatment was the patient's plan to seek additional medical attention and the support from her family for doing so. She adhered strictly to a medical model of her pain and continued to act on this belief. Pain patients who have not exhausted all medical possibilities often are unmotivated to invest themselves heavily in a psychological approach to pain management.

Although they often agree to be involved in such a program, they do so only to "get it over with" and sometimes to prove its ineffectiveness (e.g., "See there, I knew it would not work").

This final alternative, not to see the patient in the pain clinic, is the one that would probably have been selected under most circumstances. However, given the rather recent history of clinical depression and the possibility that the pain might be a depressive symptom, dismissing her entirely might encourage a clinically significant relapse.

Solution Implementation and Verification

One alternative that was selected for implementation involved bringing in Ms. P.'s family members for conjoint meetings. There were several important reasons for this selection. It was apparent from collateral contacts, as well as from the review of her inpatient records, that Ms. P. was quite involved with her children. In this light, family involvement seemed a good way to "hook" her into treatment. Gaining her interest and support seemed particularly important given her generally negative orientation toward the clinic. Another reason for the choice of this alternative was that the family seemed to play a critical role in helping to maintain Ms. P.'s chronic condition. Specifically, her daughter continued to search for new and innovative medical treatments, and her son frequently altered his behavior (e.g., spending the night at her house) when his mother verbalized significant distress. Finally, it was thought that family members might be instrumental in helping the patient develop goals (e.g., ways to increase her activity level) and in monitoring her involvement in working toward such goals.

Ms. P. and her son were seen conjointly for a series of sessions. This time was used for education, especially for the son, who was the most accepting of an interactive approach to pain management. The therapist tried to get Ms. P. to stop doctor shopping by setting specific rules: For example, any further attempts to seek medical advice regarding the pain would have to be carried out solely by the patient because family members would no longer participate in this search. The son's presence in the sessions was helpful in decreasing the patient's self-focus, which in turn led to a better working relationship between therapist and client.

On the basis of Ms. P.'s positive reactions thus far, a second alternative was implemented, in keeping with the interactive approach of multiple causality. Specifically, the patient was seen individually for a series of sessions that emphasized education and support, and she was helped to identify activities that she could continue despite her pain and depression. Conceptually, these sessions were viewed as preparatory because they were geared toward facilitating the patient's ability to benefit ultimately from treatment. In essence, these two initial treatment alternatives were designed to overcome the significant initiation problems (see chapter 3) identified during the assessment phase.

Because it appeared that the patient's negative orientation had changed substantially, a third treatment option was then carried out. Ms. P. was referred to a pain group, where she stayed for several months. At termination, Ms. P. was less self-focused and less preoccupied with her pain. She had made friends with two of the group members and routinely had coffee with them. Ms. P. left the pain group to return to her senior citizens' support group; it is noteworthy that this was her own decision.

The timing of the events in this case was important. The assessment data supported the selection of several of the generated alternatives. However, given the patient's orientation at admission, it was likely that only a comprehensive approach would keep her in treatment long enough for her to profit in any way. The utility of the decision-making model is that it forced the clinician to examine a number of alternatives and systematically weigh them in light of the patient's orientation.

The Case of Ms. K.

In this case, the patient's orientation to treatment, far from creating initiation obstacles, served to facilitate treatment goals. Ms. K. was very willing to participate in treatment, although she did not know quite what to expect. She was happy to be turning her attention away from a purely medical approach to her pain. Her case shows how the decision-making model can be useful in prioritizing several sound clinical alternatives.

Ms. K. was a 72-year-old retired nurse when she entered treatment. She had been married for 45 years to a physician. The couple had three children, two of whom lived within a 5-minute drive from their home. The patient had been referred to the pain management clinic by a drug rehabilitation center, where she had been an inpatient for 8 weeks. She was addicted to Demerol, which she had begun taking to decrease the pain associated with peripheral vascular disease in her right leg. The leg was eventually amputated. However, the pain continued, as did her use of Demerol.

Except for taking aspirin as needed, the patient had been drug free for 10 weeks at the time of the first interview. Although she described herself as in continuous pain, she was committed to a life without prescribed medications, frequently stating that the Demerol provided only short-term relief.

Ms. K.'s premorbid level of functioning was quite good. She had worked for many years as a registered nurse and a nursing supervisor, and had served as the primary nurse in her husband's private practice. She described herself as a "go-get-ter," always striving for perfection and frequently setting very high goals for herself. After retiring, she had become very active in her community, stating that she was very proud of her ability to organize people. She had many friends, whom she had seen regularly until a year prior to the first session, when it had become apparent that she was addicted to Demerol. Her contact with these people became minimal at that time.

She respected her husband and characterized their relationship over the years as being very good. However, during the intake session, Ms. K. expressed the feeling that her husband was depressed. She viewed him as blaming himself for her addiction to Demerol. In addition, he had recently made some major life-style changes that involved retirement from a very active private practice. At the time of his retirement, he had made no plans; he was currently spending days generating activities that often were unsuccessful. Ms. K. described this as stressful for her because he was frequently irritable and angry. She was worried that her husband's recent change from a very active life to a state where nothing was planned would have a significant impact on his health and general well-being. He had developed some visual problems that made many activities difficult or impossible to pursue, and this exacerbated his negative mood and level of distress. A final stressor for the patient involved the constant illness of her eldest daughter, who suffered from Crohn's disease. At the time of Ms. K.'s admission to the pain clinic, the daughter's medical condition was under control.

Problem Definition and Formulation

The initial evaluation included a physical examination with the primary focus being a reevaluation of the existing medical problem. Several paper-and-pencil measures were also administered: two specific to the pain (West Haven–Yale Multidimensional Pain Inventory, pain ratings on a Likert-type scale), one specific to the patient's current mood state (Beck Depression Inventory), and one general measure (Multimodal Life History Questionnaire; Lazarus, 1980). In addition, Ms. K.'s husband and the therapist from her inpatient admission were interviewed. Self-monitoring of daily activity level and medication usage was also employed.

Ms. K.'s pain history indicated a duration of 3 years; the onset of pain seemed clearly precipitated by an organic impairment. Currently, there seemed to be numerous additional factors that served to maintain her level of pain. First, medical assessment revealed atrophy of the stump, as a result of which her prosthesis had become ill fitting and pain inducing. Although she was able to walk, she did so very slowly and with extreme caution. Second, certain environmental and behavioral stressors appeared to be present; these included her husband's poor emotional state, her own decrease in activity level, and the pressure from her family as they continued to look to her for resolution of their own problems. Finally, it was apparent that certain cognitive variables specific to the pain (e.g., "My medical condition will get the best of me"; "My friends are no longer interested in me"; "My friends see me as different now"; "I can't take care of my family anymore") also played a role in maintaining the patient's high pain level.

Ms. K. seemed to be harboring a sense of guilt about her addiction to Demerol and about having insisted that her husband prescribe it. During the initial screening sessions, she seemed tense, annoyed, and angry. Although there were no vegetative signs of depression, she seemed sad and quite concerned about her present life. She stated that she often worried about losing the use of her left leg, becoming completely incapacitated, having something "bad" happen to her husband, further deterioration of her daughter's physical condition, and the well-being of her granddaughter. She had not shared these feelings with her family, stating that personal feelings should not be disclosed.

Ms. K. had also become quite self-focused on her condition. Self-monitoring data regarding activity level, pain intensity, and the amount of medication taken over a 3-week period suggested that the patient spent a significant amount of her time attending to her condition. This assessment also suggested a correlation among the three variables. Specifically, as her activity level increased, the pain intensity decreased, as did her use of over-the-counter medications.

It is important to reiterate that Ms. K. had previously been a very active person but during the past 2 years had become isolated. This decrease in activity level was not totally a function of pain intensity (although she verbalized this to be the case in her effort to avoid old friends and other situations) but rather was due to her fear that others would no longer see her as the "in control" person who invariably had the answers to most of their problems. However, at the time of her admission to the pain management clinic, she had not had the opportunity to test out this apprehension. Moreover, Ms. K. made other negative and irrational self-statements. For example, she believed that she could direct the course of her daughter's illness, although she could not specify how she was capable of accomplishing this. Although she was harboring some guilt, anger, and depression, she felt that it was important that her family and friends not be aware of these feelings.

In summary, a number of problems were identified that included actual physiological damage (atrophy of the stump), family and marital stressors, a significant decrease in activity level that was not necessarily due to pain involvement, and various cognitive factors (i.e., excessive self-focus, negative and irrational self-statements).

Generation of Alternatives/Decision Making

In deciding how to proceed with this case, the therapist generated a number of alternatives based on the initial assessment. Some of these are noted in the following paragraphs, along with important decision-making criteria.

1. Teach the patient progressive muscle relaxation skills.

This option might give the patient a sense of control because she would be doing something about her pain and would be consistent with her history of being a "go-getter" and taking charge of her life. Also, because she was self-focused, learning relaxation skills might serve to distract her (Holzman, Turk, & Kerns, 1986). However, this strategy was not employed because of the lack of evidence of significant muscle tension and generalized arousal.

2. Given the number of family stressors (e.g., depressed husband, medically ill daughter), implement a family approach.

A family intervention was not employed for a number of reasons. First, although it seemed clear that family members' behavior influenced the patient, the reciprocal influence was not as clear; this suggested that there might not be reasons for the others to change. More important, the family members who seemed to have the most impact on Ms. K. also had medical conditions (i.e., the husband's visual problem and the daughter's Crohn's disease) that would have limited their ability to participate in treatment on a regular basis. Furthermore, the patient's belief that certain information should not be disclosed to other family members could interfere with the success of family treatment.

3. Offer individual psychotherapy.

Implementing this option would involve patient education regarding the impact of stressful events on physical problems, cognitive restructuring, and problem-solving training to increase the patient's activity level (see Nezu, Nezu, & Perri, 1989). This approach, however, would be likely to foster the patient's preoccupation with illness and would also reinforce her isolation.

4. Offer individual psychotherapy for the patient's husband.

This option would involve educating Mr. K. about pain, problem solving ways for him to help his wife become more independent, and helping him address his current difficulties surrounding retirement. Mr. K., however, was not ready for a one-to-one therapeutic relationship. He thought of himself as self-sufficient and not requiring help from anyone. A suggestion that he engage in individual therapy would appear to pose a risk to his self-esteem at the present time.

5. Refer Ms. K. to a cognitive-behavioral pain group.

This alternative was considered for a number of reasons. First, except for relations with her family members, the patient had become increasingly isolated, partially because of her discomfort with having others see her deteriorate. Second, the patient had done quite well in group therapy during her inpatient drug program. Third, a group would be a means to increase the patient's activity level in a nonthreatening way, and it would give her the opportunity to test out her negative perceptions about how others saw her. Finally, observing how others solved problems similar to her own (e.g., changes in life-style due to the onset of pain) might have a significant impact on the patient's well-being.

Solution Implementation and Verification

A number of variables were inferred to be maintaining Ms. K.'s current level of pain; all of them seemed critical. A key question, then, was "Where should treatment begin?" This is a difficult question, one that has prompted much discussion among those interested in behavioral assessment (e.g., Barlow, Hayes, & Nelson, 1984; Hawkins, 1986; Wilson & O'Leary, 1980). Several guidelines have been offered for this initial decision; one might see them as alternatives generated to address the question of where to start when all identified problems seem equally pressing.

The following are offered as potential guidelines for such decision making: First, intervene in the area that seems to account for the most variance in the causation and/or maintenance of the pain. In other words, of all the problems identified, pinpoint the one that is likely to have the greatest impact on the patient's report of pain. Second, address the area that most seems to cloud the overall picture. Specifically, if the assessment data suggest that a variable has an impact but the extent of that impact remains unclear, then it may be good to address this area initially. Elimination or management of this problem may help reveal the impact of the other problem areas on the patient. Third, address the target area that is likely to give the patient access to naturally occurring reinforcers (Hawkins, 1986). With a depressed individual, for example, the goal is often to get the person into the real world so that others can be involved in reinforcing the patient's active participation and socialization.

One initial treatment target for Ms. K. was the management of her stump atrophy. If this problem was, as hypothesized, contributing significantly to the patient's pain, changes in other areas were likely to have little or no impact on the pain experience and would probably cause her further frustration. It was also the target problem that was easiest to address and that involved the shortest process. It was thus the ideal place to begin because it promised a likely decrease in pain that could serve to reinforce further patient involvement in the treatment process.

In the case of Ms. K., a critical variable in discerning where to begin treatment seemed to be in the patient's history. She had had a long and productive work life. Upon retiring, she had become very active socially in her community. Moreover, she described herself as a very happy person. Any treatment plan should, then, focus on increasing Ms. K.'s access to reinforcers related to her habitual activities. Specifically, gradually exposing her to the world that she was avoiding might serve a number of purposes, including decreasing her excessive self-focus and feelings of isolation, distracting her from family stressors, and increasing her ability to help her husband be more active.

To achieve the goal of reinvolving Ms. K. in her world, the therapist decided to refer her to a time-limited group program that emphasized teaching realistic goal-setting and problem-solving skills to chronic pain patients. A time-limited behavioral group was expected to help her to regain social support from her community, as well as to cope better with various stressors in her life. An open-ended group treatment, in contrast, might have been an inadvertent source of social reinforcement that would have run counter to Ms. K.'s desire to become more active in her own environment.

In keeping with a multidimensional, interactive model of pain, additional alternatives were implemented. First, a series of conjoint sessions were held with Ms. K. and her husband. These sessions focused on overall goal setting; education about the interactive model of pain; and joint problem-solving tasks regarding resolution of current stressful problems, including Mr. K.'s difficulty adjusting to his retirement. Another treatment alternative that was implemented involved a referral for the husband to a retired professionals group that offered peer support and activities. Although the latter two alternatives were not on the original list of treatment options, they were generated later when the clinician recycled through the model after being dissatisfied with the utility ratings of the original alternatives. This change highlights the clinician's need to be flexible in treatment planning in order to adjust to clinical reality.

To fulfill the verification component of the decision-making model, the clinician used several dependent measures to assess treatment effectiveness. These included the Beck Depression Inventory, subjective ratings of pain intensity, self-monitoring of activity levels for both Ms. K. and her husband, and an assessment of the patient's overall well-being. At treatment termination, all of these areas showed signs of improvement. At a 1-year follow-up initiated by the patient, she continued to describe episodes of pain but reported that she felt more in control of her symptoms. Moreover, she had become increasingly active in her community and had taken a 2-hour flight to visit her son.

The Case of C. F.

The case of C. F. illustrates the use of the decision-making model in a pediatric context.[2] Whereas the emphasis in the previous cases was on the utility of the model in discerning treatment alternatives, the present case shows how the model can be useful in clarifying alternatives for assessment as well as for treatment. With children, several additional people are typically involved (e.g., parents, teachers), and they often need to be included in the assessment process; this means that special problems may need to be addressed.

> C. F. was 10 years old when he entered treatment for headaches. His symptoms included severe pain encompassing the entire head, with pain around the eyes; in addition, he experienced photophobia. The pain often resulted in nausea and vomiting. Collectively, these symptoms were consistent with a diagnosis of migraine headaches. The time of onset of

---

[2] I would like to thank Dr. Steven Klee for bringing this case to my attention.

the headaches was unclear, but the patient and his mother estimated that he had been complaining of headaches for at least a year. Although C. F. was taking aspirins as needed, they seemed effective only in managing the milder symptoms. More recently, the headaches had become so severe that he had required emergency room treatment at a local hospital on several occasions. His mother also had a long history of migraines, as well as a seizure disorder. In addition, C. F. had a history of significant head trauma.

Problem Definition and Formulation

The most remarkable feature of the patient's mental status at admission to the pain management clinic was his anxious and depressed mood and paucity of speech. According to the mother, C. F. had become increasingly isolated and withdrawn during the few weeks prior to his admission. She also expressed concern regarding his deteriorating school performance.

On the basis of an initial assessment, it seemed that several problem areas were involved in C. F.'s complaint of headaches. The clinician decided to begin with a full physical evaluation, especially given the intensity of the more recent headache episodes. The history presented by the mother suggested that her son's headaches were sporadic and not situation-specific. A strong affective component was suggested by the patient's recent isolation and current mental status. The factors contributing to the deteriorating school performance would need to be assessed further, as this might have been an etiological variable or the result of the headaches. In short, at least four areas (physical, socioenvironmental, affective, and academic) would need to be investigated further before a clear understanding could be obtained.

Assessment with a pediatric population is complicated by the fact that children often do not possess the vocabulary to describe their physical sensations accurately. Moreover, they may describe them quite differently from adults. Therefore, many of the techniques commonly employed in the evaluation of pain with adults may not be suitable for use with children. For example, an assessment technique such as self-monitoring in the natural environment is less likely to yield valid information because it requires sustained attention over a period of time, usually 1 to 2 weeks. In addition, pediatric headaches represent a particularly complex problem because of the frequent involvement of socioenvironmental factors such as stress and secondary gain (Varni, Katz, & Dash, 1982). Such factors would need to be considered in the evaluation of C. F.

The following paragraphs list several alternative assessment strategies that might be used in the case of C. F.; they focus primarily on psychological issues because the medical/physical assessment seemed clear. This list of alternatives is consistent with the decision-making model as it applies to the identification of potential problems related to assessment (see Table 3.1).

1. Rely on the verbal report of the child and the mother to assess the frequency, intensity, and duration of the headaches.

Because evidence suggests that many factors might influence a child's self-report of physical sensations (Varni, 1983), this did not seem an appropriate strategy by itself. Also, because the mother had a history of migraines, rater bias might be likely. In other words, given that the mother was very aware of the pain associated with migraines, it was probable that she would respond in a way that she perceived would maximize treatment.

2. Involve the school (e.g., nurse, guidance counselor, teachers) in the assessment of various parameters associated with the headaches.

Given the subjective nature of the pain experience and the numerous distractors that might occur in the school setting, this strategy would be likely to yield invalid information. School personnel might, however, be quite useful in describing broader school behavior, such as the child's academic performance and social behavior.

3. Utilize a structured interview.

This approach might be useful for gathering information about C. F.'s pain and family history, school performance, and socialization, but it would not help in evaluating specific parameters concerning his headaches. For example, controlling or maintaining variables would be difficult to elucidate clearly in a structured interview.

4. Review school records.

Such a review might be helpful in identifying potential areas of strength and weakness. Also, an examination of school records across time could be useful in identifying situational variables (e.g., life stressors) that might influence the presenting problem of headaches.

5. Conduct a psychological evaluation.

Given that potential school problems existed, a psychological evaluation could be useful in identifying problem areas. Further, this patient had a history of head trauma, and there was a history of migraines in the patient's family. Thus an emphasis on neuropsychological testing might also be useful in identifying subtle cognitive deficits.

In keeping with the interactive model, a multidimensional assessment was performed. A full medical evaluation was initially carried out; it included data from specialists in ophthalmology, pediatrics, and neurology. Further, a decision was made to collect data from three sources—the school, the mother, and the child himself—to assess the specific parameters associated with the headaches. Because there was concern about the validity of the data from any one of these sources, it was thought that the combination might yield more valid information. This approach is also consistent with the self-monitoring literature, which suggests that subjects provide more accurate data when they know others are monitoring the same target behavior (Lipinski & Nelson, 1974). School records were obtained, along with the results of a recent psychological evaluation. The patient's teachers completed several structured interviews. These focused on C. F.'s academic performance and socialization in the school.

The reports from both neurology and pediatrics, including an EEG, were unremarkable regarding an organic etiology. Therefore, a diagnosis of migraine was recommended. The report from ophthalmology suggested the need for corrective lenses. Self-monitoring data revealed that, although C. F. did have headaches at home, most of the episodes seemed specific to the school. The patient's report of headaches seemed more consistent with the school data than did the mother's report, which tended to overestimate the frequency of the headaches as well as the extent of the school problems. The headaches at school were typically followed by C. F.'s being sent home or the mother's being called to take him home. His school behavior was characterized as mildly disruptive, with poor overall academic performance. Further, he was thought to be quite anxious, especially in relation to his school performance. Additional evidence suggested that the anxiety was specific to any task presented in a test form.

Between the first and second visits to the clinic, C. F. had run away from home when he discovered that a meeting had been arranged between his mother and the school personnel. According to C. F., he thought that he would get a bad report. The results of the psychological evaluation suggested an average level of intellectual functioning with difficulties in basic academic areas such as reading and spelling.

Several factors were identified as potentially maintaining C. F.'s headaches; the condition of his eyes was one specific factor. The headaches often resulted in removal from anxiety-provoking situations (i.e., school or situations where he would be evaluated). Finally, as a function of time, the patient's school performance had deteriorated, and this was now a significant source of stress for him.

Generation of Alternatives/Decision Making

Because a visual deficit had been identified, correction of this problem was necessary before other interventions could be implemented. In an effort to manage the more psychological aspects of the treatment, the therapist generated a number of alternatives for treatment of the headaches. They are listed in the following discussion along with important clinical decision-making criteria.

1. Offer the patient more potent forms of medication.

Although medication might be a later alternative, it was not the first choice. The more potent forms of medication (e.g., Fiorinal, amitriptyline, Dilantin, and phenobarbital) have side effects such as dizziness and sedation that could certainly have an impact on school performance.

2. Offer the patient relaxation and/or biofeedback training.

The efficacy of these two intervention approaches in the management of migraine and tension headaches in general (Turner & Chapman, 1982) and for children (Varni et al., 1982) has been established. However, these approaches have been criticized because a simplistic conceptualization of pain often underlies their use and because they are often used as a sole treatment (Turner & Chapman, 1982).

3. Develop a contingency management program.

It is very likely that time away from school was a powerful reinforcer in maintaining C. F.'s headaches. Specifically, when he reported headaches, he was often allowed to return home. An approach to treatment that eliminated this consequence might have a significant impact on the frequency of the headaches.

4. Provide individual therapy.

Given the anxiety level reported by the school and observed during the intake evaluation, it was likely that C. F. might benefit from anxiety management training. This might take the form of relaxation training, antianxiety medication, cognitive restructuring, and problem-solving training that would focus on building test-taking skills and coping with performance issues.

5. Recommend tutoring.

Given the deterioration in C. F.'s school performance and the fact that he was currently performing below grade level in the basic academic areas, as assessed by the Wide Range Achievement Test (Jastak & Jastak, 1978), tutoring seemed warranted.

Solution Implementation and Verification

Several factors make the case of C. F. representative of that of most pediatric headache patients. Specifically, there was a strong history of migraine in his family and, during a headache episode, there typically was a marked decrease in his social and academic functioning. C. F. did not feel that he could control these headache episodes, especially the more severe ones. At the time of the initial evaluation, he was withdrawn and irritable. Furthermore, there appeared to be significant socioenvironmental stressors that might have maintained the migraines.

Treatment for C. F. began with a consultation with his mother to discuss and plan a treatment strategy. In keeping with the decision-making model, several alternatives made up the overall treatment plan. First, school personnel were contacted and involved in management of the case. The teachers were asked to do three tasks. Specifically, they were to monitor C. F.'s academic performance and the frequency of his headaches, as they had already been doing. In addition, the school also became involved in the contingency management of the case: C. F.'s teachers were not to send him home during headache episodes, but were instead to try to manage him in the classroom. If this solution became unworkable, then an alternative was to call in the school nurse, who would allow C. F. to rest in the office until the episode had terminated or the school day ended.

Another treatment component involved relaxation training, which was implemented as a way of increasing C. F.'s ability to cope directly with the headaches. C. F. did quite well with this training, and it was likely that relaxation would have been a sufficient coping strategy. In addition, in an effort to facilitate therapeutic rapport (and in the expectation that the patient would find pleasure in it), the therapist also implemented training in thermal biofeedback. Again, C. F. was quite good at relaxing and within a few sessions was able to increase peripheral fingertip temperature several degrees. Yet another component of C. F.'s treatment involved working directly on his test-taking behavior. This entailed desensitizing him to test situations, problem solving ways of responding to difficult test items, and increasing his acceptance of not always knowing the answer to a test item.

Several measures of treatment effectiveness were employed. These included the Brief Psychiatric Rating Scale for Children (Overall & Pfefferbaum, 1982), headache frequency count, and reports of academic performance and school behavior. At the end of treatment, the frequency of the patient's headaches had decreased significantly. C. F. experienced one occasionally, but he no longer required an emergency room visit. There was a significant decrease in affective symptoms as well, with no evidence of depression and only minimal anxiety symptoms. This progress was also reflected in C. F.'s academic skills, about which the school had noted "much improvement." He had successfully made it through a number of tests, including the citywide achievement tests that would determine whether or not he would be promoted to the next grade level. In general, his teachers described him at that point as nonproblematic. Although the mother's report concerning the headaches was consistent with that of the school, she continued to feel that there were problems with C. F.'s school performance. Further individual treatment was conducted with the mother around this issue. Termination of treatment for C. F. was gradual; the time between sessions was increased progressively from a week to a month. Follow-up data indicated maintenance of treatment gains.

It is significant that, of the five treatment alternatives generated for this case, components of four of them were eventually determined to be suitable for implementation.

SUMMARY AND CONCLUSIONS

This chapter has attempted to illustrate the clinical decision-making processes often involved in the behavioral management of chronic pain. For each of the three cases presented, several treatment alternatives were generated on the basis of a multidimensional assessment that included samples from at least four areas: physiological, affective, verbal-cognitive, and behavioral. Alternatives were selected according to the unique characteristics of each case, although the three patients presented with similar sets of symptoms. Specifically, they all reported unrelenting pain with a duration of more than a year, during which time they had obtained little or no symptomatic relief through a purely medical approach. In addition to the pain, these patients shared several other qualities. All had had reasonably good premorbid histories prior to the onset of the pain, consisting of stable employment or academic performance and a stable home life. At the time of admission, significant depressive symptomatology was noted in all three patients. Ms. P.'s pain seemed to be a function of her depression. Ms. K.'s depression seemed to be a function of the way in which she now viewed her life as a consequence of the pain. In the case of C. F., the depression seemed to be a function of his feelings of being overwhelmed by both perceived and real stressors, of which pain was just one.

The alternatives generated during the decision-making analysis addressed the depressive symptoms, but, because of the decision criteria employed, these symptoms were not always targets for treatment. In the case of C. F., for example, it seemed clear that the patient was depressed. He had become increasingly isolated, withdrawn, and disruptive at school, and, during the early admission sessions, he appeared depressed. In some settings, he would have been an excellent candidate for a pharmacological treatment, especially in light of the data suggesting that antidepressants might have analgesic properties. However, the depression was not dealt with directly because assessment data suggested that it was mainly a function of other factors that could be addressed without medication or a longer term therapy. As it turned out, this was a good decision in that C. F.'s depressive symptoms covaried with other variables that were addressed directly.

In each of the three cases, a family systems approach seemed relevant. In the case of Ms. P., the patient's children played a part in influencing her report of pain in that they responded with attention when she complained. For Ms. K., the problem was more one of perceived failure with respect to family and friends. Finally, for C. F., school seemed to reinforce pain behaviors by making time away from school contingent on pain complaints, and his mother was a source of stress in that she seemed to have a biased view due to her own pain history. For all three patients, system variables were therefore consistently included as treatment targets. However, because of various additional factors (e.g., prioritization of symptoms, orientation problems, problems with a system), these variables were approached in very different ways. For Ms. P. and C. F., a systems change was necessary before a treatment effect could be observed. For Ms. K., the needed change was not so much a change in the family system as a change in her way of viewing the system.

The three case studies presented here illustrate the use of the clinical decision-making model. In each case, a variety of treatment alternatives were initially generated on the basis of information gathered during an assessment phase. These alternatives were then evaluated in terms of their advantages and disadvantages with regard to the unique characteristics of the case. Although the clinical decision-making model guiding this progress awaits further systematic evaluation, it clearly represents a meaningful way to enhance the effectiveness of treatment planning. Even though clients experiencing chronic pain exhibit similar overt symptoms, they especially require tailor-made interventions.

References

Aronoff, G. M. (Ed.). (1985). *Evaluation and treatment of chronic pain*. Baltimore: Urban & Schwarzenberg.

Barlow, D. H., Hayes, S. C., & Nelson, R. O. (1984). *The scientist-practitioner: Research and accountability in clinical and educational settings*. New York: Pergamon.

Beck, A. T., Ward, C. H., Mendelsohn, M., Mock, J., & Erbaugh, J. (1961). An inventory for measuring depression. *Archives of General Psychiatry, 4,* 561–571.

Block, A. R., Kremer, E., & Gaylor, M. (1980). Behavioral treatment of chronic pain: The spouse as a discriminative cue for pain behavior. *Pain, 9,* 243–252.

Bonica, J. J. (1985). Introduction. In G. M. Aronoff (Ed.), *Evaluation and treatment of chronic pain*. Baltimore: Urban & Schwarzenberg.

Chapman, C. R., & Wyckoff, M. (1981). The problem of pain: A psychological perspective. In S. N. Haynes & L. Gannon (Eds.), *Psychosomatic disorders: A psychophysiological approach to etiology and treatment*. New York: Praeger.

Derogatis, L. (1977). *Manual for the Symptom Checklist-90, revised*. Baltimore: Johns Hopkins University, School of Medicine.

Flor, H., & Turk, D. C. (1984). Etiological theories and treatments for chronic back pain: I. Somatic models and interventions. *Pain, 19,* 105–121.

Flor, H., & Turk, D. C. (1989). Psychophysiology of chronic pain: Do chronic pain patients exhibit symptom-specific psychophysiological responses? *Psychological Bulletin, 105,* 215–259.

Fordyce, W. E. (1976). *Behavioral methods for chronic pain and illness*. St. Louis: Mosby.

Fordyce, W. E. (1983). The validity of pain behavior measurement. In R. Melzack (Ed.), *Pain measurement and assessment*. New York: Raven.

Fordyce, W. E. (1986). Learning process in pain. In A. Sternbach (Ed.), *The psychology of pain*. New York: Raven.

Gotestam, K. J., & Linton, S. J., (1985). Pain. In M. Hersen & A. S. Bellack (Eds.), *Handbook of clinical behavior therapy with adults*. New York: Plenum.

Gray, C. L., Lyle, R. C., McGuire, R. J., & Peck, D. F. (1980). Electrode placement, EMG feedback, and relaxation for tension headaches. *Behaviour Research and Therapy, 18,* 19–23.

Haley, W. E., Turner, J. A., & Romano, J. M. (1985). Depression in chronic pain patients: Relation to pain, activity, and sex differences. *Pain, 23,* 337–343.

Hawkins, R. P. (1986). Selection of target behaviors. In R. O. Nelson & S. C. Hayes (Eds.), *Conceptual foundations of behavioral assessment*. New York: Guilford.

Hendler, N. H., Long, D. M., & Wise, T. N. (1982). *Diagnosis and treatment of chronic pain*. Littleton, MA: John Wright & Sons.

Holroyd, K. A., & Andrasik, F. (1981). A cognitive-behavioral approach to recurrent tension and migraine headache. In P. C. Kendall (Ed.), *Advances in cognitive-behavioral research and therapy* (Vol. 1). New York: Academic.

Holroyd, K. A., Andrasik, F., & Westbrook, T. (1977). Cognitive control of tension headache. *Cognitive Therapy and Research, 1,* 121–133.

Holroyd, K. A., Andrasik, F., & Westbrook, T. (1978). Coping and self control of chronic tension headache. *Journal of Consulting and Clinical Psychology, 46,* 1036–1045.

Holzman, A. D., & Turk, D. C. (1986). *Pain management: A handbook of psychological treatment approaches.* New York: Pergamon.

Holzman, A. D., Turk, D. C., & Kerns, R. D. (1986). The cognitive-behavioral approach to the management of chronic pain. In A. D. Holzman & D. C. Turk (Eds.), *Pain management: A handbook of psychological treatment approaches.* New York: Pergamon.

Jastak, J. F., & Jastak, S. (1978). *The Wide Range Achievement Test.* Wilmington, DE: Jastak Associates.

Kerns, R. D., & Haythornthwaite, J. A. (1988). Depression among chronic pain patients: Cognitive-behavioral analysis and effect on rehabilitation outcome. *Journal of Consulting and Clinical Psychology, 56,* 870–876.

Kerns, R. D., Turk, D. C., & Rudy, T. E. (1985). The West Haven–Yale Multidimensional Pain Inventory. *Pain, 23,* 345–356.

Lazarus, A. A. (1980). *Multimodal Life History Questionnaire.* Kingston, NJ: Multimodal Publications.

Lindsay, P. G., & Wyckoff, M. (1981). The depression-pain syndrome and its response to antidepressants. *Psychosomatics, 22,* 571–577.

Lipinski, D., & Nelson, R. O. (1974). The reactivity and unreliability of self-monitoring. *Journal of Consulting and Clinical Psychology, 43,* 637–646.

Lipton, J. A., & Marbach, J. J. (1984). Ethnicity and the pain experience. *Social Science and Medicine, 19,* 1279–1298.

Melzack, R. (1973). *The puzzle of pain.* Hammondsworth, England: Penguin.

Melzack, R. (1975). The McGill Pain Questionnaire: Major properties and scoring methods. *Pain, 1,* 277–299.

Melzack, R., & Wall, P. D. (1965). Pain mechanisms: A new theory. *Science, 50,* 971–979.

Melzack, R., & Wall, P. D. (1973). *The puzzle of pain.* New York: Basic.

Melzack, R., & Wall, P. D. (1983). *The challenge of pain.* New York: Basic.

Nezu, A. M., Nezu, C. M., & Perri, M. G. (1989). *Problem-solving therapy for depression: Theory, research, and clinical guidelines.* New York: Wiley.

Overall, J. E., & Pfefferbaum, B. (1982). Brief Psychiatric Rating Scale for Children. *Psychopharmacology Bulletin, 18,* 10–16.

Roberts, A. H. (1986). The operant approach to the management of pain and excess disability. In A. D. Holzman & D. C. Turk (Eds.), *Pain management: A handbook of psychological approaches.* New York: Pergamon.

Romano, J. M., & Turner, J. A. (1985). Chronic pain and depression: Does the evidence support a relationship? *Psychological Bulletin, 97,* 18–34.

Sternbach, A. (Ed.). (1986). *The psychology of pain.* New York: Raven.

Todd, E. M. (1985). Pain: Historical perspectives. In G. M. Aronoff (Ed.), *Evaluation and treatment of chronic pain.* Baltimore: Urban & Schwarzenberg.

Turk, D. C., Meichenbaum, D. H., & Genest, M. (1983). *Pain and behavioral medicine: A cognitive behavioral perspective.* New York: Guilford.

Turner, J. A., & Chapman, C. R. (1982). Psychological interventions for chronic pain: A critical review. *Pain, 12,* 1–46.

Varni, J. W. (1983). *Clinical behavioral pediatrics: An interdisciplinary bio-behavioral approach.* New York: Pergamon.

Varni, J. W., Katz, E. R., & Dash, J. (1982). Behavioral and neurochemical aspects of pediatric pain. In D. C. Russo & J. W. Varni (Eds.), *Behavioral pediatrics: Research and practice.* New York: Plenum.

Wernick, R. L., Jaremko, M. E., & Taylor, P. W. (1981). Pain management in severely burned patients: A test of stress inoculation. *Journal of Behavioral Medicine, 4,* 103–109.

Wilson, G. T., & O'Leary, K. D. (1980). *Principles of behavior therapy.* Englewood Cliffs, NJ: Prentice-Hall.

Wooley, S. C., Blackwell, B., & Winget, C. (1978). A learning theory model of chronic illness behavior: Theory, treatment, and research. *Psychosomatic Medicine, 40,* 379–401.

Worthington, E. L., Jr. (1982). Labor room and laboratory: Clinical validation of the cold pressor as a means of testing preparation for childbirth strategies. *Journal of Psychosomatic Research, 26,* 223–231.

Chapter 13

Clinical Stress Management

Thomas J. D'Zurilla
Arthur M. Nezu

INTRODUCTION

In recent years, there has been growing recognition of the important role that stress often plays in the etiology and/or maintenance of both psychological and somatic disorders (Bloom, 1985; Dohrenwend & Dohrenwend, 1985; Hamberger & Lohr, 1984; Lazarus & Folkman, 1984). Consequently, the demand for effective stress management programs has been increasing in clinical psychology as well as in medicine. Unlike many of the other treatment approaches described in this volume, stress management is not targeted for any particular symptom syndrome or diagnostic category. Stress may play a role in any disorder or illness. In general, stress management is appropriate, either as the primary treatment or as an adjunctive method, in any case where stressful life events or the client's maladaptive attempts to cope with these events are causing excessive emotional arousal, which in turn is producing psychological or somatic symptomatology. Some disorders that are often found to be stress related are anxiety states, depression, anger, migraine and tension headaches, chronic fatigue, backaches, asthma, insomnia, essential hypertension, bruxism, and gastrointestinal disorders (Woolfolk & Lehrer, 1984a).

A clinician who searches the current literature on stress and stress management for guidelines in developing an effective stress management program for a particular client may become a bit confused. For many years, the dominant view has equated stress with *anxiety arousal*, with an emphasis on physiological responses (Benson, 1975; Selye, 1983). As a result, stress management has often been equated with *anxiety management* in one form or another (e.g., progressive muscle relaxation, meditation, biofeedback, pharmacological treatment; Woolfolk & Lehrer, 1984b). Recently, however, a broader concept of stress has emerged, one that places more emphasis on environmental variables (e.g., stressful life events) and on person variables (e.g., cognitive appraisals, coping activities) that mediate or moderate physiological-affective stress responses (Lazarus & Folkman, 1984). An important clinical implication of these recent developments is that anxiety reduction strategies alone are not likely to be adequate or appropriate for all clients in all stress situations. Thus the trend has been toward the development of stress management programs that emphasize a variety of coping skills and stress reduction techniques (Meichenbaum & Cameron, 1983). Some empirical evidence supports the theoretical rationale for this approach. According to a review of comparative stress management research by Lehrer and Woolfolk (1984), combinations of stress management techniques have proven more effective than the application of any single technique. Moreover, other recent research has suggested that the best combination of coping techniques is likely to vary with individual clients and particular stress situations (Compas, Forsythe, & Wagner, 1988; Folkman & Lazarus, 1980; Forsythe & Compas, 1987).

The problem for the clinician is that the stress management literature has not yet provided any clear decision rules or principles for determining what particular coping or stress reduction strategies and techniques are likely to be most effective or adaptive for what particular clients in what particular stress situations (Woolfolk & Lehrer, 1984a). This chapter will deal with recent developments in stress theory that have important implications for clinical stress management. Considering these implications, we will then show how the clinical decision-making model described in chapter 3 of this volume can facilitate the planning and development of more effective, individualized stress management programs.

RECENT DEVELOPMENTS IN STRESS THEORY

Despite more than 50 years of stress research, there is still no universally accepted definition or conceptualization of stress. However, an interactional model of stress has emerged recently and has been rapidly gaining widespread acceptance (Lazarus, 1966, 1981; Lazarus & Cohen, 1977; Lazarus & Folkman, 1984; McGrath, 1982; Sarason, 1980). In this model, stress is viewed as a multifaceted, dynamic process that involves reciprocal interactions among a number of variables related to both the environment and the person (e.g., external and internal demands for readjustment, cognitive appraisals, physiological-emotional states, and coping activities). Thus, in the interactional model, stress is not defined simply as a characteristic of the environment, nor as a characteristic of the person. Instead, stress is a complex relationship between the person and the environment that evolves and changes over time with changes that occur in the environment and/or the person.

Richard Lazarus's Transactional Model of Stress

The most popular version of this approach to stress is the transactional model of Richard Lazarus and his associates (Lazarus, 1981; Lazarus & Cohen, 1977; Lazarus & Folkman, 1984). According to this model, stress is seen as a person-environment relationship in which the person appraises adaptive demands as taxing or exceeding coping resources and endangering well-being (Lazarus & Folkman, 1984). As this definition implies, the model emphasizes two important mediating processes: (a) cognitive appraisal and (b) coping. *Cognitive appraisal* is an evaluative process in which a person assesses the "meaning" or significance for well-being of a particular encounter with the environment. Two main forms of cognitive appraisal are *primary appraisal* and *secondary appraisal*. During primary appraisal, the person assesses the specific impact (actual or potential) of the encounter on well-being—for example, harm or loss, threat, "challenge," or potential for benefit or gain. Secondary appraisal is the person's evaluation of his coping resources and options with regard to a particular stressful encounter.

In this model, *coping* refers to the cognitive and behavioral activities through which a person attempts to manage the specific demands that are appraised as stressful, as well as the emotions that these demands generate (Lazarus & Folkman, 1984). Coping may be problem focused or emotion focused. *Problem-focused coping* is aimed at changing or controlling the stressful situational demands. According to Lazarus, *social problem solving* (i.e., real-life problem solving) is one form of problem-focused coping that helps a person achieve mastery or control over the environment. *Emotion-focused coping*, on the other hand, is aimed at managing the emotions that are associated with stressful situational demands. Emotion-focused responses are seen as the adaptive alternative to problem solving and other forms of problem-focused coping when situational demands are appraised as unchangeable or uncontrollable.

The Transactional/Problem-solving Model of Stress

More recently, D'Zurilla and Nezu (D'Zurilla, 1986; Nezu & D'Zurilla, 1989) have described a transactional/problem-solving model of stress that places special emphasis on the role of social problem solving as a general coping strategy. This model integrates Lazarus's transactional model with the social problem-solving model described elsewhere by D'Zurilla and his associates (D'Zurilla, 1986; D'Zurilla & Goldfried, 1971; D'Zurilla & Nezu, 1982). The transactional/problem-solving model retains all the basic assumptions and most of the essential characteristics of the Lazarus model; however, these characteristics are cast within a general social problem-solving framework. The process of problem solving is given an expanded and more important role as a general coping strategy on the basis of substantial research suggesting that problem solving is one of the most important coping skills a person can possess (see D'Zurilla, 1986; Nezu, 1987; Nezu & D'Zurilla, 1989; Nezu, Nezu, & Perri, 1989).

In the transactional/problem-solving model, stress is viewed as a function of the interaction among stressful life events, emotional states, and problem-solving coping. *Stressful life events*—occurrences that present a person with strong demands for readjustment, whether personal, social, or biological (Bloom, 1985)—fall into two main categories: daily problems and major life changes. A *daily problem* is a specific problematic situation characterized by an imbalance or discrepancy between adaptive demands and coping response availability (D'Zurilla, 1986). A daily problem may be considered the equivalent of Lazarus's *stress situation* (Lazarus & Folkman, 1984) when it is appraised by the person as significant for well-being—for example, as a threat or a challenge. A problem may be a single time-limited event (e.g., losing one's wallet in a strange city), a series of related events (e.g., repeated unjustified criticism from one's spouse), or an ongoing situation (e.g., chronic arthritic pain). Such problems occur in most people's lives virtually every day; some of them are trivial, although others are quite significant for well-being. In contrast with a specific daily problem, a *major life change* is a life event that demands broad-scale personal, social, or biological readjustment (e.g., divorce, death of a spouse, major career change, major physical disability). Although major life changes are much less common than daily problems over the course of the lifespan, their occurrence usually produces extremely intense and widely generalized emotional effects, which often result in significant impairment in daily personal-social functioning.

Major life changes and daily problems tend to influence each other. A major life change often means a proliferation of daily problems with which the person must cope: The death of one's spouse, for instance, results in frequent feelings of loneliness, more domestic responsibilities, increased financial pressures, and so forth. Conversely, an accumulation of unresolved daily problems might result eventually in a major life change: Repeated disputes with one's boss and co-workers could ultimately mean the loss of one's job.

The transactional/problem-solving model of stress focuses more on daily problems than on major life changes. Although daily problems are not as dramatic as major life changes, research has shown that the frequency of daily stressful events is more strongly related to psychological and somatic symptomatology than is the number of major life changes (DeLongis, Coyne, Dakof, Folkman, & Lazarus, 1982; Kanner, Coyne, Schaefer, & Lazarus, 1981; Nezu, 1986; Nezu & Ronan, 1985; Weinberger, Hiner, & Tierney, 1987). Moreover, research also suggests that the relationship between major changes and long-term health and psychological outcomes is often mediated by an accumulation of poorly resolved daily problems that result from the major changes (Nezu & Ronan, 1985; Weinberger et al., 1987). Therefore, in clinical stress management based on the transactional/problem-solving model, the focus is on teaching individuals ways of coping with specific problematic situations.

A major life change, then, is viewed as a broad, complex problem that a person cannot cope with successfully in its entirety. It must first be broken down into more manageable subproblems (i.e., current and anticipated daily problems), which are then dealt with one at a time. Consider, for example, an individual who comes to treatment experiencing distress associated with being laid off from a job. Rather than attempting to cope with this life change as a whole, it is preferable to identify various subproblems that may have resulted from this major stressful event. The subproblems may include finding a new job, managing restricted funds, coping with lowered self-esteem, reevaluating career goals, learning to use newly found free time productively, and dealing with the embarrassment of being unemployed. When broken into component parts, the complex situation becomes more manageable. More important (and consistent with the notion discussed in chapter 2 of addressing a problem from multiple perspectives), such analysis of the situation ultimately permits identification of a broad range of alternative coping strategies, thus potentially increasing the efficacy of the overall stress management program.

In the transactional/problem-solving model, the term *emotional state* refers to the emotional responses associated with stressful problematic situations. These responses include perceived autonomic activity and other physical sensations, along with their cognitive, affective, and motoric concomitants. Emotional states may be generated by stressful life events, cognitive appraisals, and/or coping activities and outcomes. The affective component of emotional stress is usually described negatively as *distress*, meaning pain, suffering, or discomfort. Emotional distress includes such feelings as anxiety, anger, and depression. Such negative feelings are most likely to occur when the person (a) appraises a problem as a significant threat to well-being, (b) doubts his ability to cope successfully with the problem, or (c) makes coping attempts that are ineffective or maladaptive. Within our model, negative emotional states are not simply stress effects. They may also influence stress by actually reducing the efficiency and effectiveness of coping attempts (D'Zurilla, 1986; Janis, 1982); this situation may then serve to increase emotional distress and create new problems. For example, following a major argument with her spouse, a wife may experience myriad emotions, including anger, hurt, anxiety, and sadness. If she believes that little can be done to rectify the situation, this negative orientation may actually influence her willingness and/or ability to attempt reconciliation. Moreover, an intense emotional response, such as severe anger, may lead her to engage in attempts that only serve to worsen the original problem or to create new ones—for example, attempts to prove that her spouse, in fact, was really at fault and should therefore apologize first.

Although emotional distress is a common form of emotional stress, the emotions associated with stress situations are not always negative. A stress situation may generate a positive form of emotional excitement, which may be termed *emotional prostress* (where the prefix *pro* means "favorable"). Emotional prostress is most likely to occur when the person (a) views a problem as a positive challenge (i.e., an opportunity for benefit or gain), (b) believes that he is capable of coping with the problem successfully, and (c) makes coping attempts that are effective or adaptive. Thus we might assume that, if a person concentrates on the potential benefits that coping efforts might produce instead of focusing only on the possible harm or loss that the problem might cause, then emotional distress might be minimized and emotional prostress enhanced. This circumstance might occur for the individual who, upon learning that a layoff is imminent, regards the event as an opportunity to find a more challenging and financially rewarding new job. Focusing on the potential benefits, as opposed to losses, would likely engender feelings of positive anticipation and excitement rather than sadness and apprehension.

The most important concept in the transactional/problem-solving model is that of *problem-solving coping,* the combination of problem solving and specific coping performance. *Problem solving* is defined as the general strategy by which a person attempts to identify, discover, or invent an effective or adaptive coping response or response combination for a particular problematic situation (D'Zurilla, 1986; Nezu & D'Zurilla, 1989). Thus problem solving is seen here as the general coping process that mediates the specific responses that enable a person to reduce or control stress in a particular problematic situation. In the terminology of social problem-solving theory (D'Zurilla, 1986), the specific coping responses constitute the "solution," or the outcome of the problem-solving process. *Coping performance* refers to the performance of these specific responses in the actual problematic situation. Thus coping performance is the equivalent of solution implementation in social problem-solving theory.

The difference between the problem-solving process and coping performance is important for both assessment and treatment in the practice of stress management. An assessment might show that a client is competent in identifying effective solutions for a particular stressful problem. However, additional assessment might reveal that she lacks the specific performance skills needed to carry out any of these solutions optimally. Thus, although the client may possess the important coping strategy of effective problem solving, the problem is unlikely to be resolved adequately if she cannot implement a solution. For this reason, assessment should be geared to identify both problem-solving and performance skill deficits. Such evaluation can facilitate clinical decision making as the therapist chooses the intervention components that will constitute the overall stress management package, and more effective treatment is likely to result.

A therapist who focuses on training in specific stress reduction techniques (e.g., relaxation, deep breathing) while ignoring problem-solving training fails to capitalize on the effective coping skills the individual already possesses. Moreover, unlike problem-solving training, the stress reduction approach gives only minimal attention to issues of generalization and maintenance. In keeping with a multiple causality framework, distress symptoms can result from deficits in problem solving, coping performance, or both. A comprehensive assessment, such as that described in chapter 3, allows the clinician to obtain an accurate and complete picture of an individual's "stress profile" and to design treatment to address those areas in need of change. Moreover, as is consistent with the notion of including future-oriented intervention components, problem-solving training helps facilitate goal attainment and the maintenance of stress reduction effects.

Problem solving is viewed here as a broad, versatile, and adaptive coping strategy. As noted earlier, Lazarus defines problem solving more narrowly as one form of problem-focused coping, which limits problem-solving goals to mastery goals—that is, meeting, reducing, or changing situational demands. The present concept of problem solving has greater adaptive flexibility: The problem-solving goals may be problem focused, emotion focused, or both, depending on the nature of the specific problematic situation and how it is defined and appraised. When the situational demands are appraised as changeable or controllable, then problem-focused goals can be adopted. If emotional stress is high, it may be adaptive to include emotion-focused goals as well in an attempt to minimize emotional distress and its disruptive effects on functioning (D'Zurilla, 1986). On the other hand, if the situational demands are appraised as unchangeable or uncontrollable, then it may be necessary to abandon problem-focused goals altogether and instead to adopt emotion-focused problem-solving goals like acceptance, distraction, reappraisal, and relaxation.

The goals may be changed at any point during the problem-solving process if and when the problematic situation is redefined or reappraised. For example, repeated attempts by a client (and therapist) to overcome marital difficulties may have little impact on the spouse's desire to maintain the relationship. If it becomes evident that the spouse actually wants a divorce, emotion-focused goals and coping strategies may be more appropriate at this point in treatment. Encouraging the client to continue with strategies aimed at marital reconciliation would likely engender more harm than benefit. Whereas the original goal may have been to increase marital satisfaction, indicating an emphasis on problem-focused strategies (cf. chapter 7 in this volume), the problem now must be reformulated to include emotion-focused goals (e.g., "How can I tolerate the stress of a divorce?"; "How can I maintain my self-esteem?"). The reevaluation would lead to different coping strategies that are likely to be more appropriate and adaptive (e.g., acceptance/resignation, seeking social support).

In general, the transactional/problem-solving model of stress provides a particularly useful framework for clinical stress management. Because of the model's heavy emphasis on the interaction among its variables, it is also consistent with the emphasis on a systems approach underlying the clinical decision-making model. In addition, both models advocate an exhaustive and expansive search for the variables that potentially affect the individual's distress symptomatology. The transactional/problem-solving model of stress is thus quite compatible with the goals of the clinical decision-making framework. On the basis of this model, for example, a stress-management program can be tailored to meet the needs of a particular client in specific stress situations. This approach involves a careful, comprehensive assessment of each client's current and anticipated stress situations and the use of a problem-solving approach to determine what particular coping strategies are most effective or adaptive for what particular stress situations, with an emphasis on the client's personal criteria for effectiveness or adaptation.

With the transactional/problem-solving model in mind, we can now turn to the application of problem-solving principles to clinical decision making in stress management. Considering the importance of problem solving as a general coping strategy, we will not only focus on the use of problem-solving principles by the clinician, but will also recommend problem-solving training for the client in order to facilitate the maintenance and generalization of stress reduction effects (D'Zurilla, 1986, in press).

APPLICATION OF PROBLEM-SOLVING PRINCIPLES TO STRESS MANAGEMENT

The model of clinical decision making described in chapter 3 consists of five problem-solving processes: (a) problem orientation, (b) problem definition and formulation, (c) generation of alternatives, (d) decision making, and (e) solution implementation and verification. As the authors emphasize, these processes are interrelated and interdependent; they should not be viewed as a simple one-directional sequence of problem-solving steps. The content of these components as applied to clinical decision-making in stress management will be described in more detail in the remainder of this chapter. Because of the importance of problem-solving skills for the client, it is recommended that the therapist and client work as a team in applying the model. When appropriate, we will describe specific problem-solving training procedures for the client that follow the general problem-solving principles.

Problem Orientation

As applied to clinical decision making, *problem orientation* is the generalized cognitive set that the therapist brings to the clinical situation concerning the client's stress problems and the overall stress management process. This cognitive set may either facilitate or inhibit effective clinical decision making. An inhibitive orientation is one that contains negative biases such as unswerving allegiance to a questionable stress model; rigid commitment to a single stress management technique; or treatment preferences that are based primarily on clinical intuition, clinical experience, or clinical tradition. For example, as stated earlier in this chapter, stress management has often been equated with anxiety management; adherence to this view might result in a narrow focus on anxiety reduction techniques alone (e.g., progressive muscle relaxation, biofeedback). Although this treatment strategy might ultimately be identified as the most appropriate one for a given client, another client with different stress problems might benefit more from coping skills training that emphasizes problem-focused techniques.

In addition, when first encountering a client who complains of excessive stress, the clinician must guard against the availability bias (see chapter 1). For example, if a previous client who complained of excessive stress were treated successfully with biofeedback, the therapist should be wary of prescribing the same treatment once again simply because of the similarity in presenting problems. As noted earlier, both the clinical decision-making model and the transactional/problem-solving approach emphasize the need for comprehensive assessment before treatment is begun.

A positive, facilitative orientation, on the other hand, is an empirical orientation that involves the cognitive set to (a) conduct an objective and comprehensive assessment of each client's stress problems, (b) make clinical decisions about treatment that are based on this assessment and on the results of comparative stress management research, (c) take into account both the strengths and deficits unique to the client (e.g., presence or absence of existing coping responses), (d) take into account the therapist's ability to implement a particular stress management method optimally (e.g., qualification to conduct biofeedback treatment), and (e) be willing to consider a wide range of potential alternative intervention methods rather than relying on a favorite stress management technique.

From the client's point of view, problem orientation refers to the generalized cognitive set that the client brings to a new problematic situation. Just as the therapist's particular problem orientation may facilitate or inhibit clinical decision-making performance, the client's particular problem orientation may have a positive or negative influence on real-life problem-solving performance. Therefore, the client is taught to distinguish between a facilitative problem orientation and one that is inhibitive or maladaptive (D'Zurilla, 1986). A person with an inhibitive or maladaptive problem orientation tends to (a) deny or avoid problems, (b) attribute problems to some general and stable personal defect, (c) appraise problems as a serious threat to well-being, (d) appraise problematic situations as unchangeable, (e) appraise his problem-solving ability negatively, and (f) depend on others for solutions to problems. A person with a facilitative problem-solving orientation, on the other hand, tends to (a) recognize problems when they occur, (b) accurately attribute problems to environmental factors or relatively benign and changeable personal factors, (c) appraise problems as a challenge or an opportunity for benefit or gain, (d) accurately appraise problematic situations as changeable, (e) appraise her problem-solving ability positively, and (f) commit time and effort to independent problem solving.

Given the importance of this factor to actual coping performance, the therapist should assess the client's orientation as soon as possible and provide training, if needed, to foster a more positive problem-solving cognitive set. To complement the clinical interview, two useful self-report methods for assessing problem orientation are the Social Problem-Solving Inventory (SPSI; D'Zurilla & Nezu, 1988) and the Problem-Solving Self-Monitoring method (PSSM; D'Zurilla, 1986); both will be described later in this chapter. Identification of the most appropriate training procedures and assessment tools can be facilitated through the use of the overall problem-solving process.

At times, a client's negative orientation can represent a significant initiation difficulty: A cognitive set questioning the viability of any stress management protocol (e.g., "Nothing can help me") reflects a major obstacle to the implementation of treatment. In such a case, the therapist—in addition to identifying the maladaptive problem orientation as one factor that potentially contributes to the client's distress and maladaptive behavior—must also regard that orientation as an obstacle to overcome if the client is to benefit maximally from treatment. In other words, the clinician should view the client's negative orientation as a problem to be solved through the use of the decision-making model.

As an illustration, consider the case of Alan, a client who sought therapy because of excessive anxiety and distress on the job. Although he was a successful systems analyst, Alan was constantly being passed over for promotions within the company. A careful and comprehensive assessment revealed that he had substantial difficulties in relating to people in both social and work situations. These difficulties involved problem-solving deficits, communication skill deficits, and social anxiety. Upon hearing the therapist's observations and recommendations concerning the possibility of improving his social skills, Alan immediately felt that the therapist did not completely understand his situation. Further probing revealed Alan's strong belief that, despite his difficulty relating to people, he should still be promoted because of his competent work (e.g., "Life isn't fair! I shouldn't have to be a good conversationalist in order to get a promotion! The bosses should just evaluate my work."). His view that life isn't fair not only caused more distress and prevented him from engaging in any adaptive ways to overcome his problems, it also represented a major initiation obstacle: All attempts by the therapist to encourage constructive behavior change were met with "You just don't understand." In the face of this obstacle, the therapist had to rephrase the initial therapeutic goal from "How can I help Alan overcome his interpersonal difficulties?" to "How can I solve this initiation problem?" Applying the decision-making model, the therapist eventually identified a strategy that facilitated Alan's cooperation and motivation during the initial phases of assessment and treatment.

Although a pool of potentially useful approaches to improving client motivation may be identified, it is essential to acknowledge individual differences among clients and the reasons underlying their poor motivation (e.g., fear of changing, low reinforcement for changing, competing reinforcement for not changing). These differences require the therapist to apply the entire decision-making model rather than "charging in" with the first promising technique that comes to mind.

Problem Definition and Formulation

As noted earlier, clinical stress management based on the transactional/problem-solving model focuses on specific problematic situations that are appraised by the client as significant for well-being. Thus the problem definition and formulation component of the model aims to (a) identify significant current and anticipated problematic situations; (b) gather as much relevant, factual information about each problematic situation as possible; (c) clarify the nature of each problem; and (d) set realistic stress management goals.

It can be difficult to identify specific problematic situations: Clients are not always sensitive to such events in their lives, and they frequently deny or avoid problems because of the emotional distress associated with facing them. To facilitate problem identification, it is often helpful to begin by administering some self-report measures of general life stress. Two useful inventories are the Life Experiences Survey (LES; Sarason, Johnson, & Siegel, 1978) and the Derogatis Stress Profile

(DSP; Derogatis, 1980). The LES assesses major stressful life events, including such life changes as the death of a loved one, a job change, and leaving home for the first time. The DSP, a multidimensional measure of stress based on interactional stress theory, provides an assessment of three major stress domains and 11 stress dimensions within these domains. The three stress domains and their related stress dimensions are: environmental stress (domestic, vocational, health), personality mediators (time pressure, driven behavior, attitude posture, relaxation potential, role definition), and emotional stress (hostility, anxiety, depression). After administering these self-report inventories, the therapist can probe during a clinical interview for possible specific unresolved problems that are suggested by the results. The LES and DSP are particularly useful because they are broad-based assessment tools that can yield information across a multitude of life areas. Additionally, the DSP assesses a variety of stress-related variables.

Another procedure to facilitate problem identification is self-monitoring by the client. The client should be instructed, when implementing this procedure, to use emotional distress and ineffective behavior as cues to identify the specific problematic situations that might be associated with these maladaptive responses. In addition, the use of problem checklists such as the Personal Problems Checklist (Schinka, 1984) and the Mooney Problem Checklist (Mooney & Gordon, 1950) can facilitate problem recognition.

When a significant problematic situation is identified, the next step for the therapist-client team is to gather as much concrete, factual information as possible about the situation and then to analyze the problem using the general transactional/problem-solving framework. As described earlier, a problematic situation is an imbalance or discrepancy between adaptive demands and coping response availability (D'Zurilla, 1986). In keeping with the concept of multiple causality (see chapter 2), a complete analysis of a problematic situation includes the identification and description of specific adaptive demands (external and/or internal), cognitive mediators (e.g., cognitive appraisals, causal attributions, personal-control expectations), emotional states, and coping attempts. In addition to identifying specific stress determinants in particular problematic situations, it is important to assess general stress determinants and moderating factors such as general problem-solving skills (D'Zurilla, 1986), social support resources (Thoits, 1986), self-esteem (Pearlin & Schooler, 1978), and certain social roles and life-styles (e.g., relaxation potential, good health habits, "hardiness"; Derogatis, 1980; Kobasa, Maddi, & Kahn, 1980). The importance of problem-solving training in clinical stress management has already been emphasized. If assessment reveals deficiencies or obstacles with regard to other general stress-moderating factors, they also are viewed as problems to be solved (i.e., target problem areas), and attempts to correct the deficiencies or overcome the obstacles are included in the client's stress management program. For example, a problem statement for a specific deficit in self-esteem might include "What can I do to feel better about myself as a parent (friend, lover, etc.)?" A problem statement for a specific obstacle to a healthy life-style might include "How can I control my drinking (get more exercise, avoid high-calorie snacks, etc.)?"

Construction of an individualized stress-related Clinical Pathogenesis Map (CPM) can be quite helpful at this point. The CPM, illustrated in Figure 3.3, is a graphic representation of the therapist's hypotheses concerning the major variables that contribute to the initiation and maintenance of the patient's problems. It also serves as a stimulus for the generation of treatment alternatives. In stress management, delineation of the obstacles to overall stress reduction and control (e.g., lack of social support, poor health habits) also fosters better understanding of the interactional nature of stress-related variables. Moreover, construction of the CPM encourages the clinician to search for multiple determinants of stress responses rather than relying on stress models with unidimensional causative frameworks.

Consider the case of Susan, a 29-year-old single woman who worked as an office manager for a major corporation. She initially came to therapy complaining of work-related stress that included symptoms of anxiety, depression, severe abdominal pain, and fatigue. A comprehensive assessment based on data from clinical interviews and self-report measures (e.g., SPSI, DPS, LES) yielded the following information: Susan displayed problem-solving skill deficits across the five major components of the problem-solving process. This was particularly evident in her strong tendency to avoid facing problems when they occurred. A previous medical examination had revealed a biological propensity to experience gastrointestinal problems under stress. Recent stressful events included a warning from her boss that her work was less than adequate, particularly in terms of resolving intraoffice personnel problems, a responsibility that was part of her job description but that she especially disliked and avoided. In addition, because of poor money management (resulting from the problem-solving deficits), she was having serious financial difficulties. The threats to her job security, coupled with the increased financial problems, finally prompted Susan to seek therapy in an attempt to reduce the stress in her life, especially the feeling of being overwhelmed by all her pressures.

Self-monitoring data indicated that Susan's stress symptoms (anxiety, depression, abdominal pain, etc.) became particularly intense when she engaged in the following activities: paying bills, going to work on Mondays, dealing with difficult work tasks, hearing about a personnel problem at work, and seeing her boss. From a transactional perspective, it was also apparent that, as the stress symptoms worsened, they tended to trigger self-deprecating and hopeless thoughts (e.g., "I'm no good"; "I deserve to get fired"; "Maybe I should just quit work and become a bag lady"). Moreover, the combined cognitive-affective-physiological distress led to increased avoidance behavior (e.g., not paying bills, taking more days off from work). Susan's attempts to cope with her problems usually involved taking long naps, drinking alcohol, and watching television. These ineffective coping attempts resulted in both the creation of new problems and the worsening of current ones. Thus a vicious cycle emerged in which the pattern—the current dysfunctional system—was characterized by a negative reciprocal impact among stressful events, emotional responses, and maladaptive coping attempts.

On the basis of this analysis, the therapist, rather than intervening with a packaged stress-management program to reduce the stress symptoms, could construct a CPM that would permit identification of the variables uniquely involved in maintaining Susan's difficulties. Whereas relaxation training, for example, might help to reduce the negative physiological consequences of stress, in isolation it would not address the complex of factors related to adaptive problem solving and coping. Given the reciprocity among the relevant stress-related variables, such a narrow approach would probably result in future relapse. A more effective overall stress management approach for Susan would include different strategies designed to address the multiple determinants of stress. A broad-based approach would both increase the likelihood that her stressful problems would be resolved successfully and facilitate generalization and maintenance of stress-reduction effects.

Because problem-solving coping is considered to be the major stress-moderating factor in the transactional/problem-solving model, it is important to assess carefully for deficits in problem-solving ability and performance. Two useful assessment measures for this purpose are the SPSI (D'Zurilla & Nezu, 1988) and the PSSM method (D'Zurilla, 1986), mentioned earlier. The SPSI is a 70-item multidimensional self-report measure of general problem-solving ability that is based on the model of social problem solving described in chapter 2. This inventory was designed to provide for a comprehensive assessment across the five major problem-solving components. Subscales encompass cognitive, emotional, and behavioral aspects of problem orientation, in addition to the four problem-solving skills. The SPSI can thus provide information about the full range of specific problem-solving deficits.

The PSSM method (D'Zurilla, 1986) is a self-monitoring procedure designed to assess specific real-life problem-solving performance. Using a special form, the client records information about his own problem-solving behavior and coping performance with regard to a specific problematic situation. This record form is organized according to the following format.

A: *Problem information.* The client describes all the relevant facts about the situation (who, what, when, where, etc.).

B: *Emotions.* The client describes the feelings and emotions that he experienced when first confronted with the situation.

C: *Alternative solutions considered.* If the client considered alternative ways of coping with the situation before deciding on a particular approach, he lists the alternatives here.

D: *Solution choice.* The client describes the coping response(s) that he decided to use and the reasons for the choice.

E: *Solution implementation and outcome.* The client describes his performance and its consequences. The client also rates his satisfaction with the coping outcome at this point.

Table 13.1 represents a PSSM form that Susan, the client in our illustration, completed early in the assessment phase. Note that the PSSM allows for a comprehensive evaluation of her coping attempts in response to a specific problem. The information on Susan's form suggests that she tends to avoid problems; her coping responses (e.g., watching TV to distract herself, drinking alcohol to tranquilize herself) are consistent with this overall orientation.

In addition to being a useful assessment device, the PSSM method offers an important procedure for training in problem solving. It provides tasks for the practice of problem-solving skills in the session as well as in real-life situations. In addition, as a self-monitoring procedure, the PSSM method provides immediate feedback concerning the client's real-life problem-solving performance.

The final step in problem definition and formulation is to set realistic stress-management goals for the problematic situations that have been identified. The major decision for the therapist-client team at this point is whether, for a particular problematic situation, to adopt

Table 13.1 PSSM Form Completed by Client during Assessment

A: PROBLEM INFORMATION

The other day my boss started talking to me about one of the new secretaries in the office who wasn't really working out. I know that it's my job to talk to her, but as he continued talking about her poor performance and how I'd better do something about it, I started to get real nervous.

B: EMOTIONS

At first I began to get real anxious, with sweaty palms and hot flashes—I could really feel my stomach start to get real sick. Afterwards, I started to get those feelings of being overwhelmed, as if the whole world was on my shoulders. That's when I want to crawl into a hole or have the world swallow me up so I don't have to deal with this problem anymore.

C: ALTERNATIVE SOLUTIONS CONSIDERED

I really didn't think of any alternatives other than just avoiding the problem—I just don't know what else to do!

D: SOLUTION CHOICE

I didn't really choose any solution. I just did what I usually do—run away! I tried hard not to think about it the rest of the day and avoided Joyce, the secretary. That night, I went home and watched TV and drank a bottle of wine. The next morning, I felt nervous and my stomach hurt. So I just called in sick and stayed home.

E: SOLUTION IMPLEMENTATION AND OUTCOME

The consequences were that my work continued to pile up, and I felt really depressed and angry at myself again for being so pathetic! I really want to deal with these problems, but I just don't know the answers!

---

a goal that is problem focused, emotion focused, or both. In making these decisions, the therapist-client team is advised to follow the entire problem-solving process as a means of developing appropriate treatment goals. For example, they should brainstorm a list of possible goals and objectives, both emotion focused and problem focused, and then evaluate and rate each item on the list according to the major decision-making criteria outlined in chapter 3. The goals selected should be ones that have received high utility scores (positive likelihood and value ratings). Both types of goals are often selected as a means of addressing the problem from multiple vantage points; their inclusion is consistent with the principle of maximizing treatment effectiveness.

For Susan, possible emotion-focused goals might be to increase relaxation and reduce drinking. Possible problem-focused goals might include improving problem-solving, communication, and assertiveness skills. For each of these objectives, various treatment strategies could then be identified.

Generation of Treatment Alternatives

Within the decision-making model, the generation of treatment alternatives sets forth stress management strategies and techniques for various problematic situations. The purpose of this component is to maximize the likelihood of developing the most effective overall individualized stress management plan. In generating such alternatives, both therapist and client should observe three rules or principles: quantity, deferment of judgment, and variety (see chapter 2). These principles are designed to enhance the creativity and flexibility of the stress management program as well as its effectiveness.

In the generation of alternatives, stress management or coping strategies can be conceptualized at different levels. At a general level, therapist and client will often consider both a *problem-focused strategy* and an *emotion-focused strategy* when both types of goals have been set for a particular situation. Subsumed under each of these general strategies are a variety of substrategies and specific techniques and coping activities (see Table 13.2 for a list of examples). For Susan, two possible substrategies in the emotion-focused category might be (a) reducing physiological arousal directly (e.g., via relaxation or pharmacological methods) and (b) reducing anxiety indirectly by modifying cognitive mediators (e.g., via cognitive reappraisal or distraction). Possible substrategies in the problem-focused category might include (a) changing behavior to meet situational demands (e.g., by improving communication skills) and (b) changing situational demands to match present behavior (e.g., by developing appropriate assertiveness to reduce unreasonable job demands).

A useful distinction can also be made between a *passive treatment strategy* and an *active coping strategy*. The passive treatment strategy requires minimal client participation, effort, and self-control. It includes such techniques as progressive muscle relaxation, meditation, hypnosis, pharmacological methods, and various types of social support (e.g., emotional support, informational aid, instrumental aid; Thoits, 1986; Woolfolk & Lehrer, 1984b). Although some of the techniques used in this approach are relevant for problem-focused stress management goals (e.g., some forms of social support), most of them focus on

Table 13.2 Common Coping Skills for Use as Coping Solutions

COMMON PROBLEM-FOCUSED SOLUTIONS

Assertiveness skills
Communication skills
Interpersonal conflict resolution skills
Social-influence skills
Self-management skills
Time management skills
Childrearing or parenting skills
Job skills
Academic skills
Financial management skills
Housekeeping skills
Sexual skills
Self-instructional skills
Motivational self-statements
Covert (imaginal) rehearsal
Behavioral rehearsal or role playing

COMMON EMOTION-FOCUSED SOLUTIONS

Cognitive restructuring techniques
Positive reappraisal
Relaxation skills
Breathing exercises
Meditation
Desensitization techniques
Prolonged exposure (extinction)
Catharsis (expressing feelings and emotions)
Seeking social support
Seeking religious support
Distraction/escape
Thought stopping
Humor
Pleasant and interesting activities
Eating and drinking
Physical exercise
Relaxing or calming self-statements
Pleasant or relaxing imagery
Personal growth ("making lemonade out of lemons")
Rational self-statements
Acceptance/resignation

direct anxiety reduction. In addition, most of these techniques involve specialized therapist skills and/or client skills that often require considerable in-session training.

In contrast to the passive treatment strategy, the active coping strategy emphasizes active client participation, effortful coping, and self-management. This approach centers more on coping with specific stress situations in vivo and places equal emphasis on problem-focused goals and emotion-focused goals. Specific coping skills and techniques include applied relaxation in vivo (Bernstein & Borkovec, 1973; D'Zurilla, 1969; Goldfried, 1971); cognitive control techniques, such as self-instruction and cognitive restructuring (Meichenbaum, 1977; Ellis & Harper, 1975); and instrumental coping skills, such as assertiveness skills and time-management skills. In addition to these specialized coping skills, this approach draws heavily on the client's existing repertoire of coping responses and activities, both cognitive and instrumental. The goal is to help the client find the best "fit" or match between stress situations and the coping responses already available. Thus problem-solving skills for the client, as well as the therapist, are very important in the active coping approach.

In applying problem-solving principles to a new stress situation, the therapist-client team attempts to identify, discover, or invent the best possible coping response or response combination, using the client's existing response repertoire as identified during the assessment phase. This procedure capitalizes on the client's unique coping strengths and resources. Doing so is especially important when the individual's repertoire of coping skills is relatively weak. Moreover, with the problem-solving approach, the "best" coping response is determined individually, using the client's own personal criteria for effectiveness (personal goals, values, feelings, etc.). This approach can be expected to increase the likelihood of personal satisfaction with coping outcomes. The relative advantages and limitations of the passive and active stress management strategies will be examined in subsequent discussion.

By applying the principles just described, the therapist and client have generated a wide variety of potentially effective stress management techniques and coping activities for a particular problematic situation. The next step in the clinical decision-making model is to evaluate the utility of these stress management alternatives.

Decision Making

The purpose of the decision-making process is to evaluate systematically (judge and compare) the stress management alternatives for each problematic situation and select the best technique or combination of techniques for the particular client to use in the actual situation. Together, the stress management techniques and coping activities for all significant stress situations, current and anticipated, constitute the client's overall stress management plan. This does not mean that a plan must be developed for all stress situations before any stress management techniques are implemented; rather, decision making is ongoing. Stress management plans are developed and implemented for particular stress situations continually throughout the stress management program. Thus the therapist is constantly using the clinical decision-making model.

Decision making, as applied to the therapeutic situation, is based on an expected utility model of choice behavior, where expected utility is a joint function of the value of expected stress management (or coping) outcomes and their likelihood of occurrence. A stress management or coping outcome consists of all significant effects or consequences of a particular strategy or technique, including social as well as personal consequences and long-term as well as short-term consequences. Moreover, in evaluating potential strategies and techniques, the therapist must consider consequences for herself (e.g., ethical considerations, professional reputation) as well as consequences for the client. To determine the value of an expected outcome, therapist and client must distinguish between positive consequences (benefits, gains) and negative consequences (unwanted side effects, costs, risks) and attempt to weigh the two. To predict the likelihood of a particular outcome, the therapist-client team must consider not only the likelihood that the strategy or technique will produce specific short-term and long-term effects if implemented optimally (as recommended in the literature), but also the likelihood that the team will be able to implement that strategy or technique optimally. This judgment requires an evaluation of relevant abilities, skills, and resources. For example, is the therapist competent to train the client in relaxation techniques? Does the therapist have access to biofeedback equipment?

Use of the deferment of judgment principle in the generation of treatment alternatives usually results in a list of strategies and techniques that vary greatly in effectiveness and feasibility. At this point, therefore, the therapist and client should conduct a rough screening of the alternatives for each problematic situation and eliminate any that are obviously inferior because of unacceptable risks or a lack of requisite abilities or resources. Then they can go on to a more formal and systematic evaluation of the remaining alternatives.

To illustrate this evaluation process, let us consider the possible advantages and limitations of a passive treatment strategy as opposed to an active coping strategy. The major potential benefits of most passive stress management techniques (e.g., drug therapy, biofeedback, meditation) are their prompt and powerful anxiety reduction effects. Therefore, these techniques merit strong consideration when anxiety is so severe as to cause extreme distress and a serious disruption in problem-solving and coping performance. Pharmacological treatment or progressive muscle relaxation training, for example, might alleviate the disruptive effects of anxiety until the client can learn the coping skills needed to deal more effectively with the problems in life. On the other hand, the major limitations of the passive techniques include dependency on the therapist or the treatment and a lack of maintenance and generalization of anxiety reduction effects after treatment has ended. Although passive stress management techniques often help to reduce anxiety, they do not teach the client how to cope more effectively with stressful problems in living. Pharmacological treatment has the added risk of negative physical side effects (Lader, 1984). If passive treatment is used as the sole stress management strategy, the immediate benefits may not outweigh the long-term costs.

In contrast to the passive stress management strategy, the active coping strategy has as its major advantage the potential for facilitating the maintenance and generalization of stress management effects—and the prevention of future stress—by increasing personal-social competence and self-control. The problem-solving coping strategy, in particular, is likely to encourage maintenance and generalization by enhancing self-management ability, adaptive flexibility, perceived control, and a positive orientation to problems in living (i.e., approaching a stress situation as a challenge or problem to be solved instead of viewing it as a threat to be avoided, as Susan did when approaching problems at work). Effective problem solving promotes self-management or self-control because it enables the client to identify or discover effective or adaptive coping responses for new situations independently, instead of relying on the therapist or others for coping assistance. Problem-solving coping fosters adaptive flexibility because it can be applied successfully to a broad range of present and future stress situations. It also provides the client with a wider choice of coping options for a particular stress situation. Successful independent problem solving is likely to result eventually in a strong perception of personal control, which has been found to be an important moderator of stress effects (Hamberger & Lohr, 1984; Kobasa, 1979). In addition, successful problem solving tends to create a positive orientation to problems in living, which also acts as a buffer against the effects of daily life stress (Kobasa, 1979; Kobasa et al., 1980). A further advantage of the problem-solving coping strategy is that it may minimize the amount of time and effort required for training in specific coping skills because it capitalizes on the client's existing coping strengths and resources.

The major limitation of the active coping approach is that it does not usually produce strong, immediate anxiety reduction effects. An active strategy like problem-solving coping tends to produce a gradual improvement in stress management ability as a result of the cumulative effects of dealing more effectively with specific problematic situations in everyday living. Therefore, when a client is suffering from acute, severe anxiety, it may be necessary to couple a more powerful anxiety reduction method with the active coping approach until the client's own coping efforts begin to result in significant stress reduction. In certain cases, the therapist may need to be particularly sensitive to this type of clinical decision.

Using the results of the decision analysis, the therapist can construct a Goal Attainment Map (GAM; see Figure 3.4) that delineates an initial overall treatment plan, linking specific intervention strategies to specific goals or objectives. A GAM for our client Susan, for example, would specify both emotion-focused and problem-focused goals. Because of her immediate, intense feelings of anxiety in response to work problems, one important emotion-focused goal would be anxiety reduction. Treatment strategies addressing this goal might involve deep breathing skills and applied relaxation (Bernstein & Borkovec, 1973; Goldfried, 1971). Such strategies might not only help decrease Susan's overall anxiety in both emotional and physical realms but also allow her to engage in active, adaptive coping attempts instead of trying to avoid problematic situations. Depending upon the initial results of this approach, various cognitive restructuring techniques (Beck, 1984; Ellis & Grieger, 1977; Meichenbaum, 1977) might then be incorporated as a means of enhancing her feelings of self-esteem and self-efficacy.

More important, the stress management package should also include strategies that address certain problem-focused goals, such as improving problem-solving ability, communication skills, and assertiveness. These strategies would not only be helpful in resolving Susan's current difficulties at work, but would also be geared to preventing future stressful situations.

This combination of problem-focused and emotion-focused strategies is based on a comprehensive assessment of Susan's stress problems guided by the clinical decision-making model. Rather than simply applying a favorite (or available) stress management method, the clinician should base treatment design decisions upon the unique life circumstances of the client. For example, if Susan's anxiety symptoms had been more life threatening (e.g., exacerbating severe respiratory or cardiac problems), a referral to a physician for medication might have preceded further stress management therapy. Or, if the physical anxiety symptoms had been moderate and tolerable, emotion-focused strategies might not have been necessary at all.

Treatment Implementation and Verification

The culminating phase of the clinical decision-making model is treatment implementation and verification. Its purpose is to put various aspects of the stress management program into practice and to allow an objective evaluation of their immediate long-term outcomes. This procedure has two components: (a) treatment implementation or coping performance, and (b) outcome assessment.

Treatment implementation or coping performance means the actual performance of the treatment procedures (as implemented by the therapist) or coping activities (as implemented by the client) that make up the stress management plan for the various problematic situations. Possible obstacles to performance include deficiencies in specific coping skills or abilities (e.g., deficits in assertiveness skills, deficits in relaxation skills or habits), emotional inhibitions (e.g., specific fears, disruptive general anxiety level), and motivational deficits (e.g., reinforcement deficits). If such obstacles exist, two possible alternatives are (a) to return to the decision-making model and identify an alternative coping strategy or technique that might be implemented more effectively and (b) to apply a treatment or training procedure designed to overcome the obstacle or obstacles (e.g., assertiveness training, relaxation training).

In Susan's case, initial implementation of muscle relaxation training revealed that she had substantial difficulty in concentrating on the therapist's instructions. During the training, her mind would often wander back to some of her difficulties at work; consequently, the relaxation exercises often produced an actual increase in tension. As a result, the therapist decided that a more cognitively based approach might be more effective, serving not only as a means of self-controlled anxiety reduction but also as a cognitive distraction technique. With this new bit of information in mind, therapist and client again consulted and reevaluated the previously generated list of alternative treatment strategies. A decision analysis then led them to try visual imagery (i.e., imagining a safe, relaxing scene) as the predominant emotion-focused strategy. Monitoring proved this new approach to be substantially more effective for Susan than the muscle relaxation exercises.

Susan's example underscores certain important points concerning the clinical decision-making model. It was apparent with Susan that stress management was not simply a matter of selecting a promising treatment approach, implementing it, and evaluating its effectiveness. Rather, on the basis of preliminary treatment results, decisions were made that led to changes in the intervention plan, implementation of a different approach, and another outcome evaluation. This case thus illustrates the notion that clinical decision making is a continual process throughout treatment. Moreover, for stress management to be maximally effective, the therapist must take a flexible overall approach to treatment. Finally, any clinical decision-making model must be fluid and dynamic, rather than static and unidirectional.

The second component of this final phase of the decision-making model, outcome assessment, involves the observation, measurement, and evaluation of treatment or coping effects. This process includes an immediate assessment of stress responses and coping outcomes for particular problematic situations, as well as a general outcome assessment immediately upon termination of the formal stress management program and again after a follow-up period. A useful self-report measure for assessing emotional and physical stress responses in specific types of stress situations is the S-R Inventory of Anxiousness (Endler, Hunt, & Rosenstein, 1962). Consistent with the problem-solving coping approach, outcome assessment should likewise emphasize training in self-monitoring and self-evaluation. A useful self-monitoring technique for this purpose, the PSSM method, was described earlier in this chapter. To facilitate an accurate and objective self-assessment of outcome, the therapist should also instruct the client in the use of appropriate behavioral measurement methods (frequency counts, time sampling techniques, data charts, etc.). In self-evaluation, the client judges the actual coping outcome using the criteria employed during the decision-making process (e.g., effects on situational demands, effects on emotions, etc.) and then compares this outcome with the predicted outcome. If the match is judged satisfactory, then the client can terminate the problem-solving process and provide self-reinforcement for successful performance in the form of self-praise or some tangible reward. On the other hand, if the outcome is judged unsatisfactory, then the client follows instructions to troubleshoot and recycle (i.e., return to the various problem-solving processes to identify and correct deficiencies and seek a better coping method). If this procedure does not produce successful coping or stress management after a few attempts, it might be necessary to recognize the futility of further stress management attempts and consider alternative treatment approaches.

For a general assessment of stress management outcome at treatment termination and follow-up, a useful self-report measure, derived from interactional stress theory, is the DSP, also described earlier in this chapter (Derogatis, 1980). Another good self-report measure for assessing general stress effects is the SCL-90-R (Derogatis, 1975), which measures general psychological distress or psychological symptomatology. In addition to self-report measures, physiological measures of stress responses (blood pressure, heart rate, electromyographic responses, etc.) are useful for assessing stress management outcome and should be included if appropriate to the particular client's case.

In general, the choice of evaluation measures should reflect a thorough decision analysis relevant to the particular client. In addition to general stress-related inventories, evaluation should incorporate assessment measures that logically relate both to the client's specific problems and to the specific treatment techniques that were implemented. In Susan's case, for example, additional procedures included (a) the PSSM method, focusing on her actual coping attempts in work-related situations; (b) continuous Subjective Units of Disturbance Scale (Wolpe, 1982) ratings for assessing anxiety levels as a function of relaxation exercises; (c) a daily log of alcohol consumption; (d) the SPSI; (e) an assertiveness inventory; (f) in-session role plays for assessing both coping and communication skills; and (g) frequency counts of abdominal pain. On the basis of data across all these measures, therapist and client reached mutual agreement regarding termination of the stress management program with follow-up visits scheduled to monitor maintenance of stress reduction effects.

Maintenance and Generalization

As noted earlier, problem-solving training for the client is recommended because it facilitates the maintenance and generalization of stress reduction effects by increasing self-management ability, adaptive flexibility, perceived control, and a positive orientation to problems in living. It is also consistent with the emphasis on future-oriented goals. The therapist can further facilitate maintenance and generalization effects by taking the following steps in the last few stress-management sessions: (a) providing positive reinforcement for effective problem-solving and overall coping performance; (b) reviewing the components of a positive problem-solving cognitive set and praising the client when he makes statements that reflect this set; (c) directing the client's attention to the wide range of daily problems to which the problem-solving coping strategy is applicable (e.g., work problems, domestic problems, interpersonal problems, community problems); (d) asking the client to anticipate future problems and plan strategies for dealing with them; (e) discussing ways of preventing old problems from recurring; and (f) encouraging the client to self-monitor and self-evaluate his problem-solving performance, using the PSSM method, once or twice each month.

SUMMARY

This chapter highlighted important issues related to the application of the clinical decision-making model to the practice of clinical stress management. It introduced a transactional/problem-solving model that offers an expansive and comprehensive framework within which to understand the nature, etiology, and consequences of stress and to address certain problem orientation issues. This model is quite compatible with the clinical decision-making model in facilitating the therapist's flexibility concerning the wide range of potential sources and moderators of stress. Moreover, both models underscore the importance of conducting a comprehensive assessment unique to a particular client and of tailoring of a stress management program to the particular problems of that client.

In addition, it was argued that general problem-solving principles are important, both to the therapist's decision-making strategy in the development of an idiographic stress management protocol and to the client's general coping strategy with regard to future stress situations. It is concluded, therefore, that knowledge of problem-solving principles and skill in applying them are critical for therapists and clients alike.

References

Beck, A. T. (1984) Cognitive approaches to stress. In R. L. Woolfolk & P. M. Lehrer (Eds.), *Principles and practice of stress management*. New York: Guilford.

Benson, H. (1975). *The relaxation response*. New York: Morrow.

Bernstein, D. A., & Borkovec, T. D. (1973). *Progressive relaxation training: A manual for the helping professions*. Champaign, IL: Research Press.

Bloom, B. L. (1985). *Stressful life event theory and research: Implications for primary prevention* (DHHS Publication No. AMD 85–1385). Rockville, MD: National Institute of Mental Health.

Compas, B. E., Forsythe, C. J., & Wagner, B. M. (1988). Consistency and variability in causal attributions and coping with stress. *Cognitive Therapy and Research, 12*, 305–320.

DeLongis, A., Coyne, J. C., Dakof, G., Folkman, S., & Lazarus, R. S. (1982). Relationship of daily hassles, uplifts, and major life events to health status. *Health Psychology, 1,* 119–136.

Derogatis, L. R. (1975). *The SCL-90-R.* Baltimore: Clinical Psychometric Research.

Derogatis, L. R. (1980). *The Derogatis Stress Profile (DSP).* Baltimore: Clinical Psychometric Research.

Dohrenwend, B. S., & Dohrenwend, B. P. (1985). Life stress and psychopathology. In H. H. Goldman & S. E. Goldston (Eds.), *Preventing stress-related psychiatric disorders* (DHHS Publication No. ADM 85–1366). Rockville, MD: National Institute of Mental Health.

D'Zurilla, T. J. (1969). Reducing heterosexual anxiety. In J. D. Krumboltz & C. E. Thoresen (Eds.), *Behavioral counseling: Cases and techniques.* New York: Holt, Rinehart & Winston.

D'Zurilla, T. J. (1986). *Problem-solving therapy: A social competence approach to clinical intervention.* New York: Springer.

D'Zurilla, T. J. (in press). Problem-solving training for effective stress management and prevention. *Journal of Cognitive Psychotherapy: An International Quarterly.*

D'Zurilla, T. J., & Goldfried, M. R. (1971). Problem solving and behavior modification. *Journal of Abnormal Psychology, 78,* 107–126.

D'Zurilla, T. J., & Nezu, A. M. (1982). Social problem solving in adults. In P. C. Kendall (Ed.), *Advances in cognitive-behavioral research and therapy* (Vol. 1). New York: Academic.

D'Zurilla, T. J., & Nezu, A. M. (1988, November). *Development and preliminary evaluation of the Social Problem-Solving Inventory (SPSI).* Paper presented at the annual meeting of the Association for Advancement of Behavior Therapy, New York.

Ellis, A., & Grieger, R. (1977). *Handbook of rational-emotive therapy.* New York: Springer.

Ellis, A., & Harper, R. A. (1975). *A new guide to rational living.* Englewood Cliffs, NJ: Prentice-Hall.

Endler, N. S., Hunt, J. McV., & Rosenstein, A. J. (1962). An S-R inventory of anxiousness. *Psychological Monographs, 76* (Whole No. 536).

Folkman, S., & Lazarus, R. S. (1980). An analysis of coping in a middle-aged community sample. *Journal of Health and Social Behavior, 21,* 219–239.

Forsythe, C. J., & Compas, B. E. (1987). Interaction of cognitive appraisals of stressful events and coping: Testing the Goodness of Fit Hypothesis. *Cognitive Therapy and Research, 11,* 473–485.

Goldfried, M. R. (1971). Systematic desensitization as training in self-control. *Journal of Consulting and Clinical Psychology, 37,* 228–234.

Hamberger, L. K., & Lohr, J. M. (1984). *Stress and stress management.* New York: Springer.

Janis, I. L. (1982). Decision making under stress. In L. Goldberger & S. Breznitz (Eds.), *Handbook of stress: Theoretical and clinical aspects.* New York: Free Press.

Kanner, A. D., Coyne, J. C., Schaefer, C., & Lazarus, R. S. (1981). Comparison of two modes of stress measurement: Daily hassles and uplifts versus major life events. *Journal of Behavioral Medicine, 4,* 1–39.

Kobasa, S. C. (1979). Personality and resistance to illness. *American Journal of Community Psychology, 7,* 413–423.

Kobasa, S. C., Maddi, S. R., & Kahn, S. (1980). Hardiness and health: A prospective study. *Journal of Personality and Social Psychology, 42,* 168–177.

Lader, M. (1984). Pharmacological methods. In R. L. Woolfolk & P. M. Lehrer (Eds.), *Principles and practice of stress management.* New York: Guilford.

Lazarus, R. S. (1966). *Psychological stress and the coping process.* New York: McGraw-Hill.

Lazarus, R. S. (1981). The stress and coping paradigm. In C. Eisdorfer, D. Cohen, A. Kleinman, & P. Maxim (Eds.), *Theoretical bases for psychopathology.* New York: Spectrum.

Lazarus, R. S., & Cohen, J. B. (1977). Environmental stress. In I. Altman & J. F. Wohlwill (Eds.), *Human behavior and environment* (Vol. 2). New York: Plenum.

Lazarus, R. S., & Folkman, S. (1984). *Stress, appraisal, and coping.* New York: Springer.

Lehrer, P. M., & Woolfolk, R. L. (1984). Are stress reduction techniques interchangeable, or do they have specific effects? A review of the comparative empirical literature. In R. L. Woolfolk & P. M. Lehrer (Eds.), *Principles and practice of stress management.* New York: Guilford.

McGrath, J. E. (1982). Methodological problems in research on stress. In H. W. Krohne & L. Laux (Eds.), *Achievement, stress, and anxiety.* New York: Hemisphere.

Meichenbaum, D. H. (1977). *Cognitive behavior modification: An integrative approach.* New York: Plenum.

Meichenbaum, D. H., & Cameron, R. (1983). Stress inoculation training: Toward a general paradigm for training coping skills. In D. H. Meichenbaum & E. Jaremko (Eds.), *Stress reduction and prevention.* New York: Plenum.

Mooney, R. L., & Gordon, L. V. (1950). *Manual: The Mooney Problem Checklist.* New York: Psychological Corporation.

Nezu, A. M. (1986). Effects of stress from current problems: Comparison to major life events. *Journal of Clinical Psychology, 42,* 847–852.

Nezu, A. M. (1987). A problem-solving formulation of depression: A literature review and proposal of a pluralistic model. *Clinical Psychology Review, 7,* 121–144.

Nezu, A. M., & D'Zurilla, T. J. (1989). Social problem solving and negative affective conditions. In P. C. Kendall & D. Watson (Eds.), *Anxiety and depression: Distinctive and overlapping features.* New York: Academic.

Nezu, A. M., Nezu, C. M., & Perri, M. G. (1989). *Problem-solving therapy for depression: Theory, research, and clinical guidelines.* New York: Wiley.

Nezu, A. M., & Ronan, G. F. (1985). Life stress, current problems, problem solving, and depressive symptoms: An integrative model. *Journal of Consulting and Clinical Psychology, 53,* 693–697.

Pearlin, L. I., & Schooler, C. (1978). The structure of coping. *Journal of Health and Social Behavior, 19,* 2–21.

Sarason, I. G. (1980). Life stress, self-preoccupation, and social supports. In I. G. Sarason & C. D. Spielberger (Eds.), *Stress and anxiety* (Vol. 7). New York: Hemisphere.

Sarason, I. G., Johnson, J. H., & Siegel, J. M. (1978). Assessing the impact of life changes: Development of the Life Experiences Survey. *Journal of Consulting and Clinical Psychology, 46,* 932–946.

Schinka, J. A. (1984). *Personal Problems Checklist.* Odessa, FL: Psychological Assessment Resources.

Selye, H. (1983). The stress concept: Past, present, and future. In C. L. Cooper (Ed.), *Stress research: Issues for the eighties.* New York: Wiley.

Thoits, P. A. (1986). Social support as coping assistance. *Journal of Consulting and Clinical Psychology, 54,* 416–423.

Weinberger, M., Hiner, S. L., & Tierney, W. M. (1987). In support of hassles as a measure of stress in predicting health outcomes. *Journal of Behavioral Medicine, 10,* 19–31.

Wolpe, J. (1982). *The practice of behavior therapy* (3rd ed.). New York: Pergamon.

Woolfolk, R. L., & Lehrer, P. M. (1984a). Clinical applications. In R. L. Woolfolk & P. M. Lehrer (Eds.), *Principles and practice of stress management.* New York: Guilford.

Woolfolk, R. L., & Lehrer, P. M. (Eds.) (1984b). *Principles and practice of stress management.* New York: Guilford.

Author Index

Subject Index

About the Editors

Arthur M. Nezu received his Ph.D. in clinical psychology from the State University of New York at Stony Brook. He has recently been appointed professor and director of the Ph.D. program in clinical psychology at Hahnemann University in Philadelphia. Dr. Nezu previously served as Chief of Psychology and Director of Research for the Department of Psychiatry at Beth Israel Medical Center in New York. He is also associate professor of psychiatry at the Mount Sinai School of Medicine and is a frequent contributor of research and theoretical articles to professional journals. Currently, he is a consulting editor for the *Journal of Consulting and Clinical Psychology* and a member of the editorial board of the *Journal of Dental Practice Administration*. His areas of clinical and research interest include clinical decision making, stress, coping, depression, problem solving, developmental disabilities, and obesity.

Christine M. Nezu was awarded her Ph.D. in clinical psychology from Fairleigh Dickinson University. She recently joined the faculty of the Ph.D. program in clinical psychology at Hahnemann University as an assistant professor. Previously, she served as Supervising Psychologist and Director of the Developmental Disabilities Project in the Department of Psychiatry at Beth Israel Medical Center and as assistant professor of psychiatry at Mount Sinai School of Medicine. Dr. Nezu's publications and presentations span a wide variety of topics, including depression, stress, personality disorders, psychotherapy integration, humor, and behavior therapy with dually diagnosed mentally retarded individuals.

Collectively, the editors have taught and supervised scores of psychology graduate students, externs, interns, medical students, and psychiatric residents in behavior therapy associated with a wide variety of psychological disorders and patient populations. Co-authors with Michael G. Perri of *Problem-solving Therapy for Depression: Theory, Research, and Clinical Guidelines* (Wiley, 1989), they have presented workshops on clinical decision making both nationally and abroad. In addition, each maintains a private practice and consults extensively to mental health agencies and industry.

About the Contributors

Neill S. Cohen is Supervising Psychologist at Beth Israel Medical Center and a clinical instructor in psychiatry at Cornell Medical School.

Thomas J. D'Zurilla is an associate professor of psychology at the State University of New York at Stony Brook.

John A. Fairbank is Senior Research Clinical Psychologist at Research Triangle Institute, Research Triangle Park, North Carolina.

Neil S. Jacobson is a professor and Director of Clinical Psychology at the University of Washington, Seattle.

Debra A. Kaplan is Coordinator of Training in Psychology at Beth Israel Medical Center and a clinical assistant professor of psychiatry at Mount Sinai School of Medicine.

Philip C. Kendall is a professor of psychology and Head of the Division of Clinical Psychology at Temple University and a research professor of psychiatry at Eastern Pennsylvania Psychiatric Institute.

Michael G. Perri is a professor and deputy chair of psychology at Fairleigh Dickinson University and Research Coordinator for Franklin D. Roosevelt Veterans Administration Hospital, Montrose, New York.

Michael R. Petronko is Director of the Division of Psychological Services and a clinical professor of psychology at Fairleigh Dickinson University.

Lynne Siqueland is a doctoral candidate in clinical psychology at Temple University.

Adrian Sondheimer is a clinical assistant professor of psychiatry and Director of Child Psychiatry Training at the New Jersey Medical School, Newark.

Arlinza E. Turner is Assistant Chief of the Division of Psychology and Coordinator of the Behavior Therapy Program at Beth Israel Medical Center.

Mark A. Whisman is a doctoral candidate in clinical psychology at the University of Washington.